PETERSON'S

The Inside SCOOP on College Life

Kelly Bare

Michele Kornegay

Peterson's
Thomson Learning™

Australia • Canada • Denmark • Japan • Mexico • New Zealand • Philippines
Puerto Rico • Singapore • South Africa • Spain • United Kingdom • United States

About Peterson's

Peterson's is the country's largest educational information/communications company, providing the academic, consumer, and professional communities with books, software, and online services in support of lifelong education access and career choice. Well-known references include Peterson's annual guides to private schools, summer programs, colleges and universities, graduate and professional programs, financial aid, international study, adult learning, and career guidance. Peterson's Web site at petersons.com is the only comprehensive—and most heavily traveled—education resource on the Internet. The site carries all of Peterson's fully searchable major databases and includes financial aid sources, test-prep help, job postings, direct inquiry and application features, and specially created Virtual Campuses for every accredited academic institution and summer program in the U.S. and Canada that offers in-depth narratives, announcements, and multimedia features.

Visit Peterson's Education Center on the Internet (World Wide Web) at
www.petersons.com

ISBN 0-7689-0325-4

Printed in the United States of America

10 9 8 7 6 5 4 3 2 1

Contents

Introduction

If you picked up this book, you're probably thinking about applying to college sometime soon, or maybe you're the parent of someone who's getting ready to take that big step. You already know that *Peterson's Guide to 4-Year Colleges, Peterson's Guide to Two-Year Colleges,* and *Peterson's Guide to Vocational-Technical Schools* can provide you with the crucial facts and figures you'll want to know about any four-year university, two-year college, or vocational-technical program in which you may be interested. But what about what it *feels* like to go to college? Where can you find out about those aspects of college life that can't be measured with data—about all those intangibles that add up to a portrait of the average college student's life?

If that's what you're looking for, you've come to the right place. *The Inside SCOOP on College Life* gives you an insiders' glimpse at life at five different kinds of university and college campuses across the country. We've gathered together the best articles from the nation's best college newspapers to show you exactly what to expect at different types of institutions. You'll read firsthand about the concerns these students face; explore the myths and traditions that give each type of institution its identity; and get a taste of both the good and the bad parts of college life.

To make it easier, we've divided the book into five chapters, each dealing with a different type of college:

- First are *large state schools*, those that enroll 7,000 or more students, are publicly funded, and offer both undergraduate and graduate work.
- These are followed by *highly competitive colleges*, those that answered "most difficult" or "very difficult" to the admissions requirement questions on Peterson's Annual Survey of Undergraduate Institutions (we'll explain more about the survey later).
- The third chapter on *small liberal arts colleges* covers private four-year colleges with enrollments under 6,000 students. Most of these schools do not offer graduate programs.
- Next are *religious colleges*—private colleges of varying size that are affiliated with a specific religion.
- Finally, we take a look at *two-year schools*; these are community colleges, junior colleges, and vocational-technical schools where you can earn an associate's degree or receive career training or certification.

Each of the five chapters is further broken down into three sections: Academics, Beyond the Classroom, and Life on Campus. In Academics, you'll go behind the scenes and find out how college students really feel about admissions policies, class size, teaching, research, funding, academic resources, advising, academic dishonesty, grade inflation, retention, and, most importantly, the academic opportunities at their schools. *Beyond the Classroom* takes a look at all the great extracurricular activities you'll find waiting for you at college—student groups, sports, Greek life, and interesting speakers. And *Life on Campus* gives you a behind the scenes tour of the factors that contribute to the atmosphere you'll find at any school, including dorm life, diversity, drinking and alcohol policies, activism, student services, fun stuff, and much more.

How did we decide which schools went into which chapter? Each four-year school's placement is based on data from Peterson's Annual Survey of Undergraduate Institutions, an annual questionnaire filled out by the more than 2,000 accredited colleges and universities in the United States. You'll find a more in-depth definition of the classification criteria we used at the beginning of each chapter. Keep in mind as you read through these articles that what you'll find, while representative of college life, is just a small sample of the ongoing events that characterize different campuses. *The Inside SCOOP on College Life* will give you a pretty good idea of what it will be like should you choose to enroll at any one of the five kinds of colleges you'll find here, but remember that each college is a world all its own.

Getting the Scoop

It's 11:48 a.m.; you're two minutes from the end of your "Economy of the Ancient Mediterranean" discussion section, and, as your growling stomach reminds you, ten minutes away from lunch.

Class is dismissed, and you gather up your books and stroll across the leafy campus to the dining hall. You grab a tray, line up, navigate the minefield of crusty macaroni and cheese with rubbery hot dogs and make it safely to a table with your usual PB&J.

Looking around for your steadfast lunch companions, you realize that you'll be eating alone. Your roommate has a lab this afternoon, and your friend from down the hall has class on the other end of campus.

Don't panic—you've got reading material. You bypass "Hamlet," who, along with professor James, would like a word with thee by 3:00 p.m. Instead, you open your campus newspaper.

In it, you learn who's up for Homecoming King and Queen. You read about how much the trustees want to raise tuition and which leaders in your student government want to fight it every step of the way. You peruse the scores from last night's soccer and football games, and see with disbelief that Prof. James' new book, "To be or not to be: Hamlet and the Modern Urban Identity Crisis," is selling like hotcakes.

Or maybe it's not at lunchtime, but in the evening, at the gym riding a stationary bike that you pull out your campus paper. Or maybe you're at the computer lab, sitting down to type that dreaded *Hamlet* paper, and you pull up your school newspaper's Web site to read the news online.

Whenever and however you get your campus news, when you start college you'll join the legions of students for whom reading the campus paper is a daily or weekly ritual. It's a way to keep up on news and gossip and feel like you're more than just a student ID number. It makes you feel like a part of the campus community and all that goes on in and around it.

The College Quest

The hard part, as you know, is finding the one single post-secondary educational institution (read: college) out of thousands at which you really *want* to be a part of the campus community.

Finding a college that perfectly suits your particular needs is tough. You're not a "well-rounded" person; you're a sharp person with lots of different, sharp edges. You want to double major in biochemistry and opera. You like big cities but you don't want to live in a high-rise dorm. Small schools seem less scary, but you're crazy about big-time football.

And when you're spending as much money as a college degree costs (according to the National Center for Education Statistics, from $3,500 for a 2-year to $18,000 for a 4-year private school), you should be picky. But since colleges aren't as customizable as Saturns or ice cream sundaes, the best you can do is conduct a thorough college search, check as many requirements off your list as possible, and try to find out how a school will *feel* when you're a student there.

The Search

Enter "The Inside SCOOP on College Life," a way to get a glimpse of what life is *really* like at different types of schools before you visit a single campus. By reading the newspaper articles in this book, you'll learn what actually happens on college campuses and see how real students feel about issues at their schools on a daily basis, not just when the college guide interviewer comes around.

The articles you'll read weren't written for this book. They were written in the course of normal school days by real students working for real college papers. They reflect the feelings of the writer and the people quoted in the story and the campus at that time. This is the real thing, folks, and these stories are similar to what you'll read in a year or two over your lunchtime PB&J.

This book will show you what happened during the last school year on different types of college campuses nationwide so you can decide for yourself how you'd fit in. Think about how these stories make you feel. Imagine yourself cheering amidst a sea of blue at a Michigan U. football game or playing croquet on the lawn of St. John's College.

Other books will give you the average SAT score and male-to-female ratio; this book won't. That stuff is important, but it comes later in your search or should be used in

conjunction with a book like this one so your college search doesn't become a numbers game.

Whether you're using this book as a place to start when you begin to think about college or are simply trying to learn more about college life, let "The Inside SCOOP on College Life" help you look at the big picture by showing you why different types of schools feel different.

> Please don't accept one or two stories from a particular school as the gospel on what life is like there. We are using individual schools as examples of a type, showing you what the general campus atmosphere is like so you can decide where you'll fit best.

What is U-WIRE?

All the papers whose stories appear in this book are members of University Wire or "U-WIRE," a membership organization and free wire service for college newspapers that aims to connect all college media to each other and the world. We read over 450 campus papers every day and collect and sort their stories into news packages that appear on Web sites like Yahoo!,

USA Today Online, Excite, and AOL's Digital Cities. We also create a searchable database of these stories, accessible only to college paper editors, who can select which ones they want to print to show their readers what's happening on campuses across town or across the country.

U-WIRE does all this because we believe that college news is important not only to the people who write it or their classmates who read it everyday but to everyone, because colleges and universities are America's centers of thought and culture.

We're thrilled to work with Peterson's, a company that shares our respect for helpful information about higher education. Peterson's has an excellent reputation for providing prospective college students with the tools they need to make solid choices about their education and their future. I hope you enjoy reading "The Inside SCOOP on College Life" as much as I enjoyed putting it together, and that it gets you closer to the school that fits you best.

—Kelly Bare
General Manager
University Wire

> After reading this book you should have a good idea of what life is like on many different types of campuses across the country. Whether you find yourself drawn to a small liberal arts college, a large state school, or maybe a two-year institution, be sure to check out CollegeQuest at www.collegequest.com. You'll find valuable information and advice on preparing for standardized tests, hunting down the best financial aid options, identifying schools that fit your criteria, and even applying on-line through CollegeQuest eApply. *The Inside SCOOP on College Life* will help you figure out what kind of school is right for you; CollegeQuest will help you get there.

Contributors

U-WIRE STAFF
Kelly Bare, General Manager
Julie J. Piotrowski, Associate Editor
Lisa M. Flores, Assistant Editor
Sarah Grubb, Assistant Editor
Ryan Sulkin, Assistant Editor

U-WIRE MEMBER PAPERS
The Eagle, American University
Jeremy Feilera
TVI Times, Albuquerque
    Technical-Vocational Institute
Donovan Kabalka
Scott Quintanilla
The Arizona Daily Wildcat, Arizona State
    University
Tanith L. Balaban
Kristy Mangos
Jennifer Holmes
Karen C. Tully
The Bates Student, Bates College
Jennifer Griblin
Jennifer Merksamer
Shawn P. O'Leary
Joanna Standley
The Lariat, Baylor University
Angie Tello
Patricia Demchack
Luke McElmurry
Brittney Partridge
The Quarter Tone, Belhaven College
Haley Rice
Voice of the Voiceless, Borough of Manhattan
    Community College
Jacqueline Forde-Stewart
The Heights, Boston College
Ann Chaglassian
Brian M. Cohen
Adam Smith
The Daily Free Press, Boston University
Amber Hansman
Tracey Sharp
The Bowdoin Orient, Bowdoin College
Stacy Humes-Schulz
C.W. Estoff
Kathleen Parker
The Bradley Scout, Bradley University
Melissa McClure
Kimberely Barnhart
The Daily Universe, Brigham Young
    University
Misti Pincock
Janette Jefress
Pamela Jo Grundvig
Mali Hegdahl
Esther Yu
Mark Morris
Kelleigh Cole
Kristen Sonne
The Brown Daily Herald, Brown University
Helen Willard
Caitlin Armistead
Shannon Tan
Sumaiya Balbale
The Bi-College News, Bryn Mawr College
Carmen Jardeleza
Janet Bunde
Christine McCluskey
The State Hornet, California State University,
    Sacramento.
Christine Lally

The Guardsman, City College of San
    Francisco
Nate Cohen
Pedro Tuyub
Nino Padova
Lara V. Desmond
Mike Kushner
Evan Ross
Amanda Wheeler
Louise Knapp Bowser
Margarita Chavez
The Tiger, Clemson University
Kristi Devlin
Rocky Mountain Collegian, Colorado State
    University
Jonathan Rice
Adam Woodroof
The Columbia Daily Spectator, Columbia
    University
Eli Lassman
Lisa Szymanski
Rachel Cohen
The College Voice, Connecticut College
Tiffany Taber
Jeanine Millard
Kate Woodsome
Karen O'Donnell
Brian Bieluch
Abby Carlen
Jennifer DeLeon
Nicole Manevice
The Cornell Daily Sun, Cornell University
Andrew Schinder
Melissa Hantman
Missy Globerman
The Cowley Press, Cowley County
    Community College
Charlie Potter
Dena Cosby
Zabrina Wilson
The Creightonian, Creighton University
Heidi Juersivich
Kamahria Hopkins
Andre Nathaniel
The Dartmouth, Dartmouth College
Jacob T. Elberg,
Jen Taylor
Giulia Good Stefani
Danya Pincayage
The DePaulia, DePaul University
Mark McCarrell
The DePauw, DePauw College
Emily Fox
Michele Geary
Abby Lovett
Jessica McCuan
Mary Anne Potts
Emily Lowe
David Clucas
Jen Neilsen
The Acorn, Drew University
Lara Shaljian
Shannon Gould
The Chronicle, Duke University
Katharine Stroup
Maureen Milligan
Campus Voice, Florida Community College
Hannah Crawford
Rabiah Ryan
The Hatchet, George Washington University

Justin Barney
Liz Latwin
Tammy Imhoff
The Hoya, Georgetown University
Andy Amend
The George-Anne, Georgia Southern
    University
Sarah Trucksis
Cory Brooks
The Voice, Glendale Community College
Jayne Nixon
Rachel Jacob
Victor Allen
Matt Batman
Evan Marshall
Denise Williams
The Spectator, Hamilton College
Matthew Brand
Suzanne Dougherty
Tait Svenson
The Harvard Crimson, Harvard University
Matthew Vogel
Robert B. Davis
Robert K. Silverman
Vasant M. Kamath
Sarah E. Hendrickson
Samantha Goldstein
Paul S. Gutman
The Argus, Illinois Wesleyan University
Anne McConnell
Dave Rupp
Diane Tasic
John C. Vrakas
The Buccaneer, Independence Community
    College
Jayme Lickteig
Katia Ushakova
Charissa N. Struble
Adam Viceroy
Indiana Daily Student, Indiana University
Aline Mendelsohn
Andy Gammill
Iowa State Daily, Iowa State University
Gloria D. Stewart
Daily Kent State, Kent State University
Jennifer Fiala
The Linfield Review, Linfield College
Mary Jo Monroe
The Commuter, Linn-Benton Community
    College
Lizanne Southgate
Jeremy Parker
E.J. Harris
The Reveille, Louisiana State University
Stacie Majoria
The Maroon, Loyola University
Katie Vieceli
Danny Layne
Chips, Luther College
Matt Becker
Sean M. Helle
Matt Becker
Seth Ansorge
The Marquette Tribune, Marquette University
Ann Hanson
Pamela Williams
Dave Young
Brian Salgado
The Tech, Massachusetts Institute of
    Technology

Susan Buchman
Doug Heimburger
Mesa Legend, Mesa County Community College
Donna Taffe
Dylan Fields
Teri Dillion
Dennis Welch
Dana Archibald
Jeremy Williams
Kim Larson
The State News, Michigan State University
Fred Woodhams
Melissa Burden
Amy Sinquefield
Michael Hauck
The Decaturian, Millikin University
Alyssa Sherman
Darren McGill
The Minnesota Daily, Minnesota State University
Jayme Halbritter
The Daily Northwestern, Northwestern University
Arthur Janik
Ellie Phillips
Michael Hope
Michael Hope
Michael Hope
Juan Hernandez
Christopher S. Own
Paul Bongaarts
Kameron Flynn
The Observer, Notre Dame University
Christopher Shipley
The Lantern, Ohio State University
Lindsey Brown
Erik Clark
Maybelle Trocio
The Bison, Oklahoma Baptist University
Alisha Bellene
Oklahoma Daily, Oklahoma University
Robyn Conder
Daily Collegian, Pennsylvania State University
Angela J. Gates
Don Stewart
Khyber Oser
Mark Parfitt
The Collegio, Pittsburgh State University
Brian Holderman
The Daily Princetonian, Princeton University
Chris Yakaitis
Ian Shapira
Stephen Fuzesi
Liz Nye
Andra Manui
Nabarun Dasgupta
The Daily Targum, Rutgers University
Cathleen Lewis
Aliza Sacknovitz
Sameer Khan
David Krantz
Bumper DeJesus
Tony Cho
The City Collegian, Seattle Central Community College
Joseph Drake
Rita Heapes
Terez Wea
Lisa Sutter
The Bona Venture, St. Bonaventure University
Michael Bigos
Brett Fagan
The Defender, St. Michael's College
Kim McCray
Ben Murray
Alethea Renzi

The Stanford Daily, Stanford University
Marcella Bernhard
Miler Lee
Patrick Bernhardt
The Crusader, Susquehanna University
Branden Pfefferkorn
Brian Ianieri
Rebecca Lee
The Battalion, Texas A&M
Jennifer Wilson
The Daily Skiff, Texas Christian University
Katy Graham
Jeri Petersen
The Towerlight, Towson University
Tom Gildon
Megan DeMarco
The Tufts Daily, Tufts University
Daniel Barbarisi
Lauren Heist
Daniel Rodrigues
The Daily Trojan, University of Southern California
Claire Luna
Michael Levine
The Daily Californian, University of California Berkeley
Dan Evans
Daniel Hernandez
The Daily Bruin, University of California, Los Angeles
Caridad Lezcano
Christi Schuler
Claire Luna
The Guardian, University of California, San Diego
Jeremy Gray
The Chicago Maroon, University of Chicago
David G. Schultz
Joe Burnett
Kary Kelly
Colorado Daily, University of Colorado, Boulder
Matt Sprengeler
The Daily Campus, University of Connecticut
Jennifer Clair
The Flyer News, University of Dayton
Dan Ketterick
Karaline Jackson
Mary Beth Luna
Lisa Calendine
The Daily Cougar, University of Houston
Jason Caesar Consolacion
The Kentucky Kernel, University of Kentucky
Karrie Ralston
The Maine Campus, University of Maine, Orono
Dilnora Azimova
The Diamondback, University of Maryland
Rochelle Kohen
Mark Matthews
The Massachusetts Daily Collegian, University of Massachusetts
Brian McDermott
The Michigan Daily, University of Michigan
Daniel Weiss
Mike Spahn
Janet Adamy
Jeffrey Kosseff
Melanie Sampson
Minnesota Daily, University of Minnesota
Coralie Carson
Jake Kapsner
Sarah Hallonquist
Robin Huiras
Daily Nebraskan, University of Nebraska, Lincoln
Lindsay Young
Ieva Augustums

The Rebel Yell, University of Nevada Las Vegas
Heather Grady
Daily Lobo, University of New Mexico
Stephen Rabourn
The Daily Pennsylvanian, University of Pennsylvania
Amara Levine
The Campus Times, University of Rochester
Kelly Egan
Jonathan Skolnick
Sarah Apgar
The Oracle, University of Southern Florida
Joe Humphrey
The Daily Egyptian, University of Southern Illinois
Ted Schurter
Justin Jones
The Daily Texan, University of Texas, Austin
Suzannah Creech
Sergio Chapa
The Daily Utah Chronicle, University of Utah
Eva Michelle Hunter
Brent Olson
Josh Pourmizaei
The Cavalier Daily, University of Virginia
Leah Loftin
Tengku Bahar
Corey Barber
The Washington Daily, University of Washington
Joe Nicholson
Badger Herald, University of Wisconsin, Madison
Joel J. Nelson
The Daily Cardinal, University of Wisconsin, Madison
Mike Staab
Judy Massuda
Adam W. Lasker
Jenny Freemyer
The Vanderbilt Hustler, Vanderbilt University
Holly Eagleson
Joanna Pluta
The Miscellany News, Vassar College
Charles Pugliese
Nicholas Loss-Eaton
Melissa Walker
Kevin Aldridge
M. Tye Wolfe
The Villanovan, Villanova University
Gary Grochmal
Kelly Blevins
Irene Burgo
Leah Urbaniak
The Old Gold & Black, Wake Forest University
Jared Klose
Sarah Rackley
Brad Gunton
The Bachelor, Wabash College
Chris Cotterill
The Student Life, Washington University
Liz Bower
The Daily Herald, Yale University
Adrienne Lo
The Yale Daily News, Yale University
Christopher Mooney
Glenn Hurowitz
Jennifer Arthur
Letitia Stein
Meghan Casey
The Observer, Yeshiva University
Sara Kostant
Susan Jacobs

The Perfect Fit

When you're a kid, you want to grow up to be President of the United States. And you tell anyone who will listen that you are going to land on the moon. In fact, you are going to be the first President of the United States to land on the moon. But you have to get through medical school first.

Some days you want to be an actress. Or a plumber. When you were twelve, you told your next-door neighbor that you were going to be a fashion illustrator so you could design suits for the President of the United States because the ones he wore on TV seemed kind of boring.

OK, OK, maybe that was just me. Growing up, I doodled on everything from paper towels to my mother's best cookbooks. My father never said anything about the condition of our Sunday paper, which often arrived in his hands with beards drawn on front-page pictures of Margaret Thatcher, sunglasses and gaudy jewelry sketched on movie stars in the entertainment section, and penciled-in pictures of items for sale in the classifieds.

In high school, I took art classes and thrived as a design editor on the yearbook staff. More school in art history and graphic design seemed like the natural thing to do. And so my high school guidance counselor advised me to look at art schools and some smaller conserva-tories where I would be able to pursue my passion for doodling and design.

But I wanted to go to a larger school, complete with rowdy tailgates, a massive student body, and a skating rink. Having been a competitive ice skater for almost ten years, I was determined to continue lacing up my boots in college. But the art schools I looked at didn't have skating rinks. Or tailgates.

And after flipping through course catalogs filled with the unusual and alluring programs that larger colleges offered, I forgot all about art history. Suddenly, I wanted to study abroad in Switzer-land and take classes in subjects like international relations, medical sociology, and especially in journal-ism. Writing was something that I had always been good at and truly enjoyed. And so I spent dozens of free periods in high school sorting through stacks of dog-eared guide books in the career center, waiting for some grand vision of what I was supposed to do next. The college application process felt overwhelm-ing, and there were many days when I seriously considered taking a year off to go skate in the Ice Capades.

I was also terrified of making a major mistake by choosing the wrong thing to study. After weeks spent exploring the possibilities with family and friends, I decided to apply to several larger schools that offered not only solid art departments but also strong programs in political science and communications. I wanted the option of changing majors without changing schools, unlike a good friend of mine who started out in Maine studying marine biology but transferred to UCLA to major in playwriting.

While I didn't want to move from one coast to another because I changed my major, I did like the idea of traveling. After growing up in Chicago for 18 years, I wanted to explore a different part of the country. After months of debate with my guidance counselor, I applied to eight schools: Washing-ton University in St. Louis, Boston College, Boston U., George Washington, Georgetown, Miami U. in Ohio, Northwestern and Brown. Sure, I'd miss Lake Michigan, the Cubs, and Chicago's world-famous deep-dish pizza, but the Smithsonian or Boston's baked beans didn't sound half bad either.

Seven of the eight schools had what I considered to be a large student body—more than 5,000 students—and were located in or near a big city. Beyond that, the reasons I was attracted to each school were diverse.

I chose both George Washington and Georgetown because of their strong communication departments and well-respected programs in international relations. Each school

2is within walking distance of a good ice rink, and Washington, D.C., is a fun, young city.

Miami University boasts the best collegiate figure skating team in the country and also has a well-known graphic design program; Boston College and Boston University have top-notch programs in both politics and communications.

Brown was appealing because it allows students to create their own majors. Since applicants can design their own curriculum and requirements, I figured I could explore a number of interests at once. (I think we students sometimes forget that's what college is all about. You're supposed to be confused— and thrilled—by the number of available opportunities.) And because the President still wears boring suits, I was excited to learn that Brown students can take classes at the Rhode Island School of Design.

Finally, I applied to the Medill School of Journalism at Northwestern, which offered one of the strongest journalism programs around. Northwestern didn't have an ice rink on campus, but the tailgates were rumored to be rowdy. On the day I visited the campus with my dad, the Wildcat marching band was busy parading across town in preparation for the school's first trip to the Rose Bowl in decades. I was swept up in football fever, and I fell in love with the school's

lakeside campus and with its promise of a thriving social scene.

Since all the schools I applied to required SAT scores, I sweated through a couple months of standardized testing, something that is not my forte. I felt like I fared better in the face-to-face interviews required by some schools.

My first interview was also the first for the alumni doing the interviewing; for three hours he questioned me on everything from the school's history to the last novel I read. I later learned from the school's admission's office that the interview shouldn't have taken more than 30 minutes.

But I became a pro at displaying personality, and my remaining two interviews were much shorter and more informal. Although my high school marks were pretty good, I learned that some colleges place more weight on your ability to carry a conversation or what you can contribute to the campus community than on your grades.

In the end, I was fortunate. I was accepted to seven of the eight schools. Then the real decision making began.

Of the factors I considered— size, student life, and academics— academics was most important. After realizing that journalism was what I wanted to pursue for the next few years, I decided to attend the Medill School of Journalism at Northwestern, where I am now a

senior. I dropped my double major in political science and declared a minor in film studies. I'm skating at a nearby rink and taking elective courses like Latin American Politics and Documentary Film Criticism.

And although I no longer dream of being President, I am still unsure of what I really want to do when I graduate. What I do know is that attending college at a place where I am free to change my mind as often as I like has been the best thing for me.

What's the best thing for you? Maybe this book will take you one step closer to finding out. When I visited the campus, I realized Northwestern was a perfect fit. While you may have a long way to go in your college search before you find your perfect fit, this book is like stepping onto five different types of campuses, exploring them, and talking with students.

Exploring and having the kind of experiences you'll read about in this book are what college is all about. Take the time to look at all the options when you apply to schools, but remember what George Eliot wrote: "It's never too late to be what you might have been." People say that college is one of the best times of your life. I couldn't agree more.

Julie J. Piotrowski
Northwestern Class of 2000

Alabama
Auburn University
The University of Alabama
The University of Alabama at Birmingham

Alaska
University of Alaska Anchorage

Arizona
Arizona State University
Northern Arizona University
The University of Arizona

Arkansas
University of Arkansas

California
California Polytechnic State University, San Luis Obispo
California State Polytechnic University, Pomona
California State University, Chico
California State University, Fresno
California State University, Fullerton
California State University, Long Beach
California State University, Los Angeles
California State University, Northridge
California State University, Sacramento
San Diego State University
San Francisco State University
San Jose State University
University of California, Davis
University of California, Los Angeles
University of California, San Diego
University of California, Santa Barbara

Colorado
Colorado State University
Metropolitan State College of Denver
University of Colorado at Boulder

Connecticut
University of Connecticut

Delaware
University of Delaware

Florida
Florida Atlantic University
Florida International University
Florida State University
University of Central Florida
University of Florida
University of South Florida

Georgia
Georgia Institute of Technology
Georgia Southern University
Georgia State University
Kennesaw State University
University of Georgia

Hawaii
University of Hawaii at Manoa

Idaho
Boise State University

Illinois
Eastern Illinois University
Illinois State University
Northern Illinois University
Southern Illinois University Carbondale
University of Illinois

Indiana
Ball State University
Indiana University Bloomington
Indiana University–Purdue University Indianapolis
Purdue University

Iowa
Iowa State University of Science and Technology
The University of Iowa
University of Northern Iowa

IN THIS CHAPTER

California State University
Clemson University
Colorado State University
Indiana University
Iowa State University
Kent State University
Louisiana State University
Michigan State University
Minnesota State University
Ohio State University
Oklahoma State University
Pennsylvania State University
Rutgers University
Texas A&M
University of California
University of Colorado
University of Connecticut
University of Houston
University of Kentucky
University of Maine
University of Maryland
University of Michigan
University of Nebraska
University of New Mexico
University of Southern Florida
University of Texas
University of Utah
University of Virginia
University of Wisconsin

Kansas
Kansas State University
University of Kansas
Wichita State University

Kentucky
Eastern Kentucky University
Northern Kentucky University
University of Kentucky
University of Louisville
Western Kentucky University

Louisiana
Louisiana State University and Agricultural and Mechanical College
Southeastern Louisiana University
University of New Orleans
University of Southwestern Louisiana

Maryland
Towson University
University of Maryland, College Park
University of Maryland University College

Massachusetts
University of Massachusetts Amherst

Michigan
Central Michigan University
Eastern Michigan University
Grand Valley State University
Michigan State University
Oakland University
University of Michigan
Wayne State University
Western Michigan University

Minnesota
Minnesota State University, Mankato
St. Cloud State University
University of Minnesota, Twin Cities Campus

Mississippi
Mississippi State University
University of Southern Mississippi

Missouri
Southwest Missouri State University
University of Missouri–Columbia
University of Missouri–St. Louis

Montana
Montana State University–Bozeman
The University of Montana–Missoula

Nebraska
University of Nebraska at Omaha
University of Nebraska–Lincoln

Nevada
University of Nevada, Las Vegas

New Hampshire
University of New Hampshire

New Jersey
Rutgers, The State University of New Jersey, Rutgers College

New Mexico
New Mexico State University
University of New Mexico

New York
State University of New York at Albany
State University of New York at Buffalo
State University of New York at Stony Brook

North Carolina
Appalachian State University
East Carolina University
North Carolina State University

Continued on page 87

Large State Schools

Let's start by defining just what we mean by "large state school." For the purposes of this book, a large state school is one that enrolls 7,000 or more students, is publicly funded, and offers both undergraduate and graduate work. The schools listed on the left page meet all of these criteria. More important than the numbers, however, is what it *feels like* to attend a large state school—what makes a large state school special, different from smaller, private schools. That's what this chapter is all about.

Simply put, at a large state school there's more of everything. First of all, there are more students. Many of the schools in this chapter enroll well over 7,000 students; a few have student bodies numbering in the tens of thousands. But we're not just talking about numbers. On the campus of a large state school, you'll find more *kinds* of students—in other words, more diversity. Diversity is what makes large state schools great. You'll be able to meet and make friends with other students from all over the country and around the world, from all different backgrounds and all different lifestyles. Kids at large state schools have a great opportunity to learn something beyond the classroom, to gain perspectives that will prove invaluable in today's increasingly globalized world. And this diversity isn't limited to geography or ethnicity; students with physical challenges, older students with children, gay and lesbian students, students from all socioeconomic backgrounds, and students repesenting the religions of the world flock to the campuses of large state schools nationwide. You'll find students who work, students who live with their parents, students who attend part time, students who've transferred from another school, and more—in fact, there's probably no one definition of a "traditional" large state school student!

Often, state school campuses are big—really big. They can span acres and constitute small towns in and of themselves. Large state schools are so large that they often have their own bus systems (believe us, you'll need to use a bus). There won't be just one library; in all likelihood, there will be ten or twenty, in addition to the main library, which will house millions and millions of books, periodicals, and other research aids. Dormitories can look like skyscrapers; so can academic buildings (and we're talking 100 academic buildings at some large schools). Which one of the ten gymnasiums is hosting tonight's big game? What fine arts theater has the opera this weekend—the one on the east end of campus or the west? (Which way's east?) These are the questions you'll hear at a large state school. In fact, the campus often spills over and becomes indistinguishable from the town it's in. Shops, restaurants, and bars are geared toward college students and professors; landlords try to attract the best college tenants; and it's a ghost town when students are on break. You'll hear students complaining about "townies" and townies griping about "those kids," but all in all, the campus and the community will be tight-knit.

If you choose to attend a large state school, be prepared to hear some of the following from friends and family members who like to put in their two cents:

- "You'll just be a number at a large school; you'll never be able to stand out from the crowd."
- "You won't get the same high-quality education at a large school that you would at a small, private college."
- "With all the focus on research going on at large campuses, you'll be ignored academically; only graduate students who don't care about you will be teaching classes."

Let's dispel these myths.

First, yes, you will be one of many students, especially in your freshman year, but that doesn't mean that you won't learn or be noticed. If you take an active interest in your classes and introduce yourself to your profs—in short, if you're proactive—you'll come to be known as "Sue, that smart kid who sits in the front and always volunteers to answer questions in my freshman English class," not "ID# 074-372-58." And there will be plenty of other ways to make your mark on campus life. You can run for student government, volunteer to help with campus tours, or be first in line to rally for more parking spaces. If you want everyone on campus to

know your name, believe us, you'll have no problem doing it.

Second, have no fears about getting a top-notch education at a large state school. Classes at state schools are just as academically rigorous as those at private schools, and, because of their large and diverse student bodies, large schools offer a wider selection of classes from which you can choose. The only thing that could possibly limit you is your imagination. Honors and advanced classes challenge the academically gifted, and if you are

Tengku Bahar/*The Cavalier Daily*

your high school class valedictorian, it's likely that you'll get an academic scholarship to attend a large state school.

Finally, just because your school is focused on research doesn't mean that you'll be pushed to the side. On the contrary, you might even have a chance to participate in the research. There are plenty of opportunities for advanced undergraduate students to assist professors with research; you could even get your findings published! Similarly, it isn't necessarily a bad

thing if a graduate student is teaching one of your classes. Remember that these students are professors-in-training, so to speak, who have a professional interest in the subject matter as well as years of study under their belts. They're often young and enthusiastic about what they're teaching, which can only be good for you.

Now what you really want to know: what it *feels* like on a large campus. With all those students, there's a lot of hustle and bustle. When 40,000 people are trying to get somewhere at any given time, expect a certain amount of chaos. When you have to get across campus from 8 a.m. biology to 10 a.m. calculus, you'll rush, too. As you cross campus, you'll see all kinds of faces engaged in all kinds of activities—from fraternity brothers pitching horseshoes in front of their house to campus musicians giving impromptu performances to the latest student body candidate expounding on her platform in the middle of the campus quad. A quick glimpse at a campus bulletin board will find it packed to the gills with all kinds of information—the next meeting of the Young Republicans, advertisements for day care for students' children, information about a campus anti-fur rally, an invitation to a concert by the school's gospel choir. As you write down the e-mail address of someone selling a bicycle (something you definitely need here), you notice that everyone's wearing the school colors. How could you forget? It's game day. In fact, you can feel the excitement in the air—everyone knows your team has made it to the Division I finals.

With so much to divert you, it's amazing you get to class at all.

You can expect many things your first year at a large state school. Expect to live in a dorm, share a bathroom, and have no privacy. Expect to have big classes taught in auditoriums by professors or grad students equipped with microphones and overhead projectors. Expect long lines—to register for classes, to buy books, to eat lunch. But most of all, expect to be confused. You'll want to get involved in campus life, but you'll be bombarded with things to do: Should you go Greek, join the business students' club, try out for the campus play, or all of the above? You may need or want to get a job, so you'll have to figure out how to fit in the time for that, too. You'll have to start thinking about what your major will be: that'll be tough, with the hundreds from which you can choose. And you'll want to take advantage of all the great activities your school is offering that semester—the concerts, the speakers, the festivals, the parties. It will be a juggling act, but that's life at a large school.

Once you get through your freshman year, you'll begin to settle in. You can choose your roommates in years to come, or maybe you'll decide to live off campus or join a sorority or fraternity and live there. As you hone in on your major and begin to take more specialized courses, your class sizes will drop dramatically (then there'll be no hiding from your professors!). You'll come to know the ins and outs of campus life—the best time to grab lunch, when the machines in the computer lab closest to you are free, how to beat the crowd on registration day. You'll find your niche, make friends, and become a member of the clubs you're most interested in and have the time for. Or you can choose not to join any of them or start your own. You'll have a job you love that fits into your schedule. In short, you'll be a perfectly well-adjusted, but busy, large school student.

Academics

If you plan to attend a large state school, keep in mind that the academic environment at the school you choose will more than likely be dominated by two factors: big classes and big research. These can be overwhelming if you're not prepared for them. It's almost guaranteed that you'll be sitting in an auditorium with at least 200 other freshmen in all of your first-year survey courses. And these courses will probably be taught by graduate students, not professors, who are up to their ears in their University's latest groundbreaking research project. ("Scholars Under Fire" examines both sides of the complex issue of research at big universities.) You'll be identified by number, not by name, and if you have problems with a class, you could feel uncomfortable approaching a professor (or graduate student) who doesn't even know your name. This isn't meant to discourage you, but it is a reality of life at a large state school, especially your freshman year. Fortunately, it's a concern that everyone at large state schools is addressing. Penn State's *Daily Collegian* reports on how their school's students—all 40,000 of them—work with faculty on specific methods to combat this problem.

But don't think that the large number of students and emphasis on research diminish the academic opportunities and facilities you'll find at a big school. In this case, bigger *is* better. At a large school, you'll have more classes from which you can choose. For example, in the spring of 1999, Ohio State University offered over twenty classes in undergraduate chemistry alone! And at a big school, you can choose from unusual as well as traditional subjects. The out-of-the-ordinary programs described here that are offered at UT Austin and the University of Michigan are just the tip of the iceberg. The University of Minnesota is the first in the nation to feature a feminist economics class. If you're academically gifted, look into Honors Programs at large state schools, such as the one described in "More brains for your buck at U. Utah." If you have a taste for adventure, service learning and study abroad programs like those offered by big schools like Colorado University and Ohio State University are included in the curricula of most large schools. Whatever your tastes, you're sure to find a large school with the right courses for you.

Academic facilities at large schools, specifically libraries and computer facilities, are among the largest and best in the nation. Indiana University Bloomington's library system (made up of the main library and over twenty-five auxiliary libraries) is home to nearly 6 million bound volumes, 4 million micro-forms, and 2 million audiovisual materials, including audio, music, video, and film. Here the *Indiana Daily Student* informs you about IU's plans to put all of its library resources on the Internet to better reach students and the world. Computer facilities at big schools, too, are second-to-none. Did you know that Penn State has twenty-five separate computer labs, with Macintosh and IBM-compatible computers, Unix workstations, Internet connections, printers, and laptop ports, as well as multimedia instructional facilities, at locations all over campus? Accommodating their student bodies technologically has become a top priority at large state schools, and because of the number of students involved, this is a massive undertaking. The *Daily Targum* reports on Rutgers University's plans to wire all University sites together via an impressive communications network. Rutgers University's efforts can be considered representative of what's going on in big schools nationwide.

Read on to discover how these elements and more—including advising, cheating, grade inflation, and graduation rates—work together to create the academic atmosphere at a big state school. You may think you'll be just a face in the crowd, but, starting with the admissions process, big school reps like Wayne Sigler at the University of Minnesota have recognized helping you make a name for yourself is their number one task.

Admissions

These days, attracting prospective students is a top priority at colleges and universities around the country. With so many institutions for high school students to choose from, admissions departments have found it necessary to beef up staffs and budgets, using magazine, newspaper, radio, and even television ads in an attempt to make their school stand out from the crowd.

Large state schools have found it necessary to enter the fray. Because these schools offer reduced tuition to students from their state, it's important that they also enroll students from out of state, who will pay higher tuition fees. Furthermore, equal opportunity and affirmative action laws at large state schools require that admissions staff members work hard to attract young men and women who will guarantee diversity in their student body. Finally, every university wants the best and the brightest on its campus, and large state schools are no exception. All of these considerations can lead to a balancing act on the part of admissions directors. Some universities, like the University of Minnesota, have found that the best way to reach out to the large number of potential students is with a personal touch.

U. MINNESOTA'S 'BIGGEST FAN' KEEPS FRESHMAN CLASSES GROWING

By Coralie Carlson

MINNESOTA DAILY (Minneapolis, Minn.) 09/28/1998

While high school seniors sat timidly with their parents in the Office of Admissions Friday morning, Wayne Sigler bounded from family to family, offering Tootsie Pops and a taste of the University.

"How y'all doing? Where y'all from?" he beckoned with a slight Southern drawl, breaking the ice and putting the visitors at ease.

After extending greetings and candy to every person in the room, the former social studies teacher stood before the group in his navy blazer and gold wire-rimmed glasses.

"I want to welcome you to the University of Minnesota. My name is Wayne Sigler and I'm the director of admissions here at the University," he began.

Under his guidance, applications to the University from high school seniors have jumped 60 percent. This year's freshman class of more than 5,000 students is the largest in 12 years. In fact the surplus is so large, about 209 incoming freshmen were forced to stay at the Days Inn last week in lieu of available dorm rooms.

Sigler achieved success by believing in his product, the University, and serving his customers, the students.

"You don't get numbers by treating people like numbers," Sigler said.

A quick walk through Williamson Hall reveals the tangible results of his customer-service philosophy: The 2-year-old admissions office sits as a gold and maroon oasis for current and future students among the gray concrete backdrop.

Inside, the admissions staff holds small group sessions like the one Sigler leads every Friday morning, twice daily and on Saturdays. Convenience for interested students and their families is at the heart of the schedules, Sigler said.

Admissions employees shape custom tours for visitors, specific to their particular interests. Following the tours, the guests can use private interview rooms to voice concerns rather than exposing fears in front of the group.

"It's really meant to enhance their dignity," he said.

Sigler said he and his crew carry the same ideology off campus as they "spread the Minnesota story" at college fairs and high schools.

He also shoulders responsibility to ensure the University's customers include minorities and disadvantaged students. Although the school does not fill admissions quotas, officials strive to meet predetermined goals to enhance diversity.

The admissions office itself is one of the most diverse workforces at the University, said Whyte, who formerly headed up minority recruitment.

Sigler said the makeup of the admissions office staff mirrors the population University officials want to draw to the school.

Unfortunately, with so many applicants—16,666 for 1998—Sigler can't sell the University to everyone interested in buying.

"The absolute worst part is having to tell a student that I can't admit them," he said. "I don't like it any more today than I did 25 years ago." ∎

Class Size

Making each student feel recognized as an individual is one of the hardest challenges admissions directors at large state schools face. And with an average of 5,000 freshmen arriving each year, these schools need to maintain that emphasis on the individual as students begin their studies. With such incredible numbers, you may wonder how you'll be able to stand out from the crowd. Keep in mind that your concern is not uncommon or unfounded; this is often the most daunting prospect of attending a large state school. But plenty of advice from students and professors can help you make your way.

PENN STATE FACULTY ADVISE HOW TO STAND OUT IN A LARGE CLASS SETTING

By Angela J. Gates

DAILY COLLEGIAN (State College, Penn.) 11/16/1998

With more than 40,000 students enrolled at University Park this fall, several Penn State professors and instructors agree it is still possible for them to stand out in the crowd. Despite the large volume of students, D. Scott Bennett, assistant professor of international politics, said there are things students can do to make themselves known.

Students need to say hello to their professors, Bennett said. While it is difficult to remember a student's name in a large class, it is easier to remember their faces, he said, which gives them a little more context for their next meeting.

Bennett also said it's the students with legitimate concerns, not just complaints about grades, whom he remembers.

"People I'm happiest to see and happiest to remember are the people with a real, legitimate question, who don't understand or missed a class," Bennett said.

Part of the problem in becoming just another number may have to do with the fact many students don't introduce themselves to their professor when they do make an attempt to talk to them, said grad student Michele Lee Kozimor-King, who is teaching a social psychology class.

In her two classes of about 185 students, she said it's difficult to remember students when they don't tell her their names.

Kozimor-King said she mentioned this to her class. Afterwards, they told her they never realized they left out their names in conversation.

"Now, they make a point to tell me their names before they address me with concerns or problems," she said.

Some students, however, feel professors in large classes don't make efforts to get to know their students.

Freshman Nicole Cowley, an advertising and public relations major, said she feels a lot of professors sometimes pass students on to their teaching assistants instead of dealing with them directly.

"I feel like a number, lost in the crowd," she said of one of her classes, which has about 400 students.

In large classes, it may be difficult for teachers to get to know their students, but it is possible, said Annie McGregor, assistant professor of theater arts.

McGregor, who has taught about 800 students per semester for the past three years, said students must be participants in their education.

Students who make a conscious effort to talk to her tend to do better in class, she said, because they make a personal investment in their own education.

"If you want to talk, the door is open," McGregor said. "There's no reason for you to feel like a number." ∎

Teaching & Research

If you find your self in a class of 200, or even 400, students, the onus is on you to set your self apart from the rest. Professors really do want to know you, and sometimes introducing yourself and showing your interest in the class can make all the difference.

In some cases, however, a "professor" per se won't be teaching your class. As we saw in the Penn State article, an important issue affecting students who attend large state schools is teaching assistants, who are often graduate students, conducting classes.

Is this fair to you? Many undergraduate students, such as those at the University of Utah—one of the nation's largest "research universities"—feel that their education is being given short shrift in light of their school's emphasis on research and, relatedly, graduate education, over undergraduate education. These students have spoken up to get their School's policies on teaching and research changed, and it seems as though the School is taking their concerns seriously.

SCHOLARS UNDER FIRE: REDEFINING THE ROLE OF RESEARCH IN UNDERGRAD EDUCATION

By Eva Michelle Hunter

DAILY UTAH CHRONICLE (Salt Lake City, Utah) 09/30/1997

Wild-haired professors stare into bottles containing the mysteries of the universe. Students run about like rats wandering an endless maze, clad in gleaming white lab coats and skintight latex gloves. Grant proposals and midterm exams run neck and neck in the race for faculty attention.

Welcome to the world of the research university; welcome to the University of Utah.

Though higher education has long been inseparably united with academic research, the concept of the research university is an area of heated debate. Most critics agree that research universities greatly benefit graduate students seeking degrees in such fields as science and medicine; however, the effect of this particular college environment on undergraduate instruction is an area of some concern—and controversy.

The U embodies a threefold mission including service, teaching, and research. Some believe that inquiries made by the Utah state legislature into faculty teaching workload are an attempt to remove some of the U focus from research.

"Criticisms have been levied against excessive use of teaching assistants as classroom instructors, professors whose English proficiency is inadequate, and reward systems that are unbalanced because of too much attention to scholarly productivity and insufficient emphasis on classroom teaching," according to a report to the legislative Executive Appropriations Committee in September.

The recommended improvements include a provision that "greater priority be given to the teaching component of their mission," and that "teaching productivity be increased at the research universities." According to the report, this includes adjusting the mix of regular full-time faculty to include more teaching faculty who have little or no research expectations, and expect permanent faculty to have heavier teaching loads.

As a sophomore, Alison Schick joined her department's Student Advisory Committee to have a voice in recommending faculty for retention, promotion and tenure.

"When it comes to evaluating professors for tenure or retention, I thought the SAC would have some voice. It's just a formality," she said," we really don't have any power."

Schick recalls two professors who won teaching awards and weren't retained. For one of the instructors, "students signed petitions and cheered like crazy at graduation," but to no avail.

"We have all of these great teachers winning teaching awards, and our university doesn't keep them," she said.

Schick spoke glowingly of the research efforts in her academic department, but added, "they're all wonderful researchers, a lot of them just can't teach."

Research universities are undeniably different from their traditional counterparts. The Carnegie Foundation for the Advancement of Teaching defines the U's class of research universities as those which offer a full range of baccalaureate programs; are committed to graduate education through the doctorate, awarding 50 or more doctoral degrees each year; give high priority to research; and annually receive $40 million or more in federal support.

The primary focus of research institutions, according to Carnegie, falls on the shoulders of graduate teaching and faculty research.

Undergraduates at major research universities are often also heavily involved in research, according to Richard K. Koehn, vice president for research at the U.

"One of the major benefits of a research university is its opportunity for undergraduates," said Koehn, "I think there should be more opportunity for undergraduate research even at this university."

Koehn believes that a mandated faculty teaching workload "would impact virtually everything negatively."

Faculty find themselves required not only to fulfill the traditional roles of teacher and mentor for their students, but must also meet the demands of research and teaching in their chosen fields. In many cases, including the U, tenure depends on it.

McIntyre believes that these hours are well spent in faculty efforts to further the service mission of the U.

"When you mandate a certain fixed amount in the classroom," said Koehn, "what you really want to ensure is that you have a quality education. That is simply not determined by the amount of time spent in the classroom, either for students or faculty." ∎

PATENTS PAY OFF FOR MICHIGAN STATE U.

By Fred Woodhams

STATE NEWS (East Lansing, Mich.) 02/19/1998

Thanks to its cancer drugs, MSU ranks fourth in the nation for the amount of money it received from its patents, according to a report from a university association.

MSU's royalties amounted to $17.2 million in 1996, placing below the University of California's $63.2 million, Stanford University's $43.8 million and Columbia University's $40.6 million.

No other Michigan university made the top 10, according to the report released by the Association of University Technology Managers.

Almost all of MSU's patent funds come from its two cancer drugs, cisplatin and carboplatin, which were patented in the 1970s, said Fred Erbisch, director of MSU's Office of Intellectual Property. The inventors of the drugs and other related parties all received their share of the royalties, which is separate from the money received by the university for the patents.

Erbisch said the university has about 100 patents.

"Since 1992, when the office was set up, we have been trying to pursue patents aggressively," he said. "We're trying to tell (researchers) that if they have something new to give us a call and try to identify if it is a new invention."

The university's money from its inventions goes to the MSU Foundation, which was founded to support research. All of the foundation's funds come from patent monies, said George Benson, director of the MSU Foundation.

In 1996-97, the foundation, which is an independent, nonprofit organization, gave the university $5.6 million and has total assets of $152 million to further fund research at MSU.

"We've been putting it into our endowment so the university will have continuous funding long after the patents have expired," Benson said.

The foundation provides the university with grants for such programs as more research laboratories to recruit faculty and grants to individual professors, Benson said.

MSU Trustee Bob Traxler, who serves as one of the foundation's directors, said the foundation is an important component of the university community and provides the extra funding for research.

The foundation has looked ahead to the time when the drug patents run out, he said.

"We recognize that we hit the jackpot with a couple of patents," Traxler said. "We want the endowment to be protected and not seen as a solution to all of the university's financial problems."

Still, Erbisch said just because something is patented doesn't mean it will make the university money.

"It took seven years before a company finally decided that they would license it," he said.

The Associated Press contributed to this report. ∎

Adam W. Lasker/*The Daily Cardinal*

Obviously, universities need money, lots of it, to keep their doors open, and tuition simply does not pay all the bills, especially at big state schools where fees are lower. Research dollars, and money generated from patents on research, go a long way toward providing much-needed funds. What is often the case with research money, however, is that it gets put back into *more research*. Other sources of revenue must therefore be considered, so each year, big universities compete for attention from both the federal government and private industry.

Funding

Large grants of federal money for universities are rare, but they are there to be had by a few lucky institutions, such as the University of Minnesota. Because of the huge amounts of dollars at stake and what that could mean to the school, competition for these grants is hot. Sometimes, the review and acceptance process can take years. In this case, the payoff for Minnesota U. was worth it; the federal grant they received has created scholarships, fellowships, and research opportunities for scores of students and professors.

$9 MILLION NATIONAL SCIENCE FOUNDATION GRANT WILL FUND MINNESOTA U. SCIENCE CENTER

Jake Kapsner

MINNESOTA DAILY (Minneapolis, Minn.) 10/22/1998

University scientists are taking interdisciplinary research to new heights with a federal grant, bringing together Midwestern college undergraduates and corporate scientists at the University of Minnesota.

The National Science Foundation awarded the University $9 million over five years for a new Materials Research Science and Engineering Center, one of about 24 in the nation.

The money enables research into materials science and engineering, such as the study and production of more environmentally friendly plastics and artificial tissues to supplement natural bone and blood vessels.

"It's very hard to break into this game, and we're in," said H. Ted Davis, dean of the Institute of Technology, where the center resides.

Although the award is notable in terms of dollar amount, he said, it is especially significant as one of only two new awards the federal science agency made this year.

While the center focuses on materials science and engineering, about 20 faculty from various fields like physics and medicine will work in teams to study the properties of such materials as semiconductors, metal alloys and ceramics.

Goals of the polymer research, one of the center's two core programs, include making biodegradable plastics and creating water-dissolvable polymers to replace polyethylene, the most commonly used polymer, said Tim Lodge, group leader and University professor.

Grant money funds 30 to 35 fully paid graduate and post doctoral positions and the purchase of equipment like an electron microscope and x-ray scatterer, Bates said.

The renewable grant also provides three-month fellowship opportunities for students and faculty aimed to integrate science and education. The outreach arm will bring Native American undergraduate students from 13 Midwestern tribal colleges to the Twin Cities each year, Ward said.

Outreach also entails summer fellowships for student-faculty teams from 19 four-year colleges in Minnesota and Wisconsin to work on projects rooted in materials science and engineering, he said.

"Materials science is essentially non-existent for

undergraduate students and even faculty at these schools," Bates said.

In the last phase of the program, the new center joined the Center for Interfacial Engineering, a grant-based program operated through the Institute of Technology for the past 10 years, to bring in private revenue.

Interfacial center director Fennell Evans said 38 companies now bring in more than $1 million to the University.

So far, 12 companies have paid $30,000 to $40,000 to join the new materials science center, money that

goes back into programs and materials costs, Bates said.

Attracting private industry not only supplements revenue, it links students with potential employers and lets companies do work in an academic research environment, Bates said.

"This is one of the most successful programs in the country in terms of collaborative and nonproprietary research," Lodge said. "So it's the pursuit of knowledge, not the pursuit of profit." ∎

Notice here how, even though U Minn received a multimillion-dollar federal grant, they still found it necessary to join with the private sector to bring in even more money. This relatively new practice of universities joining forces with, and accepting money from, private corporate interests has not escaped the attention of students, who appreciate the perks gained from the money but wonder whether their schools aren't "selling out" to big corporations for the sake of money. In an attempt to build their budgets, universities have accepted research funding from private corporations and have even, in the case of Colorado University, developed courses specifically for corporate clients, resulting in huge profits for the schools. While such specialized classes teach valuable skills and bring big money into the school, at least one CU student can't help but question this phenomenon . . .

PRIVATIZING UNIVERSITY OF COLORADO

Matt Sprengeler

COLORADO DAILY (Boulder, Colo.) 09/21/1998

Ladies and gentlemen, welcome to the University of Colorado—brought to you by Lockheed Martin?

As the university soars into the next millennium, the wind beneath its wings will be the Total Learning Environment, brainchild of CU President John Buechner. The TLE is his blueprint for reshaping CU's four campuses over the next few years, making it "the premier public learning university in the United States," and money from the corporate world will play a major role in that change.

"We cannot rely on current state support to reach this initiative; we cannot rely on private philanthropy," Buechner said as he explained the TLE to CU's Board of Regents in June. To fill the gap between state money and out-and-out charity, Buechner is steering CU toward "strategic partnerships or joint ventures with the private sector," where corporations support CU and get something they want in return.

"It doesn't seem dollars from the state are going to keep up with our ambitions," Buechner said in August.

Of course, CU already works with the private sector. Professional programs, like business and engineering colleges, are turning out students specifically for certain careers, which leads to more overlap with the corporate world than a degree in dance usually does.

"The more progressive schools and the more progressive faculty are reaching out to the community, at least in the business community," said Denis Nock, director of the Center for Entrepreneurship, a joint effort of the Boulder campus business and engineering schools. "That is the foundation of our program."

So far those partnerships aren't as pronounced on the Boulder campus as elsewhere in the CU system. Part of the difference is focus—Boulder is supposed to be a general education and research university, while the Denver and Colorado Springs campuses are oriented more to serving their communities' needs and employers—but according to university spokesman

David Grimm, these community-friendly programs are good examples of what life under the TLE will be like.

One of the most prominent examples is the Denver campus business school, which offers specialized classes for specific employers like StorageTek and Lockheed Martin. Under their dean, Yash Gupta, the school is reaching out to give employers the classes they want.

"Professors need to be involved in the real life world so they can relate to the students," Gupta said. "How can you have a medical school without a hospital? By the same token, how can you have a business school without the business community?"

StorageTek and Lockheed Martin both get specialized MBA classes from the business school—they're taught on company premises and for company employees, and they deal with the company's problems. It's good for the company, Gupta said, and it's also good for professors to get out of the ivory tower.

The programs are completely funded by their private partners, Gupta said, at a cost of about $1,000 per student. Employees in the programs work together, tackle problems affecting their company as team projects, and improve their communication skills. ■

Academic Resources

Fortunately for students at large state universities, money coming in from research, federal grants, and corporate funding means that their schools can offer the latest in technology to all who attend. Remember that every university needs money to operate, and, all controversy aside, these types of funding enable big state schools to compete with smaller private colleges and universities. Without this money, large state schools would be forced to raise tuition or offer substandard facilities. Colleges and universities with the best technology will be the ones that succeed as we enter the new millennium. But high technology is not cheap.

Indiana and Rutgers universities are at the forefront of bringing high technology to three key facets of big campus life: the library, the dorm, and classroom. Big university libraries are often massive and intimidating, but imagine having all of your school's library resources at your fingertips over the Internet. That's what IU's massive digital library program is working toward. And RutgersUniversityNet 2000 will eventually wire all of that campus's 100 academic buildings and dormitories together—literally creating a small city in contact via computer.

IU DIGITAL LIBRARIES PROVIDE RESOURCES TO ONLINE USERS
By Andy Gammill

INDIANA DAILY STUDENT (Bloomington, Ind.) 02/04/1998

Old books, photographs and ragtime sheet music from the Indiana University Lilly Library might soon be available to the rest of the world via the Internet.

The digital library program, which acts as an online "complex museum exhibit," would give access to numerous historical and cultural works for any computer user, said Gerry Bernbom, the special assistant for digital libraries to the Office of the Vice President for Information Technology.

The different parts of the IU digital library program are spread out to various IU schools and departments. But as the effort becomes more centralized, these libraries could be tied together and become more centrally located.

IU's effort is part of a national trend at colleges and research institutions to put more primary source documents on the Internet. In fact, IU is a part of a federation of schools putting different collections on-line.

"We are trying to build digital libraries collaboratively so we don't duplicate each other's efforts," Dean of University Libraries Suzanne Thorin said.

The Library of Congress decided several years ago to make some of its collections available online. Thorin was a part of the original team that created the program.

When Thorin came to IU, building a digital library program became a part of her job description.

"(IU President) Myles Brand was very enthusiastic about building digital library resources at IU and sharing those resources nationally and internationally," she said.

Thorin said IU's digital library program is in the top 20 digital libraries in the country.

Those involved in the IU digital library program foresee bigger and better things for digital libraries.

Bernbom agrees digital libraries will have an important role in the future.

"Places like Indiana University have a tremendous amount of very interesting materials with high quality historical information that isn't seen because it cannot be circulated," Bernbom said.

IU is planning several projects to add to the program. The next project will be a collection of photographs of southwestern Indiana from the Lilly Library. Thorin said they are also planning to scan collections of sheet music and miniature books from the 19th century housed at the Lilly Library.

The digital library program is a joint effort of the IU Libraries, the Office of the Vice President for Information Technologies, the School of Library and Information Sciences and several IU schools and departments. ∎

RUTGERS U. SEES FIRST CLASSROOMS WITH HIGH SPEED CONNECTIONS
By Cathleen Lewis and Aliza Sacknovitz

DAILY TARGUM (New Brunswick, N.J.) 11/05/1998

Some University students yesterday saw the benefits of RutgersUniversityNet 2000 for the first time when a presentation was made in the newly finished Ethernet-connected classrooms on the College Avenue campus.

Work on the RUNet 2000 work—which now hooks up 10 classrooms and six residence halls University-wide—began this summer and was completed yesterday, although some buildings have been connected since September, Keith Sproul, student housing network coordinator, said.

The wiring will provide high-speed Ethernet connections, along with 40 entertainment-oriented television channels and 20 channels of educational programming, Sproul said.

At a meeting to orient tour guides to the assets of the program, Sproul said the goal of the work is to "wire all dorms and all 100 academic buildings."

RUNet 2000 is intended to wire all University buildings together with a video, voice and data systems communications network over the next few years.

Members of the Scarlet Key, a group that leads campuswide tours to prospective students, organized the program to better inform curious prospects.

"They want to know about housing and computers—stuff that is important when choosing a school," College of Pharmacy third-year student Jesua Rosen, president of Scarlet Key, said.

Sproul said the orientation was "the first time one of the network connections has been used in these classrooms."

"A lot of academic buildings are already partially wired," Sproul said.

Sproul said it has not been decided which buildings will be wired next.

We "have to worry about which residence halls we can do when students are there," Sproul said. "We are making a lot of effort not to disrupt student life too badly. We are trying to minimize the disruption." ∎

Academic Opportunities

It's a common misconception that large state schools can't compete with smaller universities when it comes to academic offerings. Actually, quite the opposite is true. You've just read how two big schools are spearheading their own technological revolutions, and the area of academics is no different. Because they're larger and have a student body who exhibit a diversity of interests, large state schools can offer a great number and wider variety of academic subjects. Let's face it, you're more likely to find a group of students interested in a specialized subject—say, the economics of fishing in the South Pacific—at a school where the student body numbers 40,000 than at a 2,000 student small liberal arts college. And there is strength in numbers. Students at large schools have successfully campaigned to get the classes *they* want into the curriculum.

The most important thing is for you to find a school that suits your academic needs and talents and then take advantage of all it has to offer. For instance, because their schools are often research facilities, some undergraduates at large state schools, like UT Austin, can work closely with graduate students and professors in specialized areas of study. And engineering students at the University of Michigan boosted their resumes, and had a lot of fun, by building a genuine race car. It just goes to show you that there's something for everyone at a large state school.

U. TEXAS UNDERGRAD RESEARCH CHARTING NEW WATERS

By Suzannah Creech

DAILY TEXAN (Austin, Texas) 06/15/1998

When Rachael O'Brien graduated from the University of Texas at Austin in May she had a degree in civil engineering and a semester of individual research in environmental engineering behind her.

O'Brien was a spring recipient of a UT undergraduate research fellowship. This fellowship enabled her to begin conducting a bottle study she designed on bacteria and gas pollution.

In August, O'Brien will head to the University of California at Berkeley for graduate studies in environmental engineering, and she said she feels much better prepared for her future studies thanks to the undergraduate research she did at the University.

With 37,000 undergraduates, many likely to pursue graduate studies, the University has joined other large universities in recognizing the importance of undergraduate research, said Jon Dollard, associate dean of graduate studies.

"People are realizing this is a kind of thing that can work for undergraduates," Dollard said. "It's a wonderful opportunity for undergraduates to associate with people doing research."

And while graduate students have always been associated with academic research, many undergraduates are recognizing that the opportunities are out there for them as well.

"All you have to do is talk to a professor," O'Brien said. "If they don't have any research opportunities for you they might have a colleague who does."

But a report issued last month by the Carnegie Foundation for the Advancement of Teaching stated that universities underuse their resources when it comes to undergraduates. "Thousands of students graduate without ever seeing the world-famous professors or tasting genuine research," the report stated.

Jennifer Cooper, a zoology/anthropology senior and winner of a UT fellowship for undergraduate research, said her research experience has taught her things students don't learn in class.

"It's prepared me for graduate school more than anything else," Cooper said. "I've found it's helped me sharpen my ability to analyze problems and to design and carry out research."

Cooper agreed that undergraduates deserve to be given as many research opportunities as possible.

While scientific research often receives high acclaim, research opportunities are also available in the liberal arts and the humanities.

Meier said these two areas are just as important as scientific research.

"It's not just scientific research that's beneficial to society," Meier said. "It's important for universities to understand great creative works, the history of our culture and the histories and languages of other cultures. For undergraduates to be involved in that process, not only will they understand it better, but they may help us to understand it better."

Many UT undergraduates are working either on research projects of their own or on those of graduate students and faculty.

O'Brien participated in the Undergraduate Research Fellowship Program, one research program offered at the University.

What originated as a student government campaign promise in 1996 is now a $100,000 program, which gave fellowships to 47 students this spring, said Dianne Ruetz, administrative associate for the office of the vice president for research.

"The main value of this is the experience," Ruetz said. "It is to get students more involved in their area of study rather than have them sit in class and take notes—to be more than just a number."

Besides being a factor in creating a well-educated graduate, Dollard said, research can be a major determinant in a student's career path.

"If you start with undergraduate research, you may learn exactly what you want to do," Dollard said.

For O'Brien, who plans a career in environmental engineering, the research she has done has helped to make the concepts she learned in class concrete.

"I have a better grasp of the figures and data involved in environmental energy, understanding exactly what pollution limits are and what I'm detecting," O'Brien said.

While the Carnegie report says it is the universities who underuse their resources, Cooper said students do the same thing.

"The instructors at UT are underutilized by the students," Cooper said. "You owe it to yourself to take advantage of what your instructor has to offer you." ∎

U. MICHIGAN ENGINEERING TEAM DESIGNS RACE CAR

By Daniel Weiss

MICHIGAN DAILY (Ann Arbor, Mich.) 12/01/1998

Resumes do not come much better than this: "Member of a team that designed, built and raced a car capable of accelerating from zero to 60 in 4.7 seconds."

For some University students, this is no idle dreaming. It describes a year-long project taking place in the North Campus' Autolab. About 45 students, many in engineering, have joined as a team to design and build a race car for a national competition to be held May 19–23 at the Pontiac Silverdome.

The team comes together under the campus chapter of the international group Society of Automotive Engineers (SAE). This project, one of four sponsored by the society, is referred to as Formula SAE. The project aims to design and build a new race car each year, making the fastest car possible.

At the national competition, judges evaluate cars not only on how well they perform, but on their design as well. No more than $9,000 must be spent on the car, and teams must show they can produce more cars at or below the target cost.

Todd Brittingham, co-captain of the team and an engineering senior, said the business aspect of the competition complements the engineering side.

While the car costs approximately $9,000, the year-long project is budgeted in the neighborhood of $40,000. Financial contributions come from a variety of sources such as the University's School of Engineering, which gives $3,000 to the project and provides space in the Autolab for the team to work. Ford Motor Company also donates $5,000.

The project is divided into five groups—chassis, electronics, body, business and engine—each with its own leader. John Matsushima, a Engineering graduate student, leads the group responsible for the engine. Matsushima spent five years in Japan working for Toyota, where he coordinated the production of the RAV4 engine.

He said working for the formula team differs greatly from his work in Japan.

"This is actually more fun," he said. "We can spend as much money as we can to go as fast as we can."

Brittingham said the project will help make the team members stronger job candidates.

"This project is a big resume booster," Brittingham said.

He recounted a story of a Ford recruiter interested only in hiring engineers with masters or doctorate degrees who said he would accept someone with a bachelors degree if the applicant had worked on the formula car. The recruiter called participation in the project "a golden ticket," Brittingham said.

Resume booster or not, the team takes the competition seriously.

Kharmai recalled that before the competition last May, some team members put in incredibly long hours. "We would come in here at eight a.m. and leave at one a.m.," he said.

A sign posted in the team shop may best indicate the team's will to win.

"What have you done to beat Cornell University today?" the sign reads. ■

Besides offering a wide range of interesting—and different—subjects to students, large state schools compete academically with smaller, private institutions through their Honors Programs. In these programs, academically gifted students pursue intense studies in areas of interest, most often their majors, receiving instruction from experts in the field and delving into subjects more deeply than the regular curriculum requires. You usually have to maintain a higher GPA to be admitted to an Honors Program, but the benefits gained from such an opportunity are well worth the effort. Successful honors students like those at the University of Utah receive scholarships for further study and enjoy extra activities open only to them, among other rewards (almost makes hitting the books fun).

MORE BRAINS FOR YOUR BUCK AT U. UTAH

By Brent Olson

DAILY UTAH CHRONICLE (Salt Lake City, Utah) 02/01/1999

You may have thought you forfeited the right to take stimulating classes from interesting professors who know your name (in classrooms smaller than Mammoth cave) when you decided to come to the University of Utah instead of selling your left kidney to attend a prestigious small liberal arts college.

However, there is a way to take classes just like those offered at small liberal arts college at the U, thanks to the honors program.

According to assistant director Esther Radinger, "The Honors program is considered the equivalent of a small liberal arts college within a large university."

In order to join the honors program, U students need a minimum 3.4 GPA; there are no other requirements. Approximately 850 students are currently part of the honors program.

Of course, the classes, taught by over fifty hand-picked professors, are what the program is all about. The professors come from different departments and backgrounds, and some are business professionals who bring "real world" experience to the classes.

Before a professor can teach with the honors program, he or she must be recommended by students and their departments.

The professors create unique classes they want to teach which are approved, before they are taught, by the honors program Advisory Committee (HPAC) and the Honors Student Advisory Committee (HSAC).

Professor Ann Engar, who teaches in the program, explained part of why professors enjoy teaching in the honors program. Engar said, "there are good students in all classes . . . but what is true of honors students is they do recognize the importance of coming to class and they engage in the material [presented]."

In addition to regularly scheduled classes, the program offers dozens of courses that vary year to year. This semester's choices ranged from "Enemies Within: The Idea of Conspiracy in American History" by Professor Robert Goldberg of the Department of History, to "Confirmation of Spiritual Diversity in Love and Community" by Professor David Derezotes of the Graduate School of Social Work.

There is a class for just about everyone in the program. Joanna Joyner, chairwoman of HSAC, said that her favorite class was a five-quarter series of classes team-taught by two teachers who deal with both the scientific and cultural developments of the Western world.

For HSAC member Tiffany Merrill, it was Professor Bob Croyle's class, "Life and Work of Freud," that "got me interested in my major."

Joshua Nelson, the Vice Chair of HSAC, loved Martha Bradley's class "Image of the City" because of its examination and discussion of actual cities in Utah.

The Student Directed Seminar is one of the unique features of the U's honors program. With the approval of HPAC and HSAC, seniors in the program can design a class and teach it with a professor's help. According to Radinger, this has happened about 35 times in the program's history.

The honors program also gives scholarships to help offset the costs of honors foreign studies programs. There is an ongoing six-week Cambridge, England summer study program with three scholarships available for one-third of the total cost of the program.

The program has also arranged summer programs to Germany, France, Austria, Greece and Switzerland in previous years and will continue to do so in the future.

The program holds activities for program members. In December, the program provided discount tickets to one evening performance of the Nutcracker ballet and held a reception afterward.

HSAC member Daina Graybosch said that the honors program is for students "if you really want to come out of college with a liberal education," but added "if you don't want your ideas and ethics challenged, don't take Honors classes."

Freshman Sunny Nakae agreed: "It's an opportunity to explore new horizons. It's a challenge but it's a challenge that's fun." ∎

The Honors Program at the University of Utah is just one of many ways that undergraduates at large state schools can enhance their studies. Out-of-the-ordinary learning experiences are not uncommon at large state schools. In fact, while Utah's honors students burn the midnight oil to achieve an academic edge, the young men and women in the University of Colorado INVST program burn calories—pulling weeds, fishing, and more—as they learn.

U. COLORADO STUDENTS LEARN BY SERVING

By Matt Sprengeler

Colorado Daily (Boulder, Colo.) 07/27/1998

Can you achieve social justice by pulling knapweed? Some CU students and instructors hope so.

As temperatures climbed toward triple digits, a band of about 15 hardy souls climbed Flagstaff Mountain on July 17 and spent half the day attacking knapweed, a persistent vegetable invader that crowds out native plants. The group, mostly CU students, labored away under the watchful eyes of hawks cruising on midday thermals.

This was just a taste—the weed-pullers, as well as a similar band who spent the day working elsewhere on the mountain, were kicking off a summer of hard work across the country, and in some cases beyond. The students are all members of INVST, a special CU program that combines academics with community service.

INVST stands for International and National Voluntary Service Training, and service is exactly what this two-year program provides. Knapweed is a warm-up; later this summer INVST students will do everything from travel around Mexico studying issues like NAFTA to live in a Denver homeless shelter.

"Being in the city with no money, nothing like that, gives you a completely different perspective," said Kristen Greco, a second-year INVST student who lived in the shelter last summer. "All the stores, all the people with money, are in a completely different plane of existence."

That's the sort of education INVST tries to impart. In the summers, participants experience worlds different from their own. During the school year, they take courses about community change and social justice.

"Basically, our goal is to create the next generation of community leaders," said Kevin King, INVST's outreach coordinator. King is a graduate student in education and an INVST alumnus—he liked the program so much that he came back. Program participants are undergraduates, usually juniors and seniors, he said.

King is coordinating the trip to Mexico, which is the summer program for second-year INVST students. Students will see the effect that NAFTA, the multina-tional trade agreement, has on both sides of the U.S.-Mexico border, he said, particularly the environmental and social consequences.

The second-year students will also live in a small Mexican fishing village for several weeks, working with a Mexican group called Familias Unidas which King said is similar to Habitat for Humanity.

The first-year students will roam the West this summer. They will start in New Mexico, helping revitalize areas damaged by fires, then go to the Samaritan House homeless shelter in Denver, and will wrap up on a Navajo reservation in Arizona.

"Our mission is to train a group of young leaders who will take on the task of community service," said INVST director Jim Downton as he surveyed his knapweed-bearing charges. "It's really about this group of amazing young people."

Sweating under his pith helmet, INVST student Andy Johnson said his experience in the program has widened his vision. "This is what I think of when I think of a liberal arts education," he said. ∎

Of course, learning in another country needn't involve casting a fishing line. At many large state schools, students can take the same classes they would on campus at universities around the world. Large state schools are known for their study-abroad programs. Because of their size and the number of students they send abroad each year, big schools can enter into study-abroad relationships with virtually any university worldwide. And most credit earned abroad is transferable back home. What better way for an international relations major to brush up on Japanese than by studying in Tokyo for a semester? And while most students enroll in classes abroad to enhance language skills, others look at study abroad as a great chance to see the world before graduation.

OHIO STATE U. STUDY ABROAD PROGRAM BENEFITS FUTURE, STUDENTS SAY

By Lindsey Brown

THE LANTERN (Columbus, Ohio) 06/02/1998

The summer before her senior year of high school, Suzanne Parks took part in an exchange program to Germany.

Four years later, Parks, a junior majoring in international studies, is preparing to study abroad for six weeks this summer in St. Petersburg, Russia.

Parks is leaving June 21, and she has been preparing by working on her language skills and taking classes to better understand Russian.

"It's a huge mental preparation," Parks said. "It's going to be hard to be away from people I am around all the time."

Carlo Colecchia, coordinator of education abroad, said Ohio State University's Office of International Education offers 80 programs in 30 countries on a year-long basis. Some of the countries include Argentina, Denmark, Ecuador, Germany, Ireland, Japan and Spain.

Colecchia said there are many reasons why students study abroad.

"I think it's a great way to meet people both abroad and from Ohio State because we have a number of group programs," he said. "It attracts a certain student with good grades. They are interested in expanding their horizons and this is a great way to do that."

Parks said she is studying abroad to improve her language skills and because it is related to her major. She said she has also gotten to know the people she is traveling with.

Brian Zaharack, a graduate student majoring in comparative studies, said he has studied abroad twice in Israel and is going back this summer to study the Hebrew language.

"It's a great experience to get involved in a different culture," Zaharack said. "I love learning different languages, and it's an education in itself."

Colecchia said students also study abroad as a practical career builder. "Having international experience is a very common attribute employers are looking for, especially with the globalization of the economy," he said.

Aaron Retish, a graduate student majoring in Russian history, said he is studying in St. Petersburg, Russia for two months this summer. He said he wants to study the language and also start research for his dissertation.

Colecchia said students who study abroad earn between eight and 15 credit hours per quarter. He said students sometimes earn fewer credits because the program is shorter.

"Students do earn graded OSU credits, regular transfer credits, as if they were taking their courses here on campus," Colecchia said. "Study abroad students usually make regular academic progress towards graduation."

Colecchia said students find the programs surprisingly affordable, and grant money and financial aid is available to students going abroad.

"We have programs as inexpensive as just tuition, but we have other programs like an exchange to Japan where the program fee might not be so high, but the cost of living in the country can be substantial so you have to factor that in," he said. "We try to keep our programs as inexpensive as we can. We're not for profit."

"It doesn't cost as much as one would think," Retish said. "It comes out to be about the same amount as taking classes at OSU."

About 693 students received academic credit for some type of overseas study last year, Colecchia said. He also said students should speak to a study abroad coordinator to see what program is the best for them.

"Certain programs are suited for different students," Colecchi said. "Some programs just require good academic standing, and other programs, like our exchange program, tend to be a little bit more competitive."

Zaharack said studying abroad is a wonderful experience and he recommends it to everyone.

"The first time I studied abroad I was really happy to get out of Columbus," he said. "I made friends, learned the language and learned a lot about myself. I can't wait to learn more this year." ∎

Outstanding Professors

Of course, what will make or break your academic experience at any university you choose is the quality of the instruction you receive. We all know that a great teacher can make even the most difficult subject come alive. On the campuses of large state schools, such great men and women inspire and enlighten students every day. If you think that professors at large state schools probably don't compare to those teaching at prestigious private colleges, these stories of two men teaching at Michigan state universities will change your mind. Both men were rewarded for their exemplary credentials with positions of national prestige. Thankfully for their students, both plan to keep on teaching.

U. MICHIGAN PROFESSOR ADVISING CLINTON

By Mike Spahn

MICHIGAN DAILY (Ann Arbor, Mich.) 09/11/1998

While most University professors traversed campus to get to work this morning, Kenneth Lieberthal strolled across the White House grounds to meet President Bill Clinton and introduce him to a new set of Asian ambassadors.

Lieberthal, a political science and business administration professor, took a two-year leave from the University and accepted a job this summer as special assistant to the president for Asian affairs and senior director for Asian affairs on the National Security Council. The position makes him the chief adviser to Clinton on issues involving countries from North Korea to Australia to Burma.

The economic crisis in Japan, nuclear testing in North Korea and the increasing importance of China in world affairs have forced Lieberthal to hit the ground running in Washington, D.C.

"The Asian financial crisis is the fundamental problem we will have to deal with in my two or 2 1/2 years here," he said.

Just one month into his term, Lieberthal has already played an integral role in the Clinton administration's

Tony Cho/The Daily Targum

daily negotiations with North Korea with regard to its development of nuclear weapons.

He is also coordinating Japanese Prime Minister Keizo Obuchi's Sept. 22 visit to the United States.

"I'm by no means working alone, but I will provide final briefings for the President and attend the meeting," Lieberthal said. "I'll basically be the note-taker."

Lieberthal said his expertise in Chinese politics, which he taught during his 15 years at the University, qualified him for the position.

He's been visiting China for the last 30 years.

Lieberthal's colleagues at the University say he is the perfect man for the job. John Campbell, a political science professor who went to graduate school with Lieberthal and has taught with him for years, said Lieberthal is a great man and a super teacher.

"He is very knowledgeable, very smart, and well respected in China," said Campbell, who specializes in Japanese politics. "He has, for a long time, worked on foreign relations with China, but also worked quite hard at broadening his knowledge of the entire region."

Students have also praised Lieberthal. First-year law student Casey Thomson said the professor's temporary leave is a great loss for the University.

"He was an absolutely great teacher," Thomson said. "I didn't even want to take his class, but I went to the first lecture and he totally won me over."

While National Security Adviser Sandy Berger selected Lieberthal for the post August 10, this is not the professor's first contact with Washington. Lieberthal has served as an adviser to the State Department for nearly two decades, largely because of his trips to China and his great expertise in foreign relations.

"I had briefed Sandy Berger and his predecessor Tony Lake several times on issues affecting China," Lieberthal said.

Lieberthal keeps a humble—or at least humorous—aura among international policy makers.

"But maybe I got the job for lack of other good candidates," he joked. ■

NATIONAL AFRICAN ASSOCIATION NAMES MICHIGAN STATE U. DIRECTOR ITS LEADER

By Melissa Burden

THE STATE NEWS (East Lansing, Mich.) 11/30/1998

A member of the African Studies Association for 30 years, the director of Michigan State University's African Studies Center was recently named president of the national association.

For a year term that began this month, David Wiley will serve as the leader of the more than 3,000-member organization. The African Studies Association, which consists of mainly U.S. university faculty members, is the world's largest scholarly association regarding African studies. Formed in 1957, it also has members from Canada, Europe and Africa.

Wiley, vice president of the association in 1997, said he hopes during his term the association will strengthen relations between the United States and Africa.

"I'm hoping that the association can find ways it can interact with the media, can strengthen the African universities and increase the exchange between African and U.S. libraries," he said.

Wiley said he plans to help spread African teachings in American colleges and schools.

He said the association also encourages more accurate media coverage of Africa because Africa is often misrepresented in U.S. media and film. Even so, interest in Africa is growing rapidly in the United States, he said.

"This is a very important moment for this associa-tion to remind Americans of how much of their language, art, music and culture came from Africa," Wiley said.

Before he came to MSU in 1977 to direct its African Studies Center, Wiley directed a similar center at the University of Wisconsin at Madison from 1972 to 1977.

Wiley, who edits the quarterly "African Rural and Urban Studies" journal, has conducted research in Zimbabwe, Zambia and Kenya and also has lectured at the University of Zambia.

MSU history and African studies professor David Robinson said the president runs an annual meeting and oversees several association committees.

Robinson, the association's president in 1992–1993, said Wiley has done a good job in acquiring library materials for libraries in Africa. He said Wiley will put his position as president a high priority.

"He's extremely bright and well-organized and works hard, probably too hard," Robinson said.

John Hudzik, dean for International Studies and Programs, said Wiley is an expert on sub-Saharan African issues.

"He not only has a message, but he captures people's attention when he talks about it," Hudzik said. "David has for years been a very instrumental force nationally and internationally in shaping policy and programs for Africa and the relationship between this country and Africa." ■

Advising

Faculty members at big schools are involved in more than teaching. You've already read that many conduct academic research in addition to teaching. Other faculty members get involved directly with students as advisers. Your college adviser most often will be a professor but could also be a graduate or older student. He or she will help you select classes that best suit your needs and interests, lend an ear when you have concerns, and guide you through the treacherous—and confusing—process of choosing a major. You'll invest a lot of faith in these people.

Not surprisingly, students at big schools like the University of Maryland often complain about advisers. They question whether their best interests can possibly be given priority when each adviser may have many advisees. While this is a problem on many big campuses, advisers themselves aren't totally to blame. As with anything else, students need to be proactive with their advisers, especially if they attend a big school.

U. MARYLAND ADVISORS' PERFORMANCE NOT UP TO PAR, SOME STUDENTS SAY

By Rochelle Kohen

THE DIAMONDBACK (College Park, Md.) 11/4/1998

Once again, spring registration time is here.

In a rush to plan next semester before their registration date, students flip through pages of the Schedule of Classes, searching for the right courses to meet requirements, not forgetting to select back-up courses in case the classes they want are filled.

All the while, they compare notes with each other to find good teachers and interesting classes and meet with advisors to discuss their options.

While some students look forward to the advice they receive during advising appointments, others say the experience causes more harm than good.

"My advisor told me to take English 101 because it would be easy and it's not. It's causing me lots of stress and lack of sleep," said Alia Lamborghini, a freshman letters and sciences major.

While advisors are responsible for making sure each student progresses over the years, most of the responsibility lies with the student to be prepared and informed about academic requirements, said Wayne McIntosh, director of undergraduate studies for the government and politics department in the College of Behavioral and Social Sciences. Students are quick to blame advisors for their academic problems, he said.

"Students are adults and they should take responsibility," McIntosh said. "An advisor can help a student make a decision but can't make it for them."

Sometimes students receive advice which they choose to ignore, said Robert Hampton, associate provost for academic affairs and dean of undergraduate studies.

In some cases, students do not even show up for their advising appointments and still complain about advising, he added. "More often than not, you hear from students who are disappointed," Hampton said.

While negative comments regarding advising tend to be more common than positive feedback, according to Hampton, there are also students whose advising experiences are consistently good. These students say advisors provide them with the assistance and advice they need.

Advising is tailored specifically to each college, school or department on campus, Hampton said. Each has its own qualifications for its advisors and offers its own training for advisors. Some require that their advisors be faculty, while others have students advising, he said. In some schools, advising is mandatory for all students and in other schools, advising is done on a voluntary basis, Hampton said.

In the College of Journalism, advisors are graduate students who have a good GPA and are outgoing, said Meg Brewer, an administrative assistant in the college.

Advisors must study a lot to understand the way credits and requirements work, she said. "We want people who interact well with others," Brewer said.

Hampton's office hosts an annual advising confer-

ence to discuss advising policies and issues on campus. The conference covers items such as student expectations of advisors, the role of parents in advising and student complaints, Hampton said. ∎

Academic Dishonesty

Say you're enrolled in Intro to Statistics, which you're taking very seriously since you know you'll need it for the major in psychology you just declared. You attend Big State U, so there are 200 other students in your class; you notice during the first exam that the professor can't see that many of the students are cheating. Do you tell? At some schools, you may have to. Because of the rampant cheating problem at many big schools, some, like Clemson University, have voted in honor codes and other rules concerning cheating. Previously the domain of smaller, more academically competitive colleges, honor codes have become a part of life at many big schools.

CLEMSON U. STUDENT GOVERNMENT LOOKS TO IMPROVE ACADEMICS BY PREVENTING DISHONESTY

By Kristi Devlin

THE TIGER (Clemson, S.C.) 01/22/1999

Student government members passed a statement of Academic Integrity through the Academic Council on Dec. 9. Clemson College was founded as a military school, and like most military institutions, honor was a treasured virtue. Somewhere between now and then, some students, faculty and administration think that any code of honor has fallen to the wayside.

The following statement will be seen in all new University publications such as the 1999 Student Handbook and University announcements:

"As members of the Clemson University community, we have inherited Thomas Green Clemson's vision of this institution as a 'high seminary of learning.' Fundamental to this vision is a mutual commitment to truthfulness, honor and responsibility, without which we can not earn the trust and respect of others. Furthermore, we recognize that academic dishonesty detracts from the value of a Clemson degree. Therefore, we shall not tolerate lying, cheating, or stealing in any form."

The University is not attempting to instate an official honor code as University of Virginia, Vander-

bilt or Washington and Lee have. "This is just a baby step towards what we would like to see," said Matt Dunbar, student body president.

A committee was formed last year by Dunbar to approve a draft of this statement. He also suggested that professors read the statement to students on the first day of classes, and mentioned the possibility of its addition to course syllabi.

The next step is a meeting of student government leaders and the Faculty Senate. The idea of a statement of integrity came out of a concern of a lack of structure in the current policy, explained Dunbar.

Buried deep in the pages of the student handbook are current guidelines for academic dishonesty. Among the illegal violations are plagiarism and receiving or using unauthorized aid. Academic dishonesty also includes the unauthorized use of another person's student online account.

The outline of what constitutes an offense is relatively self explanatory, but the procedure gets much less clear cut concerning what a faculty member is to do if they catch a student violating the policy.

The handbook states, "When, in the opinion of a faculty member, there is evidence that a student has committed an act of academic dishonesty, the faculty member should contact the Ombudsman in the Office of Undergraduate Academic Services to discuss the evidence and see if the seriousness warrants a formal charge of academic dishonesty."

Dunbar's concern is that many teachers do not report cases of dishonesty and take matters into their own hands. He feels there is no standardized procedure that teachers follow when they catch a student cheating. If you get caught cheating in one class, he explained, the penalty may be very different than in another. ■

Grade Inflation

There are a lot less dishonest ways than cheating to get good grades; grade inflation may be one of them. At many schools, big and small alike, grade point averages (GPAs) have risen steadily over the years. Some blame grade inflation—the tendency for professors to award high grades to more students—for the trend. Others claim that since today's students are better prepared for college than those in years past, higher grades are deserved. At the University of Minnesota, GPAs have risen steadily over the last 10 years. Some look at this as something other than a cause for celebration.

GRADE INFLATION TREND GETS HIGH AND LOW MARKS FROM OFFICIALS
By Sarah Hallonquist

MINNESOTA DAILY (Minneapolis, Minn.) 02/23/1998

As far as grades go, a B just isn't what it used to be—and at the University, that's raising a few eyebrows.

An analysis of the University's grades shows a steady climb in high marks over the last 10 years. During the next few months, a committee will look into rising grade point averages, an issue which plagues colleges and universities across the nation.

At Princeton, a report released this month documents a definite grade inflation trend. The average GPA rose to 3.42 in 1997 from 3.08 in 1973.

Similarly, the mean GPA at the University of Washington reached 3.12 in 1996, up from 2.31 in 1964. And at Stanford University, As and Bs make up 80 percent of the grades earned.

Compared to the higher grades at these schools, the University might be only at the doorstep of the grade inflation problem. Reasons for the increases are difficult to pin down, and school officials are reluctant to offer concrete answers.

Possibilities include better academically prepared students, increasing instruction and grading by non-tenured professors, and changing philosophies about what grades measure.

A subcommittee of the University Senate's Committee on Educational Policy is examining whether grade inflation is a problem at the University.

"There have been concerns raised around the University for decades about the unreliability of the current grading structure," said Judith Martin, the subcommittee's chair.

Since 1989, the average fall quarter grade point average for University undergraduates has risen to 2.96 from 2.83.

"This isn't any monumental increase," said John Kellogg, a senior analyst in the Office of Planning and Analysis. But he added, "It's a definite trend."

And with that trend comes an increase in the percentages of As and Bs earned in several of the University's undergraduate colleges.

The Carlson School of Management tops the list with

the largest change. This fall, 49 percent of the school's grades were As, compared to 30 percent in 1987.

Jerry Rinehart, director of undergraduate programs for the Carlson school, said the increase can be attributed partly to higher-achieving incoming students.

"Students are doing better before they come to us, and they continue to do better," he said. "We have students who are used to doing well in the classroom."

Rinehart's view is not far from those of other faculty members and administrators. Many say the University is admitting students who are better prepared for college study, leading them to perform at higher levels.

This fall, the University admitted its largest and smartest freshman class. Eighty-seven percent of entering students met preparation requirements compared with 74 percent in 1992. About 17 percent would have met current requirements in 1985.

"Definitely over time it's a strong class academically," said admissions director Wayne Sigler.

But smarter students aren't the only plausible interpretation for the school's higher grades.

'Escape from the curve'

Concerns over grade inflation arose during the Vietnam War, when students and professors who opposed the war clung to draft deferment loopholes. High-achieving college students weren't drafted, so some professors intentionally inflated grades for the sake of keeping students off the battlefield.

"My suspicion is that people just got used to giving higher grades at that point and never got out of it," Martin said.

Since the Vietnam period, grade inflation has been a topic of discussion and interest, said Marvin Marshak, a physics professor and former top aide to Hasselmo.

Having taught at the University for 23 years, however, Marshak said he believes the quality of students has improved, but also that strategies have changed in undergraduate education in the last few decades.

In the past, professors often tried "quota killing"— flunking a specific percentage of students to foster competition—to demonstrate the appearance of being a tough grader. In Marshak's view, those days are gone.

"There's more interest in seeing the students succeed than there used to be," he said. "And when you do that, you'll get better performance." ∎

Graduation Rate

While grade inflation may be on its way to becoming a problem at large state schools, a larger, and more justifiable, concern is with retention rates. Large state schools, on average, see fewer students return from freshman to sophomore years than do smaller, private schools. Many factors contribute to lower retention rates at large schools, including the greater likelihood for these students to live off campus and have jobs. At the University of Nebraska, concerted efforts to work with first-year students and make them feel connected to the school made a big difference in increasing their retention rate.

STUDY SHOWS MORE U. NEBRASKA FRESHMEN ARE STAYING
By Lindsay Young

DAILY NEBRASKAN (Lincoln, Neb.) 09/30/1998

Top administrators are pleased that more than four out of five freshmen who arrived on campus last year decided to return for their sophomore year.

The University of Nebraska-Lincoln increased its freshman retention rate by about two percentage points from 78.7 percent in the fall of 1996 to 80.6 percent in 1997, officials have announced.

Vice Chancellor for Student Affairs James Griesen attributed the new rate to increased admissions standards.

The standards, which began in the 1997–98 academic year, require freshman applicants who graduate from high school in 1997 or after to have a composite ACT of 20 or higher or a combined SAT of 950 or higher, or to rank in the upper half of their graduating class to be guaranteed admission.

After the standards were put in place, the number of freshmen decreased. But those numbers are being made up with an increasing number of students returning for their sophomore year, Griesen said.

In Chancellor James Moeser's State of the University address in August, Moeser set a goal of having more than 80 percent of freshmen return for their sophomore year.

"It just so happens I didn't set the goal high enough," Moeser said.

In his August address, Moeser said an increase in freshman retention would be a result of an all-university push to increase academic rigor.

To address retention issues, Moeser announced the formation of the Freshman Year Experience Task Force in his August address. The task force will look at the quality of life of first-year students and at how well UNL is mentoring those students, Moeser said.

Information included things such as working hours, gender, ethnic background and whether a major was declared. Ted Pardy, task force committee chairman and biological sciences professor said the committee may do another more detailed, up-to-date survey.

The 1993 data raised concerns, he said. If students work, especially off campus, it affects the possibility of their return. Work is connected to whether students are having financial trouble as well, he said.

Also, freshmen who live off campus may be less likely to return, Pardy said.

Looking at those aspects and others will help the task force prepare to give an honest appraisal to high school counselors, parents and students, detailing risk factors for freshmen, Pardy said.

People often tell students, "You did well in high school," Pardy said. "If you work hard, you'll make it. But that's not as helpful."

Bumper DeJesus/*The Daily Targum*

Efforts that could have played a role in UNL's recent increase also include the new residence hall learning communities and the expansion of the Supplemental Instruction program, Griesen said.

Donald Gregory, director of the Division of General Studies, said the residence hall learning communities allow a group of freshmen to live on the same residence hall floor and take general education classes together.

Freshmen are more likely to stay if they feel like they are part of a community, Gregory said.

Supplemental Instruction involves undergraduates who assist students in understanding a course's content and in developing effective study strategies, he said.

Pardy said programs like the learning communities and Supplemental Instruction are only a few of the services provided in an effort to keep freshmen at UNL.

Moeser said he hoped the task force would look at such services to give students a connection to UNL.

"I strongly suspect that the students who fall out are the ones who never establish any point of meaningful contact with the university," Moeser said.

Moeser said though his goal of 80 percent retention has been met, the university's retention efforts won't slow.

"We want to keep moving up," Moeser said. "We're never satisfied. Anything less than 100 percent retention gives us room to shoot for." ■

When UNL put the extra effort into making freshmen feel like part of the campus community, the freshman retention rate rose. But keeping students coming back for their junior and senior years and graduating them in four years are other problems at large state schools. Nearly 50% of students do not graduate in four years, the length of time most people think it takes to get a degree. Again, this problem is more prevalent at big public schools, where students have to balance work with classes to make ends meet. In fact, many students at large state schools say that it's impossible to get a bachelor's degree in four years. The University of Maine begs to differ . . .

U. MAINE PLAN GUARANTEES FOUR-YEAR DEGREE

By Dilnora Azimova

THE MAINE CAMPUS (Orono, Maine) 11/24/1998

The University of Maine is offering students a chance to get their tuition free after four years, but many students aren't taking advantage of the opportunity.

The offer is part of the University of Maine's guarantee for students to graduate in four years, called the Four-Year Degree Guarantee Program.

The program was created in response to some students' belief that U. Maine students cannot complete their education and earn their degrees in four years, said Douglas Gelinas, vice provost for undergraduate education.

"Many students have an idea that they cannot graduate in four years," Gelinas said. "I have not seen any student who got the right courses and could not graduate."

"There are probably many reasons why little more than 30 percent of students complete their degrees in four years," said John Beacon, dean of enrollment management. "Primary reasons are because students change their major after being enrolled for a year or more and need to take additional classes in their new disciplines to meet specific degree requirements. If students decide to change their majors, they will need to consult with an adviser to make sure the degree program still applies."

Beacon said other students find it difficult to graduate in four years because they also work.

"For many students," he said, "the burden of working to help make ends meet overcomes educational goals as a priority and students either drop out entirely or cut back to less than full-time and take more years to complete degree requirements."

In order to participate in the program students must follow certain guidelines. If the guidelines are met and the student is unable to graduate in four years, the tuition for their remaining required courses is free.

Russ said students have a responsibility to see their advisers every semester and take courses the adviser and student agree on if they want to participate in the program.

Students will also have to take courses whenever they are offered, including evenings and weekends, in order to be in the program, Russ said.

The university is responsible for providing students with advisers and offering the required courses so the students in the program can obtain their degree in the allotted four years, Russ said.

"The advisers have to know the rules and regulations of the program and give a student proper advice," he said.

Advisers help students select courses that meet their degree requirements, but they aren't fully responsible for a student graduating.

Students are required to have a minimum of 15 credit hours, maintain a certain grade point average and identify their majors in order to be in the program. Students who do not maintain a 2.0 cumulative GPA may no longer be in the program.

The program does not cover double majors, double degrees and minors because of the need for students to take more classes.

"We do not make a blank promise that it will work all the time," Gelinas said. "Most of the time it would."

Students who decide to study abroad should discuss with their advisers whether their time away will affect their ability to meet the requirements of the program.

Some students agree they could graduate in four years, but they are not in a hurry to leave the college.

"I do not think I would," said John Davis, sophomore elementary education major who is currently taking 14 credits. "I'd rather take my time and go in a slower pace."

While it is possible to graduate in four years, Davis said it is too much work for him.

"Too many classes, too much work," he said. "If I really work on [graduation], I could graduate in four years."

The University of Maine is not the only state with low graduation rates. Beacon said U. Maine's rates are similar to those of other land-grant, public universities across the nation. ∎

U Maine has found a way to graduate students in four years. But what's the rush, really? The editors of the Daily O'Collegian at Oklahoma State University would prefer to take their own sweet time to graduate:

EDITORIAL: FIFTH YEAR'S THE CHARM
Staff Editorial

DAILY O'COLLEGIAN (Stillwater, Okla.) 06/08/1998

Graduation is here, but many Oklahoma State University seniors are deciding to stick around for another year . . . or two.

Not that there's anything wrong with that.

American College Testing polls show that 52.8 percent of college students require at least five years of classes to earn a bachelor's degree.

It isn't unusual for students to not decide what career they want to pursue until they are sophomores and juniors. In fact, freshman orientation students are told that the average student changes majors three to four times.

Students who change majors or switch colleges often lose credit hours and find themselves a little behind.

The four-year plan has become a thing of the past, and, in reality, an extra year to graduate may actually be better for college students in the long run.

Taking more time to take more classes allows the opportunity for students to find out what their talents and interests are.

The five- or six-year plan also gives students more time to gain work experience at summer internships. This can be a definite advantage when interviewing for jobs after graduation.

The cost of college is constantly on the rise, and more and more students are finding it necessary to work their way through college. This causes many students to limit the amount of hours they take and declare part-time status.

Parents should not be concerned if their child needs a little extra time to finish college.

It is better to take as much time needed and enjoy the time at school, rather than rush through and find out maybe that major wasn't the right one after all. ∎

BEYOND THE Classroom

earning is not just an academic endeavor, and opportunities to expand your horizons at large state schools range from political activism and volunteerism to athletics and Greek life—and everything in between.

At large state schools, student clubs and organizations come in all shapes and sizes. Opportunities are out there to learn, explore, let loose, support a cause, show your stuff, meet others with similar interests, help your fellow man—and so much more. Campus groups can be run under the auspices of the university and receive school funding, like KVRX, the University of Texas radio station you'll read about. Others are chapters of national student organizations, like Students for Industrial Hemp, described in "Hemp gets help at U. Kentucky rally." Some, like La Sociedad Latina at the University of Virginia, are smaller and not as high-profile. For some students, campus government, music, or religion really get them going. If you're one of them, you'll have no problem finding a niche on a large college campus. Arizona State University alone has hundreds of clubs and organizations to join, from the College Republicans and the Hip-Hop Coalition to KASR Radio, the Gay and Lesbian Legal Alliance, and the Burmese Student Association. And since large schools are a huge presence in the town in which they're located, most have clubs that bring together students and townspeople for special events, like UCLA's TheaterFest, described here by the *Daily Bruin*.

If you attend a large state university, athletics will most certainly dominate life beyond the classroom. At these schools, athletics are taken very, very, seriously. If your school moves to the top of the NCAA Division I college football rankings, the air of excitement will be palpable. If they go on to win the "big game," expect a schoolwide celebration like that described by the *Michigan Daily*; if they lose it all, heads will be hung in disappointment around campus for days. "Penn State Student-Athletes Balance Books" examines the plight of athletes at large state schools. With the hopes of tens of thousands (millions, if you count fans off campus) riding on them with every game, some big school athletes find the pressure to juggle winning and learning overwhelming. Still, large schools give talented athletes a chance for a higher education that they may not have otherwise had. According to the NCAA over $640 million in athletic scholarships were handed out in 1997. And it's not just the big sports that give out scholarships at state schools. Twelve full scholarships are there to be had by talented women softball players at Purdue University. And while women athletes may not get the press, or the prestige, that men competing in college football, basketball, or baseball do, large schools are seen as the training grounds for future Olympians and professional athletes of both sexes.

On most large college campuses, Greek life vies with athletics for the hearts and minds of the student body. Greeks are a huge force on the campuses of large state schools. The University of Kentucky alone is home to thirty-seven fraternities and sororities; the largest, Kappa Alpha Theta, has 139 members. Greeks have historically been social organizations focused on unity and friendship. More recently, however, in an effort to build membership, new sororities and fraternities have formed with students' professional interests and ethnic backgrounds in mind, like Kappa Delta Phi, spotlighted in "Greek Profile: Powerful Women Uniting at Cal State Sacramento." Recent years have seen much change, or attempts at change, in the Greek system at large state schools. Trying to overcome the *Animal House* reputation they've been saddled with for decades (as well as several tragic incidents involving alcohol), some Greek organizations are considering "going dry," or banning alcohol, in all of their chapters. "Delta Sigma Phi Goin' Dry at Colorado State" examines one fraternity's foray into alcohol-free existence.

No matter what your tastes, at a large state school you'll be sure to find a group where you'll fit right in. And if you don't, why not start your own club? Each year, hundreds of new organizations pop up on big campuses nationwide—so there'll be lots of support for your cause.

Student Groups

Through student clubs and organizations, you can enhance your major area of study or learn something completely new. You can enjoy an activity for a semester, a year, all four years, or a lifetime. Because large state schools have a diverse study body, your choices will be limitless.

Student government on large college campuses is serious business. Campaigns have to reach a lot of students, and competition can be fierce. But the rewards are incredible. Student government representatives don't just lobby for more Doritos in vending machines. They effect real change in campus life. And when they have the opportunity to travel halfway around the world to learn about student governments in other countries, as this University of Nebraska student body president did, the results can be tremendous. Student government offers young men and women the chance to serve and learn about others, come to appreciate our democratic way of life, and develop a sense of resolve to change their world.

GOVERNMENT

NEBRASKA STUDENT BODY PRESIDENT BRINGS IDEAS BACK FROM ISRAEL

By Ieva Augstums

DAILY NEBRASKAN (Lincoln, Neb.) 08/26/1998

Soldiers walked streets with machine guns, watching every move she made.

She noticed the lack of security while visiting the U.S. Embassy in Israel, a couple of days after U.S. Embassy bombings in Africa.

She learned conflict negotiating with Israelis and Palestinians peacefully.

Those were some of the situations the Association of Students of the University of Nebraska President Sara Russell came face-to-face with during a nine-day student government seminar Aug. 6–14 in Israel.

Russell, a senior math major, met with 12 other university student body presidents from the Midwest, Rocky Mountain and Plains states to heighten international global awareness and discuss diversity in Israel's society, people and history.

"Life is not the same after you are ripped out of your comfort zone," Russell said. "It's uncomfortable and scary."

Organized by Project Interchange, an educational institute of the American Jewish Committee, Russell visited Jerusalem, Tel Aviv, the West Bank and Christian holy sites near the Sea of Galilee and in Bethlehem. She was selected to attend the travel seminar through an application and interview.

ASUN Director of Development Marlene Beyke said ASUN fully supported Russell's endeavor to go to Israel.

"Anytime when we have the opportunity to expose our students to other cultures and experiences, it is a growing experience, which cannot be refused," Beyke said.

The $7,000 trip, paid by Project Interchange, offered participants an overview of challenges within Israeli society, including human relation conflicts.

Meeting with elected Palestinian Authority representatives, Arab community leaders and U.S. government officials, Russell said, helped her learn about national politics, the U.S.-Israel relationship and the Middle East peace process.

"It was a crash course in U.S. international relations," Russell said. "It was more intense learning than any university course could have offered me."

Touring the U.S. Embassy, Russell heard presentations from U.S. government officials regarding the process of third-party peace negotiations.

While on tour, Russell said there were many times in the building when she didn't think security measures were strict enough, especially considering the devastating bombings of U.S. embassies in Kenya and Tanzania on Aug. 7.

"The metal detector would go off, and no one would care," Russell said. "They just thought because we were a tour group, everything was fine."

Visiting Hebrew University, Jerusalem, Russell discussed with other students the strong apathy on that campus over political issues regarding the Israeli-Palestinian conflict.

"There are two rights clashing creating one wrong—war," she said. "They say they need to go to war, but I don't think war is ever an answer."

Russell, who was ASUN Human Rights Committee chairwoman last year, said she still has a strong belief for other alternatives to war and equality for all people.

Russell said her excursion to another country made her aware of possible issues at the University of Nebraska–Lincoln and reinforced support for resolutions on current issues.

Russell said the American Jewish Committee's goal of eliminating bigotry and promoting tolerance in the United States taught her how to build tolerance among students.

"Yes we have problems upon problems here at UNL, but if people could sit down and discuss matters, things can be solved," she said. "Everyone can and needs to learn to tolerate others."

Other issues discussed among Israeli students and Russell included trying to keep tuition low, student representation in student government and lack of student parking on campus.

"It's nice to see parking is not just an America problem," Russell said. "It's universal and not just UNL."

Russell said she is planning to convey to the ASUN Senate a sense of how lucky students are living in the United States.

Subtle cultural differences made all the difference in Israel, she said.

"I was fascinated, but very nervous of the machine guns on the streets," she said. "You learn fast to respect and tolerate others and their beliefs."

Russell said students need to learn to respect and tolerate each other and realize there are always compromises when conflicts arise.

"We do have a lot of problems in the U.S.," Russell said. "But we are really quite amazing if you just sit and think about it." ■

Jeffrey Chen/*The Highlander*

Sara Russell traveled to another country to learn more about campus government and changed the way she saw her university, and the world, in the process. One wonders how many more students could have benefited from the Project Interchange program if the project's meetings had been broadcast around the world to anyone who wanted such an awesome experience.

Few schools or programs have such capabilities, but the ultra-modern radio station at UT Austin can make such a scenario possible. The lucky student members of KVRX learned that UT's commitment to their station could put them on the information superhighway—and at the forefront of broadcasting technology.

U. TEXAS STUDENT RADIO STATION BEGINS NETCASTING

By Sergio Chapa

DAILY TEXAN (Austin, Texas) 06/16/1998

Utilizing state-of-the-art telecommunications technology, KVRX (91.7 FM), the student radio station for the University of Texas, has augmented its broadcasting capabilities. The student-run radio station can now be heard 24 hours a day, anywhere in the world.

As of Thursday, June 11 at approximately 5 p.m., the station joined several college and commercial radio stations when it began sending its signal over the Internet through a live RealAudio server located in the basement of the Texas Student Publications building at 25th Street and Whitis Avenue.

"This has been a long time in the making," said KVRX station manager, Mark Miller. "KVRX once again has proven their commitment to excellence in broadcasting. By Netcasting, we are able to enter a whole new medium and perhaps reach a whole new audience. We can reach people in Norway or Hong Kong, but more importantly people in the computer labs on campus."

RealAudio is a form of streaming audio files through Internet connections into small packets rather than through huge files. The standard method before RealAudio was to have whole sound files, which were downloaded from various Web sites.

To listen to a whole song in those formats would require about three megabytes of memory, which, on a 28.8 band modem, would take an hour to download.

"With the technology from Real Networks, the makers of RealAudio, you receive only packets of data in streams, which are read by a program, then discarded, not saved onto your computer," said Gary Dickerson, designer of the KVRX Web page and one of the people behind the station's transition to Netcasting. "RealAu-

dio is incredibly efficient, revolutionizing the way audio—and video—can be used online."

KVRX's move to Netcasting comes at a critical time for the station, which celebrated its 10th anniversary in April. In May, cable service provider Time-Warner decided to discontinue providing its cable stereo service for the station in order to use the bandwidth for tests.

With the funds provided, the station purchased a $1,300 server and $600 RealAudio server software. Goodwill Computerworks of Austin gave the station a monitor in exchange for underwriting spots on the station.

That was just the beginning. To broadcast KVRX over the Internet, Dickerson and the station staff had to find a place with Ethernet connections to house the new server.

"KVRX, despite the fact that it sat right next to the MicroCenter for years, has no Ethernet connection," Dickerson said. "That was a big problem."

The station faced additional adversity.

"Because KVRX is an all-volunteer organization, with everyone there going to school, such things were done when we could find the time," Dickerson noted. "A couple of months after the funds were allotted, we found a nice local business, the Logic Approach, which built a server for us. We purchased the software from Real Networks to have a live server."

"Only time will tell if this will be a successful venture," Dickerson said. "More people have computers than cable radio, I think. Plus, there's the added bonus of being able to have listeners in Hong Kong. I should think that the former cable deejays would be thrilled. They can listen to the station no matter where they are." ∎

While student-led events at large state schools may attract thousands of people, other campus events and organizations aren't so big. But the dedication of the members is often the most important lesson learned. Sometimes results are small and come less quickly, as students at the University of Virginia could tell you, but all in all, students of all cultures at big schools have incredible opportunities to make their voices heard. Because large state schools exhibit a student body with a diversity of backgrounds, it's more likely that all students can speak their minds at a large state school.

CULTURAL GROUPS

U. VIRGINIA LATINOS REVISIT PAST, CELEBRATE ETHNIC CULTURE

By Nicola M. White

CAVALIER DAILY (Charlottesville, Va.) 10/1/1998

Quick: What's the oldest city in the United States?

"Most people think Jamestown," La Sociedad Latina President Sam Eder said. "But it's St. Augustine, [Fla.]—a Spanish, not English, settlement. "We have an Anglo-centric notion of history," Eder said.

U.S. Census data predicts that in the future, Latinos will be the country's largest minority group. Now, the Latino population is about 26 million—or 10 percent of the nation.

To the University's Latino community, realities like the misrepresentation of Latino history and a surge in population underline the significance of Hispanic Heritage Month, lasting from Sept. 15 to Oct. 15.

Because the University's Latino population remains between two and three percent, the month's events have so far gone largely unnoticed.

"It's easy to be discouraged," Dean of Students Robert T. Canevari said. "But they have to keep their eyes further down the road . . . because if they continue to work like this, there'll be a dividend at the end."

During the past year, LSL established an alumni association, lobbied for increased recruitment of Latino students and has been increasingly vocal about getting support from the administration—in the form of a dean to represent Latino students' needs.

"There have been successes that may not be tied into Hispanic Heritage Month," Canevari said, referring to LSL's accomplishments. "But it's important to share these successes with the University community."

The University theme for Hispanic Heritage Month is "Confronting Identity," a topic Eder said is often raised in the Latino community because members find it difficult to pinpoint their own identity.

"We have a lots of Latinos who may or may not look like [a stereotypical image] or may not speak Spanish," he said. "We have so many different interests."

Events slated for Hispanic Heritage Month include a presentation by Pedro Medina. Medina, a Darden graduate, is the regional director of all McDonald's restaurants in Colombia. Additional events include Latino movies at Clemons, a Dia de la Raza Think Tank discussion and in conjunction with University Union, a Mexican Folkloric Ballet at the Charlottesville Performing Arts Center.

"It's a time in which we get to remember our heritage and make it known to the University," former LSL President Alexandra Minoff said. "It's a time to share our culture with people that don't necessarily know a lot about Hispanic heritage or culture."

Hispanic heritage is sometimes difficult to define, Eder said. Columbus Day, which falls at the end of Hispanic Heritage Month, is known in Latin America as Dia de la Raza or "day of the race."

"It's a schizophrenic holiday for us," he said. "We're a part of that founding of the new race but we're a part of the demolition and eradication of indigenous cultures. We're all involved in the big mix.

"We're still considered immigrants," he added. "We're a culture that's been here, but still hasn't mixed. The month demonstrates how outside the 'norm' we are that we need a month to showcase our culture."

Hispanic Heritage Month emerged from a weeklong celebration—Sept. 10 to Sept. 16—honoring the Latino contribution to U.S. history, implemented by Congress in 1968.

Twenty years later, in 1988, Hispanic Heritage Month became law. ■

True, as the students of UVA discovered, joining a campus organization doesn't necessarily mean that your group's message will get recognized far and wide. On the other hand, sometimes it does.

Imagine the shock when the members of UH's Wind Ensemble were nominated as semi-finalists for an unprecedented four Grammy awards. As is often the case with campus extracurricular groups, when students with a common love come together, the sky is the limit. The group may not have won, but the experience was truly once-in-a-lifetime.

MUSICAL GROUPS

U. HOUSTON WIND ENSEMBLE CD NAMED SEMI-FINALIST FOR A GRAMMY

By Jason Caesar Consolacion

THE DAILY COUGAR (Houston, Texas) 01/21/1999

The Moores School Wind Ensemble recently found its name among the most talented performers in the world when it became a semi-finalist for four 1999 Grammy awards.

Last spring, the group recorded a compact disc of Gustav Holst's work "The Planets in the Moores Opera House" under the Mark Records label. In December, Wind Ensemble Director Eddie Green received the news that the CD was a semifinalist in four different Grammy categories.

Sarah Apgar/*The Campus Times*

"I was stunned," Green said. "I just couldn't believe the announcement. It's great to be recognized, but it's even more gratifying to be recognized on the same list as internationally renowned professional groups."

The CD, which featured the music of Holst and American composer Aaron Copland transcribed by Moores School of Music staff member Merlin Patterson, was nominated for Best Classical Performance, Best Classical CD and Best Classical Production by David Burks and Joe Dixon.

The big surprise for Green was the fourth nomination the CD received for Best Orchestral Performance alongside such names as the New York Symphony.

The Moores School Wind Ensemble was the only nonprofessional collegiate group to be nominated in the classical categories.

"That's what surprised me the most," Green explained, "because we're not an orchestra, much less a professional group. We're a collegiate wind ensemble. Also, the other names on the list included some of the best symphony orchestras in the world. The recognition is greatly appreciated."

A few years ago, the Moores School Wind Ensemble was selected by the International Percy Grainger Society to make the official recordings of the Grainger Wind Ensemble pieces. Volume I of those recordings was selected CD of the Year by Stereophile magazine.

Prior to that, the wind ensemble has not been recognized with an honor as highly touted as a Grammy.

"I'm just proud of the hard work and attention that our students put into getting the best performance result on that CD," Green said. "Once again, the recognition is quite an honor, and I can't explain how happy I am for our group."

The wind ensemble will record another CD, scheduled to be released in July. ■

Students in Houston translated their love of classical music into four Grammy nominations, which goes to show the power of a group united in their passion for a subject. So what's your passion? Acting? Music? . . . How about hemp?

POLITICAL GROUPS | HEMP GETS HELP AT U. KENTUCKY RALLY

By Karrie Ralston

KENTUCKY KERNEL (Lexington, Ky.) 03/24/1998

Students for Industrial Hemp, one of the newest organizations on campus, will be lobbying at the capital tomorrow to show support for a bill that will allow hemp research to be conducted in Kentucky.

The group planned on holding a small rally with about 50 students from the Students for Industrial Hemp organizations at Transylvania University, Eastern Kentucky University, and Morehead College.

The rally was canceled after Senate bill 99 was removed from tomorrow's docket.

"Even though the bill has been removed from yesterday's docket, we are still going to Frankfort to try and win some representatives over to our side," said Rick Bertelson, a third-year graduate law student and vice president of SIH.

If Senate bill No. 99, which is sponsored by Richmond area Senator Berry Metcalf, is passed it will allow research of the plant to be conducted, most likely at the UK College of Agriculture.

There are over 25,000 uses for industrial hemp including paper products, clothing, textiles, diesel fuel and cooking oil.

"Because 40 percent of all wood products can be made with industrial hemp, hundreds of thousands of trees could be saved," said Katharine Steel an information studies junior at LCC and member of Students for Industrial Hemp.

Growing marijuana and hemp has been illegal since the passing of the 1937 Marijuana Tax Act.

Because of limited technology, a distinction could not be made between hemp and marijuana, who are part of the same family, so both were outlawed. The distinction was made in 1979, but the law was never changed.

Students for Industrial Hemp do not take a stand with legalization of the marijuana. ∎

Who would've thought that students who attend a state-sponsored, public school could rally in favor of hemp? Or religion, for that matter. Isn't there supposed to be separation of church and state? Fortunately, even those who attend public state schools supported by taxpayers cannot be denied their right to assemble or their freedom of religion. Religious groups representing a variety of faiths exist on the campuses of most state schools. Impact Bible Study at Colorado State is one such group.

RELIGIOUS GROUPS | CSU BIBLE GROUP FINDS PEACE AND DIRECTION IN GOD AND EACH OTHER

By Jonathan Rice

ROCKY MOUNTAIN COLLEGIAN (Ft. Collins, Colo.) 02/24/1998

The feeling was so powerful, they decided to bring it to Colorado State University.

"It was a serenity, a peace," said Kevin Moore, a junior in exercise and sport science at CSU who was surrounded by 2,000 young, mostly African American Christians. They were attending Impact96, a conference for high school and college students "for the cause of Christ" in Atlanta in December 1996.

One month later, Impact Bible Study at CSU had its first gathering, the result of the efforts of Moore, Tylanda Johnson, Zerina Davis and Shallon Coleman. All are CSU students who attended the conference together and saw the need for a new Bible study.

Although there are at least 25 other Bible study groups already on campus, Impact is different.

The group is geared toward African Americans, the first group of its kind at CSU. The group practices traditional African American worship styles and incorporates their religious values and traditions into the gatherings.

Impact, which is non-denominational, is also one of only a few opportunities at CSU for African Americans to come together in a formal group setting.

"Before Impact, there was a need for someone to reach out to African Americans, and specifically African American Christians," said Johnson, a junior in microbiology who co-founded the group and who is a co-facilitator. "At CSU, African American Christians didn't have anywhere to plug in to."

Campus Crusade for Christ, a national, interdenominational organization with chapters on college campuses across the United States including CSU, sponsored the Atlanta conference and initiated the Impact movement.

Mah-rya Apuzzo, who works for the CCC regional office in Denver that covers Rocky Mountain campuses, and Jon Nitta, a member of the CSU ministry of CCC, recognized the gap at CSU and approached Moore, Johnson, Davis and Coleman with the idea of attending the Atlanta conference.

"CSU is predominantly white and not representative of the population in general and of Christians," Apuzzo said. "We needed to reach out to that segment of the community."

Now, on Friday nights in the basement of Parmelee Hall, African Americans can come together to worship and study in the ways some learned from their parents or at predominantly African American churches while growing up.

The group gathers to rejoice and find solace and strength in God and each other. These feelings in part are found through music, an important component of African American worshiping.

"Our (worship) style is different; our music is different," Johnson said. "The way we praise God in music is different. It's like getting the message across in classical music versus rock."

Impact also creates an opportunity for African Americans simply to come together and fellowship.

"The African Americans on campus have no connection or unity," Moore said. "At Impact, we can come together, bond, lift each other up and support each other." ■

Sports

Many college students join clubs and other student groups to relax, get involved, learn more, and have fun. For those who participate in big time college athletics, however, it's a different story. At big state schools, athletics are taken very seriously. Coaches like Penn State's Joe Paterno and Indiana University's Bobby Knight are quite literally legends on campus and in their schools' states. And that's just the coaches—at large state schools, high-profile athletes put the "big" in "big man on campus," reaching a lofty status that is idolized by some and scorned by others. Whether these students are really learning anything is a subject of much debate. Hours of practice per day are the norm. Schools want a good team, which fills the seats in the stadium, which brings in millions of dollars to the school. Accusations of giving undeserved passing grades to student-athletes have often been leveled at large state schools but haven't often been proved. Read on for both sides of the story.

PENN STATE STUDENT-ATHLETES BALANCE BOOKS

By Don Stewart

Daily Collegian (State College, Penn.) 02/24/1998

Describing the task student-athletes face in attempting to juggle both sports and academics is, well, academic.

It's a challenge.

In most cases, being a student-athlete is like having two full-time jobs. In addition to keeping up with classes, athletes have to deal with the responsibilities of being a member of their teams.

"It's real tough," redshirt sophomore football player Chafie Fields said. "I don't think people realize how tough it is to be a student-athlete. It's a lot more than just playing ball. There's never free time for you so you can't really have a social life."

Athletes have plenty of reasons to care about their grades. They must meet certain academic requirements in order to play their sport. In addition, most college athletes won't go on to play their sport professionally. Knowing this, they push themselves in the classroom in order to improve their chances of getting a job.

In pushing themselves, however, student-athletes are forced to deal with the issue of time management.

"I don't think it's really that hard if you just know how to manage your time," junior women's basketball player Christine Portland said. "When I first came here I was so overwhelmed, and my grades showed that."

Like Portland, many student-athletes find their freshman year to be tough. Courses are harder and coaches are more demanding than they were in high school.

"I guess all freshmen go in and get that reality check," redshirt sophomore volleyball player Sergio Pampena said.

Tanith L. Balaban/*Arizona Daily Wildcat*

As a freshman, senior basketball player Pete Lisicky was determined to study every day and never miss class. He said he learned quickly he didn't live the same life as regular students.

"What happened was I just got burned out," Lisicky said. "I got mono(nucleosis) my freshman year."

Now, Lisicky focuses more on keeping himself sharp physically, mentally and emotionally. He said missing a class once in awhile is worth it if you aren't feeling well.

"Sometimes it's just better to take that nap just to make sure you're physically OK," Lisicky said.

David Yukelson, the Academic Support Center's coordinator of student athlete programs, said time management is a skill, not a maturity issue. To help teach this skill to freshman athletes, Yukelson said the Academic Support Center runs an informal peer helping program in which older athletes guide younger ones.

"It can be quite difficult (balancing academics and athletics), but for all the help we get we shouldn't have an excuse for not to be able to do it," freshman gymnast Dominic Brindle said.

Time-management skills are tested the most during athletes' seasons—their busiest times of year. During this time, athletes have to focus even more time on their sport.

Road trips present a big hurdle for student-athletes to leap during their season. They sometimes have to miss days of classes while on the road. So, in order to stay on top of their course work, student-athletes have to work closely with their professors.

Many student-athletes, like junior wrestler Clint Musser, take fewer credits during their season. Musser said he usually takes 18 credits in the fall and 12 in the spring.

"There's so much focus on the season, I don't want to overload on academics," he said.

Even with the lighter course load, however, Musser said it's a challenge to keep his grades up during the season. When he comes home after practice and opens a book, Musser is so tired he often falls asleep.

"You've just got to say to yourself, 'It's gotta be done,' Musser said. "It's not the funnest thing in the world, but it's gotta be done."

The toils of student-athletes aren't fruitless, however. In addition to keeping themselves eligible and earning an education, most student-athletes get a chance to compete and experience the glory that comes with winning. They usually get a scholarship for their troubles as well.

"I think it's really rewarding to be a student-athlete," junior volleyball player Christy Cochran said. "I know people say it over and over, but it's the truth." ∎

Obviously, student-athletes don't have an easy road. The pressures to win, to keep that athletic scholarship, to balance studies and sports (and what about free time?) are enormous. In fact, some claim that all they really know of their school is athletics; with all the demands on their time, they really don't get to enjoy college like a "traditional" student does. But it does seem, from the last article, that schools like Penn State go out of their way to help these students succeed. This perceived favoritism has created feelings of animosity on many campuses. At large state schools, students often feel second to athletics, especially when the school's team—not its academic achievements—is receiving national media coverage. One student asks the big question: Is the importance given to sports at large state schools misplaced?

COLUMN: UNIVERSITIES LOSING TRACK OF ORIGINAL MISSIONS

By Robyn Conder

OKLAHOMA DAILY (Norman, Okla.) 10/29/1998

Universities are our culture's centers for scholarship, the arts and the natural sciences. They are the heart and foundation of cultural achievement. Without the academic rigor of university life, achievements ranging from technological and medical breakthroughs to social triumphs such as the civil rights movement would not have come to pass.

Accordingly, a university should strive for academic excellence. Students must be primarily challenged to think critically, to question the status quo and to explore new realms of

Cory Brooks/*The George-Anne*

knowledge and thought. Their minds must be developed to their full potential in order to maintain academic excellence.

The body, as the vehicle of the mind, should be kept in good condition, and the rigors of academics need to be relaxed occasionally. Recreation is necessary to healthy function of the whole self. For that reason, universities sponsor sports programs.

At least, in an ideal world, that would be the reason why universities sponsor sports programs. In reality, this is all too often not the case. At many schools, including OU, sports programs eclipse academics. The focus of the school becomes its sports teams, not academics.

When most non-students, as well as many students, think of the ranking of OU, they automatically consider its football ranking. Academic ranking is some kind of secondary consideration, a sort of afterthought. The football team has become the all-important center of university life and thought.

We all know that this is true. Football players are offered lucrative scholarships based not on academics, not on need, but on athletic ability. National Scholar freshmen are required to march onto the football field at halftime of a game to pay homage to the football gods. The opinion page of *The Daily* mirrors the sports page during football season.

Why is football so important to this university? Why are academics thrown by the wayside? Is the university's mission to provide great entertainment, or great academics?

It could be argued that the sports teams bring added income to the university through ticket sales. With the Athletic Department deeply in debt, however, this argument rings hollow.

Some might say that the sports program increases the regional and national exposure of the university, bringing publicity that ultimately benefits the school. But is this the kind of publicity that we want to bring in? Does having OU be known best for its football and basketball further the university's academic mission?

Why do invocations to "support the university" always imply that we can show our loyalty by attending football games? It's because many American universities have lost sight of their primary objective—to educate students and to foster scholarly thought.

We need to bring OU's focus back to where it should be—academics. The athletic program should be preserved, but it should move away from the center of our attention. Only then will the university's mission be furthered. ∎

Obviously, not everyone agrees about the importance of athletics at large state schools. Are they emphasized over academics? Are men's athletics given more importance than women's? Do they really bring money into the schools? And moreover, do student-athletes really learn? The debate will likely rage on forever, but whatever your opinion, it's hard to dispute the enthusiasm a winning team can generate at a large state school. Imagine a sea of thousands of fans, all dressed in blue (or red, or green), joined together on a Saturday afternoon in the hugest display of school pride you can imagine. And when your team wins—well . . .

MICHIGAN FANS STORM FIELD, STREETS IN CELEBRATION

By Janet Adamy & Jeffrey Kosseff

Mᴄʜɪɢᴀɴ Dᴀɪʟʏ (Ann Arbor, Mich.) 11/24/1997

Emotions surged through Ann Arbor on Saturday as fans celebrated The University of Michigan's victory by rushing the field, crowding outside the University president's house and packing campus bars.

"I came to school here just for this moment," said senior Jeff Williams, as he celebrated on the field with an estimated 8,000 other students.

"I've been waiting 21 years to do this and it feels great," said senior Dave Hebert. "Oh, my God, it feels great. It's like I've been reborn as a Michigan fan."

When the game clock reached zero, handfuls of fans

braved the 7-foot drop from the stands onto the field. A few minutes later, thousands of fans rushed down the stairways to crowd onto the stadium grass.

Fans took victory laps around the stadium, lit cigars on the 50-yard line and carried football players high above their heads.

"I couldn't move after the game. It was so crowded," said Michigan cornerback Charles Woodson. "All the fans were grabbing me. . . . So far it's so great, and we're going to Pasadena."

Fans hugged and kissed strangers and friends alike as they stayed on the field for nearly an hour after

Michigan's triumph. Others took pieces of the actual field as a souvenir, digging up chunks of the turf to save for posterity.

"I got sod from the 50-yard line, two pairs of players' gloves—No. 97's and No. 42's gloves," said fan Terry McClellan, who later sold a wristband he picked up while on the field. "I feel great. . . . The best part is that we won."

"I've been waiting for this day ever since I got here," senior Rob McLeod said as he hugged his friend in celebration.

"It's fantastic," said sophomore Matt Plumb, a trumpet player in the marching band. "It has to be one of the greatest moments of my life."

During the on-field melee, Plumb turned to his fellow band members and said, "I love you guys."

Outside the stadium gates, thousands of students rushed down South University Avenue and crowded onto University President Lee Bollinger's lawn.

"I came to meet the big guy," said senior Safdar Bandukwala. "I came to congratulate him."

Exuberant Wolverines surfed through the crowds, climbed trees, jumped on moving cars and videotaped the moment. One student fell 40 feet from a tree outside the president's house and was rushed to the hospital, where he remained yesterday in fair condition.

One car carried nine screaming fans on its hood and roof as the crowd surrounded it, chanting "Go Blue" as they pounded on the car. A person driving a jeep honked its horn and allowed strangers to jump into the car.

Five excited Michigan fans doused a Buckeye flag with lighter fluid while students cheered as they watched it burn.

Along South University, indignant Ohio State fans and rowdy Michigan fans exchanged insults and victory cheers, while firefighters and police stood by to monitor the situation.

Another large crowd of more than 100 students and fans gathered at the corner of South University and East University avenues, one side shouting "Go" while the other responded with "Blue."

Junior Kevin Fogelberg, who screamed from atop a circular bench, said he felt "amazing" with so many students gathered in one location.

"I've never seen this much energy and this much life in this school since I've been here. It's like (your) birthday and Christmas all in one," Fogelberg said. ∎

Sarah Trucksis/*The George-Anne*

Greek Life

Another defining element of life at a large state school—and one that is no less controversial—is fraternities and sororities. In 1998, more than 400,000 young men were members of fraternities, and sorority membership numbered over 300,000. Large state schools house the majority of brothers and sisters. What are the benefits of Greek life? What are the drawbacks? Do Greeks make a difference on campus, or are they simply social organizations with exclusive membership and bizarre rituals? Is the experience worth the money you'll pay in dues, which can sometimes amount to hundreds of dollars a year? It's something that everyone who attends a large state school has an opinion about. Some fraternities and sororities believe they've gotten a bad rap and are taking actions to change their bad image. That won't be easy, as the next article suggests.

DELTA SIGMA PHI GOIN' DRY AT COLORADO STATE

By Adam Woodroof

ROCKY MOUNTAIN COLLEGIAN (Fort Collins, Colo.) 10/02/1998

Many people say that the words beer and fraternities have been synonymous since the movie *Animal House* debuted in the late 70s. However, several fraternities across the nation, including Delta Sigma Phi at Colorado State University, may change that image by requiring all chapters be alcohol-free, transforming fraternities back to what they were first intended for—friendship and brotherhood.

"It's not just about alcohol," said John Lister, President of the Delta Sigma Phi fraternity chapter at CSU. "It's about academics and getting back to the beliefs that we were founded on in 1899. Originally, we were the guys who had the higher GPAs. It's really gone downhill."

Delta Sigma Phi chapters from across the nation are teaming up for Challenge 2000. The fraternity, with its 5,000 undergraduate members and 109 different chapters nationwide, is requiring members to focus on academics and make the house alcohol-free by Dec. 10, 2000—the 101st anniversary of the founding of Delta Sigma Phi.

Academically, each chapter's grade point average must be higher than the all-campus average for the university and the chapter's graduation rate also must exceed the campus average. In addition to the alcohol-free chapter living, there will be absolutely no hazing, harassment or abuse of any individual or group.

All members must participate in a community-service activity and maintain an active, values-centered leadership program for all members.

"Our fraternity is determined to improve academic performance, increase membership and end the misuse and abuse of alcohol," Delta Sigma Phi national president Thomas E. Decker said. "Alcohol is not our only problem, but alcohol is an overwhelming obstacle to our success in many areas—our grades, our leadership, our reputation. We cannot deny that any longer.

"Our chapters are not bars; they are homes where our men live and learn. Our houses need to once again become an environment where men can consistently lead healthy, clean lifestyles conducive to academic achievement and personal success. They are in college and they are students first and foremost."

"To reach our fullest potential, we need the partnership of other men and women's fraternities and sororities—and the partnership of the host universities," Decker said.

In the push for alcohol-free facilities, Delta Sigma Phi is joining several other international fraternities that have taken the same challenge since 1997. The fraternities make up nearly one-fifth of undergraduate fraternity chapters in both the United States and Canada.

"It's not just our fraternity," said Lister, "it's a nationwide effort."

For CSU's chapter of Delta Sigma Phi, turning the house into an alcohol-free environment won't be an easy task to accomplish.

"It's going to be a challenge," Lister said. "I really think it's going to be something that could be very positive for fraternity life. Right now we are gradually starting to work toward that. A lot of our guys are against alcohol anyway."

Lister said the number one reason people join fraternities or sororities is for the friendships, not the beer.

"For every single person in our house, it's not about the drinking so much," he said. "It's about the brotherhood. I joined because of the brotherhood with all these guys."

While alcohol may not be the sole reason to join a fraternity, raging parties may be an appeal for freshman and transfers seeking out the best house. Lister said he doesn't know if the house can give it up completely.

"I can guarantee that almost any fraternity will have some alcohol," he said. "It's too difficult to regulate something like that. We won't be totally dry."

While Lister doesn't think Delta Sigma Phi can become alcohol-free by the deadline set by the national chapter, he does see the trend of fraternities and sororities moving in that direction.

"I don't know if you'll see the changes by 2000," Lister said, "but I think that in five or 10 years there will be some serious changes from the *Animal House* style." ■

The guys at Delta Sigma Phi have their hands full, and they're not alone. As the debate about Greek life rages on, many Greeks have seen their chapters shut down for policy violations or lack of interest. As universities begin to offer a wider range of activities to students, membership in traditional fraternities and sororities have not kept pace with rising college enrollment numbers. Fraternities have suffered the most; according to a recent article in *U.S. News*, UT Austin has seen a 29 percent drop in fraternity recruits since 1990.

At some big schools, Greek life is still going strong; it has just taken on a different face. Greek organizations that better meet students' diverse cultural and professional—as well as social—needs have popped up all over the country. At Arizona State University, for example, you can join the Lambda League, which promotes gay and lesbian issues; Gamma Alpha Omega, a Hispanic organization; Alpha Kappa Psi, for business students; and Gamma Beta Phi, a national honors society—to name just a few. Kappa Delta Sigma at Cal State is one such organization.

GREEK PROFILE: POWERFUL WOMEN UNITING AT CAL STATE SACRAMENTO

By Christine Lally

THE STATE HORNET (Sacramento, Calif.) 10/01/1998

At a time when some sororities at CSUS are stressing over the possibility of their chapter dying out due to a lack of membership alpha Kappa Delta Phi just keeps getting bigger, according to Rush Chair coordinator Allia Cavero.

KDPhi was established in UC Berkeley in 1989, to give Asian-American women the opportunity to participate in the Greek system. The chapter became one of two Asian American interest sororities at CSUS in 1995.

Pledge educator and founding sister Auzon Acena

said it is amazing to see how quickly her sorority has grown in just three years.

"When I was working to get KDPhi started at CSUS, I never dreamed it would turn out this way. It succeeded all of my expectations," she said.

With more than 20 chapters and 700 members, the sorority has expanded nationally to universities such as Johns Hopkins, Cornell and Michigan University. It currently reigns as the largest Asian-American sorority in the nation.

"It gives me shivers to think of the original founders," said Cavero. "They took action and gave

Asian American women a voice at a time when they weren't really heard from, especially at the Greek level."

By carefully balancing service and social activities, with the hopes of promoting Asian American awareness, the academically focused sisterhood at CSUS can only get stronger, according to Cavero.

"In this society, the words minority and women are a double strike," said Cavero. "Gathering women together, as KDPhi does so well, creates a big voice that otherwise might not be there. KDPhi makes the words minority and women incredibly strong when they stand together."

She pointed out that KDPhi is not a sorority solely for Asian American women, as is often assumed by students. The nationalities of current members, ranging from Vietnamese, Chinese, Filipino and Turkish, make the personalities of the sisters very diverse and approachable, she said.

"We focus on Asian American awareness," Cavero said. "Any woman from any background is welcome to join who wants to learn more about Asian Americans."

According to Jennie Quan, KDPhi's athletic chair,

Asian American awareness is her sorority's biggest contribution to CSUS. Asian Americans are making their presence known on campus, as well as with other sororities and fraternities.

Quan said KDPhi encourages individualism and participation in the college experience through sisterhood, scholarship and leadership.

According to Acena, KDPhi has created a very positive and memorable college experience for her.

"Through KDPhi, I have created a life that will go on after college, through my memories and my sisters," she said.

As part of the complete college experience, KDPhi includes community service.

The sisters of KDPhi motivate each other to further Asian American awareness through projects, such as the AIDS Walk-a-thon and volunteering time at the Sacramento Food Bank and the Asian American Youth Center.

The sorority's national philanthropy is breast cancer awareness. They will sponsor a speaker on the subject in November, according to Cavero.

"From the original founders' example, it is our duty to affect our community and give the younger generations something to strive for," she said.

Leah Loftin/*The Cavalier Daily*

Part of being well-rounded is having a social life. According to Cavero, the KDPhi sisters have this side of college life mastered.

Attending the sorority's national convention every May gives the sisters of KDPhi the opportunity to interact and network with people from all over the nation.

"It is an amazing experience to look around the room at the convention and realize that you share a common bond with each of them, and they are all your sisters," said Cavero. ■

It's clear that Greeks are proud of their organizations. Belonging to a group that has traditions and responsibilities has an amazing impact on some. Fraternity brothers and sorority sisters defend each other and their organization vehemently, especially in the face of protest, as the fraternity brother in the next article does.

COLUMN: FRATERNITIES-WITHOUT ALL OF THE FICTION

By Josh Pourmizaei

DAILY UTAH CHRONICLE (Salt Lake City, Utah) 02/11/1998

I have a confession to make. I am an active member of the Pi Kappa Alpha fraternity and, though it may be surprising to many, I am happy to say I have never drank goat's blood and never been ritually beaten over the head with tequila bottles and ceremonial paddles.

My statement may seem comical and absurd, but due to many of the assumptions and stereotypes made about fraternities and their practices, I personally feel the announcement was all too necessary.

The simple fact is this: Fraternities are not cult-like factions created to promote primal behavior; they are nothing more than a unification of friends . . . but perhaps I'm getting ahead of myself. We should address the issue first.

A couple of weeks ago an article was published in the Chronicle concerning a documentary made about a fraternity and its barbaric ways. The author of the column described horrific hazing rituals, female-degrading principles and how this movie was indicative of the maliciously unnecessary habits of the fraternity as an organization.

One thing has always been crystal-clear for me: If I ever want to learn about a culture, organization or individual, I listen to the source. If you want to learn about fraternities, ask a member of a fraternity. It makes absolutely no sense to me to learn about the IRA from the Prime Minister of Vietnam.

My experience with the Pi Kappa Alpha fraternity has been filled with nothing more than the building of unbreakable friendships and the creation of unforgettable memories.

I understand, though, that bad things have happened in fraternities before, and the last thing I want to do is dismiss blame where blame is due. But this is another example in which logic seems to take the back seat to anger. Individuals must be held accountable for their individual decisions.

As a member of a fraternity, a position which one would think should hold some clout when describing fraternities, I am proud to say I have seen more acts of magnanimity by my brothers than anything else for the simple fact we are always together and we are always demanding the best of ourselves.

It is when individuals are left alone, are not held accountable for what they do by friends who are watching and are not seen as a reflection of a group, that their judgment can stray and their motives can be tainted.

There is one last issue to address: Fraternity members do not pay for their friends; they pay for their activities. I know where every dime I spend in the fraternity goes, and I never think twice about paying. Perhaps, though, I shouldn't have said that, for I really don't care whether or not others think I'm "buying my friends," for what I have gained as an individual from being a part of a fraternity is absolutely priceless. ■

Makes Greek life sound incredible, right? Depends whom you ask. While some find fraternities and sororities to be esteem-building ventures where young men and women can learn the value of friendship. Others, like the former Greek in the next column, find them to be institutions of conformity-mores at large state schools, where high membership rates result in a greater chance of anonymity. How can you put "the real you" forward if you're wearing the same sweatshirt that 100 other young women are wearing?

COLUMN: RUSH WEAK

By Jeremy Gray

THE GUARDIAN (La Jolla, Calif.) 01/11/1999

Fraternities hate being called "frats"—it is considered disrespectful. That being said, let me tell you why rushing frats is a big mistake.

Rather than promoting lifelong friendships and skills that can be useful in the real world, fraternities are an extension of high school for people who can't move past gossiping, student government and conformity. At least, that was the case when I was in one.

Fraternities work if you buy into the concept of "brotherhood," and I do mean buy into it. There are several pledge fees to pay (running up to about $200), and that's before you're even guaranteed a spot in the fraternity. Once you get in, the dues range from $140-$170 a quarter, depending on the particularities of each fraternity. Each pledge and active member is also expected to buy t-shirts made for Greek-related events at $8-$10 a pop. The puffy-lettered sweatshirts are even more, running $30-$40. But hey, paying through the nose is OK if it means having access to the mysterious concept of brotherhood, right? Not exactly.

For some individuals, myself included, membership in the fraternity was symbolic of overcoming challenges in pledging and managing to get decent grades (and I will say, in defense of fraternities, that they do make pledges go to

Maybelle Trocio/*The Lantern*

mandatory study hours every week). But most of that private symbolism went right out the window when I stepped outside and realized I looked like 70 other guys and automatically had the "duh" stigma that goes with being Greek at UCSD.

Furthermore, rush is a mirage. If you wondered why every active member greeting you seemed like he knew your family, dentist and insurance salesman, your suspicions have merit. For one or two weeks beforehand, fraternity members actually train for rush week in high hopes that they will attract the most potential pledges. The strategy is simple: the larger your fraternity, the better it looks. Why would so many people join a bad fraternity?

Perhaps fraternities work at other universities where they have actual fraternity houses and the support of the campus. Maybe they just aren't for everybody. They certainly aren't for people who don't like gossiping, dressing alike and acting like every planned event is going to be bigger than Noah's Ark.

At UCSD, fraternities are for insecure individuals who need to feel like they belong. However, there are better ways to belong than to pay for friends. Besides, if you're going to get involved in a social club, you may as well join one that will give you more than a special handshake and a couple of candle ceremonies. ∎

Clearly, there are as many opinions about Greek life as there are organizations. If you choose to attend a large state school, chances are you'll consider joining a fraternity or sorority. Remember that, despite the bad press, Greek organizations do a lot of good on the campus and in the community. It's often the Greeks who are out there on a Saturday morning having car washes for charity or volunteering at hospitals. Membership in a sorority or fraternity can lead to lifelong friendships and teach you about unity and camaraderie. Just be sure you look at all sides of the debate before you "rush" in.

Interesting Speakers

Joining a fraternity, sorority, or any one of the other groups described here may become a monthlong, yearlong, or lifelong commitment, but opportunities outside of academics can be one-night-only, once-in-a-lifetime experiences as well. Because their campuses are home to auditoriums and stadiums that can hold huge crowds, large state schools are big draws for top celebrities.

CLINTON CALLS FOR STUDENT ACTIVISM DURING U. MARYLAND VISIT

By Mark Matthews

THE DIAMONDBACK (College Park, Md.) 02/11/1999

President Clinton's campus visit Tuesday brought back memories of Midnight Madness; spectators listened to fight songs and speeches, cheered and gave standing ovations. The crowd formed a patchwork of Terrapin red and AmeriCorps gray, threaded with suits and skirts of VIPs such as Ethel Kennedy and MTV's Carson Daly.

"We played the same gig as we would a basketball game with a couple of presidential tunes," said band member Andrew Parlette, a junior computer science major. "It was just a little difficult to play when the President came in because we wanted to see him."

Joining the band in Ritchie Coliseum were nearly 2,000 onlookers—so many that the audience in some bleacher areas overflowed into the aisles. Speakers seated on the stage included Gov. Parris Glendening, Lt. Gov. Kathleen Kennedy Townsend, whose mother, Ethel, was in the crowd, Prince George's County Executive Wayne Curry, campus President Clayton D. Mote Jr. and Student Government Association President Avery Straw. Daly introduced an AmeriCorps public service announcement that began airing on MTV yesterday.

The crowded atmosphere added to the excitement. Every time a speaker mentioned Clinton's name, the crowd roared back in support. Chants and applause also followed any mention of the campus, AmeriCorps or the Terrapin men's basketball team.

Jonathan Skolnick/*The Campus Times*

Security remained tight, with Secret Service members, University Police and state bomb squad members patrolling the area inside and outside of Ritchie Coliseum.

In addition to security sweeps conducted Tuesday night and restricted parking yesterday, fraternity members living next to Ritchie Coliseum in the first five houses on Fraternity Row were asked to pull down their window shades and refrain from exiting through their back doors.

Despite these security measures, the College Park Airport did not reroute its flights, which is a standard security measure during a presidential visit. Airport assistant administrator Adam Vidoni said a presidential helicopter, Eagle 1, was in the airspace during the assembly.

Before the program began, almost a dozen students and citizens stood on the opposite side of Route 1 holding signs, handing out leaflets and chanting against the bombings and sanctions against Iraq. Religious proponents and media coverage opponents spoke out as well.

While the presentation came in the waning days of the impeachment trial in the U.S. Senate, many audience members said they thought Clinton's decision to speak was genuine and not a public relations stunt.

"I was really impressed and my feelings toward [Clinton] changed. He's an amazing speaker and I think he really cared," senior communications major Janell Orr said.

"He wants to encourage young people to help in their community. A lot of people have the attitude that young people are lazy, and this is going to help end the [stereotypes] of Generation X," said AmeriCorps member Jamie Siudyla. ■

LIFE ON Campus

You must be wondering what your life will *really* be like when you attend a big school. But even before you get there you'll have to figure out how you're going to pay for your education. Lucky for you, costs at a large state school are lower than those at private schools, especially if you're a state resident. Since it's likely that you'll be paying at least some of your own way, check out "Financial aid office keeps Louisiana State students in check" for a great overview of the ins and outs of financial aid. The U.S. Department of Education gives out over $42 billion in federal financial aid yearly; add that to the amount that the state and your school can kick in, and you'll be back in the black in no time. Other solutions to your financial dilemma include work-study and scholarship programs. Work-study programs like those described in "Work study solves financial dilemma at MSU" offer students a great alternative to working as waitresses or busboys: With flexible hours, great working conditions, and—best of all—no dirty dishes, work-study can be a student's dream come true. If you think you can make the grade, check into academic scholarships like the Regents Program at the University of New Mexico. Because they're anxious to enroll the brightest students they can, large schools often have deep pockets when it comes to academic scholarship dollars.

So the check's in the mail, and you're off for your first day at college. Be prepared for crowded conditions—in some cases, *really crowded*. The scenario described in "No more room service," where University of Minnesota freshmen had to live in hotels until enough rooms opened up, presents an extreme case to be sure, but it highlights a problem at campuses nationwide. Last year the University of Nebraska enrolled over 4,700 freshmen on its Lincoln campus; Penn State University, over 12,700 on its twenty-four campuses. They've all gotta live somewhere.

You should expect a lot of diversity in all those faces you'll see, too. One of the greatest bonuses of life at a large college is the mix of students you'll find, and big schools take great steps to ensure harmony and understanding in their student bodies. Iowa State's innovative U.S. Diversity and International Perspective Requirements put them ahead of the national average by requiring students to earn 6 credits from course-work emphasizing gender, ethnicity, and cross-cultural research, among other topics. Best of all, students of all backgrounds at big schools find open forums to air grievances as well as plenty of support, as stories from the University of Wisconsin, Penn State, Indiana University, UVA, and the University of Iowa aptly point out.

All those kids have to let loose somehow, so expect lots of opportunities to party and have fun at a big school. A hard choice you'll face is whether or not to indulge in alcohol. Before you do, read "Colleges across country battle alcohol abuse." These stories bring home the problems, and the consequences, of alcohol on big campuses. Problems with students and alcohol nationwide have brought lawsuits against Greek organizations and the schools themselves, which has led to huge insurance rates for both. For this reason, large universities are cracking down on alcohol abuse. Fortunately for you, anti-alcohol campaigns have brought with them countless opportunities for alternative, non-alcohol-related events campuswide. Big campuses host scores of concerts yearly: "U. Conn hosts Dave Matthews, special Guest Popper" describes one. The trend to move away from alcohol has also encouraged students to explore other avenues for fun. Texas

A&M students whoop it up with Whoopstock and University of Michigan students run the Naked Mile to celebrate the last day of classes. Okay, you don't have to run naked, but you get the picture. If you choose, you can stay sober *and* have a good time at a large state school.

In case they're wondering, tell mom and dad not to worry; you'll be well-provided for at a large state school. Student services on big campuses do a great job of keeping everyone safe and healthy. "Model security program celebrates 25 years on Kent State campus" reviews the type of safety services you can expect, including late-night campus escorts and dormitory supervision. All of your health questions and concerns will be addressed at campus medical facilities, through excellent health insurance options and counseling. Because they must be in strict compliance with state and federal regulations, facilities at large state schools are fully accessible for those with physical challenges. Even "nontradi- tional" students—that's all you working parents out there—can take advantage of the excellent services offered by big schools, including care care options like those at the University of South Florida.

One last thing to keep in mind: The atmosphere at a large state school will be greatly influenced by the fact that the university is subject to the whims of state legislation. In these crazy political days, that can mean a lot. We begin our discussion of life on campus with the subject of state influence.

State Influence

Large state schools can keep tuition low because they're funded in large part by the state's taxpayers. While low tuition is good news for those who don't want to pay a fortune for their education, there is a price to be paid for lower rates. State schools are, in essence, controlled by the state and are subject to all laws of the state. While that may sound harmless, in today's political climate of conservatism and cutbacks, it often spells bad news. It takes time to get public school legislation pushed through state channels, especially when it concerns anything "controversial." Even more importantly, budget decisions are also made in large part by the state. Both of these can affect life on campus, as those students in Ohio found.

BILL DEFENDS OHIO STUDENTS' VOICES
By Erik Clark

THE LANTERN (Columbus, Ohio) 01/20/1999

Ohio Rep. Bill Schuck, R-Columbus, reintroduced a bill Friday that would limit restriction of student expression at Ohio's public colleges and universities. The same bill died in the Senate at least twice before when the 122nd and 121st General Assemblies ended their terms.

The bill states that a "state university or college or its employee shall not adopt any rule, regulation, or policy subjecting a student to disciplinary action solely on the basis of the student's speech or other expression."

Schuck attended a caucus retreat Tuesday with his Republican colleagues, so he was unavailable for comment. Jonathon Archey, Schuck's legislative aid, explained that the bill assures that any expression protected by law off campus will also be protected on campus. In addition, if a student believes his or her expression has been wrongly restricted, the bill allows for the student to file a civil suit against the institution.

This means that expression that is considered defamation, a threat to public safety, or any other form of unprotected speech, would not have a safe haven at Ohio's public post-secondary education institutions.

David Williams II, Ohio State's vice-president for student and urban/community affairs, said he knows of no time when Ohio State University's campus would be a place of less freedom of expression than any other public place, except possibly if a student were to disrupt the learning process in a classroom.

The university is always careful to guard against hurtful speech, but only when legal rights of expression are not compromised, Williams said.

OSU is currently working to create a specific "expression area" to ensure students have a place to speak their minds, he said. This area could be a physical room or hallway located somewhere on campus, Williams said.

The last version of the bill, House Bill 51 of the 122nd General Assembly, was passed by the House in February 1997, less than a month after it was introduced, but it did not pass the Senate before the assembly adjourned last month.

Archey said Senate consideration of that bill, which was introduced by Rep. William Batchelder, R-Medina, who retired at the end of the last term, kept getting postponed in favor of other issues.

Any bill that is not passed by both houses before the end of an assembly's term must be reintroduced by the next assembly if it is to receive any further consideration.

Archey said the bill Schuck reintroduced, essentially a verbatim copy of Batchelder's previous version, already has several cosponsors and enjoys "wide, bipartisan support" in both chambers.

However, the bill suffered the same fate at least one time before the 122nd assembly. Batchelder introduced the bill in the 121st assembly as well. It passed in the House, but the Senate did not vote on it before the assembly adjourned in December 1996.

Archey said that very often bills do not pass on their first or second times through the legislative process be-cause of the system itself, "not because of a lack of merit."

"I think [the bill] would have an excellent chance," he said.

The bill will be assigned a number after Wednesday's House voting session. ■

EDITORIAL: BUDGET PLAN PUTS PROFIT ABOVE LEARNING
Staff Editorial

THE LANTERN (Columbus, Ohio) 02/05/1999

Ohio State University administrators call it "incentive-based budgeting," but ignore the double talk: It's profit-based budgeting.

In considering a system that funds colleges according to the amount of revenue they generate, OSU is letting big business set its agenda and placing profit above the traditional values of higher education. The board of trustees is expected today to approve installing a shadow budget in the next school year, so administrators can study how the university would look under the new system before implementing it.

OSU will look a lot like a business. Colleges will receive increased funding based on the revenue they generate through enrollment, research grants and partnerships with companies. For the board, whose members are mostly from the business community, making profit the goal that drives OSU must seem entirely logical.

OSU currently operates on an historic budget system in which each college receives a set amount of funding plus an increase for how much it grew from the previous year. Provost Ed Ray said the system is inadequate because it doesn't provide a mechanism that rewards colleges enough that help the university grow.

"Helping the university grow" is more academic jargon, meaning making the university as much money as possible. It's not hard to figure out what colleges do that, because they're the ones with nice new buildings and facilities.

During the state budget cuts of earlier this decade, many colleges were slashed to prevent having to hike tuition. To survive, colleges had to look to alternate means of funding. Getting multimillionaire alumni to help out was one way.

Research grants also proved to be an important way to bring colleges, such as engineering, cash as well as OSU prestige. Liberal arts majors and others could only sit back and watch as the gap between the educational haves and have-nots grew larger.

If your college didn't have wealthy alumni or couldn't bring in research grants, chances are that after the axe dropped, so did enrollment. With profit-based budgeting, low enrollment, no research grants and lack of money from business equals lower funds from OSU. Which is one of the big problems with profit-based budgeting: It's a Catch-22.

Colleges that were devastated in the budget-cutting onslaught, like social work, are likely to get ransacked even worse under the new system. These colleges then face the fate of any division of a business that doesn't make a profit—They're eliminated.

Issued last year, the Carnegie Report included OSU in a group of universities that endanger undergraduate education by placing too much emphasis on research. It's beyond comprehension why OSU would consider putting even more reliance on research, unless teaching undergraduates just isn't part of its mission anymore.

Running universities like businesses has frightening implications on our democracy. Higher education shouldn't be about just churning out students who can make a lot of money. It should be about making people able to think and communicate, whether or not their base of knowledge can earn them or their college a profit. ■

Paying for College

Even with lower tuition at state schools, some students must work to pay for college. This needn't be a bad thing. Work-study—receiving a paycheck or tuition remission for working on campus or in the community—enables many students to get paid for interesting jobs with flexible time schedules. Since most jobs are for the university, employers are understanding of the other demands on your time, and your education is given top priority.

WORK STUDY SOLVES FINANCIAL DILEMMAS AT MSU

By Amy Sinquefield

THE STATE NEWS (East Lansing, Mich.) 09/23/1998

For many students, the trials and triumphs of campus life go far beyond the classroom and into some not-so-deep pockets. The high price of higher education leaves a large number of students searching for jobs to suit their fiscal needs.

Michigan State University work-study program offers a solution to this student dilemma.

"They appreciate the fact that you are working while you go to school," said Lisa Czarnecki, an epidemiology graduate student, who is enrolled in the program. "They are flexible and work around my schedule."

Work study is a financial aid option in addition to loans, grants and scholarships. Financial aid participants who choose the work-study program and meet all the qualifications are granted an award, which makes the student eligible for a number of jobs designated for program participants.

Applicants for the program must be part-time or full-time students who receive some form of financial aid. Work-study awards are granted on the basis of financial need.

"I like (work study) because it helps me pay for school and I get to play on the computer a lot," said food management senior Marlon Sharpley, who works in Brody Hall's computer lab. Sharpley has been enrolled in the program for five years.

Linda Sigh, assistant director of the Office of Financial Aid, said last year the work-study program granted approximately 3,000 awards to MSU students.

"I encourage all financial aid students to work," she said. "It helps them get more acquainted with the university and to manage their time better."

Once students are given the work-study award, it is up to each individual to find a job. This is done with the help of the Student Employment Office, which posts openings on the Internet. Positions in campus computer labs and libraries are among the office's options.

The jobs, however, are not always on campus. Students also can collaborate off campus with non-profit organizations, ranging from local day care centers to various national establishments.

Employers also benefit from hiring work-study students because the employers do not supply the entire wage. Under the program, 70 percent of a student's pay comes from the work-study fund, 30 percent is paid by the employer.

Average pay depends on where and in what position the student works.

Pre-med freshman Yasmin Lena Myah is happy with the options in the program and said the time she spends in the computer lab gives her experience with computers and the Internet.

"I would recommend work study because it is good experience and it's not a lot of work," Myah said. "It's kind of like the perfect job."

The same flexible schedule is what attracted nursing senior Ann White.

"You can work a couple of hours and then you can go study and then come back and work some more," said White, who is working in the Main Library for the second year. "They know school is most important." ∎

Much better than flipping burgers, you'll agree. But if you still don't want to work your way through college, maybe you can apply for one of the many scholarships offered at large state schools.

Each year, millions of dollars are awarded to academically talented, socially involved, community-minded students. Because large state schools want to attract the best students, they often offer partial, or even full, tuition (plus room and board and more, in some instances) to deserving students. UNM's Regents' Scholars program is one such fabulous scholarship.

SCHOLARS MAKE U. NEW MEXICO PROGRAM A SUCCESS
By Stephen Rabourn

DAILY LOBO (Albuquerque, N.M.) 11/30/1998

What happened to the valedictorians, straight-A students and otherwise academically revered people in your high school? If they came to University of New Mexico, there's a chance they received the privilege of being named Regents' Scholars.

Every year, the University finds 15 of the brightest, most promising students and gives them a full four-year ride, including tuition, fees and room and board, said Rita Padilla, director of the University's Scholarship Office.

Regents' Scholars must meet one of these criteria—score 31 or above on the ACT, be class valedictorian, maintain at least a 3.9 GPA or be a National Merit finalist.

They also must be involved in school and community activities, Padilla said, and once at UNM they must continue to be involved. Students choose what activities they take part in, she added.

Two of UNM's more conspicuous Regents' Scholars are Fred Melendres, president of the Associated Students of UNM, and Guillermo Caraveo, ASUNM's vice president.

Melendres, who was Valley High School's valedictorian, came to UNM in the fall of 1995. Since then, he has played on the soccer team for three years, fulfilled the roles of ASUNM attorney general and senator and last year won the Truman Scholarship, a $30,000 grant to be used for graduate school.

Melendres said the scholarship program helps students form a community at the University. The program also provides students with mentors who direct the scholars in areas that interest them and introduce them to students with similar interests, Melendres said.

"It's a really good program," he said.

Melendres said the scholars get involved at UNM out of gratitude for their scholarships.

"I think Regents' Scholars feel an obligation to give back," he said.

Caraveo, a senior, was also his high school's valedictorian. He also said the community aspect of the program makes it unique. The students find an immediate link to other students, he said. Of the 60 current Regents' Scholars, one can always find a "shoulder to cry on or someone to talk to," he said.

Everyone would agree, Caraveo said, students benefit from the program. He added that the most important part of the program is that students learn from each other.

The Regents' Scholarship Program was started in 1989 by Robert Sanchez, then-president of the Board of Regents. Padilla said Sanchez hoped to use the program to recruit students with exceptional talents in academics. The program also was designed to offer students special, peripheral services, she said, such as specialized advising, mentorship programs and automatic admittance to the General Honors Program.

Padilla said the scholarship program is quite successful and is the best one on campus. It allows the University to compete with other schools for top students.

Freshman Amanda Smith said the scholarship was one of the main reasons she chose UNM over the University of Southern California and the University of Oklahoma.

Smith also said the sense of community among the scholars is what makes the program successful.

"The whole group is really close," she said. ∎

UNM Regents' Scholars represent the cream of the crop; what about the regular guy (or girl) who needs money for college? For the rest of us, thank heaven for Pell grants, PLUS loans, Stafford loans, and any other of a number of ways federal and state governments can help you get through college. Since the majority of students attending public schools receive these awards, having a financial aid office that's up to speed is vital on these campuses. Louisiana State's Student Aid and Scholarships office is a well-oiled machine when it comes to getting you the money you deserve. They'll help you sort out your FAFSA from your SEOG from your TOPS and get you to the bank on time.

FINANCIAL AID OFFICE KEEPS LOUISIANA STATE U. STUDENTS IN CHECK

By Stacie Majoria

THE REVEILLE (Baton Rouge, La.) 02/01/1999

Approximately 45 percent of Louisiana State University students depend on one university office to help keep them in school each year.

The office is Student Aid and Scholarships, and it has coordinated financial aid requests and helped to deliver funds to over 13,000 students this year alone.

Students must complete a Free Application for Federal Student Aid to be considered for federal aid, said Judith Vidrine, assistant director of student aid and scholarships.

All federal financial aid eligibility is based on a family need analysis and determined by the government, she said.

"That is all pre-determined by sending the application in. So when we get it, the story's already told," Vidrine said.

A formula is used to estimate the expected family contribution to the student, she said.

Variables such as the family's income from the previous tax year, number of family members, number of family members in college, and the family's assets and expenses are used to determine the expected family contribution, she continued.

A second formula is then used by the student aid office in deciding the precise amount of financial aid a student will be offered, Vidrine said.

A budget, which combines the costs of tuition, books, room and board, personal travel expenses, and miscellaneous expenses, is tabulated, taking into account the student's living arrangement and whether or not they are a Louisiana resident, she said.

The expected family contribution and any Pell Grant or scholarship funds are subtracted from the

budget, leaving the amount of additional aid needed, such as loans, she said.

"There are certain populations of students who we feel are not best benefitted by the formula," Vidrine said. For example, working students who must report their parents' income because they are classified as dependents may not receive some grants because of the combined incomes, she said.

Students can always look into borrowing money if they do not qualify for "free money," Vidrine said.

"You always have an option. It may be a loan, it may be an unsubsidized loan, but you always have the option," she said.

Additional criteria a student must meet to receive federal student aid are maintaining a 2.0 GPA, making satisfactory progress towards a degree, and enrolling in the appropriate number of hours, Vidrine said.

Students must register for at least six hours of classes to be eligible for loans, and the amount of the Pell Grant is proportionate to the student's course load, she said.

The maximum award for the work-study program is $1000 per semester, Vidrine said. Students are also limited to a 20-hour workweek with this program, she said.

Workers who do not earn the full amount of their award in the fall may make up the money in the spring, she said. Remaining funds at the end of the academic year are put back into the work-study program, she continued.

Student wages cannot be raised to allow students to earn their award more quickly, Vidrine said. "The federal government in allocating work study says you pay minimum wage," she said.

A few exceptions exist to this statement, such as off-campus jobs requiring additional transportation costs or positions included in departmental budgets, she added.

Although eligible students may receive work study and grants as long as they are enrolled in school, a cap exists on the amount of money they can borrow, Vidrine said.

A dependent undergraduate may borrow up to $23,000, and an independent undergraduate may borrow an additional $23,000 in unsubsidized loans. Graduate students may borrow up to $138,500 for undergraduate and graduate studies combined, she said.

PLUS loans, or parent loans, are an option for students who have exceeded the limit on Stafford loans, Vidrine said.

All lenders belonging to the student loan program are required to be consistent with interest rates and loan terms, Vidrine said. The interest on a student loan can never exceed 8.25 percent, she said.

Students should file their aid applications as soon as possible after Jan. 1, Vidrine said.

March 1 is the recommended deadline for full consideration of limited-funding programs, such as work study or the Supplemental Education Opportunity Grant, she added.

The priority deadline for TOPS, also applied for with the FAFSA, is April 15, and the final submission deadline is July 15 for the following academic year, Vidrine said.

Pell Grants and the loan programs are not limited funding programs, and students may apply for this aid throughout the school year, she said.

Students who are taking out loans must watch an entrance video before they receive the funds, Vidrine said.

"It is an effort for us to inform students of their rights and responsibilities of borrowing," she said. "We try to instill in them to borrow conservatively."

Consequences of student loan default include bad credit ratings, garnished wages and seizure of tax refunds, Vidrine said.

Vidrine said her advice to students is to apply for financial aid early, keep in touch with the office, read the aid materials and reply to correspondence.

"Let us know when there's a problem, because we are willing to help," she said.

Tabitha Rice, a teaching certificate student, said she has never had a problem with the financial aid process.

"It's pretty straightforward, you just fill out a paper," she said.

One flaw with the program is its exclusion of some dependent students from consideration for Pell Grants due to their parents' income, since sometimes they do not receive funds from their parents, said Rice.

Adolfo Escobar, senior in mechanical engineering, said he likes the way the University handles the volume of students who need financial aid assistance.

The financial aid program could be improved by making funds available for international students, said Escobar. ■

Housing

Now that you've figured out how to pay for college, it's time to head off for your first semester. If you decide to live on campus, your parent's minivan won't be the only one pulling up to the freshman dorm that first day of school. And after you've lugged all your worldly possessions up to your room, you might find that your living quarters aren't as cozy as you'd hoped them to be. And forget about a private bathroom—you may need to share that with half of your floor. Chances are the laundry room will be in the basement, and your cafeteria (if your dorm has one) will look like the one in your high school—only much, much larger. To add to these less-than-ideal circumstances, record numbers of students being accepted at large state schools have led to a serious housing shortage. One of the more novel ways of solving this problem has been to house students in local hotels until rooms are available.

U. MINNESOTA STUDENTS BEGIN DORM LIFE

By Robin Huiras

MINNESOTA DAILY (Minneapolis, Minn.) 01/04/1999

After more than three months of hotel living, the last students housed at the University Days Inn moved into residence halls for the beginning of winter quarter.

The University Days Inn housed about 200 overflow students until vacancies within the halls allowed for more permanent accommodations.

For the past few years, the University has converted study lounges into temporary rooms for overflow students. However, because of an increase in the number of incoming freshmen this year, officials needed to look to alternatives outside residence halls for overflow housing.

Mary Ann Ryan, director of Housing and Residential Life said the University knew space was available for every student in the halls before the end of fall quarter, but wanted to wait to physically move the students.

"We're sensitive to the fact that students during finals week have other priorities," Ryan said.

With the highest freshman enrollment in 10 years and a guarantee of housing to those freshman who get their applications in before May 1, placing all of the students in traditional rooms was difficult. However,

Bumper DeJesus/*The Daily Targum*

Housing and Residential Life officials are moving to accommodate next year's class by providing upwards of 600 additional beds in the next two years.

"As it looks now, we will not need to go back to the Days Inn," Ryan said.

Decorated to look like any other hall, hotel life had both its advantages and disadvantages. Most students enjoyed the private bathrooms, but having to walk further for food and laundry services disgruntled many hotel residents, Ryan said.

"For different people there were different complaints," said Dave Nistler, Days Inn hall director. "The most frequent was the inconvenience of not having an established place to stay."

Elisa Keck, a freshman who moved out of the Days Inn and into a dorm on Oct. 31, agreed. She said many hotel mates shared her sentiments. Additionally, having to walk to the campus to eat, do laundry and use computers was a big annoyance, Keck said.

With no-shows in the halls and residence hall students choosing other living options, the hotel rooms slowly became vacant, Nistler said. Roughly 25 students remained in the hotel during the last two weeks of the quarter. ■

Diversity

One of the strengths of large state schools is in their diversity. You'll see it in the student body living in your dorm and the professors teaching your courses. You'll be living and taking classes with and being taught by men and women of all ethnic, religious, and sexual orientations. In most states, that's the law. Many see this as a great chance to learn beyond the classroom—about other people and other ways of life. Life on a large state school campus mirrors life in the "outside world," where you'll interact with people of all persuasions on a daily basis. On many campuses, ensuring a diverse student body promotes tolerance and understanding.

But diversity sometimes creates controversy. Many decry affirmative action as a means of giving preferential treatment; some laud it as one of this country's greatest social advances. And as in the world beyond your school's gates, racism and bigotry exist on many campuses, affecting the lives of minority students. It's an area of concern, and different schools are tackling the problem in different ways.

Race is a controversial issue in the nation at large and on college campuses in particular. It's safe to say that no other subject can arouse the intense feelings that discussions of race can. And as in the country as a whole, college campuses are struggling with racism. On the campuses of large state schools, the problem is particularly prevalent. Affirmative action laws, where they exist, may ensure a diverse mix of students and faculty, but resolving the struggles of minorities on campus is left in the hands of individual schools themselves. Fortunately, great strides are being made at schools across the country, which are reaching out to students of all ethnic backgrounds. The University of Wisconsin and Penn State University are two schools making concerted efforts to combat racism.

RACIAL TENSION KEY POINT OF DISCUSSIONS

By Joel J. Nelson

BADGER HERALD (Madison, Wis.) 09/21/1998

In an effort to reveal racial problems at University of Wisconsin–Madison, university officials have begun looking at the climate in which students of color must live.

The Dean of Student's Office, through a presentation entitled "Revealing Racism: The Campus Climate for Students of Color," intends to raise awareness about the experiences of students of color and match their needs with available programs and services.

The goals of the study are to better understand the experiences of students of color in the classroom, at home, on campus and in the Madison community.

One of the major underlying problems discovered by four focus group studies was "aversive behavior" among whites towards students of color. Many of the students of color felt it was difficult to form social bonds with white students and faculty, the study found.

"They won't even talk to you. They won't look at you," a male Puerto Rican who took part in the study was quoted as saying. "The thing about the college environment that's really different for a lot of us is that they are very cold and reserved. They don't try and make the effort for outreach."

Elton Crim, student services coordinator for University Health Services, said students of color are tolerated on this campus, but they need to go beyond tolerance to inclusion within the student body.

"The isolation of students of color is not a misperception," he said.

The study was conducted through a series of four

Mike Staab/*The Daily Cardinal*

focus groups, three groups of undergraduates and one group of graduate and professional individuals.

A total of 24 students took part in the group discussions. Sixty-seven percent of the students involved were female, 29 percent were male, and four percent gave no response.

The results of the finding were released during an informal presentation at Memorial Union Thursday. While few students turned out for the event, UW officials said they are only beginning to study the problem and hope to increase student involvement through future discussions about race at UW. ∎

HANDBOOK OFFERS MINORITY STUDENTS GUIDE TO LIFE ON CAMPUS

By Khyber Oser

DAILY COLLEGIAN (State College, Penn.) 02/05/1998

Imagine a white student at the University of Ghana.

Walking around campus or sitting in the classrooms, it would be a struggle for the student to blend in, fit in or feel comfortable.

This is an example given by Marc Levey, a principal author of "How to Succeed on a Majority Campus: A Guide for Minority Students," of what minority students often experience at a predominantly white institution.

Levey, senior diversity planning analyst at the University, said the pressures and scrutiny attached to being a minority student can make the adjustment to college even more difficult for incoming freshman.

"You get tags or associations that are often negative and false," Levey said. "Many times, minority students think about themselves as different. It never leaves their minds."

The guidebook's goal is to offer successful strategies for making the most of minority students' experiences at predominantly white schools, Levey said. All three principal authors are diversity officials at the University and the book is based on more than 100 interviews with minority students and minority student counselors across the country, according to a news release.

Complete with checklists, question-and-answer exercises, photos taken at the University and quotes from minority students, the guidebook resembles an interactive "how-to" book. It was released nationwide and in Canada in mid-November, Levey said.

The guide addresses broad subjects that apply to all minorities such as study skills, dating, health concerns and racism. But it also contains chapters devoted specifically to the experiences of international students and lesbian, gay and bisexual students of color.

"It's a book that hasn't been written before," said Michael Blanco, director of the Multicultural Resource Center at the University. "There is no other book that I know of that is a comprehensive guide on the experiences of minority students attending a predominantly white institution."

Blanco and Terrell Jones, associate vice provost for educational equity, are the other principal authors.

Joseph Selden, director of multicultural affairs for the College of Communications, said he read the book and would recommend it to students, faculty and staff.

"It's got a little bit of something for everyone," Selden said. "(The guide) is something everyone ought to add to their reading list."

However, Jameel Quarles (sophomore-marketing and international business), a member of Black Caucus, said he thinks the book may only be applicable to a certain audience.

"For freshmen and people who are about to enter college, I think the book is good," he said. "But for students who've been here for two or three years, we've already learned the stuff we need to survive."

Toshie Faloye (junior-insurance and international business) said she thinks being outnumbered is a constant issue for University minority students, adding that she is the only minority student in some of her classes this semester. Faloye, a member of the Caribbean Student Association, said many minority students hang out together because they can relate to one another.

"The Black community is more motivated to stick together," she said. "Sometimes I feel more comfortable with people of color."

The guidebook discusses the fact that some minority students cope by sticking together in large groups, but the book also addresses that some minority students at predominantly white institutions seclude themselves instead.

Quarles said he sees minority students who fit the latter mold.

"There's not that much for minorities to do on this campus, so some minority students will stay in their rooms and some go home," he said. "I know people who go home every weekend."

The guidebook is intended to help minority students deal with the difficulties of adapting to a predominantly white institution, Levey said, but he

Tengku Bahar/*The Cavalier Daily*

said the book can be a valuable resource for incoming non-minority students because they will be able to relate to many of the same situations.

"I think the notions of alienation, separation, fear of a new atmosphere, competition, the bigness of this place and getting lost in a crowd are examples that will ring true to the vast majority of new students," he said. ■

On some campuses, homosexuality and bisexuality are even more controversial than race. Young men and women who are gay, lesbian, or bisexual tackle ignorance and even hostility as well as their own, often conflicting, feelings about their sexuality. As with race, big schools that pride themselves on diversity have reached out to these students. On the campus of Indiana University, peer support and counseling are provided for students struggling with their sexual identity.

PEER SUPPORT AVAILABLE AT INDIANA U. FOR GLBT STUDENTS

By Aline Mendelsohn

INDIANA DAILY STUDENT (Bloomington, Ind.) 11/05/1998

Several years ago, as a student at Miami University of Ohio, Carmen Wargel realized she was a lesbian. During that confusing and emotional time, Wargel would have appreciated the opportunity to discuss the issues with a peer.

Brian McDermott/*Massachusetts Daily Collegian*

Although she didn't have that chance, Wargel is helping coordinate this kind of effort at IU—the Peer Support Project.

"Sometimes we need to talk to someone our own age," said Wargel, library coordinator for the Gay, Lesbian, Bisexual and Transgendered. "Our friends don't always listen to us in that way."

The program, which is in its third year, consists of 12 diverse peer supporters, who range from freshmen to graduate students. Peer supporters, who must be GLBT, are linked to a student according to interests, experience and concerns. Supporters contact the students via e-mail, phone or have face-to-face meetings.

Wargel stressed that the program does not necessarily exist to provide answers. Often, she said, individuals beginning the delicate coming out process just need a sympathetic ear. Others need guidance in developing a plan to tell their parents. Some don't even know if they are GLBT. Through talking to a supporter, Wargel finds that students clarify their thoughts.

Sophomore Andy Erne, a peer supporter, knows firsthand the benefits of a support program. As a high school student, when Erne was coming out of the closet, he sought assistance through the youth gay organization. He also confided in a teacher. But he realizes not everyone has these resources.

"I don't think you could have too much support," Erne said.

Law student Lasca Holcomb, another peer supporter, attended a liberal women's college. Holcomb feels the program on IU's campus has an added significance, since the conservative atmosphere might not always be conducive to a supportive environment.

Freshman Mandy Hyndman has yet to be assigned to a peer. But she has been a peer supporter on an informal basis, helping GLBT friends through difficult times.

"Too many people are afraid to talk to just anyone," Hyndman said. "When there is a program with the title of 'peer supporter,' people feel like they can trust it, and that's the first step to helping themselves." ■

To ensure equal treatment of minority students, big schools have enacted policies banning discrimination, have put counselors in place, and have encouraged formation of groups promoting these students' agendas. Women are not a minority in this country, yet some studies have shown that men excel in certain academic areas, especially math and science, because of gender-biased treatment by teachers in these fields (who are, in turn, largely men). The University of Iowa is dealing with this discouraging statistic through a vanguard program that will encourage women to stick with studies in computer science.

U. IOWA COMPUTER DEPT. TESTS ALL-FEMALE SECTIONS

By Sam Achelpohl

IOWA STATE DAILY (Iowa City, Iowa) 01/27/1999
— A year ago, the University of Iowa Department of Computer Science undertook an experiment never before attempted at the university or, for that matter, in the Big Ten.

The department began a unique initiative to attract and retain women in computer science, a field traditionally dominated by men.

In response to the lack of women in the field, two all-female discussion sections were offered for the course Computer Science I during the past two semesters.

The experiment is in its last stage of a three-semester trial period. At the end of this semester, the results will be reviewed by Linda Maxson, dean of the College of Liberal Arts.

Marie Roch, a teaching assistant in Computer Science I, knows first-hand how hard it is for women to stick with the major.

"Some women have a tendency to speak up less in computer science," she said. "It's important for women to have support in a classroom like this without feeling overshadowed by men."

Steven Bruell, professor of computer science and chairman of the department, brought the problem to the attention of Big Ten schools' computer science departments in September 1997, at their annual meeting in Chicago. All agreed that the lack of women in the field is a major problem and that something had to be done about it, he said.

"Retaining women in the computer-science field is a nationwide problem," Bruell said. "We want to counteract that problem."

He said he knew of tests that had been done with single-gender high school classrooms showing female students scored equal to or better than males in science and mathematics-related courses, in which men have traditionally done better.

At the meeting, Bruell said he asked if any of the universities had tried offering all-female discussion sections; though none had explored the possibility, all thought it was a good idea.

"I had no preconceived notion of what to expect when we first decided to start (the experiment)," he said. "We've been pleasantly surprised."

Aside from a few complaints by some male students who inadvertently registered for the all-female discussion sections, no protests have been raised, Bruell said.

"There is no special treatment in these sections whatsoever," he said. "It's strictly voluntary. (Women) can register for whichever (section) they want."

Last semester, the women's section performed, on average, better than many of the mixed sections, Bruell said.

Although he can't foresee how this will affect higher-level courses in the department, Bruell said it's definitely something his department will look at this semester.

"The bottom line is that we need more women in this field," he said. "This is a step in that direction." ■

Drinking

No matter what your background, one thing's for sure: There will be plenty of chances for you to party once you reach college. Your parents may not want to accept it—and the school's admissions counselors probably won't admit it—but the consumption of alcohol is a fact of life at college.

Although laws prohibiting anyone under the age of 21 from drinking have been on the books for years in most states, the majority of colleges have turned a blind eye toward underage drinking in years past. Now that scenario is changing as lawsuits have been brought against colleges whose lax enforcement of drinking laws have led to hospitalization and—in a few tragic cases, death—because of student drinking.

Because students at large state schools live both on and off campus, the problem with student drinking affects not just the school itself, but the entire community as well. In the worst cases, riots fueled by drinking have broken out in communities across the country. And parties at fraternities and sororities that serve alcohol continue to wreak havoc on campus, especially at large state schools.

The time to crack down on alcohol abuse among college students has come, so be forewarned. If you choose to party (and it will be hard not to), the consequences may be severe.

COLLEGES ACROSS THE COUNTRY BATTLE ALCOHOL ABUSE
By Mark Parfitt

DAILY COLLEGIAN (State College, Penn.) 07/23/1998

It has been said again and again—alcohol abuse is a problem at Penn State. Every time a major alcohol-related incident makes the news, the topic resurfaces. But alcohol abuse is not just a problem at Penn State, it's a growing problem facing colleges across the country.

From coast to coast, many students view alcohol as part of a college culture. But as this culture continues to grow, some communities have said that what would be considered out-of-control drinking in the rest of society has been tolerated and ignored simply because it has always been regarded as part of a college lifestyle.

In the past, colleges used two main ways to prevent students from participating in high-risk alcohol situations—alcohol education and alcohol enforcement.

But as violent alcohol-related situations like the July 12 Beaver Avenue riot continue to occur across the United States, students, administrators and community members are discovering that the old methods against college alcohol abuse are no longer working and are looking for new, productive solutions.

The Beaver Avenue riot in the early morning of July 12 was an event that will most likely be a part of college history and memories for all Penn State students who were in town during the weekend of the 32nd Annual Central Pennsylvania Festival of the Arts.

It took seven police agencies about 2 1/2 hours to disperse a crowd of at least 1,500 people on East Beaver Avenue. Rioters turned over vehicles, ripped lampposts and parking meters out of the ground, smashed storefronts and set fires fueled by furniture, tree limbs and trash. Early estimates of the damage are around $150,000.

The State College Police Department officially attributed the cause of the incident to too many people abusing alcohol. Twenty-one people have been charged with violations related to the riot, including failure to disperse upon lawful order, disorderly conduct and resisting arrest.

Alcohol abuse is not a problem confined to Penn State. Nationally, many college campuses, both large and small, have seen a rise in student alcohol use and alcohol-related incidents, like the Beaver Avenue riot.

Police in Durham, N.H. had to use pepper spray to disperse a crowd of 400 to 500 University of New Hampshire students in a riot last September, according to The New Hampshire, the university's newspaper. During the riot, participants chanted obscenities and tossed bottles and rocks at police offers.

A similar outbreak took place at the University of Oregon about a month later.

Police in Eugene, Ore. originally arrived at a party to enforce alcohol violations. But when police tried to take action, people began throwing bottles at the officers, according to The Oregon Daily Emerald. Officers in riot gear then turned to tear gas after a 30-minute standoff with the party participants. Of a crowd of about 300, four arrests were made and charges filed included disorderly conduct, rioting, drug violations and attempted assault.

These were only two of many riots involving alcohol that have occurred at campuses nationwide.

A study released by the Harvard School of Public Health, which studied binge drinking at 140 colleges, said 84 percent of the students drank during the school year, and almost half of those were binge drinkers. The study also found that the binge drinking of some students had a impact on students who do not drink, like the Beaver Avenue riot.

One of the largest college riots in recent history took place two nights in a row in May 1997 at University Hill, a student section of Boulder, Colo. During the first night about 1,500 people participated in a riot that resulted in 12 injured police officers, 60 damaged vehicles and 20 smashed parking meters, according to Colorado Daily.

As this national issue becomes a local problem for many college communities, universities and towns have decided that what worked in the past is no longer effective at battling alcohol abuse.

Karen C. Tully/*Arizona Daily Wildcat*

Like in Boulder, large alcohol-related incidents have brought universities and their neighboring towns together to form committees, programs and centers that all try to reduce alcohol abuse among students.

The solutions being designed at many universities are experimental and controversial, but those involved feel something new is needed and that these ideas are worth a try.

Some universities believe that if they can control the alcohol supply, they will see an overall decrease in alcohol abuse.

Colleges across the country are looking at the University of Delaware, which in recent times has been considered a pioneer in battling student alcohol abuse on many fronts.

The university received a grant from the Robert Wood Johnson Foundation to create educational ways to reduce binge drinking. However, as part of that grant, the university had to toughen its alcohol policies and enforcement, said Jane Moore, assistant dean of students at the university, which is located in Newark, Del.

What resulted was a new alcohol policy in the fall of 1997 that is essentially a "three-strikes and you're out" rule.

Five behaviors would violate the university's alcohol policy: underage possession and/or consumption, open container of alcohol in public, hosting a party involving the illegal use of alcohol, dispensing alcohol to minors and intoxication.

Since its enactment less than a year ago, Moore said the university has suspended 48 students from dorms and 21 students from the university. Once a student is found guilty of a first offense, she said, he or she rarely participates in the banned behavior again.

"We see less second offenses," Moore said. "We really get through to these kids."

Unlike Penn State, an alcohol violation off campus that violates the policy at the University of Delaware also always results in academic sanctions for students.

"The Newark police report (off-campus alcohol violations) to our dean of students office and it is considered one of the three strikes," Moore said.

But the University of Delaware is not only battling alcohol through enforcement measures. It was also able to use the money from its grant to educate students and attempt to reform the alcohol culture among its students.

"It's changing a culture," Bishop said. "You don't change a culture overnight." ■

It's a mistake for university administrators to think that changes in alcohol policies like these will pass unnoticed by the student body. Many students battle against changes in campus regulations concerning alcohol, especially when they feel that their opinions concerning new rules have not been heard. Sometimes the battle over alcohol can get ugly, as it did in East Lansing, Michigan.

STUDENTS RIOT AT MICHIGAN STATE AFTER ALCOHOL IS BANNED AT TAILGATES

By Michael Hauck

DAILY NORTHWESTERN (Evanston, Ill.) 05/13/1998

Thousands of Michigan State University students protesting a campus alcohol ban clashed with police the evening of Friday, May 1, and continued rioting into the morning.

Police used tear gas to disperse the students who lit bonfires, threw stones and bottles and stormed streets between the Michigan State campus and downtown East Lansing, Mich.

Students were protesting the university's decision to ban alcohol in Munn Field, a popular spot for student tailgate parties before and after home football games.

The riot at Michigan State is not the first problem involving alcohol the campus's police have faced—Michigan State ranked No. 1 in a study recently released by the Chronicle of Higher Education that measured arrests involving alcohol on college campuses.

The report indicated that such arrests rose 10 percent in 1996, the fifth consecutive year substance law violations have increased among American college students.

Michigan State reported 574 violations involving alcohol in1996. Other schools in the top five included University of California-Berkeley, University of Wisconsin-Madison, University of Minnesota-Twin Cities, and Purdue University.

The study looked at 487 universities with 5,000 or more students and compared the total number of arrests involving alcohol with the number of students attending the university.

The report also found that drug arrests in 1996 increased 5 percent nationwide.

Arrests involving alcohol at Northwestern are usually associated with underage drinking, unlawful possession of fraudulent identification, driving while intoxicated and drinking in automobiles, said Lt. Glenn Turner of University Police.

More than 65 people were cited by UP in 1996. Most citations involved alcohol. Six of these were NU students, Turner said.

Arrests for drunken driving and drinking in automobiles have decreased recently following a crackdown by University Police on these two types of crimes, Turner said.

"People realized they would go to court," he said.

Administrators at Michigan State said they are trying to find a peaceful solution to students' complaints about the university's policies on alcohol.

But Terry Denbow, Michigan State's vice president of university relations, said the student violence in early May did not convince the administration to change its policy.

"Anybody who thinks that this incident will lead to a re-evaluation of our decision is wrong," Denbow said.

Michigan State University police Capt. Tony Kleibecker said student protests may have ended because of final exams and summer vacation, not because students agree with the university's position on alcohol.

"Problems brought forth by students are far from resolved at this point," Kleibecker said Tuesday. "Students feel oppressed by the administration and the way in which alcohol incidents have been handled."

The university has formed an action team composed of students, administration, and university police to try to resolve issues before classes begin in the fall, Kleibecker said.

"The real test will be when students return next school year," Kleibecker said. ■

Activism

Of course, college students united for a cause can serve far more constructive ends than those at MSU did. Big college campuses are known as places of student activism. On big campuses, students with different viewpoints can come together to rally for what they believe in. Because their schools' policies are likely to be affected by state and national legislation, large state school students, like those at the University of California, are tuned into the political pulse of their surroundings.

HUNDREDS AT U. CALIFORNIA-BERKELEY WALKOUT, TEACH-IN FOR AFFIRMATIVE ACTION

By Daniel Hernandez

DAILY CALIFORNIAN (Berkeley, Calif.) 10/22/1998

More than 1,000 UC Berkeley students and faculty refused to teach or attend regular classes yesterday, and instead took part in the long-awaited UC-wide walkout in defense of affirmative action.

The protest, led by more than 60 professors and

dubbed "Affirm With Action," included several symposia, rallies, teach-ins and forums, and is expected to continue today with more than 30 additional student-led teach-ins on various topics concerning affirmative action and higher education.

The rally, considered the highlight of the event,

filled Sproul Plaza with hundreds of students whooping, cheering, chanting and carrying signs representing various student organizations and political views.

"There was a good turnout (at the rally), lots of motivation, lots of people voiced their opinions," said junior Josh Diosomito, a coordinator for the Filipino Academic Student Services, who led one of the teach-ins on Lower Sproul.

Speakers at the rally included UC Berkeley Ethnic Studies professor Carlos Munoz, Diane Chin, executive director of Chinese for Affirmative Action and Barbara Christian, a UC Berkeley African American Studies professor.

Sara Chavez, a senior at Castlemont High School in East Oakland, spoke at the rally on behalf of OLIN, a Bay Area youth organization that sponsored last month's high school student walkout.

"It's hard enough for us to go to college with affirmative action, and without it it's even harder," she said.

The events at UC Berkeley began with a symposium in Barrows Hall titled "The Realities and Politics of Affirmative Action."

Chin rebuked the notion that Asians are hurt by affirmative action. "Asian Americans will not be used to eliminate equal opportunity for people of color," she said. "We support affirmative action and stand with you in the fight against discrimination."

Other symposia and teach-ins were held throughout the day at various locations, including the intersection of Bancroft Way and Telegraph Avenue and Lower Sproul Plaza.

While many students said they were generally receptive to the walkout, others said they felt the event detracted from the educational process at Berkeley. Many of them made their opinions known at yesterday's rally by brandishing signs with slogans such as "Education Not Politics" and "I Want A Refund."

Another sign, alluding to the state's 1996 passage of Proposition 209, read, "The People of California Have Spoken."

Ishmael Reed, who teaches in UC Berkeley's

Dan Evans/*The Daily Californian*

English department, said that students who displayed the signs misunderstood the meaning of the walkout.

"Whatever tactics that are civilized and nonviolent should be used to overturn this decision," he said.

Others said Prop. 209 has not benefited the state, nor has it been embraced by all Californians.

"Before Prop. 209, we didn't have enough underrepresented minorities on campus," said Professor Alex Saragoza of the Chicano Studies department. "All it did was make a bad situation worse."

Walkouts in conjunction with those within the UC system occurred in Washington, Michigan, Arizona, Illinois, at several California State Universities and at schools such as Yale, Johns Hopkins and Stanford, according to speakers at the rally.

"I urge people to not let the whirlwind stop, to keep following the tail wind and keep fighting," Diosomito said. "By whirlwind, I mean voting, grass-roots organizing and getting consciously involved in the movement."

According to Ricardo Montenegro, student body president at San Francisco State University, well over one hundred students from San Jose State and San Francisco State universities attended yesterday's rally.

"SFSU faces the same problems," Montenegro said. "Students need to educate themselves on the seriousness of the issues. SFSU stands in solidarity with the UC system's strike."

"If it happened to (the University of California), it could happen to the Cal State system," he added. ∎

Student Services

Because of the large numbers of students on their campuses, large state schools must meet a dizzying array of needs. All students must be provided with an environment that is conducive to learning—one that is safe and supportive. At big schools, this means that you will feel comfortable walking across campuses that cover miles and within dormitories that resemble high-rises. Hundreds of thousands of students receive medical care, and all facilities are available to students with physical challenges. Counseling services are there if you have questions or concerns. All in all, if you attend a big school, you can be sure that the administration is looking out for each and every one of its many students.

You've just finished a paper at the library and need to get back to your dorm, which is halfway across campus. It's after midnight, and you're not sure you feel comfortable walking home alone. Thankfully, most large state schools have escort services to get you home safely. And once you arrive at your dorm, chances are that security personnel will be on watch. Because large campuses and huge dorms and academic buildings are scary to some students, big colleges go out of their way to make you feel safe and comfortable. Security services like those at Kent State are representative of what you'll find on big campuses nationwide.

MODEL SECURITY PROGRAM CELEBRATES 25 YEARS ON KENT STATE CAMPUS

By Jennifer Fiala

Daily Kent Stater (Kent, Ohio) 08/12/1998

Kent State was one of the first universities in the country to start the Security Aide Program, and now it is celebrating 25 years of using the program to keep Kent's campus one of the safest in Ohio.

The Security Aide Program is a partnership between the Kent State Police Department and Kent State Student Security Aides. The security aides patrol residence halls and academic buildings in search of unusual behavior. They also run an escort service to safely accompany students to and from residence halls and academic buildings.

About 70 students work as security aides and are on shift duty from 8 p.m. to 4 a.m. Monday through Friday. They are the eyes and ears of the Kent State Police Department, carrying radios that police monitor.

Kent State Police Chief John Peach said the police department and resident security has had a "wonderful marriage" that has been in place for over 20 years.

"Our system is the prototype for higher education residential security systems within the United States," Peach said.

Peach said the student security aides receive some training from the police department on a regular basis so they understand how the police department runs.

"(The students) learn a lot on how to deal with people and the system in the police department, and there are a number of officers that we have that started out as security aides," he said. "A security aide has training background and seems to have the tempera-ment that's needed to become a police officer. They work well with people, relationships and know how to react to situations intelligently, respectively and responsively."

Kimberly Macon, security manager for Residence Services, said other universities often inquire about Kent State's security system and try to model programs after it.

"It's great that we have a program that other schools want to model," Macon said. "We train our staff for routine security (problems) on campus. They use general proactive patrolling and do not look to do a police officer's job. If there's a situation we can't handle, the police are called, and they're in charge."

Security aides must be Kent State students and have a 2.2 grade point average. Student security aides are paid $5.40 an hour, and they can work up to 30 hours per week. ∎

Having made it back to your dorm safely, you jump into the shower before hitting the sack. Clumsy as ever, you slip on the tiles and sprain your big toe. Will you be able to get high-quality, affordable medical care? Health care and insurance coverage are nationwide concerns these days, but college students need not worry about the medical services that will be available to them. Medical centers on college campuses are top-notch, and basic services are covered in your tuition fees. However, you'll probably need to go to an off-campus hospital for your big toe, which means that you'll need insurance to pay for the care you'll receive there. Big colleges such as UCLA are able to provide students with low-cost insurance for noncovered medical expenses. Because they can enroll many people in the plan, big schools are better able to keep individual costs for insurance down.

UCLA STUDENTS FIND SCHOOL INSURANCE A CHEAP OPTION TO HMOS

By Caridad Lezcano

DAILY BRUIN (Los Angeles, Calif.) 02/02/1999

Many Health Maintenance Organizations (HMOs) have been scrutinized on both state and national levels because patients claim that their insurance plans don't cover all of their medical needs.

On Jan. 20, a suit against an HMO was settled in the context of the already heated debate between unhappy patients and their insurance providers.

In the case, a jury rewarded $116 million in punitive damages to a widow whose husband fought until his death against his HMO, which wouldn't pay for his experimental cancer treatment.

At UCLA, many students—10,000 of the 34,000—purchase the Medical Insurance Plan (MIP) to meet their health care needs. The plan is only available to registered UCLA students.

MIP differs from other plans because it offers "world-wide coverage," while plans of similar cost by HMOs generally are "limited coverage plans," according to Michele Pearson, director of Ancillary Services at Student Health Services.

A limited coverage plan offers only certain services at other facilities besides that of the provider, while a worldwide coverage plan extends them.

For instance, if a patient needed emergency care while on a trip, the HMO would pay for medical costs. However, if the patient needed any extended treatment, they would be required to return home for continued treatment. In contrast, MIP covers both emergency care and extended services at any hospital if the patient is over 50 miles away from UCLA Medical Center.

MIP was designed to give students supplemental services beyond the basic health services offered at Arthur Ashe Student Health and Wellness Center. These include hospitalization, emergency and surgical care and medical care away from UCLA.

The Ashe Center is available to all registered students, regardless of the kind of insurance they have. But, the services are limited to basic medical care needs. For example, the Ashe Center will take care of students with health issues ranging from colds to gynecological problems, but won't handle larger health problems, such as surgery.

At $190 per quarter, MIP is cheaper than comparable plans, which would cost at least $1,800 a year from an HMO.

"The sole purpose of the plan is to protect students by keeping profit margins for insurance companies at a minimum," Pearson said.

The low cost is due in part to the Student Health Insurance Committee (SHIC), which negotiates the MIP benefits every year and its cost to students. Members of this committee are appointed by the Undergraduate Student Association Council.

"On this campus, MIP has an insured advocate in the administration of the Ashe Center," Pearson said.

In addition, MIP is available for financial aid recipients. UCLA offers a $90 credit per quarter toward the purchase of MIP—about 50 percent of its cost.

"Being away from home and my mom's insurance plan, MIP acts as an extra safety net in case of an emergency," said Sophia Speigal, a third-year biology student.

Graduate and international students must purchase MIP if they don't have another form of coverage, Pearson said. In 1990, the Graduate Student Associa-

Rutgers University/*The Daily Targum*

tion voted by referendum to make insurance coverage mandatory for graduate students attending UCLA.

The program is recommended for uninsured undergraduates, but not a requirement.

International students must also purchase MIP if they don't have another type of American insurance plan because of the difficulty attaining medical care due to language barriers, according to Pearson.

"I was not accustomed to this country's medical policies and would have been lost without MIP," said Don Michiolvich, a second-year undeclared international student. ■

Think we've run the gamut of services provided on big college campuses? Not so. The bigger the campus, the more likely that there will be a large population of "nontraditional" students—those who don't fall into the twenty-something, unmarried, childless stereotype of the traditional student. Imagine how hard it must be to balance work *and* marriage *and* children with getting an education. Big colleges are especially sensitive to the dilemmas of "nontraditional" students. Night classes, distance learning, and, at the University of South Florida, day care are ways that big schools help "nontraditional" students juggle these responsibilities.

CENTER GIVES USF PARENTS NEW CHILD CARE OPTIONS

By Joe Humphrey

THE ORACLE (Tampa, Fla.) 01/06/1998

When Luis Belen, a University of South Florida junior business major, drops his two children off at the new USF Family Center today, he will be relieved from his duties as "Mr. Mom."

In the past, Belen would watch his 3-year-old and 19-month-old children during the day and attend school at night, while his wife, Valerie, a staff member for Student Health Services, cared for the children.

But with today's opening of the new USF Family Center, Belen will have the chance to attend school during the day and also give his children a chance to do the same.

"It's difficult to shift from Mr. Mom to student," he said. "We decided (on the center) to relieve us of taking care of kids constantly. Being with me all day and my wife at night, (our kids) didn't have any interaction."

Belen's kids are among the ones which will be utilizing a new program—drop-off care.

For $4 an hour, students, faculty and staff can drop off their children (infant through age 10) for up to 29 hours a week. The drop-off program, which is open from 7:30 a.m. to 9:30 p.m. Monday through Thursday and 7:30 a.m. until 6 p.m. Friday, can accommodate up to 22 children at a time.

"This meets the needs of a lot more kids," said Mary Poole, a coordinator for special projects. "Parents can use it for a couple hours a day or as a backup."

There were originally only 12 drop-off spots, but, according to the center's director, Tricia Sifford, 10 slots were added because of demand.

"There was a second preschool room, but we found the need was larger for drop-in," she said.

Parents without pagers or cellular phones will be provided a pager by the center while their children are in the center.

"With students, it's impossible to get in touch with them, though most of them do have pagers," Sifford said.

Full-time care will also be available for infants, toddlers and preschoolers.

But Poole said it's the drop-off center which is going to receive the most attention.

"It's only about 60 percent full right now, but as the word spreads, it'll take off," she said. "It's an option that doesn't exist anywhere else."

Sifford said with all the new toys the center has added, "It'll be like a second Christmas for the kids."

And as final preparations were made Friday, with boxes strewn about the center, the atmosphere appeared chaotic. But Holly Wilson, office manager for Corporate FamilySolutions, the Nashville, Tenn.-based company which will manage the center, said it is business as usual.

"We've done this a hundred times over," said Wilson, who represents the same company which operates the child-care center at H. Lee Moffitt Cancer and Research Institute. ■

Even with the support that nontraditional students receive at big schools like USF, it's still a difficult way of life—with plenty of long hours, hard work, and conflicting responsibilities. One student at Iowa State give us a glimpse into the life of a nontradtional student.

COLUMN: TRIALS OF BEING NON-TRADITIONAL

By Gloria D. Stewart

IOWA STATE DAILY (Ames, Iowa) 02/11/1998

Who am I? I'm a non-traditional student, just one of many on the Iowa State campus. I cannot tell the story of every non-traditional student here, but I can tell one story: my own. Perhaps it will give you a peek into some of the unique problems faced by other adult learners.

I sit next to you in the classroom. I'm the one who looks mom-type. Maybe I look blurry-eyed from the 32 mile drive I just completed in the fog or snow. Perhaps I have bags under my eyes because of lack of sleep (much like everyone else in the room). I may seem stuck-up, but I'm really just shy and not sure how you feel about adult students.

When I began my college career in Jan. 1995, I was 39 years old. I had one son attending college and another in high school. I was working nearly full time as a reporter and photographer at a local weekly newspaper, where I'd been for five years.

I had reached a point in my life when I finally had the confidence to pursue my lifelong dream of a college education. My husband and sons were very supportive, and that has made me luckier than many of the non-traditional students who made the transition alone.

I married at 18, and my first son was born within a year. Our finances were paycheck-to-paycheck. College didn't fit in the picture.

As years went by, my self-esteem got lower and lower until I suffered a severe depression, shortly after my 30th birthday. I spent 13 weeks of one year in the hospital, once following a nearly successful suicide attempt.

After a few years of therapy, changing doctors, and several tries at finding the right medication, I began to live again. My old goal of getting a degree resurfaced, and here I am in my fourth year of college.

I attended a local community college for two years to get my feet wet and to see if I really could remem-

ber how to study after 22 years. I ended up taking elementary and intermediate algebra because I had forgotten everything.

At first, I looked around the classrooms and saw all these young, energetic faces, and minds so fresh. I was intimidated. I responded by establishing a strong study ethic. I spent hours and hours reading. I was determined to do well in order to make up for not applying myself in high school, and for losing so much time.

Every new class, new room, new instructor, and new assignment was a huge challenge for me. After each hurdle, I became a little stronger. I discovered that my desire for education gave me an advantage. I was in school because I wanted to be there, and I knew I was aiming for a degree in journalism.

I also reaped benefits from years of life experiences. I didn't feel the social temptations that some students face. Instead, my conflicts for time came from work responsibilities and my family.

As I began my senior year this January, my life gained an entirely new perspective. Suddenly, my classes have become more of a burden. All my school work, especially busy-work assignments, has lost its importance.

After a stressful Christmas break, I found myself in a new role of being a caregiver to my elderly parents. I knew the time was coming, but I wasn't ready for it, and I don't like it much.

I am the youngest daughter of 84-year-old parents who still live in a big two-story farmhouse, five miles from the nearest town. Words from my pre-teen years have come back to haunt me, "I will always stay here and take care of you."

My last week of Christmas break was spent coordinating care for my mother so she could come home from the hospital instead of going to a nursing home. Dad doesn't walk very well any more, but insists on keeping a herd of sheep and a horse around that he does chores for. He has always been waited on by my mother. No more.

My once-strong and active mother lives in a frail, 97-pound body that no longer works as it should. Her heart is weak and irregular, her lungs don't process oxygen properly, and her two artificial hips are nearing the end of their 15-year life-span. She is on six liters of oxygen at all times, a low-salt diet and an overwhelming assortment of medications.

For five weeks my sisters and I have been taking turns preparing meals, doing laundry, cleaning and organizing visiting-nurse care. Miraculously, mother has improved more than we ever could have hoped for.

The health aides only come twice a week now, and for nearly a week, mom and dad have been getting their own noon meals.

Three days a week I take a short detour on my way home from Ames. I fix supper and do a few chores. Sometime after dark I venture the last ten miles to my home, and retreat in the arms of my husband.

My youngest son is attending community college now and plans to transfer to Iowa State next fall as a sophomore. If everything goes as planned, that will be my last semester here.

I'm just one of the non-traditional faces you may find in your classrooms. There is a story behind each one. ∎

Fun Stuff

No one can deny that college is hard work. It demands hours of study and unwavering dedication. At a large state school, you'll be taking classes with huge numbers of students, and you'll have to adhere to page upon page of policies regarding housing, alcohol, discrimination, and student services. You'll probably have to work part-time, and if you join a fraternity, sorority, or any other of the many campus organizations that are there to divert you, your time will be in even more demand. You'll be working so hard and have so many commitments that you'll never have any fun.

Yeah, right. If college wasn't fun, no one would go, no matter how much their parents wanted them to. You're young, and you deserve to have a good time! Luckily for you, big schools are big draws for big fun—from hip hop and rock concerts to weekend festivals to just plain goofiness. Before we leave our tour of large state schools, consider the ways some kids let loose on campuses across the country.

CONCERT REVIEW: U. CONN HOSTS DAVE MATTHEWS, SPECIAL GUEST POPPER

By Jennifer Clair

THE DAILY CAMPUS (Storrs, Conn.) 02/08/1999

Students lucky enough to have tickets to the sold out Dave Matthews and Tim Reynolds concert Saturday night got an added bonus. The legendary John Popper of Blues Traveler hopped on stage to finish the show with an excellent encore.

Popper was in town traveling with his band Frogwings, which hits Toad's Place on Friday. The band also includes members of the Allman Brothers Band and guitarist Derek Trucks. Popper, who grew up in Stamford, is a close friend of Matthews.

"I'd take many bullets for Dave, but I hope it wouldn't come to that," Popper told The Daily Campus. The master harmonica player said that he would be taking a year off from Blues Traveler, and will start to make a new solo album in two weeks.

Matthews' tour has been slightly slowed down due to illness. A show at the University of Buffalo had to be rescheduled on Feb. 1. At both of his Connecticut appearances, Matthews praised Afrin nasal spray.

At Jorgensen, Matthews seemed to overcome the illness to host a gigantic sing along. Matthews and

Brian Holderman/*The Collegio*

'Reynolds played nearly every one of The Dave Matthews Band's greatest hits during the three hour set. The crowd sang along with songs such as "Crush," "Jimi Thing" and "Proudest Monkey."

Reynolds didn't take any breaks during the show and was amazing on guitar. He played two guitar solos in which he proved that he could make any sound imaginable with the instrument. Reynolds' hands

danced up and down the guitar as the crowd watched in awe.

The full house at Jorgensen didn't take a break, either. The audience showed their enthusiasm from start to finish, yelling requests to Dave and cheering the duo on. Matthews displayed his silly personality by answering the crowd and telling short stories. ■

WHOOPSTOCK SWOOPS IN TO A&M CAMPUS
By Jennifer Wilson

THE BATTALION (College Station, Texas) 04/24/1998

The Whoopstock Unity Festival, one of the newer Texas A&M traditions, will bring students together in a celebration of diversity while listening to bands, playing games and sampling foods this Saturday at O.R. Simpson Drill Field.

Whoopstock started five years ago in response to a KKK rally in College Station. Instead of going to the rally and protesting, students decided to organize a festival celebrating diversity.

Dima Mousselli, chair of Whoopstock and a senior biology major, said the festival aims to promote diversity and unity in a relaxed atmosphere.

"We are not trying to shove diversity down anyone's throat," she said.

Mousselli said she hopes participants open their minds expand their cultural knowledge.

"We are reaching beyond ourselves to embrace our differences and share our similarities in a celebration of unity," she said.

Dumper DeJesus/*The Daily Targum*

Kristina Wright, director of administration for Whoopstock and a senior anthropology major, said the festival presents opinions and other ideas about many cultures.

"We want to get people out who want to try something different or who might not normally come," she said.

Wright said diversity is an important issue on campus because A&M lacks diversity compared to other universities.

"This [Whoopstock] helps us understand the diversity we do have," she said.

Comedians, dancing groups, music, games, art and food will highlight the festival's entertainment. ∎

STUDENTS BARE ALL IN U. MICHIGAN'S 'NAKED MILE'

By Melanie Sampson

MICHIGAN DAILY (Ann Arbor, Mich.) 5/5/1998

"Nakedness coming through!"

That's what an unidentified person shouted while running in the annual Naked Mile, which brought more than 10,000 students and spectators to the streets of Ann Arbor on April 21.

To commemorate the last day of classes, students participated in the Naked Mile tradition by running

unclothed around the University campus. The first set of runners started out at 10:30 p.m. The run ended around midnight.

For many first-year students, this year's race was their introduction to the celebration of nakedness. Many students said they preferred to watch the event rather than run.

"It brings everybody together," said Colleen

Cavanaugh, an LSA first-year student. "It's a great tradition."

Spectators came from afar to view the festival of nudity, which started at the Rock and ended at the Cube. Runners stumbled, many of them drunk, down South University St. and past the Diag. A chorus of unclothed students took part in a sing-a-long on the steps of the Museum of Art before a massive crowd.

Not everyone in attendance was amused by the naked revelry.

"I think it's one of the silliest things I've seen in my life," said Jill Perigo, an Ann Arbor resident.

Some participants described the experience as unique.

"It was . . . the biggest rush ever," said Holly Armstrong, a Kinesiology senior.

Nursing senior Jen Fitzgerald said she was excited about running exposed through the streets of Ann Arbor.

"We're born naked, let's graduate naked," Fitzgerald said. ■

North Carolina — Continued
University of North Carolina at Chapel Hill
University of North Carolina at Charlotte

Ohio
Bowling Green State University
Cleveland State University
Kent State University
Miami University
The Ohio State University
Ohio University
The University of Akron
University of Cincinnati
University of Toledo
Wright State University
Youngstown State University

Oklahoma
Oklahoma State University
University of Central Oklahoma
University of Oklahoma

Oregon
Oregon State University
Portland State University
University of Oregon

Pennsylvania
Indiana University of Pennsylvania

Pennsylvania State University University
 Park Campus
Temple University
University of Pittsburgh

Rhode Island
University of Rhode Island

South Carolina
Clemson University
University of South Carolina

Tennessee
Middle Tennessee State University
The University of Memphis
University of Tennessee, Knoxville

Texas
Sam Houston State University
Southwest Texas State University
Stephen F. Austin State University
Texas A&M University
Texas Tech University
University of Houston
University of North Texas
The University of Texas at Arlington
The University of Texas at Austin
The University of Texas at El Paso
The University of Texas at San Antonio

Utah
University of Utah
Utah State University
Weber State University

Virginia
George Mason University
James Madison University
Old Dominion University
University of Virginia
Virginia Commonwealth University
Virginia Polytechnic Institute and State
 University

Washington
University of Washington
Washington State University
Western Washington University

West Virginia
West Virginia University

Wisconsin
University of Wisconsin–Madison
University of Wisconsin–Milwaukee

Arkansas
Hendrix College
Lyon College

California
California Institute of Technology
Claremont McKenna College
Centre College
College of Oceaneering
Transylvania University
Deep Springs College
Harvey Mudd College
Occidental College
Pepperdine University
Pomona College
Scripps College
Stanford University
Thomas Aquinas College
University of Southern California

Colorado
The Colorado College

Connecticut
Trinity College
Wesleyan University
Yale University

District of Columbia
Georgetown University

Florida
The Harid Conservatory

Georgia
Agnes Scott College
Emory University
Oglethorpe University
Spelman College

Illinois
Knox College
Lake Forest College
Northwestern University
University of Chicago
Wheaton College

Indiana
Taylor University
University of Notre Dame

Iowa
Grinnell College
University of Osteopathic Medicine and
    Health Sciences

Kentucky
Centre College
Transylvania University

Maine
Bates College
Colby College
College of the Atlantic

Maryland
Johns Hopkins University

Massachusetts
Amherst College
Boston College
Brandeis University
College of the Holy Cross
Harvard University
Massachusetts Institute of Technology
Mount Holyoke College

Simon's Rock College of Bard
Smith College
Tufts University
Wellesley College
Williams College

Michigan
Hillsdale College
Kalamazoo College

Minnesota
Carleton College
Gustavus Adolphus College
Macalester College
St. Olaf College

Missouri
Saint Luke's College

IN THIS CHAPTER
Boston University
Brown University
Columbia University
Cornell University
Dartmouth University
Duke University
Georgetown University
George Washington University
Harvard University
Kenyon College
Lafayette College
Massachusetts Institute of Technology
Northwestern University
Princeton University
Stanford University
Tufts University
University of Chicago
University of Pennsylvania
University of Richmond
University of Southern California
Vanderbilt University

New Hampshire
Dartmouth College

New Jersey
Drew University
Princeton University

New York
Bard College
Barnard College
Colgate University
Columbia University
Cooper Union for the Advancement of
    Science and Art
Cornell University
Fordham University
Hamilton College
Jewish Theological Seminary of America
The Juilliard School
New York University
Rabbinical Seminary of America
St. Lawrence University

Sarah Lawrence College
Skidmore College
Union College
Vassar College
Webb Institute
Yeshiva Karlin Stolin Rabbinical Institute

North Carolina
Davidson College
Duke University

Ohio
Hiram College
Kenyon College
Oberlin College
Ohio Wesleyan University

Oregon
Lewis & Clark College
Reed College
Willamette University

Pennsylvania
Allegheny College
Bryn Mawr College
The Curtis Institute of Music
Dickinson College
Franklin and Marshall College
Gettysburg College
Grove City College
Haverford College
Lafayette College
Muhlenberg College
Swarthmore College
University of Pennsylvania
Ursinus College

Rhode Island
Brown University
Providence College

South Carolina
Furman University
Presbyterian College
Wofford College

Tennessee
Rhodes College
University of the South
Vanderbilt University

Texas
Austin College
Rice University
Southwestern University
Trinity University
University of Dallas

Vermont
Bennington College
Middlebury College

Virginia
Washington and Lee University

Washington
University of Puget Sound
Whitman College
Whitworth College

Wisconsin
Beloit College
Lawrence University

Highly Competitive Schools

Next we move on to highly competitive colleges. The definition here is a little trickier. For the purposes of this book, highly competitive colleges are those that described their admissions policies as "most difficult" or "very difficult" on Peterson's Annual Survey of Undergraduate Institutions.

The large majority of these schools are private. Many, but not all of them, originally had a religious (Christian) affiliation, but they're not defined here by religion. Some, like Columbia University in New York City's Upper West Side, are situated in urban areas; others, like Yale University, are located in the suburbs of larger cities; still others, like Cornell University, call more rural locales home. They are most often, but not always, mid-sized schools with average undergraduate enrollments of around 5,000. While other factors may vary, the defining characteristic of these schools, then, is in the selectivity of their admissions practices. If you get accepted at a highly competitive university, consider yourself one smart kid.

What can you expect your first year if you're one of the few to be admitted to a highly competitive college? Above all, expect an extremely rigorous academic program—and that's probably an understatement. Your mind will be challenged in ways you never thought possible. Expect to be taught by a faculty that includes award winners of every kind in its numbers: Pulitzer Prize winners, Nobel Prize winners, former Rhodes Scholars, and more. Expect a spirit of cooperation; at a highly competitive college, faculty members, students, and administration respect each other's intellect and work together to create an atmosphere conducive to learning. You'll be overwhelmed by the power of the almighty dollar; there are a lot of them floating around on the campuses of highly competitive schools. Everywhere you go, you'll hear about the hundreds of years of tradition that have preceded you about the alumni, faculty, and research that have made the school great. Expect to be really intimidated by all of this. The analogy that a highly selective school is like a pressure cooker is not far off the mark; trying to live up to all these expectations can result in some really stressed-out students.

In actuality, two factors distinguish highly competitive universities from the rest: academics and money. Life at a prestigious college revolves around academics, from the moment you apply to the moment you graduate. Each and every student, without exception, must be extremely academically talented to be accepted. The academic curriculum in every subject offered is innovative and difficult. Students are encouraged to explore new fields of study, to push the limits of their learning, to experiment in subjects of their choosing, and to focus on topics they love. The universities are committed to learning on a broad scale; they strive to produce well-rounded students who can think analytically about any subject. The subject of discussion is as likely to be tonight's game or where the big party is as well as where everyone's going for their semester abroad or summer internship and who the best English lit prof is.

Money also figures prominently into life at a highly competitive university. There will be no mistaking the fact that your school has a lot of money. You'll read about huge endowments from former alumni, sometimes amounting to tens of millions of dollars. If their tech fund scores, your school could bring in big money through its investments in the stock market. The caliber of the faculty will have research and grant money pouring in. Because highly competitive schools are older than most others, you may see lots of old-looking (some call them historic) buildings on campus, but inside those walls lies modern high-tech equipment. Once they choose to embrace technology, highly competitive colleges have the money to do it in

style, and their computer facilities show it. Gargantuan libraries overflow with research materials, both modern and ancient. Highly competitive schools can and do pay out considerable amounts to acquire rare works of art for their collections without batting an eye. And some students won't need financial aid to afford the $20,000-$30,000 yearly tuition these schools charge, so even the student body will ooze money.

Sarah E. Hendrickson/*The Harvard Crimson*

Let's talk about some of the myths of highly competitive colleges:

- If you don't have the financial wherewithal, you won't be able to get into a highly competitive university.
- Highly competitive schools are conservative and elitist.
- Highly competitive schools are focused on the academics to the exclusion of everything else—you'll have no life whatsoever if you attend a prestigious school.

First, it's a misconception that only the rich can attend a prestigious college. While it will help if your family can contribute something toward the incredibly high cost of enrollment at a highly competitive college, fantastic financial aid, scholarship, and grant packages are awarded to deserving students every year. Scholar-athletes can also benefit from the countless athletic scholarships offered. If you meet the rigorous standards for admission, the financial aid offices at highly competitive colleges will work with you to get you the money you need to attend regardless of your financial circumstances.

While it's true that highly competitive colleges were once the bastions of conservatism and elitism, that has changed over the years. Today these schools are known as places of great liberalism and diversity, and this is evidenced in prestigious schools' curriculums, policies, and the students themselves. Because of their emphasis on interdisciplinary liberal arts curriculums, highly competitive colleges are more likely than most to offer coursework in cross-cultural studies, for example, and to encourage students to explore subjects that will make them globally aware. The spirit of cooperation that we mentioned earlier also results in more liberal school rules. Administrators have a lot of trust in their students, so campus policies are less strict than those you'd find on other campuses. When problems arise, administrators are willing to work with students as equals to find solutions. Highly competitive schools also embrace innovative practices more readily; the unique housing options available at some prestigious schools are evidence of this. And despite what you might think, students aren't exclusively white or snobby. Prestigious schools take great pride in the diversity you'll find on their campuses. The only common denominator is a brain.

Don't despair—you will see life beyond the library walls if you attend a highly competitive university. You can get involved in countless extracurricular activities: fraternities and sororities, athletics, volunteering, student government, newspapers, and other serious *and* fun clubs geared toward all interests. Or you can attend lectures and other special events if you don't want to commit yourself to an activity for an extended period. The point is this: You'll have to make time for it in your busy schedule, but if you want to have fun (and who doesn't?), you'll be able to do it at a highly competitive university.

How will a typical day go if you attend a highly competitive school? Although no two students will have the same experience, you may be rushing off to class first thing in the morning, anxious for the next hands-on experiment your organic chemistry prof has cooked up. Students around you are gossiping about a donation from I. M. Riche, the school's most famous alumnus. What will the money be spent on? An addition to the molecular biology lab? That rare Eliot manuscript up on the auction block? A 10-lane swimming pool? The topic of conversation quickly turns to your school's latest Nobel Prize winner—doesn't that make 15 now? You're glad you signed up for her class next semester. Chemistry class is a success as always, then you're off to the library to hit the books for a few hours before your ancient civilizations class; you're totally psyched because today a curator from the Metropolitan Museum is here for a discussion on the Egyptian exhibit you'll be viewing next week. After class you drop by your advisor's office for a quick chat about the study abroad options you're considering for the summer, then back to the dorms for lunch and your soap operas (hey, you're only human, right?). Off

again to another class, more time at the library, and dinner. Final stop: the meeting of the photography club, which you're trying for a semester to see if you like it. After the meeting, you think about signing up for ballroom dance instead. Back to the dorm, brush up on your French conjugations for tomorrow's morning class, then, your mind a blur, you're asleep before your head hits the pillow.

Believe it or not, you'll get used to this hectic pace before your first year is over. Courses will become a challenge, not a chore. You'll get into the groove of studying and discover the comfiest chair at the library and the fastest PC at the computer lab. You'll establish a rapport with your professors, your advisors, and school administrators. You'll find extracurricular activities that fit into your schedule and help you blow off steam. The money, the prestige, and the traditions will no longer intimidate you. You'll realize that you *deserve* to be there. And lo and behold, you'll find you're actually having fun. ∎

Academics

Needless to say, if you attend a highly competitive school, academics will be your primary focus. If you're considering applying to any one of the schools included in this chapter, take a few minutes to think long and hard about the commitment you'll be making to study and research—hours and hours and hours of it a week. The academic programs at these schools are extremely rigorous; that's why they're held in such high esteem. If you complete a course of study at a highly competitive school, you will receive what some consider to be the finest education in the world, and you'll work hard to earn it.

But first you have to get in.

The name says it all: Getting into a highly competitive school is tough, to say the least. Each year, many apply but only a select bunch are admitted to prestigious schools. That's because the competition for every spot is fierce. Because the education they provide is so prized, these schools require more of their applicants: higher standardized test scores, higher grade point averages, more extracurricular involvement, more recommendations, more essays, and more interviews. Highly competitive schools can pick and choose exactly whom they want to admit (and whom they don't) from the cream of the crop of students from all over the world. If you choose to apply to a prestigious school, your commitment to an education will be scrutinized. So be prepared. You can get the madness out of the way early by taking advantage of some schools' early decision policies, whereby your application is examined sooner. If you're accepted, however, you may have to commit to attending that school early in your senior year. While some say this is a great chance to get the headache out of the way and enjoy your last few months of high school, see "Getting in first can mean coming in last" for another opinion on early acceptance. Not all highly competitive schools practice early acceptance; Brown and Harvard, for example, offer nonbinding acceptance wherein you can be accepted early but don't need to make your final decision until May.

Of course, one of the factors you'll consider when choosing a college will be the facilities you'll find on campus. You can expect nothing but the best at a highly competitive school. For example, students using Stanford University's libraries have access to more than 7 million volumes, 100 million archival and manuscript documents, 500,000 government printed documents, 250,000 maps, and more than 100,000 video and film items, in addition to numerous special collections of rare books, manuscripts, archives, and photographs. SUNet, the Stanford University Network, connects approximately 35,000 host computers, microcomputers, and workstations to other off-campus computers and provides direct connection to the Internet. The *Harvard Crimson* reports that the University's Chemistry Department is experimenting with putting lectures online. How are all of these fabulous facilities possible? Simply put, prestigious schools have lots of money. Alumni and others endow the schools with cash donations and other acquisitions. In his will, philanthropist Paul Mellon, a 1929 Yale graduate, bequeathed Yale University more than $90 million in cash donations and 130 works of art. "We're in the money" describes a recent $340-million donation to Vanderbilt. Corporate ties are another factor; for example, the Yale Center for International and Area Studies provides scholarships through its Coca-Cola World Fund. While students sometimes fault highly prestigious college administrators with being too conservative in spending the money that they receive, there's no doubt that these schools' high-quality facilities are the product of billions of dollars coming in from various sources.

Facilities for research and study don't mean a thing if a school's academic curriculum and instruction aren't up to par. These are other areas where prestigious colleges excel. At a highly competitive college, you will be challenged both by rigorous and innovative coursework and by professors who are Nobel Prize winners, famous authors, and internationally recognized scholars. Academic offerings focus on both breadth and depth; in fact, highly competitive colleges pride themselves on teaching students how to think critically in diverse areas while also providing them with focused studies in the field of their choice. By and large, students are given the freedom to sculpt their own course of education from myriad offerings. Because highly competitive colleges don't often focus on preprofessional training (for an in-depth look at this interesting facet of these schools' curriculums, see "Proposed finance major to be discussed at Yale U."), internships are often a great way for prestigious school students to get experience before they enter the working world. Here you'll read about great internship programs at the University of Chicago and Stanford.

In "Editorial: Anything for an A," you'll see how even these colleges are not immune to cheating. "More George Washington U. students are graduating early" describes the race to graduate that many students feel while attending a highly competitive school. And the biggest talk on prestigious school campuses these days has been regarding grade inflation. In "Compared to Princeton, Yale offers no easy A's" you'll find an in-depth look at what all the fuss is about. Get the picture? From admissions to graduation, academics reach into every single aspect of a student's life at a highly competitive school.

Admissions

Students who attend highly competitive colleges say that the hardest part was getting in. The admissions process for prestigious schools is often painstaking and always demanding. Competition for slots at prestigious schools is stiff: According to the Columbia University Fact Book, their undergraduates are culled from the top 5 percent of all students in the country. The median scores on both the verbal and the math portions of the SAT are in the low 700s for Yale applicants. And 80 percent of entering freshmen at Stanford have high school GPAs between 3.8 and 4.0. On top of this, the average number of acceptances versus applications is usually quite low at highly competitive schools: Last year, of the 13,000 students who applied to Princeton, only 1,172 enrolled for the freshman year. Needless to say, the processes and the pressures to "get in" are daunting.

Some highly competitive schools, particularly those in the Ivy League, practice "early decision," whereby they accept the best high school students before their senior year even begins. While these schools claim that early decision is in fact better for the students—those accepted can relax and enjoy their last year of high school assured that they've made it into a top-notch school—others say that early decision just means early stress. It's bad enough, they claim, that these students have to jump through hoops to get into the schools, but pushing the process earlier and earlier into their lives could just about send them over the edge. One student at The University of Southern California, which has done away with early decision, offers her view on the practice.

COLUMN: GETTING IN FIRST CAN MEAN COMING IN LAST
By Christi Schuler

DAILY TROJAN (Los Angeles, Calif.) 03/03/1998

Another year, another freshman class. As the season for college admissions once again opens up, more and more high school seniors frequent campus grounds across the country in search of the perfect college.

However, certain students are missing from the tours being conducted in the new year. These students are already sitting at home clutching their early-acceptance letters and preparing for a new chapter in their lives—a chapter that won't start for another five or six months.

Many colleges, especially Ivy League schools, participate in the early admissions process, otherwise known as the annual rat race to select what they consider to be the ideal student body. The procedure kind of resembles fishing, a sport in which one party searches for the biggest, brightest fish in the pond and throws back anything less preferable for the next party in line to collect.

Some, like USC Dean of Admissions Joseph Allen, stand opposed to this program and the stress and anxiety it causes. In addition to these down points, it plays out unfairly for supposedly second-tier schools.

Recently, Allen suggested putting it on hold for a few years. And for this, he should be applauded.

While early decision may have its advantages, I agree with Allen that it is an unnecessary practice. Furthermore, the benefits do not outweigh the negative aspects of the nerve-racking procedure. If Ivy League schools are truly the supreme institutions they claim to be, they should be able to uphold that reputation without the aid of early admission.

For one thing, the added stress that accompanies submitting an application early does not make high school seniors' first semester any easier. While they should be focusing on their grades during their last year of high school, they are worrying more about meeting their ideal college's early deadline. After all that extra work, if they still don't get in, what happens to their morale? They are forced to settle for the alternative; not the ideal attitude to take when entering another four years of education.

If they do get in, many seniors breathe a huge sigh of relief and sit back to enjoy the rest of their semester, settling for a merely satisfactory second semester rather than an outstanding one to ensure that they do not lose their status. The relief factor and the ability to relax during the second semester are the only real benefits here. Granted, there are exceptions, as some students use that extra time wisely by either devoting it to some other activity or taking advantage of squeezing financial aid out of the college to which they are already bonded.

The process only benefits students who are under the ideal circumstances. They have already made up their minds to attend a certain school; they have budgeted their time so that they can finish the early process without the added stress. Their parents are behind them every step of the way, prepared to pay should the college fail to award a high financial aid package. Colleges who consider these students obviously hold a school-spirited applicant in higher esteem, and may be more willing to award this applicant for both showing initiative through early action and securing his or her position among the ranks.

What I am saying is that these students may have the opportunity to single themselves out by applying early; however, they should apply early regardless of whether or not that option exists on paper. The college should still recognize a student's eagerness to attend simply by the fact that they submitted an application way before they were required to. Also, admissions officers should work harder to admit applicants at a more universal rate.

Allen is fighting the good fight. Unfortunately, as was the case when a proposal was made not too long ago by UC schools to consider dropping the SAT scores as a credible consideration when accepting students, the change is too radical to be nationally activated. It's just comforting to know that someone out there is thinking objectively about the politics that go into selecting students, and that someone just happens to be part of the school that I chose to attend. ∎

Some find it refreshing that the Dean of Admissions at one of the nation's most prestigious universities is advocating admissions practices that may eliminate some of the angst from the application process. Attracting students from different backgrounds to create a diverse student body is also a priority at highly competitive colleges, who are finding it necessary to revamp admissions policies to do so. Princeton University is one such institution.

PRINCETON COMMITTEE RECOMMENDS ALLOWING TRANSFERS FROM COMMUNITY COLLEGES

By Ian Shapira

DAILY PRINCETONIAN (Princeton, N.J.) 10/13/1998

The makeup of the University's student body might receive a modest facelift if the Board of Trustees heeds the advice of some of Princeton's most well-known professors and deans.

Several proposals in a report released last week, if implemented, could make landmark changes in the ways the University accepts new students.

The most striking recommendation entails establishing a transfer admission application exclusively for sophomores graduating from community colleges.

"That would be a dream come true," said Robert Pluta, a sophomore at the nearby Mercer County Community College. Pluta, 24, who is a humanities and social sciences major, said he enrolled in a community college because it was cheaper.

"The people here are just as qualified as Ivy Leaguers, and I really think Princeton should start accepting transfers," Pluta said.

Laurene Jones, the transfer guidance counselor at MCCC, said for years students have inquired about transferring to Princeton, only to be "shut out." Many of them, instead, end up matriculating at the University of Pennsylvania "because it's close and more user-friendly."

Jones argues that MCCC, which sends about

two-thirds of its graduates to four-year universities, has a "good number of students who come here for financial reasons and who all could have gone anywhere."

The committee's report also includes a proposal to increase the size of each entering class by 125 to 150 students.

While the idea could be considered generous, especially in light of the hundreds of exceptional candidates turned away each year, some are concerned that expanding an already overcrowded student body will chip away at the intimate undergraduate experience on which the University prides itself.

"We don't want to jeopardize what Princeton is justifiably known for," said Shirley Tilghman, a molecular biology professor and a member of Undergraduate Admissions Study Group.

"But we want to use these slots to bring excellent students to this University," she added. ▪

You'll have to go through a lot to get into a highly competitive college, but it will be worth it because of the quality of the education you will receive. Some students feel that small classes are the key to a superior education. Unlike large state schools, highly competitive schools rarely have freshmen courses with students numbering in the hundreds. Since they accept far fewer numbers of students, this seems only logical.

Because they work so hard to be admitted, students at highly competitive universities are understandably angry when they have to sit in a large—sometimes very large—class. The trend at highly competitive schools these days seems to be to enroll more and more students. If additional faculty members aren't hired, it isn't hard to do the math: It can only lead to larger class sizes. At Columbia University, this appears to be a cause for growing concern.

OVERCROWDED CLASSES TROUBLE COLUMBIA U. STUDENTS, FACULTY

By Rachel Cohen

DAILY COLUMBIA SPECTATOR (New York, N.Y.) 02/05/1998

Professor Peter Awn teaches a class on Islam that is limited to 75 students but has 95.

In 1992, 150 students took macroeconomics. This year 400 will.

There weren't enough seats for all the students in one School of Engineering and Applied Sciences class this semester, so some were sent to another room to watch their class on a live-feed television.

The combination of a growing student body and a shrinking faculty is making classes larger and learning more difficult for Columbia undergraduates, according to faculty and students.

Faculty members say they are worried about the increasing demands on their time as their classes get larger.

Many students have found they cannot register for the classes they want. When students do get into popular classes, they are sometimes forced to sit on the floor or stand in the hallway.

Columbia College Dean of Students Roger Lehecka said some class sizes are getting larger due to shifting student preferences for certain classes, but that the administration can handle the student demand.

"We have built in assurances that classes will not get larger," Lehecka said.

Enrollment in some economics classes increased by over 100 percent in the past six years, according to Economics Chair Richard Clarida.

"In the last seven years, the number of students taking economics has doubled [while the number of] faculty has shrunk," Clarida said.

The number of students enrolled each year in Principles of Economics, the introductory course for majors, rose from 600 students to 1,000 since 1992. The number of students in Intermediate Microeconomics went from 170 to 400 students per year.

Awn said he couldn't let any more students into his Islam class.

"I have a pedagogical problem with letting humanities classes get so big," Awn said, adding that the teachers of large classes rely too heavily on tests instead of papers.

Professor Edward Tayler, who teaches a popular Shakespeare class, estimated that in the 1985–86 academic year there were 2,800 undergraduates in Columbia College and 523 faculty members.

In 1995–96, there were 3,500 undergrads and 454 arts and sciences faculty members, he said.

"I have no objection to more students, 4,000 or more, so long as you hire the faculty to teach them," Tayler said. "It's desperately hard to get an education [in a big class] and an emotional drag to be shunted from place to place." ∎

Teaching & Research

You can see that some of the issues that affect life at a large state school can also be found at highly competitive schools, albeit on a smaller scale. Another area of concern is with the amount of research being conducted at prestigious schools. As with professors at large state schools, professors at highly competitive schools often find it necessary to teach while conducting research that could garner the school prestige and money. Since the pressure to "publish or perish" is endemic in prestigious school faculties, graduate students often must pick up the slack, just as they do at large state schools.

The problems may be similar, but it seems that the lines of communication between students and professors at highly competitive schools are more open than they are at big state schools. At Cornell, students were given a forum to voice their opinions about the quality of the instruction they were receiving; in turn, professors agreed to explore ways to solve problems. This kind of privilege is characteristic of highly competitive universities, where students and professors enjoy give-and-take relationships.

CORNELL U. STUDENTS AND FACULTY DISCUSS THE QUALITIES OF A GOOD INSTRUCTOR

By Melissa Hantman

CORNELL DAILY SUN (Ithaca, N.Y.) 02/19/1999

In a small gathering at Donlon Hall last night, students were given the chance to voice their thoughts about Cornell professors to a group of faculty that included President Hunter Rawlings III.

Prof. Bruce Lewenstein, communications, hosted the discussion.

The talk opened with students confessing they often relied upon teaching assistants more than their professors. Professors in turn admitted many graduate

students do not have much teaching experience in their fields.

"As a grad student . . . you're not trained to teach," said Prof. Meredith Small, anthropology. Rawlings acknowledged that while some departments guide TAs through the teaching process, others "let them sink or swim."

It was suggested that Cornell develop a University-wide teacher training program. As the group explored the topic of professors' devotion to and love of teaching, Small pointed out the extreme pressure on many professors to publish and conduct studies at this "research-centered university." Faculty and students debated whether research added to or detracted from classroom teaching.

Some audience members said they enjoyed hearing about their professors' research since it made course material more relevant to life. "Research enhances teaching . . . and the other way around," said Prof. Ali Hadi, statistics. Yet Small pointed out teaching is often sacrificed for research. Rawlings said, "I really do think [research and teaching] go hand in hand."

Students expressed a wish for professors to be warm and approachable—and for the material to be cogent and not intimidating. "So many times, students don't think of professors as human beings, but as teachers.

I've actually had students ask me if professors live in their offices," Rawlings said.

Faculty recommended the University's Center for Learning and Teaching as a resource for students.

At the discussion's end, students stated their disapproval of the median grade report released for every course, saying students use this as a basis when choosing classes.

"There's nothing wrong with wanting an A, but you should also want to learn," Hadi agreed.

Gideon Lin '99 enjoyed airing his concerns in the discussion. "Most people think Cornell is a large, impersonal university. A lot of students complain about their teachers," he said. "I'm glad we finally get to speak our minds." ■

Highly competitive schools have deep pockets—which is a polite way of saying that they're loaded, really, really loaded. The money these schools have comes from various sources. First are endowments, made up largely of contributions from loyal—and rich—alumni, who love their alma mater so much that they want to build a new wing onto the library (and have it named after them, of course). Prestigious schools also maintain substantial, diversified investments that bring in millions and millions each year. And don't forget grants and money brought in from research, which contribute two more pieces to the pie.

When big money comes into these schools, it often gathers national attention, as it did at Vanderbilt University in Tennessee. What would you do with $340 million? Some students dared to dream about it.

WE'RE IN THE MONEY: VANDERBILT STUDENTS CONSIDER $340 MILLION DONATION
By Holly Eagleson

VANDERBILT HUSTLER (Nashville, Tenn.) 12/10/1998

Happy holidays—$340 million has just landed in your lap.

It's in the form of one sweet stock transfer that just needs your signature and then you can have your way with it. That is, if you're Vanderbilt Chancellor Joe B. Wyatt.

Since the announcement that a $340 million gift (the largest private donation to a university) has Vanderbilt's name on it, national attention has been

directed our way and has inspired lottery fever on campus. Rumors of how the money should be spent are flying, and you may have even concocted your own plan of how to play Santa.

But finding out how students want the money spent is like opening a Pandora's box of a thousand different priorities—each reflecting a different facet of student life at Vanderbilt.

For example, Student Government president Jamaal

Nelson said he was pleased with reported plans to allocate the money to the Cancer Center at the medical center, but also had a more populist proposal for the gift.

"I think that the plans for the new Sarratt Center have gone very well, but man, with $300 million, a center equipped with a five-screen movie theater would be great," he said.

"There could be three or four coffee shops, five or six fast food places, but most importantly, an area for students to congregate where it would be so inviting, so welcoming and so warm that it would be difficult to leave to go to classes. A place that promoted student interaction against all barriers and differences."

Junior Aparupa Bhattacharya sees campus security as a pressing problem.

"As a student, I'd put it toward the escort system. I've talked to freshmen who are concerned that campus really isn't well-lit and who aren't feeling safe.

"The golf cart thing that SGA has proposed for a new escort service is pretty expensive, so it'd be a great place to put the money because campus safety should come before anything else."

Junior Kristy Blumberg, a member of the women's tennis team, said that more money for athletics is another way to improve life for a portion of the student body.

"I think better athletic facilities, like a better McGugin with more workout facilities, are important. Compared to other schools, it's not nearly as nice."

She added that more money is necessary to help defray the costs of tuition, and that the gift might be the solution to many families' budget crunches.

"It'd be neat if it was used for more scholarships, not necessarily for just sports, but to help out since this school is so expensive."

Senior Turner Inscoe, president of the Interfraternity Council, said that accommodating all Greek organizations on campus, as well as fostering faculty/student interaction through a social facility on Greek Row, would be top priorities.

"I'd like to be able to have houses for all the Greek organizations, primarily the black Greeks who don't have them now."

No matter how it's spent, students seem to advocate keeping the windfall at home, with Vanderbilt's paying customers, the students. ∎

These schools may have huge amounts of money on paper, but that doesn't necessarily mean, as students at Vanderbilt learned, that the money gets pumped directly into campus improvements. Traditionally, highly competitive schools have spent their money conservatively (you could say that's why they have so much of it). A lot of the money is put back into investments, which in turn generate even more money for the school. With all the money these schools have, some, like the editors of the *Harvard Crimson*, question their administrations' Scrooge-like attitude toward spending it.

EDITORIAL: SPREADING THE WEALTH
Staff Editorial

HARVARD CRIMSON (Cambridge, Mass.) 12/07/1998

Last week's announcement that the University will increase its endowment payout by 20 percent next year is welcome news to students and faculty alike. Finally, Harvard is dispersing just a little more of its gigantic endowment, which has nearly tripled in the last five years. Finally, Harvard is back on track with a payout of about 4.5 percent of the endowment, upping the shockingly low 3.3 percent payout of this year.

It's about time, but is it enough?

Despite the big numbers involved (the University will be spending $95 million more than it did last year, and the Faculty of Arts and Sciences will receive $40 million of the total), Harvard is merely returning to its normal spending level—a level many financial analysts agree is quite conservative.

Administrators cite the upcoming conclusion of the Capital Campaign as one of the reasons for the increased payout. Provost Harvey V. Fineberg '67 said, "A lot of people have contributed a lot of money, and I think it will be very helpful to be able to point and see how that money is having an effect today." While we agree that major University donors deserve to see the fruits of their generosity, the University should take its spending cues not from individual donors but from the needs of students.

The FAS money will be used to fund the already-implemented increases in financial aid, to hasten current construction projects including repairs to the library system and the building of the Knafel Center for Government and International Studies and to support faculty research. Aside from the very helpful increase in financial aid funding, students will see little

change in their everyday lives as a result of this larger payout.

Harvard should consider opening its purse just a little wider and pouring some millions into addressing student concerns: freezing tuition levels at current rates for the next few years; improving student facilities such as the woefully backward Malkin Athletic Center; hiring more professors to lower the student-faculty ratio and continuing to strengthen the financial aid program.

Let's hope that this move back from stinginess to mere thriftiness betokens the possibility of future generosity on the part of the University. ∎

Academic Resources

With all that money coming in every year, it's not hard to believe that the library, computer, and research facilities at highly competitive colleges are unparalleled. While some students at prestigious schools complain that administrators steeped in old traditions are slow to bring in new technology, when it does arrive, it's more often than not the best of the best. "Harvard U. Puts Lecture Videos Online" describes that school's groundbreaking digitized Real Video lectures, available on the Internet for chemistry students.

HARVARD U. PUTS LECTURE VIDEOS ONLINE

By Robert K. Silverman

HARVARD CRIMSON (Cambridge, Mass.) 11/18/1998

Joshua E. Raffaelli, freshman, has been bedridden for a week with pneumonia, unable to attend class or leave his room.

Nevertheless, he has not missed a single lecture for Chemistry 5, "Introduction to Principles of Chemistry."

Beginning this semester, all "Chem 5" lectures have been digitized and posted on the course Web site. Students can access the lectures from their rooms and view them using Real Video.

"The digitized lectures are awesome. I can't get out to go to class, [but I can view them on my computer]," Raffaelli said. "They're perfect."

The digitized lectures are designed to benefit all students, not just those who miss class. Students can

use the lectures to review their notes, clear up misconceptions or study for a test.

"If you miss a piece of information in lecture, you can go back and get it really easily. They're also good to review before a test," said freshman Tova A. Serkin.

Praise for the Real Video lectures is nearly universal, from both students and faculty members.

"Students don't have to reserve a video and the television room. It's a tremendous boost in efficiency," said Chem 5 instructor James E. Davis, a senior lecturer on chemistry and chemical biology.

"The little stuff that I saw was really neat. It was like a glimpse of the future," said Gregory C. Tucci, head laboratory teaching fellow for Chem 5.

While the new video technology has been successful, there are no long-range plans to implement the system throughout the College.

"It's too early to tell if this will become a standard College or University-wide practice, but ICG hopes to offer the service to three or four courses next term," ICG Manager Paul F. Bergen wrote in an e-mail.

Chem 5 was originally selected as a trial subject because of its large size—more than 350 students—and prior use of computer technology.

"Jim Davis has been very active in employing computer technology, and we've worked with the course in the past," said HASCS Director Franklin M. Steen. "It's a big class, so more people are benefiting."

Steen stressed that the ultimate goal is not to replace traditional videotaping of classes but simply to make the technology available to all interested professors.

"We'd like to try a few more courses," he said. "We don't go around and say, 'Hey, we've got great technology here, why don't you try it out?' It has to be faculty-driven."

The new technology has also drawn positive responses from outside of the University. Hausmann said the lectures can be transmitted over a standard modem, making them available to anyone with access to the Web.

"There's a dimension of globality," Hausmann said. "We've gotten e-mails from other universities and people asking about our resources. I think it's great." ■

Academic Opportunities

Like their research facilities, academic curricula at highly competitive colleges are without peer. Students at prestigious schools, by and large, have more freedom to choose classes. Highly competitive universities provide an incredibly wide variety of course offerings and majors. You can conduct independent research projects. In some instances, you can even custom-design your own major. A real go-getter can get complete requirements for two bachelor's degrees in four years. And most highly competitive schools offer combined degree programs, where students can get a bachelor's degree and an advanced degree in just a little more time than it would take to get a bachelor's degree alone.

At highly competitive colleges, courses of study are designed with students' needs in mind. For example, with the Dartmouth Plan, students can take advantage of a year-round calendar consisting of four 10-week academic terms. Since most students need to complete 12 terms to graduate, a certain amount of flexibility is built into the program. Students can extend enrollment to five years to take time off, study abroad, or explore career opportunities, or they can go straight through and graduate in three years if they want.

Highly competitive schools value hands-on classes that include plenty of one-on-one attention and instruction. Stanford's Field Ecology and Northwestern's Investigative Journalism classes are testaments to this philosophy.

STANFORD U. FIELD ECOLOGY TEACHES STUDENTS HANDS-ON SCIENCE

By Miler Lee

THE STANFORD DAILY (Stanford, Calif.) 05/21/1998

Under the setting Mojave Desert sun, a group of students kneels down in the sand dunes. They watch harvester ants emerge from underground and deposit seed husks and debris at their nest opening. One of the observers, Nathan Sanders, pauses for a moment, then lifts a nearby rock to find a half-dozen termites on the underside; he drops the white fleshy insects near the nest. Immediately, the ants grab the termites in their mandibles and scurry to bring their prizes back to the nest. "See," he tells the others, "they've switched tasks."

Watching ants at all, much less in the middle of the desert, may seem an unusual activity for most Stanford students. However, this is standard fare for students in Biology 181: Field Ecology.

This one-of-a-kind class, taught by postdoctoral fellow Diane Wagner and assisted by biology doctoral students Sanders and Taylor Ricketts, offers undergraduates the opportunity to engage in hands-on learning and research in ecology. For those in the class, it is a refreshing and valuable departure from the way science is normally taught, in impersonal lecture halls or laboratories.

Wagner's aim has been to give students practice doing science. "I have two goals for the class. One is to encourage students to ask questions about the natural world. The other is to equip them with the tools, the ecological methods, to answer some of those questions on their own."

To this end, students spend most of the class hours outdoors, refining their field skills. For five hours every week, they

Jenny Freemyer/*The Daily Cardinal*

examine various ecological questions at Jasper Ridge Biological Preserve. Recent field exercises have included investigation of arthropod diversity in areas infested by Argentine ants and study of plant distribution on the serpentine and sandstone grasslands.

These field methods have also proved useful on the other field trips that the class has taken. Some of the trips have been to the marshlands to observe shore birds, to Moss Beach and Pescadero Beach to study intertidal and coastal strand communities, and to the Granite Mountains in the Mojave Desert to examine desert ecology.

However, the most important component of the class is not necessarily the field exercises, but the independent projects that each student will undertake. "Doing a lab that someone else conceived is in some ways like coloring in someone else's sketch," Wagner said. "There are things you can learn that way, but it's a lousy way to figure out whether you like painting or whether you're good at it.

"You could do canned labs for years and never have any idea what it feels like to look at the results of a study you designed; it can be an absolute thrill."

Junior human biology major Lindsay Stallcup agrees. "The individual project is great because you get to create something that you're interested in . . . it's the real thing; you're doing your own field work."

Many students taking the class feel that this emphasis on individual learning is a rare opportunity, especially in the sciences. "It's more or less a one-time-only deal," Stallcup said.

Although the Biology Department has offered similar courses in the past—most notably, Prof. Harold Mooney's Biology of Natural Populations, which was offered intermittently in various forms from 1970 until a few years ago—Wagner's class fills a curricular hole in the Biology Department.

"It's a great opportunity to get hands-on experience working in the field," Stallcup added. "What I'm learning in field ecology is really important for my major . . . but it's not anything that's offered through a traditional lecture/classroom-style class."

Her classmate, junior biology major Michele Flagge, shares this sentiment. "Out of all of the classes that I have taken so far at Stanford, I have learned the most information from Field Ecology. I think this is a demonstration that hands-on learning is far superior to purely classroom-based instruction."

Sophomore human biology major Emily Yates-Doerr said, "Field Ecology is what I thought college would be like." ∎

NORTHWESTERN U. STUDENTS UNCOVER NEW SIDES TO MURDER

Arthur Janik

DAILY NORTHWESTERN (Evanston, Ill.) 02/02/1999

What if finishing a homework assignment meant saving someone's life?

For the five Northwestern Medill School of Journalism seniors investigating Anthony Porter's capital murder case, this reality confronts them every day.

"The pressure of homework in other classes is to get an 'A,'" said Shawn Armbrust, one of students involved in the case. "The pressure of homework in this class is to prevent an innocent person from being executed."

The students, all taking Prof. David Protess's investigative journalism class this quarter, were thrust into a 1982 Cook County case involving the murder of a young couple in Chicago's Washington Park. Porter, now 43, was convicted of the crime and sentenced to death.

His September execution was stayed at the last minute, and Protess said recent developments uncovered by the Northwestern student sleuths seem to point to his innocence.

At Porter's competency hearing, which began Monday, state prosecutors presented evidence to demonstrate his competency during his alleged murder and later court defense. An IQ test administered last year put his score at 51. An IQ between 80 and 120 is considered average.

Porter's score renders him barely capable of defending himself, let alone committing the crime, said Syandene Rhodes-Pitts, another member of the team.

Porter's competency is not the only part of the case the students are questioning. If the court testimony is accepted at face value, then the prosecution's star eyewitness would have had to have seen the crime take place in the dark, from 250 feet away, through a fence, at 1 a.m., Armbrust said.

"We went over much of the case paperwork and court testimony and found a lot of inconsistencies," she said. "We did a reenactment of the crime and found that the way in which the crime was supposed to have happened didn't make sense."

The students' prodding and searching led the prosecution's star eyewitness to recant his testimony. And now it seems likely that they have found the actual murderer, said Erica LeBorgne, another team member.

"It was a matter of asking the simple questions that no one bothered asking before," McCann said. "The police had the story they wanted, and [Porter's] attorney lacked basic defense skills."

Such twists and turns are reminiscent of the Ford Heights Four case. In 1996, another team of Protess's students uncovered evidence that led to the exoneration of four wrongfully accused murder suspects. Though it may seem difficult investigating in the shadow of such a monumental accomplishment, the students involved said they don't see their predecessors' success as a source of competition.

"The Ford Heights Four case is basically a model for comparison—the groundwork for our own investigation," said Rhodes-Pitts.

What was intimidating was the incredible time pressure the students had to work under, Protess said. Porter's execution was scheduled for the end of the first week of classes.

"We were working under a very tight deadline with a man's life at stake," Protess said. "Despite the tremendous pressure, the students worked tirelessly investigating a 16-year claim of innocence."

Although the competency hearing will continue this week, the defense will seek a continuance of the original case based on the students' newly uncovered evidence.

"Our mission is to find the truth, whether it finds [Porter] guilty or innocent," said Protess. "That's a journalist's job—to uncover both sides of the story.

If a wrongfully accused person is innocent, then the noblest goal is to correct that injustice."

Remarkably, because of the students' efforts, Anthony Porter—a man who spent 16 years in prison and was soon to be executed for a crime he did not commit—was eventually released from prison and cleared of all charges. ■

The *Daily Northwestern* article surely makes a case for practical classes, wherein training is given in a specific skill that is used in a specific career, in this case, investigative journalism. Surprisingly, this runs counter to the philosophy and tradition of most highly competitive colleges, who consider themselves bastions of the liberal arts tradition. Although prestigious universities usually have more than one college—for example, engineering and business colleges as well as a larger liberal arts and sciences college—for the most part theoretical coursework is emphasized over practical coursework. In other words, highly competitive colleges do not see themselves as training grounds for those seeking preparation for a particular career and so do not ordinarily offer degrees in, say, marketing or tourism—standard fare at other schools. As the *Yale Daily News* reports, Yale University is just now considering a major in Finance.

PROPOSED FINANCE MAJOR TO BE DISCUSSED AT YALE U.

By Jennifer Arthur

YALE DAILY NEWS (New Haven, Conn.) 02/09/1999

For Yale's future investment bankers and business moguls, a new major may be on the horizon.

The Economics Student Advisory Committee will meet this Thursday to discuss a faculty-proposed new branch of the economics major, called "Economics with a concentration in Finance," that could provide an organized course structure for business-minded students.

Because Yale currently has no pre-business program, students interested in pursuing a career in finance typically major in basic economics. Other universities, such as the University of Pennsylvania and the University of Virginia, let undergraduates enroll in their business schools and graduate with a degree in economics, majoring in business.

The proposed new major—which, unlike at other schools, would remain within Yale College—would not require a reshuffling of current course offerings. All of the tentative course requirements, such as Economics

252 "Finance: Theory and Applications," are currently available in the economics department. The proposed major, however, would require some extra effort, as it has 15 requirements, whereas the economics major currently has 12.

"Although the major will have 15 required courses, I think it is a great idea and will make econ with a concentration in finance students very strong candidates for leading investment banks and other business firms," Economics Curriculum Committee member Greg Hintz '00 said in an e-mail to other members.

Economics majors said they are receptive to the idea.

"I know a lot of people who are interested in investment banking," economics and International Studies major Debby Wang '00 said. "I think that if they had a background in finance it would help them a lot."

Others agreed.

"If they could have more classes or create a major it would have a lot of interest," Grant Chavin '01 said.

Economics faculty members said they would be free to comment on the proposed major after Thursday's meeting.

Current seniors and juniors would probably not benefit from the new major, but if approved, it would offer incoming students a chance to specialize.

"I think it will be useful for those freshmen who already know what they want when they come here," Maxime Ko '99 said.

Many, such as Randy Wolfe '01, said that the proposed new major would be good career preparation.

"It would be good to get something close to Wharton," Wolfe said.

Although he stressed that he recommended that those interested in business attend a business school, Robert I. Webb, senior associate dean of the McIntire School of Commerce in Virginia, agreed that the proposed major had a "high marketability." ■

Another area in which highly competitive colleges excel is in the variety and diversity of internships they offer to their students. In fact, some students look at internships as accentuating theoretical coursework by providing practical, career-related experiences. Some interns, like those from the University of Chicago who acted for Steppenwolf Theater, receive course credit; others, like those from Stanford who work at Hewlett-Packard and other Silicon Valley corporations for the summer, do not.

Students who participated in both programs, whether for credit or not, agree that internships provide excellent opportunities to meet mentors and see what life beyond college can be like.

U. CHICAGO STUDENTS RECEIVE INTERNSHIPS AT STEPPENWOLF THEATER

By David G. Schultz

Chicago Maroon (Chicago, Ill.) 10/13/1998

Wake up. Open your eyes. Take a deep breath. Step out of your lowly Hyde Park digs and step onto whatever form of public transportation takes you downtown. Now go to work at the Steppenwolf in a professional theater production with working union member actors.

For 12 U of C undergrads, this scenario became a reality. Gathering together for the first time with director Tina Landau in late August, the students began preparation for their roles as ensemble members of the cast of Charles Mee's 'The Berlin Circle,' Steppenwolf's main stage production playing now until November 13. The interns play students at the fall of the Berlin Wall in 1989.

According to third-year Saket Soni, the characters are loosely based on the photographs and paintings of

people living at the time. "These characters were created by looking at pictures and by looking at newsreels and paintings. As a part of the ensemble, we generated characters within the play," said Soni.

To the amazement of many of the interns, cast members did not merely execute the director's vision, but also acted as contributors and creators of that vision itself. Landau allowed the cast to present their interpretations of the play through exercises such as the Viewpoints method, where cast members arranged scenes with their fellow actors to present different ideas for staging certain parts of the script.

"Tina [Landau, the director] was just as interested in our ideas as the rest of the professional actors. That was great," said Lucinda Bingham, a third-year in the College.

In addition, some students said that as interns, they

benefited from the mentorship of their more experienced partners. Fifth-year student Susanna Gellert said that she noticed the "specific mentor relationships that formed between the older and younger actors."

The acting internships themselves grew out of a conversation between University Theater (UT) Director Curt Columbus and Martha Lavey, a friend of Columbus' who is affiliated with Steppenwolf, over the already established administrative internships that UT organized with the Theater.

Columbus then took the idea to Dean of the College John Boyer, who suggested that the internships be given academic content as well as an experiential aspect, and that course credit be given.

UT Educational Director Gavin Witt underlined the uniqueness of the program. "They were not just witnessing. It was a truly educational experience," said Witt. Students put on 12 previews and perform eight shows a week for five weeks in addition to two shows on Saturday and Sunday.

"That is something you just won't get at UT," Columbus said. ■

PUTTING KNOWLEDGE TO PROFITABLE USE AT STANFORD

By Marcella Bernhard

THE STANFORD DAILY (Stanford, Calif.) 09/30/1998

Ever since Stanford alumni William Hewlett and David Packard founded Hewlett-Packard next to campus in the 1930s, Stanford students have shared a symbiotic relationship with Silicon Valley.

Each year, fresh-faced Stanford students provide the lifeblood of dozens of companies in the area. In return, students get the chance to work on innovative projects on the cusp of the industries' next big thing.

The working relationship between Stanford students and the computer industry often begins with summer internships.

Judy Hay, Class of '98, worked for Hewlett-Packard in Boise, Idaho for two summers during her undergraduate days as a computer science major. She now works at Hewlett-Packard in Mountain View, updating a Web browser designed to remove glitches from the process of printing pages off the Web.

The main challenge in updating Hewlett-Packard's original software, Hay said, was to make it more user-friendly. The developers "were much more into function than user-interface," Hay explained.

Stanford students are getting their foot in the door at start-ups as well as with industry giants. Senior Chris Kramer, a computer science major, spent the summer at the Silicon Valley Networking Lab. The lab, which was launched in May, is modeled on already-existing labs at Harvard University and the University of New Hampshire, which provide services for larger computer companies.

Kramer is involved in a project that tests devices that will eventually increase the speed of Internet access over fiber-optic phone lines. The project aims to improve the 56 kilobyte-per-second speed of today's modems to a future level of one megabit per second.

Compaq, AT&T, Intel, Lucent Technologies, ADM and 3Com are among the eleven companies working to develop devices based on the original networking technology pioneered by Tut Systems. For now, Kramer and others at the lab are making sure these devices perform as fast and accurately as they can.

The shared culture of Stanford and Silicon Valley creates a generally easy transition from life at school to life in the industry—or an easy overlap, in the case of students continuing their summer internships into the school year.

Whether their work involves interactions primarily with engineers, suppliers, old hands or new blood, students and alumni working in the Valley enjoy the general dynamism and excitement of the environment.

Not all Silicon Valley jobs fit into the young, start-up stereotype, however. Hay is working with a team of men that has been together for fifteen years.

Working in Silicon Valley also has the advantage of providing all the scenic distractions of the Bay Area—providing you can leave the office to enjoy them.

Hay says she hopes to spend more time in Mountain View, though "it depends on how many upgrades they let [me] do." ■

Outstanding Professors

Whether you choose to become an intern for a semester, for the summer, or not at all, you can rest assured that if you attend a highly competitive university, the experience you'll get in the classroom will more than prepare you for life after college. Plain and simple, highly competitive colleges hire outstanding faculty members. Many are internationally renowned in their fields. Some are Nobel Prize winners. Some, like John DiIulio and Elaine Showalter, stir up nationwide controversy. But most importantly, all contribute to the kind of education for which highly competitive schools are acclaimed.

ROLLING STONE CITES TWO PRINCETON PROFESSORS AMONG ACADEMIA'S "MOST WANTED"

By Chris Yakaitis

DAILY PRINCETONIAN (Princeton, N.J.) 10/06/1998

What do John DiIulio, Elaine Showalter, and Marilyn Manson have in common?

They're all controversial figures featured in the Oct. 15, 1998 issue of Rolling Stone. Wilson School professor DiIulio and English professor Showalter are spotlighted in Rolling Stone's "1998 College Special" section. The article "Dangerous Minds" names the two University professors among eight of academia's most notorious and "most wanted professors."

Showalter, featured first in the article, said she was flattered by the title "most wanted professor."

"I got a big kick out of that, especially that I was the baddest cat in the jungle," she said. "I think the country's really safe if I'm the most dangerous."

The article focuses on the impact of Showalter's 1997 book, Hystories: Hysterical Epidemics and Modern Media. The book argues that chronic fatigue syndrome, Gulf War syndrome, recovered-memory syndrome and alleged alien abductions are psychosomatic or imagined phenomena, much to the dismay of many syndrome sufferers.

"It has had tremendous support from the medical and scientific communities," Showalter said. "It's not a heretical book, but for people who are committed to those ideas it was very startling."

The article describes some of the negative feedback Showalter has received, including an anonymous correspondent who threatened to "get" her and several sufferers who said they would " 'rip her apart' or 'assassinate' her unless she recanted," the article said.

"It was quite responsible reporting," she said. "I did have death threats, but nobody actually took a shot at me yet."

DiIulio drew Rolling Stone's attention for his take on criminology. According to the article, DiIulio believes that harsher sentencing and more prisons are necessary to address America's crime problem. He also predicts that the country will soon be overrun by "superpredators," young criminals of extreme and unprecedented viciousness, the article said.

DiIulio's views have won the interest of some senators and congressmen and the scorn of some scholars and researchers, the article said.

"[DiIulio] preaches what people want to hear in a field where myth far outruns reality," Norval Morris of the University of Chicago said in the article.

According to the article, DiIulio—who could not be reached for comment yesterday—has defended himself against this and other attacks, as well as the current drop in crime in the U.S. "I am at a loss to explain . . . why crime rates have been falling, but I am, of course, glad they are!" he said in the article.

And how do the professors feel about sharing national coverage with the infamous Antichrist Superstar?

"Why not? I thought it was absolutely terrific," Showalter said. "Especially with this picture (inside) of me looking like such a nerd . . . looking beyond harmless. I really got a kick out of it." ∎

Advising

You probably recall the dissatisfaction that many students had with advisers at big state schools. With the large number of students attending big state schools each year, personal attention can be hard to come by. As the following *Brown Daily Herald* article points out, highly competitive schools are not immune to problems with their advising systems. What's important to note, however, is that a special committee was formed at Brown to investigate student complaints about advising. As is often the case at highly competitive colleges, administrators are often more willing to listen to student complaints and work with them to find acceptable solutions to problems.

BROWN U. ADVISING SYSTEM MAY FACE CHANGES
By Caitlin Armistead

BROWN DAILY HERALD (Providence, R.I.) 02/23/1998

A new committee will attempt to reform a system that students have identified as a weak link in Brown's academic program.

Dean of the College Kenneth Sacks has formed the Committee on Academic Advising in an attempt to reform the current advising system and highlight its strengths.

According to Sacks, students have identified the advising system as a weakness in the University's academic program.

"The charge of this committee is to explore both perceptions and the mechanics of advising at Brown, and to make recommendations that may improve advising and/or define more accurately for both

Juan Hernandez/*The Daily Northwestern*

students and advisors the goals and responsibilities of advising," Sacks said.

This committee will address potential changes in the system through four specific tasks. First, it will write a number of questions for several focus groups that will consist of randomly selected undergraduates and faculty. These focus groups will try to determine the strengths and weaknesses of the current undergraduate advising system. In addition, these groups will test some hypotheses about improving advising.

The next task of the committee will be to evaluate the results of the focus groups, as well as previous campus reviews of advising and a recent Student Life exercise on advising.

In addition to addressing issues in formal academic advising, the committee will study aspects of informal advising, such as the Undergraduate Teaching and Research Assistantship program, residential counselors and career planning services.

The final task will be to look at the possible effects of the new changes in the advising system.

"I would say that we are interested in all aspects of academic advising and are eager to learn students' ideas as to the needs and wants that could be provided by our advising system at Brown," said Professor of Sociology Gregory Elliott, who is serving as the committee chair. "Our goal is to provide the best structure possible within which Brown students can make for themselves a rewarding and challenging liberal arts education in what I believe to be the best undergraduate college in the country. To this end, we are open to all serious suggestions, criticisms and compliments about the current system."

The committee will hold its first meeting at the end of this week and will meet regularly for the remainder of the semester. ∎

Academic Dishonesty

We've already established that at a highly competitive college, you have access to fabulous facilities, are taught by some of the world's finest professors, and are given guidance by advisers with your very best interests at heart. What if, despite all that, you still find you can't make the grade? Would you be tempted to cheat? At many highly competitive colleges, cheating is a big problem. Because classes are so competitive and because everyone is considered to be "the best of the best," students at prestigious schools are under enormous pressure to do well. For some, a B isn't good enough.

Students who cheat at any college do so out of desperation, but at a highly competitive college, the sense of desperation among students who cheat is probably stronger. You've made it this far, you think; failure is not an option. On top of that, your parents are paying tens of thousands of dollars for you to be here, so you can't let them down. If you're struck by this desperation, keep in mind that most highly competitive colleges have long-standing, strict honor codes regarding cheating. Cheating at a prestigious school is looked at with extreme distaste, and getting caught for it will brand you "Public Enemy #1." As the following editorial from the *Stanford Daily* points out, the burden to uphold academic integrity at a highly competitive school is placed on both the students and the professors.

EDITORIAL: ANYTHING FOR AN 'A'
By Chris Yakaitis

Stanford Daily (Stanford, Calif.) 10/06/1998

Every student knows that the pressures of college life can occasionally become unbearable. The responsibility of living independently for the first time, making new friends, sustaining meaningful relationships and succeeding academically burdens all students.

At Stanford the pressure to get good grades is particularly strong. Many parents are making great sacrifices to send their children to this reputable and expensive institution, and most students at Stanford also feel the weight of their own internal motivation. Competition for coveted consulting jobs and medical school slots frequently propels students into all-nighters and Friday nights in the 24-hour study room.

In an atmosphere of such drive, burden and expense, the temptation to find an easy way out is understandably attractive. At Stanford it is up to students and professors to ensure academic integrity by abiding by a judicial sys-

tem set up by students and faculty more than a century ago. Professors and teaching assistants are required to report any violations of the Stanford Honor Code to a judicial affairs officer, who then determines whether there is enough evidence against the student to justify a trial before peers on the judicial panel.

In light of recent research indicating that professors at most universities personally discipline students they suspect of cheating, we feel the responsibility to validate and support Stanford's objective judicial system. While instances of cheating at Stanford are reportedly low compared to most schools, cheating does occur and students often feel the pressure to make up lab data or copy a paragraph from an obscure book to save another night of missed sleep.

The problem with professors individually disciplining cheaters is inconsistency and unfairness. Say, for example, that two students turn in plagiarized papers to different professors. One professor may lower the student's final grade but still pass him or her, while the other professor may fail that student or even move to have him or her expelled from the University.

In addition to unfair and inconsistent punishments, the lack of a standard judicial process can deprive students of the right of due process and an objective investigation of a professor or TA's allegation. This right is crucial for students who agree to abide by an Honor Code before taking every exam.

The judicial process exists to ensure academic integrity among all Stanford students and faculty, and concerned students and faculty should voice any concerns they have over the fairness of the process and the conduct of its administrators. Ultimately, the judicial system works for the benefit of all students by assuring that Stanford maintains its academic reputation through the honest and original work of its students. ∎

Grade Inflation

You might think that students at highly competitive colleges wouldn't have to resort to cheating to get good grades. After all, they were smart enough to get admitted to the school in the first place. Yet it happens. Similarly, you wouldn't think that professors at prestigious schools would award their students higher grades than they deserve to make the students, and therefore the school, look smarter. Yet that, too, happens—or at least it's alleged to happen at colleges and universities nationwide, but particularly at highly competitive schools. The higher your students' grades are, the better the press for your school will be, and the more enrollments you'll get, or so the accusations say. Universities could be said to face the same kind of pressures that their students do, only on a larger scale.

After a *New York Times* article reported rampant grade inflation at Princeton University in 1998, the subject came to the forefront of discussions of grading at highly competitive colleges. Princeton professors have by no means admitted to the practice, but they plan to think more about what grades really mean, according to the *Daily Princetonian*. At the same time, Yale denies the existence of grade inflation on its campus, but note, in "Compared to Princeton, Yale Offers No Easy As," how one Yale student claims it's " 'hard to do below a C.' "

MIDTERM GRADING STANDARDS REMAIN UNCHANGED AT PRINCETON U.

By Stephen Fuzesi

DAILY PRINCETONIAN (Princeton, N.J.) 10/30/1998

Though the University's unofficial war on grade inflation continues to loom over professors, students should not expect their midterm grades to be the first casualty.

Faculty from a variety of departments said yesterday they did not expect to see changes in average midterm grades, despite the University's call to gradually stem a 25-year trend of rising marks.

The recommendation came in a faculty committee report issued in September based upon a much-publicized finding of grade inflation last spring that pushed the University's grading practices onto the front page of *The New York Times*.

But no dramatic changes are in store for students—at least as of midterms. "What will be different this year? Not much in terms of procedures and in terms of self-consciousness," said religion department chairman Jeffrey Stout, echoing the sentiments of officials from several other departments.

However, professors said they have thought more about what grades mean due to the University-wide discussion of grade inflation.

"Professors are not under specific pressure to change their grading practices," said professor Andrew Haughwout. "But, I've reflected on it . . . I probably am thinking harder about grading now than I was a year ago."

Yet, Haughwout said he doubted any professors would take dramatic actions on their own in fear of possibly jeopardizing the popularity of their classes and their marks on student course evaluations.

John Burgess, the departmental representative in philosophy and a member of the Faculty Committee on Examinations and Standing, cautioned against reading too much into midterm grades as a measure of inflation. "The first real test will be in January," he said, referring to final exams.

With semester grades in mind, several departments have focused on efforts to standardize grading practices across courses and between precepts.

"There's no conscious effort to lower the curve, but there is a conscious effort to make it more consistent," said sociology department chairman Paul DiMaggio. He added that at the end of the semester the depart-

ment will calculate the range of grades handed out by faculty and look for any trends.

Also seeking to keep grading standards constant, the history department distributed to its majors and faculty descriptions of the significance of different grades—what an A stands for as opposed to an A-minus, for example.

But Michael Mahoney, departmental representative for history, said the rapid approval of the standards signaled that they basically summarized what was already in practice. "I think most people who look at them will say, 'Yeah, that's what we thought,'" he noted.

Jameson Doig, chairman of the politics department, said the politics faculty met two weeks ago to discuss grade inflation. Among their concerns, he said, was that University students would be placed at a "relative disadvantage" if their grades declined while those of students at other prominent schools remained high.

As a result, efforts to reduce grade inflation would be most effective if conducted in conjunction with other schools, Doig said. ∎

COMPARED TO PRINCETON, YALE OFFERS NO EASY A's

By Glenn Hurowitz

YALE DAILY NEWS (New Haven, Conn.) 04/03/1998

Despite recent hype in the national press over grade inflation, many students at Yale are still struggling to bring in the Bs.

It is speculated that students can pressure professors to give them top grades, sometimes even with threats of legal action, but interviews with Yale students indicate that grade-grubbing here is not as intense as it is at some rival universities.

At Princeton, for example, sophomore math major Geoff Mitelman said that although Princeton's introductory classes have fairly tough curves that accurately reflect performance, inflation in upper-level courses is "tremendous."

"In a lot of the upper level courses, it's curved in such a way that it's hard to get below a B-," Mitelman said.

Mitelman added that at the same time, it is difficult to score above an A-.

But Mitelman said that such inflation, especially in his own top-rated department, is justified.

"It's the hardest department in the world," Mitelman said. "The Princeton math department is especially difficult. There are so few majors. There's such a rarefied atmosphere. The people who are taking the classes would be getting A's and A+'s in other classes."

Princeton, unlike Yale, also gives grades of A+, which are counted as 4.33 in grade point average calculations, which can boost GPAs above the 4.0 mark.

It is somewhat difficult to gauge statistically how Yale's grade distribution stacks up against other universities—a few years ago the University made its records secret.

Opinions on how well grades correspond with performance vary greatly among faculty members.

Political science professor Rogers Smith is known as a tough grader. But Smith said his grading distribution accurately reflects the performance of his students. And he added that in his time at Yale, he has not seen a significant rise in the quality of students' work.

Yale College Dean Richard Brodhead takes a different tack.

"The kind of students who come here have a taste for excellence," Brodhead said. "More students work harder in courses now than they did twenty years ago. The average quality of work has risen from the days when I was a student."

Brodhead attributed the quality increase to rising admissions standards and a change in attitude among students—Brodhead said it did not used to be considered "cool" to study hard.

Many students agreed with Brodhead, and some went even further, saying pressure to guard against grade inflation could lead to arbitrary grading.

Some Yale students and other Ivy Leaguers alike expressed concern that the sciences do not give the same easy grades that other courses, in the humanities and social sciences, do. In the sciences, it is often more difficult for students to come up with creative answers—no matter how you spin it, E still equals MC^2, so there's not much room for interpretation.

Molecular Biology and Biochemistry major Andrew Stadlen '98 said that even in the hard sciences, it is hard to receive truly abysmal marks.

"It's hard to do below a C," Stadlen said. "You really have to screw up pretty badly to do worse." ∎

Graduation Rates

Unlike large state schools, where a large percentage of students may take more than four years to graduate, at highly competitive colleges, most students graduate in four years, some in even less. Because the schools are costly, students (and their folks) save big money if they graduate early. Competition between students also manifests itself in early graduation—with the "prize" going to those who get their degrees in the shortest amount of time. Not surprisingly, this drive to graduate early, coupled with the fierce competition at highly competitive schools, creates a pressure-cooker atmosphere. This, in turn, makes it hard for students to make the most out of what they came to the school for in the first place. *The Hatchet* looks at the pros and cons of this trend.

MORE GEORGE WASHINGTON U. STUDENTS ARE GRADUATING EARLY

By Tammy Imhoff

THE HATCHET (Washington, D.C.) 01/21/1999

In a move to cut the cost of their education and begin their careers earlier, an increasing number of GW students are opting to earn their undergraduate degrees in less than the traditional four years.

Most early graduates cite the high cost of attending GW as the main reason they decided to leave the University ahead of schedule. Leah Probst graduated last month with a degree in biology—a semester early. She said she wanted to save her parents the extra tuition.

She's not alone. Information from the University's institutional research department shows that of the 1,539 freshmen who entered GW in 1994, 47 graduated within three years, up from 25 of the 1,490 freshmen who enrolled the year before. Forty-two of the 1,367 students who entered GW in 1995 graduated in three years or less, University data show.

But Kim Moreland, associate dean for undergraduate studies in the Columbian School of Arts and Sciences, said she hopes students who do not have financial incentives to graduate early will think carefully about their decision.

"My feeling is that a university is almost a holy space—it's four years you have to decide to explore intellectual interests, for trying things you may never pursue again, or you may discover you have a passion for," Moreland said. "If you try to rush all that you may lose something you never can regain. That doesn't mean there aren't people with good, solid reasons (for graduating early), but it seems sad to rush it."

She said the number of students who graduate with more than the 120-credit minimum also has been increasing. She said that may mean students who have the option to graduate early are choosing to remain on campus to take advantage of elective courses and the college atmosphere.

Several students attend summer school, use AP credits and register for more than 15 credit hours to receive their bachelor's degree in three years. Tara Kelly, who said she plans to graduate with an English degree in May, took 18 credit hours for two semesters and used AP credits to graduate a year early. Kelly said she thinks it may be difficult to find a job after graduation because she has less internship and job experience than some of her peers.

"I'm concerned about the fact that I don't have the extra year academically and for an internship, but I'm hoping in the end (employers) will take into consideration that I was able to do everything I needed to in three years," Kelly said. ∎

Andra Maniu/The Daily Princetonian

BEYOND THE Classroom

Odds are that you'll be spending a good deal of your time studying if you attend a highly competitive college, but don't worry, there will be plenty of other stuff to do, too—if you've got the time and the inclination.

Many students at highly competitive colleges explore life beyond the classroom through any of a number of clubs and organizations. At prestigious schools, students are perfectionists, and student-run organizations embody their quest to be the best. What often characterizes these groups is their innovation. Here you'll read how University of Chicago students went beyond the ordinary to conduct e-mail student government elections, how USC students started their campus's first magazine, and how George Washington students produced, directed, and starred in that school's first full-length film. Overachieving prestigious college students don't stop there. They also work tirelessly to support on-campus and off-campus projects that promote unity and help others.

Sports are another way that students take a break from their studies at highly competitive schools. At these institutions, athletics are characterized by tradition, fierce rivalries, and extreme loyalty—witness Duke's Cameron Crazies, and the century-plus-old Harvard–Yale football rivalry. And if you think that the sports teams at highly competitive schools aren't up to snuff, you better get ready to "Duke" it out with hundreds of thousands of loyal fans in North Carolina. At prestigious schools, you needn't be a semi-pro to play, but if you're a scholar and an athlete, athletic scholarships can be a great way for you to get into an Ivy League or other highly competitive school. It's a little-known fact that top high school athletes are recruited just as strongly by prestigious schools as they are by big state schools. The high school athlete then has a tough choice to make: Attend a large state school and maybe have a shot at making a pro team, or attend a highly competitive school and get an education that will put you ahead in the job market. Many high school athletes face such a decision every year.

Tradition extends beyond the sporting field and into attitudes about Greek organizations at highly competitive colleges. These schools vary widely in their opinions of Greeks. Columbia has 27 fraternities and sororities on campus; Harvard, on the other hand, has none. When you do find Greeks on campus, their numbers will be smaller—compare MIT's 50 Kappa Sigma brothers to the 139-member chapter of Kappa Alpha Theta at the University of Kentucky that we mentioned in the Large State Schools chapter. And it's more likely that "alternatives" to the traditional Greek organizations will find success on the campuses of highly prestigious schools.

If you don't think you have the time to commit yourself to a club, a sport, or a Greek organization but still want to do something more, you'll find that highly competitive colleges offer fabulous lecture series that require little time on your behalf for a lot of payout. Highly competitive colleges can pay the large sums that speakers in heavy demand charge, and famous prestigious school alumni come back to their alma maters regularly to share their experiences and offer advice. All told, whether they have a little extra time or a lot, students at highly competitive colleges have no problem finding extracurricular activities to enrich their college experience.

Student Groups

Highly competitive colleges are committed to offering their students opportunities to go outside the classroom for learning experiences. Because prestigious schools have the money to support them, students groups enjoy great success on these campuses.

Imagine being named student body president at Brown, Stanford or any of the other highly competitive universities across the country. The prestige of such a position will carry a lot of weight, both on campus and later in life, as you prepare your resume and venture out into the "real world." For this reason, student government is extremely important on the campuses of prestigious schools. And because candidates want to garner the most votes possible, innovative election methods are becoming popular at these schools. Take the University of Chicago, for example, where voting for a candidate required only a mouse click.

GOVERNMENT

U. CHICAGO STUDENT GOVERNMENT HOLDS ITS FIRST EVER E-MAIL ELECTION

By Kary Kelly

THE CHICAGO MAROON (Chicago, Ill.) 10/23/1998

Point and click. That is all students had to do to vote in this year's Student Government (SG) Assembly elections conducted Tuesday and Wednesday. This election marked the first time e-mail ballots appeared on the University of Chicago campus, giving students the opportunity to cast their votes from their homes.

Members of SG noted that well over half of the voters submitted ballots via e-mail.

"We switched to e-mail because everyone will get it. Everyone is set up with an e-mail account and most people check it at least every couple of days," explained Victoria True, the nominee for the Graduate Affairs chair. "It gives everyone a chance to vote."

Parag Gupta, SG president, confirmed the accessibility of e-mail, citing an increase in voter turnout from previous years.

"We had a phenomenal voter turnout," said Gupta.

True also noted the administrative ease of the e-mail ballots. "With the e-mail, we don't have to worry about setting up polling sites in every division. There are 24 divisions—that means a staff member and a student at every site, every hour, for two days. We're just not big enough to support that."

The electronic ballots also decrease the potential for fraud. Each voter is asked to provide a special authorization code, making the origin of an e-mail ballot much easier to trace than that of a paper ballot. Those who tabulated the results suspect minimal or no fraudulent ballots in this election. Votes were counted three times to ensure accuracy.

Between 900 and 1000 students voted in the election, an improvement from last year's numbers. Close to 630 of these voters cast their ballots on Tuesday as opposed to Wednesday.

"It seems important to vote, but it is not as though we are deciding some great social issue or anything. You just have to take it for what its worth," explained Greg Gurda, a first-year student in the College.

"I think this election was a success, particularly when you consider that it's the second week of classes and everyone is busy getting settled in. Apathy in SG elections is not that big of a problem, especially when the U.S. Government can't even get 33 percent of the population to vote in the presidential election," said True.

Some students were pleased with the electronic ballots, citing its convenience as the primary benefit. "I definitely prefer e-mail to having to stand in line and sit down somewhere. It will make me more likely to vote in the future," explained San Bretheim, a second-year student in the College.

"It was an easy, quick, convenient, and seemingly accurate way to vote," said first-year student in the College Aiko Onishi.

However, others were put off by the impersonal tone of the ballot.

"The e-mail ballots didn't let me get to know the candidates," said Mennatallah Eltaki, first-year student in the College. "It was just some faceless e-mail so I abstained from voting altogether." ■

Innovation—and, more importantly, having an environment conducive to innovation—are hallmarks of highly competitive schools, where students are encouraged to flex their intellectual muscles to get things done in different ways. Students at the University of Chicago saw the need to generate more interest in student government, and they solved the problem in a new way. Similarly, journalism students at USC saw a niche and started their own magazine from scratch to fill it.

STUDENT MEDIA — USC STUDENTS START NEW CAMPUS MAGAZINE

By Claire Luna

DAILY TROJAN (Los Angeles, Calif.) 11/19/1998

Since the semester started in September, a group of about 25 students has spent day and night in a computer lab creating something with little more than $4,000 and a lot of energy.

Their creation, "Tommy" magazine, is named after the Trojan mascot of the students they wish to educate, enlighten and amuse.

"Tommy," available free on campus today, will attempt to bridge the gap between news and entertainment through in-depth, analytical investigative pieces as well as essays and reviews.

"USC hasn't had a forum for the kind of articles that appear in a magazine in the past," said "Tommy" founder Leif Strickland, a sophomore majoring in print journalism, regarding why he started the publication. "When I came to the university as a freshman, I really felt there was a void in the publications at USC. This year, I finally had the energy level to pull something like this off."

After discussing the idea with students in his newswriting class, Strickland found students who were also interested in starting a magazine as an alternative to working for a newspaper.

"We found we were more excited by the idea of starting our own publication than by working for one that already existed," said "Tommy" writer Eve Troeh, a junior majoring in print journalism and anthropology. "I think the staff shares the enthusiasm and the want for a challenge of doing something different than a daily newspaper.

"With a magazine, we can be more creative and take more risks and cover all the things that the Daily Trojan can't or doesn't have the time to cover," she said.

Strickland's main goal for "Tommy" is to make a publication that will be interesting and important to students.

"We'll be taking on any issues that are of relevance to USC and to students that have some sort of impact," he said, "everything from educational issues to financial issues."

"Tommy" creators say they intend to bridge the gap between USC and other universities across the country.

"We hope to compare USC to other schools and take a bigger view of how things are on other campuses, like meal plans and practical things like that," Troeh said. "We might get ideas for change and how things might be improved to bring the university up to par with all of the good things at other universities."

Some of "Tommy's" first topics include disabled access at the university and a profile of Topher Grace, a freshman at the university last year who took a semester off to star in "That '70s Show." ■

Theater students at highly competitive schools don't always take life so seriously. Sometimes they just want to have fun—and support a good cause. Students at prestigious schools may not be as involved with the community as those at big schools are, but they do get involved in life outside the ivy-covered walls in innovative ways. Members of Yale's Children's Theater figured out a way to have fun while generating money for their great organization, which reaches out to kids in the community in a "novel" way.

CHILDREN'S THEATER GROUP TUCKS-IN YALE U.

By Meghan Casey

YALE DAILY NEWS (New Haven, Conn.) 02/03/1999

Comfy in her Winnie the Pooh pajamas and snuggled in bed, Rebecca Goodman '00 read "Curious George" aloud to attentive freshman Taylor Krauss. Justin Vaughn '02, whose blue pajamas feature pictures of bacon and eggs sunny-side-up, listened closely.

No, this scene is not a case of Yale students cracking under midterm pressure. It is the Yale Children's Theater bringing much needed comfort to students about to crack under midterm pressure.

"After a good meal and a good pipe, George felt tired," Goodman read. "He went to bed right away."

"This story is a bit dated, when it was still okay to tell kids to smoke," she added.

Goodman, Krauss and Vaughn are all members of the Yale Children's Theater.

Kameron Flynn/*The Daily Northwestern*

Though the group's official mission is to "enrich the lives of New Haven children and their families" through theater performance and teaching, the Children's Theater also serves the Yale community with its tuck-ins fund raiser.

"Tuck-in" begins when two members of the Children's Theater arrive at a student's doorstep between the hours of 11 p.m. and 1:30 a.m. They come in their pajamas bearing cookies, milk and a storybook.

In sharing a children's story, the Children's Theater tries to "bring Yalies back into that wonder and amazement that is childhood," Goodman said.

Usually, someone purchases a tuck-in for an unsuspecting friend. The buyer is presented with a list of 50 to 60 children's books. This is a list of the books in Goodman's personal collection. It includes traditional favorites like

Dr. Seuss books as well as some less-familiar stories.

After indicating any preferences for a particular story, the buyer must also specify a time when his friend will be at home. The storytellers will arrive within 30 minutes of this time.

It is not a coincidence that tuck-ins go on sale so close to Valentine's Day.

Sold from Wednesday to Saturday of this week, the tuck-ins are delivered on Tuesday, Wednesday and Thursday of next week.

The Children's Theater started using tuck-ins as a fund raiser long before Goodman can remember. Sold for $2 each, the tuck-ins help to fund Children's Theater workshops and plays to benefit the New Haven community.

These theater workshops are held in 17 different locations, including psychiatric wards, libraries, and area schools during after-school hours.

In addition to weekly workshops on theater and Sunday story hours, the Children's Theater sponsors a yearly playwriting contest for local elementary school students. The finalists' entries are published by the Children's Theater.

The Children's Theater performs several of these plays as well as their own productions. This semester's first production, "The Little Prince," will open on campus at the end of February, then tour New Haven schools and libraries.

About 30 students participate in tucking-in their classmates. Many of these are affiliated with the Children's Theater, but others, according to Goodman, just decide to join in for the fun. They want "to share the joy of theater with Yalies," Krauss said. ∎

While highly competitive schools pride themselves on the diversity of their student populations, the truth is that members of minority groups often find it hard to fit in at these schools. Diversity has come more slowly at prestigious schools, and it's a fact that all who attend are aware of. Fortunately, highly competitive schools are now more mindful of the fact that to succeed they must accommodate their minority students. To do so, they are encouraging the formation of campuswide and nationwide cultural organizations. Now, more than ever, fledgling organizations like SASA, a nationwide cultural group, are finding homes at highly competitive schools.

SOUTH ASIAN STUDENTS ALLIANCE ORGANIZERS HOPE FOR LEGACY

By Michael Hope

DAILY NORTHWESTERN (Evanston, Ill.) 01/19/1999

Organizers of last weekend's South Asian Students Alliance are hoping that it has a lasting legacy in the form of a first-ever national students organization.

Of the more than 2,000 students from across the country who attended last weekend's national conference at Northwestern, 100 sat in on a representatives conference to organize a national SASA organization, said Aakash Shah, conference co-chairman.

The national SASA network would help raise public awareness of South Asian concerns among the public at large and increase communication among South Asian students, said senior Sonya Laroia, co-chairwoman for the SASA Representatives Conference.

"We're trying to nationalize the organization to make a broad national conference that is accessible all the time, whether it comes to political support or networking or speaking out against discrimination," said Shah, a senior.

The SASA conference is the largest student-run minority conference of its kind, but once-a-year meetings don't establish a strong permanent base for South Asians, Laroia said.

"We wanted to extend SASA beyond a once-a-year event," Laroia said. "With a national system, there will be activity and communication across the country that didn't exist before."

As a result of last weekend's planning, SASA representatives elected members to regional positions and hope to finalize details for a national network soon. Each region will hold its own yearly conference, although there will continue to be a national conference, such as the one held at NU this year.

Sophomore Vishal Vaid, the newly elected Midwest regional co-chair for the SASA National Network, said the Representatives Conference was very productive, but was slowed by the bureaucracy and official business common to many student groups.

"This conference was more issue-intensive than previous conferences," said Vaid. "We're going in the right direction, but there's still a lot of work that needs to be done."

Although some of the events of the conference had a high student turnout, such as the keynote address given to a standing-room-only crowd, other events such as the affirmative action discussion attracted smaller numbers, Vaid said.

Laroia said that this year's conference had a more successful educational focus than conferences have had in years past.

"Typically the SASA conference is seen as a party event with about 80 percent of the students going to the conference to see and meet other South Asians," Laroia said. "This year the events actually applied to what students were interested in so over half of the students attended the workshops, where it's usually only 30%."

Although Laroia said that there has been a lot of work that went into the conference this year, the organizers of the conference said their work had paid off.

"We've been working since May, and the conference took a lot of dedication, but the positive feedback from students we got made all the time and effort worthwhile," Laroia said. ∎

Nabarun Dasgupta/*The Daily Princetonian*

Although steeped in tradition, highly competitive schools attract plenty of students who want to change the world, as seen in the scores of highly competitive college students nationwide who rally for social equality and diversity awareness. PEACE is one such group.

POLITICAL GROUPS

NEW STUDENT GROUP BRINGS PEACE TO BROWN U.

Sumaiya Balbale

BROWN DAILY HERALD (Providence, R.I.) 12/02/1998

Lindsay Rosenfeld '00 has long been interested in pursuing social work.

In high school, she and David Neil, a senior at Vassar College, decided they wanted to start a program to educate young kids about different communities. They called it PEACE (Promoting Equality And Community Everywhere).

PEACE has spread its branches to Taiwan, Japan, Israel, Canada, and India and across college campuses to Yale, Vassar, Wesleyan, Washington University, University of Alabama, and now, Brown.

As of October, Brown began its very own chapter of PEACE. Almost two months later, it boasts 30 members.

"We wanted to continue the work we had done in high school," said Rosenfeld of the project. "We felt there was a need to bridge the gap between different communities."

PEACE, according to its mission statement, "is an international movement created and led by young people, devoted to establishing new modes of thinking and ways of living around the world." The organization attempts to address issues of discrimination, prejudice, hatred, and coexistence, said Rosenfeld.

So far, PEACE has organized a Mentoring Program at several Providence elementary schools. Eight PEACE mentors helped students at the private Robert Bailey Elementary School and the public Mary Fogarty

Elementary school begin a letter writing program between the two schools.

The program "helps improve literacy skills and allows second graders to come in contact with other kids their age that they would have otherwise never met" said Rosenfeld.

PEACE members also are working on the PEACE Community Awareness Symposium at Brown for Black History Month in February. The Sympo-sium hopes to "bridge the conversation between Brown and the greater community" said Rosenfeld.

"The purpose of the symposium is to create safe spaces for dialogue and to raise awareness of and confront pressing local, national, and global issues ranging from social inequalities to hate crimes, from religious conflicts to sexism," she said. "The events of the symposium will reflect the experiences, concerns, and suggestions of people from diverse backgrounds." ■

Another way that concerned students at highly competitive university campuses get involved is through volunteering. Despite the intense academic demands that rest on their shoulders, prestigious school students give freely of their time for worthwhile causes. At Boston University, several young men learned a lesson outside the classroom through the Big Brothers organization.

VOLUNTEERISM

BOSTON U. STUDENTS TAKE ON BIG ROLE IN KIDS' LIVES

Tracey Sharp

THE DAILY FREE PRESS (Boston, Mass.) 11/19/1998

Lei Zuo knows how it feels to be alone.

The College of Engineering junior moved to Massachusetts from China when he was 12. He didn't know anyone and didn't speak the language.

"I'm an only child, and I had to move away from all of my friends," Zuo says.

Eight years later, Zuo speaks flawless English and spends some of his spare time with 11-year-old Benjamin "Benty" Turner, his "little brother."

Zuo is one of 600 Big Brothers in Boston and 10 at Boston University who spend a few hours each week with fatherless boys.

"Hanging out with my little brother is like being a kid again," Zuo says.

College of Arts and Sciences senior Rishi Parekh, another Big Brother, agrees.

"We've done just about everything: movies, parks, Duck Tours, everything," Parekh says of his little brother Victor. "But the best times are spent just walking and talking together."

It costs virtually nothing to be a Big Brother, and the rewards are immeasurable, Zuo and Parekh say.

"A year ago we were out walking," Zuo says," and Benty looked up at me and said, 'Lei, we learned about you in school today—we learned about role models.' "

On Saturday, Zuo and Benty played Frisbee, basketball and Nintendo. The day wasn't competitive, though Benty won a Nintendo football game 42–16.

"All it takes is a couple hours, a couple times a month, to really make a difference in a young boy's life," says Len Urso, recruitment and marketing coordinator at the Big Brother Association of Greater Boston.

"We're looking for BU students to provide positive role models," says Urso, a BU graduate and a Big Brother himself.

The Big Brother Association hopes to reduce the two-year wait for potential little brothers by recruiting more volunteers, particularly minority men, since more than half of the boys served are minorities.

The organization hopes to boost its total volunteers to 2,000 by 2002, Urso says.

"For nearly two years, Benty's younger brother didn't have a Big Brother," Zuo says. "He just got one a few months ago and he's so much happier.

"We learn a lot from each other," he says. "I go to a Korean church and his is African American, so we visited each other's and learned about our different cultures." ■

It's true that there's a certain degree of seriousness involved in life at a highly competitive school. Student groups are no exception. You've read how students at prestigious schools from Boston to Chicago to Los Angeles take campus organizations and volunteering very seriously. In everything they do, these over-achievers strive to be groundbreakers, to be the best, in and out of the classroom.

But sometimes the crème de la crème needs to let loose and do something out of the ordinary—or just plain silly. If you're the adventurous type, don't think that your life will be buttoned-down at a prestigious school. If you attend the University of Chicago, you can even jump out of an airplane (that is, if you want to).

SOCIAL CLUBS

U. CHICAGO STUDENTS TAKE TO OFFBEAT SPORTS CLUBS

By Joe Burnett

CHICAGO MAROON (Chicago, Ill.) 01/30/1998

There are two reasons for joining the Sky Diving club; the club advertises its members as people "with the moxie to jump out of a perfectly good airplane at 13,000 feet above the ground." The club was founded by Paul Heeringa, a member of the College's class of '97. Members of the club jump at Skydive Chicago, the oldest and largest drop-zone in the country. According to Roger Nolson, the program director at the drop-zone, the club comes once a month with as many as 25 students, mostly first-timers.

The most common way to get cleared to jump is tandem jumping. By jumping attached to a "tandem master," you need only 15–45 minutes of ground training before diving into a 30 second free fall and landing under a huge parachute.

For those afraid of having their last look at earth be at a high speed and a small distance, the safety of sky diving has been improved drastically since the days of military surplus gear. Parachutes are made of light-weight, extremely strong materials, and jump zones have high-tech emergency assistance technology.

For students with a sense of adventure whose budgets are a little closer to earth, there is the Outdoor Adventure Club (OAC).

The OAC is not limited to one particular sport. Instead, trips of all kinds are planned to fit the desires of the members of the club and others. Club President Courtney Hemphill said the main appeal of the club for herself and others is "meeting people with the drive to get out of the city." Apparently, many students see this as an attractive option.

The OAC owns tents, snowshoes, sleeping bags, packs, ropes, harnesses, and other gear which it lends out to members of the club. It also plans group outings, mostly for rock climbing, mountain biking, cross-country skiing, and hiking and camping trips.

For those students who prefer more personal, antiquated forms of adventure, the fencing club is one of the few inter-collegiate clubs on campus. The fencing club originated from the University's NCAA Division I Varsity Fencing Team, which was disbanded three years ago. The team boasted Olympians and national team members early in the century, as well all-Americans more recently.

The sport of fencing goes much deeper than "playing with swords." In the words of President Merrick Sheaffer, "It is a problem solving game." Others have referred to fencing as chess at 100 miles-per-hour.

There are three categories of fencing competition, each one based on a different weapon: Epee, Foil, and Sabre. Scoring is based on hits on various areas of the body and scored by electronic sensors on the sword and the duelists outfits.

Sarah E. Hendrickson/*The Harvard Crimson*

Fencers are not often injured. "Like, once a year someone's sword snaps and a kid gets stabbed," said Sheaffer, "but other than that remote danger, there is little room for harm. These swords are very flexible and dull, and the masks are tested before every meet."

Sheaffer also heads up the University Footbag Club. Footbag, also known as hackey-sack, shares nothing in common with any of the preceding clubs. However, it complements them perfectly. While most of the incentive to join the other clubs is some sort of "rush" or intense activity, footbag is all about "kickin' back."

That is not to say that there are no competitive footbaggers out there. In fact, it is one of the fastest growing sports in the nation. Illinois is home to 24 footbag clubs and some southern colleges have two separate clubs.

Sheaffer sees a lack of interest at the U of C in the competitive angle to the game. This seems to suit him and those involved. There is no permanent membership, only an e-mail list. Once or twice in the spring, the number two player in the world, Scott Davidson, comes down from his home on the North Side to kick with the club.

For those questioning the appeal of kicking a cloth ball filled with beads, Sheaffer sights the fact that it is easy to learn, you can learn some cool tricks quickly, and it's a great way to relax. To Sheaffer, the advantage of footbag over other sports is that "you can play it anywhere, anytime. You don't need any money and the equipment fits in your pocket." ∎

Maybe your idea of extracurricular fun doesn't involve sports of any kind, not even hackey-sack. If so, you still can find a way to be out-of-the-ordinary at a highly competitive school. No one says you have to be an intellectual elitist to fit in at a prestigious school. Just ask the members of UPenn's COTE club, for example.

PENN STUDENTS START CLUB TO REMEMBER 1980s

By Amara Levine

DAILY PENNSYLVANIAN (Philadelphia, Penn.) 09/28/1998

The recent celebration of 1980s pop culture in America—from last year's hit Adam Sandler movie *The Wedding Singer* to the emergence of '80s theme nights at local dance clubs—has spread to Penn's campus with the founding of the Children of the Eighties club.

College freshman Adam Sussman officiated at the gathering of about a dozen students, introducing himself to the attendants of the meeting as "founder of the COTE club and a proud child of 1980." His claim to fame, he said, is that he and singer Debbie Gibson had the same orthodontist.

Sussman hopes that the leadership board, to be elected at the next COTE meeting, will help him organize events focusing on '80s culture appreciation. Suggestions for such events included movie theme nights, such as the "Brat Pack" or Molly Ringwald, karaoke night, an '80s dance party and pop culture trivia night.

A loyal Kevin Bacon fan, Sussman posed the idea of holding a "Bacon fest" featuring many of the actor's earlier films. A "Six Degrees of Kevin Bacon" tournament is in the works as well, based on the game that tries to link all actors back to Bacon through his many movies.

The meeting concluded with a short reminiscing session where everyone shared his or her favorite '80s pop-culture memory.

"Definitely Rainbow Brite and She-Ra, princess of power," College freshman Caroline O'Reilly said. "I had all the toys and whatnot that came with them."

Tina Turner's "What's Love Got To Do With It?" was Engineering and Wharton freshman Eileen McCarthy's favorite memory.

"Joan Collins and Linda Evans duking it out," said Dental School freshman Elli Saba in reference to the prime-time soap opera "Dynasty." "Classic television."

"The Wonder Years" was definitely the greatest show, he said. "I also love . . . "The Goonies," "Saved by the Bell," and "Thundercats.""

When students interested in the COTE club asked for a phone number at which to contact Sussman, a smile burst across his face.

"I had hoped to get 7-5309," he explained, referring to the Tommy Tutone hit single "867-5309 (Jenny)."

He settled, instead, for the number assigned to him by the school. ∎

Does it surprise you that sports are an important part of life at highly competitive schools? While their teams may not get the recognition, or national television coverage, that teams at big state schools do, highly competitive schools still field teams in every sport imaginable. Harvard has 32 varsity teams, from men's baseball and soccer to women's fencing and volleyball.

Loyalty to the team is often more important than the performance of the team itself at a prestigious school. Die-hard fans cheer their team on through good times and bad, and some prestigious school teams have had a lot of good times. Any college basketball fan knows about the Duke team, which has made it to the Final Four seven times since 1988, winning twice. At Duke, being a loyal fan—aka Cameron Crazy—is a status symbol in itself, as "Camping out in 'K-Ville' at Duke U." describes. And as with more aspects of highly competitive school life, tradition and history define athletic competition. While the Cameron Crazies and tent dwellers are well on their way to beginning a new tradition in Durham, the football teams at Harvard and Yale, as you'll read in "Harvard-Yale Goes Back a Long Way, Baby," have 124 years of tradition under their belts.

CAMPING OUT IN 'K-VILLE' AT DUKE U.

By Katherine Stroup

THE CHRONICLE (Durham, N.C.) 02/18/1998

The rain that had been falling for days had finally stopped, and for the first time in nearly a week, students at the campout were expected to spend the night in their tents.

As the students hastily repack their belongings, the grumbling begins: "I can't believe they didn't grant a grace period," or, "I stayed out here all night and not a single tent check!"

New students come to take over, and the still-weary overnighters depart, trudging through the mud back to their dormitory rooms. For them, this is not just any morning in K-ville: This is judgment day, the day to survey the sprawl of nylon that has become their home, and ask themselves: "Is it worth it?"

Ask any student this question, even on the coldest or wettest of nights, and the answer is almost always the same: "I do it because I want to be a part of K-ville, part of a Duke tradition."

But these fans might be surprised to learn that tenting is a relatively new phenomenon.

"Tenting" as the University now knows it didn't begin until the 1981 arrival of basketball coach Mike Krzyzewski, who would go on to become the NCAA

Tournament's winningest active coach and whose teams would capture the 1991 and 1992 national championships. Even then, however, tenting existed only on a much smaller scale.

Nowadays, however, the bustling metropolis that currently exists in front of Cameron bears little resemblance to the pre-1990 campout sites. The campout seems to grow in both duration and size every year.

"Once the first person puts up their tent, that's it—everyone has to," says Kevin McGinnis, a 1996 graduate and a former K-ville head line monitor for Duke Student Government. "And, every year, 10 more students come to the University who are a bit more crazy than the previous class."

Many past students also argue that the University's increasing national academic ranking may be contributing to the current flare-up of tenting enthusiasm.

As McGinnis explains: "I think there's definitely this attitude of, 'I'll show you; we're taking organic chemistry, but we also have to sit in a tent for weeks on end.'"

It is exactly this kind of blind enthusiasm that has secured Duke a slot in sports lore.

"As a [high school] senior, I always knew that, if I came to Duke, there'd be the fans, there'd be people staying in tents, enduring windstorms and rainstorms to see you play," says freshman Shane Battier, forward on the men's basketball team. "Really, the fabled Cameron Crazies have legendary status across the country."

Battier acknowledges that Krzyzewskiville plays a part in the recruiting process. Mainly, he says, the tent city serves as a continual reminder that, every time a player dons his white Duke jersey, he's going to be playing in front of a sold-out crowd.

Beyond the recruiting process, however, the fans clearly have an influence upon the players who choose to come to the University.

"The fans have a huge impact," asserts Trinity senior Steve Wojciechowski, co-captain of the men's basketball team. "We have a few more home games to go, and we'll really need [the fans] then. But they've been great all season, in terms of coming out for every game. And I certainly don't expect anything less for the last few games."

When asked to speculate upon the Krzyzewskiville faithfuls' motivations, Battier seems unwilling to unnecessarily examine a good thing.

"Tenting?" Battier asks, preparing to launch into one of his trademark quotes. "Only at Duke. I don't know why that is. I really can't explain it, and I really don't want to explain it. It's just wonderful." ∎

HARVARD-YALE GOES BACK A LONG WAY, BABY
Robert B. Davis & Vasant M. Kamath

HARVARD CRIMSON (Cambridge, Mass.) 11/19/1998

As long as anyone can remember, the traditional Harvard rival has always been the snarling Yale Bulldog with his contemptuous stare. Lately that bulldog has been strangely silent, the result of a general dominance in football over the last few years.

This Saturday the Harvard Crimson hope to extend that dominance in the 115th Harvard-Yale Football Game. A win would mean a victory for the fourth time in a row. The last time either team has won more than 3 games in a row? 1947, when Yale won its fourth straight game. The teams did not play in 1943 and 1944 because of World War II.

The Harvard-Yale football match-up dates back to November 13, 1875, when the Crimson first defeated the Bulldogs 4-0 at Hamilton Field in New Haven. The first game was played under rugby rules.

In every season since 1898 except one (1919) Yale has been Harvard's final opponent of the football season.

Currently, Yale leads the series 61-45-8. The Game, as it is better known amongst those familiar with the rivalry, has had its share of memorable moments for both sides, though.

In 1894 The Game was so violent that the seven players had to be carried of the field, said to be in serious condition. The Bulldogs were victorious, winning 12-4; the schools postponed the series for two years.

Victor Chang/*The Chronicle*

In his pep talk before the game in 1908, legend has it that Crimson mentor Percy Haughton choked a bulldog to death with his bare hands and then tossed it at the feet of his players. Though it is just a legend, Harvard did shut out Yale, 4-0.

In 1915 the Crimson rolled, blanking the Bulldogs 41-0 to establish the team's greatest margin of victory ever.

Famous alumni also have left their mark on the game's history.

Massachusetts senior Senator Edward (Ted) M. Kennedy '54-56 caught the team's only touchdown pass in the 1955 contest, a 21-7 loss.

In perhaps the most famous game in series history, Harvard rallied from a 22-0 deficit, 22-6 at halftime, to "defeat" the Bulldogs 29-22. The Crimson scored 16 points in the game's final 42 seconds. Former NFL star Calvin Hill played halfback for Yale while movie star Tommy Lee Jones '69 was an All-Ivy defensive tackle for Harvard that year.

Harvard twice spoiled Yale's bid for a perfect season.

In 1974, a 95-yard touchdown in the final minutes gave the Crimson a 21-16 victory, and in 1979, the Crimson once again pulled a stunning 22-7 upset victory at the Yale Bowl.

In 1982, an M.I.T. prank briefly interrupted the game when a large black weather balloon with the letters M.I.T. painted across it landed on the 45-yard line. The balloon rose, inflated, and then exploded. Unfazed by the prank, Harvard went on to trounce Yale 45-7.

In the 100th contest in 1983, Harvard wrapped up a share of the Ivy League championship by defeating host Yale 16-7.

Last year Harvard finished a brilliant year—including an undefeated season in the Ivy League (7-0) by knocking out Yale in New Haven, 17-7. It was the Crimson's first perfect Ivy League season in history. ■

Paul S. Gutman/*The Harvard Crimson*

GREEK LIFE

You can see that athletics are a big deal at some highly competitive colleges, like Duke, and not quite so important at others. The same could also be said of Greek organizations. Highly competitive colleges have widely varying policies and attitudes when it comes to the Greek system. Harvard will not allow any Greek activity on its campus at all. At MIT, Dartmouth, and Northwestern, the Greek system is very strong and involves a large percentage of the student body. Because Greek organizations generally involve smaller numbers of students when they do exist at prestigious colleges, administrators find it easier to keep alcohol-related incidents like those described in the Big State Schools chapter to a minimum.

Problems with alcohol and Greeks do arise, however, at prestigious schools. Just last year, a fraternity pledge at MIT died while drinking. Perhaps in light of this and other tragic events, the Dartmouth Board of Trustees voted early in 1999 to "end the Greek system on campus as we know it." The Dartmouth story made big news in college circles. The history and traditions of Greeks at Dartmouth go back 150 years and mean a lot to many students and alumni. Predictably, students at the school protested this drastic change loudly. A 600-student protest march and rally that interrupted the Winter Carnival opening cermony, one of Dartmouth's most famous traditions, seemed to set the stage for future conflict. Now that the dust has settled, however, it seems as though most of Dartmouth, in particular the editors of *The Dartmouth*, have begun to look at the issue as an opportunity for growth, not dissention.

DARTMOUTH TRUSTEES TO END SINGLE-SEX GREEK SYSTEM
By Jacob T. Elberg

THE DARTMOUTH (Hanover, N.H.) 02/10/1999

In what will mark the most significant change at Dartmouth College since coeducation, the Board of Trustees and College President James Wright announced yesterday a plan which will put an end to the single-sex fraternity and sorority system which has existed at the College for more than 150 years.

The Board—which yesterday released a revolutionary list of five principles aimed at overhauling residential and social life at the College—will look for input from the community before deciding on a new social system "that's not built on single-sex houses."

Wright said both he and the Trustees are prepared to weather the student and alumni opposition they expect will result from the decision, which will change the face of social and residential life on a campus where more than 35

Danya-Pincayage/*The Dartmouth*

percent of undergraduates are members of the 25 single-sex fraternities and sororities.

"This is not a referendum on these things," Wright said. "We are committed to doing this."

In addition to a call for a social system which is "substantially coeducational and provide[s] opportunities for greater interaction among all Dartmouth students," the Trustees said they will seek significant changes to the College's residential system and improvement of campus social space when they released their statement of "five principles that will characterize the future residential and social life of students at the College."

The Trustees are prepared to spend "tens of millions of dollars" to finance the social and residential life changes, according to Wright, who said the College will hope to purchase and refurbish the houses of the Greek organizations who currently live in privately owned buildings.

"The Trustees are giving students the opportunity to reimagine social life and residential life at the College," Wright said. "And the Trustees are prepared to invest money to meet [their] aspirations."

Wright, who is known for his interest in and knowledge of the College's history, said the Trustees' social and residential life initiative will be the biggest change the College has seen since the Trustees voted to admit women in November of 1971.

"[Coeducation] would be the only thing that's happened here that probably would exceed this in terms of effecting the quality of the student experience at Dartmouth," Wright said. "And there definitely is no doubt in my mind that eight or 10 years from now the quality of the student experience as a result of these things will be far stronger than it is today."

Wright remarked that the current fraternity and sorority system is not one of inclusion—making a dramatic initiative such as this one necessary.

"By definition, a fraternity or a sorority is not inclusive of all members of the community," Wright said. "Finally Dartmouth needs to become a place that's more whole, where the entire community can share more fully in the life of the community."

Wright declined to comment on what he envisions for the future of the College's social system, but said that despite the Trustees' call to eliminate "the abuse and unsafe use of alcohol," neither he nor the members of the Board have any inclinations of making Dartmouth a "dry campus."

"I wouldn't even fantasize how to make a dry campus here," he said. ∎

EDITORIAL: THE WRIGHT OVERHAUL?
Staff Editorial

THE DARTMOUTH (Hanover, N.H.) 02/10/1999

We often hear people talking about the problems of the Greek system, but it is rare that these problems are defined. It seems that, ironically, the biggest problem with the Greek system is its own success. Members of Greek houses are strongly loyal to their letters, and Greek parties are the most highly attended social events on campus. The houses give members an intangible sense of contentment and belonging that only Greeks can fully understand.

The Greek system has come to dominate social life so thoroughly that in doing so it has created two major problems on campus. One is that there are no other mainstream social options readily available, and the other is that it has created an alienated portion of the community that feels as though they have been relegated to the fringe of College life. This is not right, and it is for the best that the College tries to remedy the situation.

Their proclamation today consisted of at the very least making Greek organizations coeducational, and perhaps doing away with them all together. The administration has wiped clean the proverbial Greek slate, but has presented no real plan for future social life at Dartmouth other than the vague idyllic principles laid out in the statement by the Board of Trustees. While bold, it seems that the social atmosphere they seek would not be achieved by this move.

The policy of coeducation will not truly address the problem that most people recognize first in the flaws of our current system. This is the fragmentation of the College into groups. Whether it is along racial or athletic lines, students here associate with those who are most like themselves, and coed houses would be no different. More problems exist between these fractured groups than do between females and males. The administration must acknowledge that the true solution to student social deficiencies lies somewhere beyond coeducation of Greek organizations.

There seems to be no turning back for the administration now. It was President of the College Jim Wright who said, "This is not a referendum on these things. We are committed to doing this."

It is a shame that the administration felt that they needed to surprise the student body with this news, and a shame that changes and improvements in the Greek system couldn't have taken a more gradual evolutionary shape. But despite this apparent lack of consideration toward student feelings, the situation that is forced upon us now also presents us with an opportunity to take all the best of our current social system and improve upon it however we can.

What we as students do now to shape social life at Dartmouth will affect life at the College forever, and we must weigh that responsibility heavily as we evaluate our system and the choices that confront us. The President and the Trustees have committed the College to funding a major overhaul of student life. We have tens of millions of dollars at our disposal to make this school into what we want. This is one chance and our time. We had better make it count. ∎

DARTMOUTH COLLEGE
Hanover, NH
The Dartmouth

By Jake Elberg

On the first night of Homecoming weekend, upperclassmen gather around the Green at the center of campus to look on as a thousand freshmen sprint around a 60-foot high stack of burning wood, better known as the Homecoming bonfire. The freshmen battle the heat of the flames and change direction as dictated by the upperclassmen as they try to run around the inferno enough times to match the final two digits of their year of graduation. Many run shirtless, or wearing even less, protected from the New Hampshire cold not only by the flames, but by more than a century of tradition.

Giulia Good Stefani/*The Dartmouth*

It seems that highly competitive schools have been experiencing their fair share of controversy these days. Because change often comes slowly at these schools, who pride themselves on tradition, any radical move can disrupt life on campus.

Interesting Speakers

Sometimes, however, students at highly competitive schools like to be shaken up, to have their ideals challenged and hear other sides of the story. The three speakers described here all invite healthy debate, whether over race, gender, or, in the case of Jerry Springer, just about anything.

NAACP PRESIDENT ADDRESSES APPRECIATIVE TUFTS U. CROWD

By Daniel Barbarisi

Tufts Daily (Medford, Mass.) 11/17/1998

Utilizing a spirited and powerful oratory to pound home his views on the place and role of African-Americans in the U.S. of today, Kweisi Mfume, president and CEO of the National Association for the Advancement of Colored People (NAACP) drew ovation after ovation from an appreciative crowd in a packed Cohen Auditorium last Thursday night.

In a wide-ranging speech touching on affirmative action programs, the situation of African-American students at Tufts, discrimination in American history, and the recent work of the NAACP, Mfume challenged both the white and black communities to work toward equal rights and equal opportunity for all.

"I hope, and I pray, that those of you who are seated here in this audience who by virtue of your birth or by virtue of your genetic cloth, happen to be characterized as white or Caucasian," Mfume said, "that you will understand the indignity of some of us who are not, at the scourge of racism, bigotry, and second class citizenship—and that you, in your own way, will become just as indignant."

Mfume then continued along those same lines, saying that, "I hope and pray also that those of you who . . . happen to be of African ancestry, that you

understand, as we must, the real need, at some point in time, to get beyond blame, to get beyond excuses, and to once again start doing for ourselves."

Mfume recounted his recent experiences as president of the NAACP, a position he has held since resigning from Congress in 1996. Telling the audience of the group's recent success in holding marches, protests, demonstrations, and in disseminating information by "congressional report cards" and other means, Mfume urged the audience to combat injustice in all forms, from an individual uttering a racial slur to discriminative practices in the offices of the Supreme Court.

"Unless we challenge what is wrong in society, we have failed in our duty as students of democracy," Mfume said.

Following the close of his speech, Mfume opened up the microphone to questions from the audience. Junior Amol Sharma brought up to Mfume the question of instituting the proposed new class on bigotry and intolerance, asking for his comments and advice.

"My first thought is that it's revolutionary, because if it's done right, it can help to cure a lot of problems of perception," Mfume said. "You want me to recommend it to your university?" Mfume asked the body while motioning to University President John DiBiaggio, seated on the main stage. "I'll do it right now. So moved."

Junior Lauren Kadi questioned Mfume, who had previously spoken of his activist collegiate career, on how Tufts' students can make their voice better heard, especially on issues of financial aid and diversity.

"We reject students who can't afford to go here," Kadi stated. "What is your advice—how do we make our voices count?"

Mfume responded by saying that a constant dialogue, and an interplay of ideas, were needed.

"One of the first things you do is engage the ideas, and talk about them like you're doing now. In the absence of a confrontation of ideas, you really don't have much to lean on, and you don't have anyone to blame. It's only through the confrontation of ideas and dialogue that you're able to broker change," Mfume concluded. ∎

FEMINIST BETTY FRIEDAN DISCUSSES CHANGING ROLES OF WOMEN WITH CORNELL U. STUDENTS

By Missy Globerman

CORNELL DAILY SUN (Ithaca, N.Y.) 12/04/1998

Betty Friedan, the woman who practically launched the feminist movement in the United States in 1963 with the publication of 'The Feminine Mystique,' is on campus for two days to discuss whether America needs "a values revolution."

In a panel discussion yesterday afternoon in Ives Hall, Friedan spoke about the changing role of women in today's workplace and in family responsibilities.

In her commentary, Friedan emphasized that American society's consciousness about women in the workplace is lagging. "Women are still defending their right to be working, but the reality is that half of the workforce is made up of women," she said. Discussing research on the role of working mothers, Friedan said "the dialogue about women in the workplace needs to move beyond its supposed detrimental effects on children, simply because it is not always accurate."

"Research also shows that children can be benefited by mothers working outside of the home, but no one talks about that," she added.

She said women are such an integral part of the workforce and are now earning as many professional degrees as men, yet men are still in the top leadership positions. "The male template for career advancement needs to be re-examined," she said.

Friedan supports a new standard called the "quality of life measure" that she said she hopes will be as important as the Gross Domestic Product measure. "There needs to be bolder thinking on how to measure the quality of life of women and men in the work force," Friedan said.

"Currently, success is measured by material advancements. . . . We need to read just the definition of success to account for time outside of work and satisfaction with life, not just the dollars-and-cents bottom line," she said.

Friedan is one of the world's foremost spokespersons on women's rights. She founded both the National Organization for Women (NOW) and the National Women's Political Caucus. She played a key role at Cornell in 1972 in launching the first women's studies courses in the United States.

Friedan joined the Cornell faculty as distinguished visiting professor in the School of Industrial and Labor Relations (ILR) in April to direct a $1 million, four-year project in ILR's Institute for Women and Work. The Institute is a nationally known research and education center for the study of workplace and gender issues.

The Washington D.C. based project, "New Paradigm: Women, Men, Work, Family, and Public Policy," is supported by a generous grant from the Ford Foundation, where a series of monthly symposia and other activities are under way. ∎

SPRINGER TACKLES A RANGE OF TOPICS AT NORTHWESTERN U.

By Michael Hope

THE DAILY NORTHWESTERN (Evanston, Ill.) 02/03/1999

Introduced as the "most controversial person on television today," Jerry Springer stepped on to the Pick-Staiger Concert Hall stage Tuesday to thunderous applause and calls of "Jerry, Jerry!"

Springer, a 1968 graduate of Northwestern Law School, spoke for an hour to nearly 1,000 people as part of the weekly Medill School of Journalism lecture series.

Springer, who spoke for free, sat on stage with Medill Dean Ken Bode and talked about his talk show, his 10 years as a television journalist in Cincinnati and his thoughts on the media's invasion of privacy.

"News exploits people," Springer said. "Journalists need to ask themselves 'Is it worth ruining people's lives?' People always say 'The public has a right to know.' We have a need to know if we're involved in a war, or if the water has been polluted. We don't need to know what Bill Clinton did with a cigar."

Springer has called his show the most stupid show on television, but he said the outrageous show doesn't claim to be anything but entertainment.

"I'm hired to conduct a circus, but it's fun." Springer said. "I'm not going to apologize for what I do. I enjoy my job."

Attendance at the speech suggested Springer is not

Justin Jones/*The Daily Egyptian*

the only one who enjoys the television show. Ratings for "The Jerry Springer Show" have climbed during its eight-year run, briefly surpassing even "The Oprah Winfrey Show" last year.

"It's an escape," Springer said. "It's outrageous. It's an hour a day to unwind with."

Last year, Springer was asked by the Chicago NBC affiliate, WMAQ-TV, to offer commentaries for the evening news. Two anchors with the station resigned in protest. Springer then gave up his commentary position.

"I now rent myself out to companies who want to downsize," Springer quipped.

During the speech, Springer said his show is a true democracy that brings people from all backgrounds to talk about various issues facing the country.

Responding to charges that his show is trash, Springer said it is unfair to characterize his guests as trashy. Rather, Springer said his guests represent a more realistic cross-section of the society.

"Just because they don't speak the Queen's English or go to the right schools, all of a sudden they're trash?" Springer asked.

One student asked Springer if he thought his education had been wasted now that he is a talk show host.

"I don't get any intellectual stimulation from this

job," Springer said. "But let's be honest. I don't think I would get more intellectual challenge from being a dentist, either."

Some audience members said they went to the speech to see if Jerry Springer, the person, was similar to Jerry Springer, the talk show host.

"I knew he was very intellectual because of his background, but you don't get that insight when he's on the show," said Tracey Wilkinson, a freshman. "He doesn't have to be that way on television."

Some students said they were pleased to see Medill host a speaker who is not a typical journalist.

"It helped Medill to bring him, because they didn't look as elitist as they sometimes do," said Hazeen Ashby, a sophomore. "Sometimes Medill seems like it's filled with people who can't empathize with the people they cover." ∎

LIFE ON Campus

From the outside, it's easy to speculate about what it must be like to attend a highly competitive college. All those brilliant minds converging in one place. All that money. All that power. The mystique surrounding prestigious colleges is part of our culture; we've stood in awe of these schools for hundreds of years. So before you even step on campus, you might think you have an idea of what it will be like there. And you're probably pretty intimidated by it. How can you possibly measure up to all of that? What you'll find, however, is that life at a highly competitive college is a lot more "normal" than you'd imagined. There's no denying that the facilities and faculty are superb, that a lot of money will be on display, and that you'll be part of cherished traditions that go back centuries. All of this will be palpable on campus, and you'll probably feel a lot of pressure. But if you're accepted at a prestigious school, don't forget that the other students there will be kids just like you—kids who want to learn, grow, and have fun.

One thing you'll all have in common is the amount of money your family spent (or borrowed) to get you there. Yearly tuition at highly competitive colleges can top $30,000. That's more than a large percentage of American families earn. What's ironic, however, is that most of these schools offer fabulous scholarship and financial aid packages that can help deserving students and their families defray some or all of these costs. For example, Vanderbilt University offers more than 90 honor scholarships and awards, most for full tuition, each year. In the 1997–1998 year, the total amount of financial aid awarded to Cornell University students was more than $133 million; over 60 percent of Cornell students received financial aid. "Quest to best each other's financial aid hits the Ivies" describes how even the most expensive of the highly competitive colleges, the Ivy Leagues, compete with each other to offer amazing financial aid packages to attract top-notch students to their campuses.

In gathering together the best students they can, highly competitive colleges also focus on ensuring diversity in their student populations. You'll find that even though these schools are small, they will be home to myriad ethnic, racial, and religious groups. You'll read here about Yale's support for Native American students, Northwestern's efforts to bring together straight and gay students, Penn's and Yale's struggles with religion, and Stanford's attempts to combat bad press regarding gender. While some schools' admissions policies regarding minority status have come under fire, particularly in light of the recent trend away from affirmative action, the efforts that highly competitive colleges make to guarantee a place for qualified applicants—regardless of income, race, religion, physical challenge, sexual orientation, or gender—are laudable. Highly competitive colleges also feature innovative housing arrangements, such as the coed dorms described in "Vandy gives go ahead on coed dorms," theme dorms, and other novel arrangements that encourage student interaction.

In making room for students of all types, highly competitive colleges have established excellent services to make your years there less intimidating and more successful. According to a 1998 article in the *New York Post*, the security department at Tufts University makes it one of the safest universities in the entire country. At MIT, which some may consider male-dominated, special forums like those discussed in "Women shown how to adjust to MIT" make women feel more comfortable. Career information is given particular emphasis at highly competitive universities; although the column included from the *Harvard Crimson* points out that the types of opportunities for employment could be diversified, the fact is that students at prestigious colleges have a wealth of career resources to draw upon. Students' health and well-being are also of prime importance, and should students find a service niche to be filled, they often take it upon themselves to do so, with the support of the school, as you'll read in "Northwestern U. students establish eating disorder support network."

In other words, administrators at highly competitive colleges want to make sure that their students are happy. They are well aware of the pressure you'll be under, and they'll work with you to make sure you have nothing to worry about—other than your studies, that is. They'll even help you unwind after a long week. "Beer trucks earn duke U. funding support" highlights one prestigious school's approach to partying on campus. Duke students and administrators found that, by working together, they could allow alcohol on campus but still keep alcohol-related problems to a minimum. If you're a teetotaler, plenty of non-alcohol-related events like the ones featured here from Cornell, Columbia, Brown, and Harvard will surely be able to divert you from your studies for just a little while.

Prestige

The aura of a highly competitive school is the product of many factors. First, everybody who's there knows how hard it was to get in and how competitive they'll need to be to rise to the top of the heap, given the academic rigor of the coursework. There's also no secret about how much this education is costing the students (and their parents), and the campuses themselves exude money. Because the outside world values this type of education highly, employers willing to pay you big bucks will flock to hire you upon graduation. And when you graduate you'll be connected to thousands of successful alumni through tradition and history. All of these endow students at highly competitive schools with a sense of prestige.

Of course you'll feel privileged; you should. Highly competitive colleges are a revered part of our culture. It's a big deal to be accepted at a highly competitive college, and an even bigger one to graduate. When you graduate you'll become part of the history and tradition that has made your school what it is. But remember that traditions change, even at highly competitive colleges, albeit more slowly. This is something that prestigious university alumni, like those at Brown, have had to come to grips with, especially in recent years.

BROWN U. DEEMED 'TOO LIBERAL TO DONATE MONEY' BY OLDER ALUMNI

By Helen Willard

BROWN DAILY HERALD (Providence, R.I.) 12/7/1998

When the February 1995 issue of the Brown Alumni Monthly (BAM) featured a tattooed Brown student on the cover and a picture of a co-ed room inside, plenty of older alumni got upset.

"I now regard Brown only as a cultural sewer emptying polluted product into mainstream America," wrote Frederick Fordon '55 in response. "I sorrow deeply for what was and is no more."

Another alum responded to a "60 Minutes" report talking about Brown courses on homosexual and lesbian issues.

Alfred I. Miranda '46 decided to stop donating to Brown until the University stopped including courses taught by gay or lesbian faculty.

"If the Brown administration will notify me when and if such courses have been discontinued, I will at that time resume my contributions via annual giving and restore my alma mater to my will," Miranda said in a BAM letter.

Although some Brown alumni might find it hard to come to grips with naked parties, coed dorms, political correctness, and homosexual faculty, most alumni still

show their support for Brown through donations despite problems with specific policies, according to Mark Nickel, director of the news bureau.

"It's really not possible to consistently please all 70,000 alumni," Nickel said. "The number of people dissatisfied with Brown as a whole is actually rather small."

Agra Monagan '99, a student supervisor at the Brown Annual Fund, agreed that many Brown alumni are willing to donate money to the University.

"Basically, once we explain where [the money] goes, and they know why they need to help, they will," she said.

Both Nickel and Monagan stated that Brown graduates are a generally open-minded group of people.

"Brown keeps alumni informed," said Monagan. "And I think they're the type to adjust, so their thinking is flexible with regard to Brown."

Most of the more unwilling graduates spent their time at Brown before the New Curriculum, when Brown was a more conservative school.

"Brown ceased being my university long years ago,"

wrote E. Howard Hunt '40 in a letter. Hunt was a Watergate operative who pleaded guilty to six counts of conspiracy, burglary, and wiretapping in 1973.

"Pre-New Curriculum Brown graduates might feel differently about the type of school Brown is now," Monagan said. "There's a whole range of reasons that people may or may not donate money to Brown. Some want to give spirit and realize it really helps the school."

Plenty of older alumni, however, still support Brown.

"But it is my Brown," wrote Stanley R. Greenberg '50 in a letter to BAM. "I identify with those students who are seedy, needy, contentious, and different. As long as they are around I know that democratic America is alive and kicking."

Some alumni voiced their opinion that other alumni were romanticizing their days at the school.

"Some of us old-fart alumni need to lighten up and remember our younger days more kindly and with honesty," wrote Richard T. Downes '45 in a letter to BAM.

Brown graduates are the kind to speak up when something, including their alma mater, bothers them, Nickel said.

"Brown cultivates an independent spirit," he said. "Graduates are willing to stand up and speak up. But I believe the actual number of Brown graduates who are dissatisfied is fairly small."

"People see in Brown a way to make a difference," he said. "Some alumni see their donations as investments, not in the monetary sense, but rather to accomplish a goal in addition to helping their alma mater." ■

You can see the pull that alumni have at highly competitive colleges. Because they endow their alma maters with billions each year, the opinions of alumni carry a lot of weight and affect not only policy but also student attitudes. Highly competitive college alumni go on to financial greatness—to Wall Street careers that garner them exorbitant wages, corner offices, and fabulous cars. There will be a lot of pressure for you to succeed at the same rate as your forebears. One student at Harvard, however, asks his fellow students to examine how they define "success."

COLUMN: FAMILY—ANOTHER OPTION
By Matthew S. Vogel

HARVARD CRIMSON (Cambridge, Mass.) 12/07/1998

One of my high school friends calls it the "Harvard complex"—the idea that because we're at Harvard we must "amount to something" and be "important." What puzzles my high school friend and me is why this complex is so focused on careers. In one of my lectures last week, a professor asked us if we saw anybody here present the idea of a family as a real option after graduation. And I really don't think we do, or at least I have yet to meet someone who does.

Samantha Goldstein/*The Harvard Crimson*

It is not good enough that we become great moms or dads. We are surrounded by pressure to earn six-figure salaries and hold prestigious titles. We feel that we must succeed in one particular way, and there's something not quite right with just being someone's spouse or parent. Marriage and children—having a family—is seen as something to be put off or avoided, as a hindrance that will prevent us from achieving success.

A couple of weeks ago, my friends were telling me they need to do well in their classes in order to get a "good" career in investment banking or consulting. Are those really the only places where good careers exist? And even beyond that, do we really need a career? What about just having a job? What about pouring all of our energy and talent into our home rather than our office?

Too often it is taken for granted that "success" means beating others to the top of our chosen field—seldom, if ever, is success seen as raising good kids. My friends outlined, step-by-step, how they wanted their lives to proceed after graduation. None included a family in that picture. That shocked me. I grew up believing the most important thing any two people can do is raise children. As a friend recently put it, "to love is to live," and what better way to love than to raise children?

Last weekend, a friend and I had dinner with a couple of guys who have lived their entire lives in the North End. They have been best friends for 30 years. It was a great dinner—pizza at Regina's—but what really made me think was a comment my friend made as we rode the Red Line back to Harvard Square. She told me that what was so special about the evening was that they didn't see us as Harvard students. They weren't intimidated by us and didn't treat us as if we were somehow different. They weren't impressed by our education or the trajectory it throws us in. Instead, they saw us, she said, as "real people."

That's what we are, real people. We don't have to be a partner in a firm or save the world from anything. We can graduate, get a job, get married and have kids—and we won't be failures. And in no way does this detract from the fact that we are still a part of this institution and are here to make what we choose of the many lessons Harvard has to offer. If anything, it reinforces it.

True, having a career and a good family are not mutually exclusive—many people have both. But having both involves sacrifice in career and family. Like any life decision, it is, in the end, a question of priorities. Why choose the career? Is it because we really want it or is it because we feel it is what we should do? People at Harvard tell us over and over again that we should do what we love. What troubles me is so few of us here ever include having a family as an option.

I may be wrong, and indeed I hope I am. By no means do I feel Harvard students are cold and heartless individuals with no use for the family. Nor am I saying that there should be no investment bankers, lawyers or doctors in this world.

What I am saying is that those careers aren't our only options. It really is okay to have a job instead of a career, to center one's life on the home instead of the office. Some would say this is a waste of a Harvard education—in fact, some already have. But I don't think it is a waste for the main beneficiaries of my Harvard education to be my kids. Nor do I think that those who do devote their lives to their kids, like my own parents, are failures. One of the greatest things we can give to the world is our children. Just don't forget that, Harvard. ■

Paying for College

Too bad you won't be able to bring in those six-figure salaries before you enroll in a highly competitive college. Bar none, tuition at these schools is the most expensive in the nation. For the 1998–1999 school year, the most expensive of the Ivy League schools, Harvard, Brown, and Yale, charged $31,132; $31,060; and $30,830, respectively. And the Ivies set the tone for what other highly competitive schools think they can charge. Tuition inflation is a huge problem at prestigious schools, a problem that keeps deserving students away and threatens the financial future of those who enroll. *The Student Life* of Washington University bemoans their school's recent tuition increase announcement.

EDITORIAL: WASHINGTON UNIVERSITY MUST REIN IN TUITION GROWTH

Staff Editorial

THE STUDENT LIFE (St. Louis, Mo.) 11/11/1998

At an on-campus forum last Monday, Chancellor Wrighton admitted that Washington University's tuition will indeed rise for the 1999–2000 school year. While university officials have not yet determined how much the already pricey fee of $22,422 will rise, the trend over the last ten years has been a raise of at least four percent, or nearly three times the current inflation rate.

Wrighton and administrators must recognize that as WU's tuition skyrockets toward $30,000, an increasing number of students will not be able to afford it.

WU is not the only school to continually test the willingness of the market to accept its raises in price. Tuition increase is a phenomenon that has taken over public and private universities and colleges nationwide. In the 20 years between 1976 and 1996, the average tuition at private universities increased from $2,881 to $15,581.

And, just like taxes, tuition increases are not all bad. The money goes toward strengthening and improving the administration, faculty, facilities, technology, regulations, as well as numerous other components of a university, to make the social, educational, and environmental experiences of the students better.

WU in particular is one of the forerunners in creating and implementing an impressive plan to improve itself, and, as a result, improve its national ranking. However, even if it means slowing down the process towards becoming a top tier institution, WU must figure out a way to decrease the financial burden placed on today's students.

In a report issued earlier this year, the National Commission on the Cost of Higher Education warned that unless colleges and universities get tuition under control, they could face government intervention. As a result, administrators at Virginia Wesleyan devised a plan to save money in other areas and not raise tuition next year. Even schools such as Yale, Princeton, Harvard and Stanford are keeping their tuition increases under four percent while adding millions of dollars to financial aid budgets at the same time.

WU continues to raise its tuition, including an outrageous increase of 5.7 percent last year. WU receives the majority of its revenue from gifts, grants, and investments. Tuition, while providing an enormous amount of income that the university is able to spend how it sees fit (unlike earmarked gifts), is not going to cripple the university if it were a little lower each year. A small decrease in the amount of money tuition provides WU would make a huge difference to individual students.

By increasing tuition but not making major changes in the reach of financial aid, WU runs the risk of decreasing the student body's economic diversity. Students who are affected the most by tuition increases are the middle class, especially those who just barely do not qualify for financial aid. These students will not even look past the school's price tag.

Finally, one of the most consistent complaints about tuition increases is that WU does not do a good enough job explaining where the money goes. Students very rarely see the direct impact of their tuition, and the administration could better justify such increases by telling the community which professorships, departments, buildings, or scholarships tuition increases

maintain or improve. Tuition increases are a part of student life, and students at WU can't expect tuition to flatten out overnight. But we can, and we should, expect the university to look at the tuition-controlling strategies at places like Stanford and Harvard, schools we are attempting to emulate in every other way.

Listen up, administrators: $30,000 (including room and board), is just too much for one year at WU. ■

As the editorial points out, highly competitive schools aren't the only ones that have seen tuition increases in years past. And one place where prestigious schools seem to excel is in the amount of financial aid they offer. If you meet or exceed all of the requirements for admission to a highly competitive school, chances are you won't be turned away for financial reasons. In fact, if you score 1600 on the SATs and graduate at the top of your class, you'll have highly competitive schools literally battling with each other to enroll you. That translates into big scholarships and financial aid packages for you. The *Yale Daily News* reports on the trend toward bidding wars between Ivy League schools looking to attract budding Einsteins.

QUEST TO BEST EACH OTHER'S FINANCIAL AID HITS THE IVIES
By Letitia Stein

YALE DAILY NEWS (New Haven, Conn.) 11/04/1998

Forget about football. The competition within the Ivy League that has received the most attention recently has been the race to provide more financial aid dollars, not touchdowns.

With the addition last week of Cornell University and Dartmouth College to the list of schools that will re-work their financial aid policies, the recent rush by top universities to improve their financial aid offerings looks to some like a bidding war.

But university administrators and higher education experts think this won't be the case. They say the current competition arose more from individual schools addressing their own needs. This appears quite different from the federal government's view of the situation a decade ago, when top universities met once a year to discuss admissions policy, provoking an anti-trust suit.

Provost Alison Richard, Yale's chief academic and financial officer, said Yale's policy will depend upon Yale's needs, not another school's policy. Yale will study other schools' financial aid changes and the effect of last year's changes before deciding what to do for next year.

"These things become a bidding war if one makes it

a bidding war," Richard said. "[But] to think of it as a bidding war is to move far away from the principles that undergird our financial aid policy."

Higher education experts doubt the Ivy League schools will engage in the risk of price competition.

David Breneman, Dean of the Curry School of Education at the University of Virginia said that a bidding war would conclude in more financial aid money to students, but would not necessarily benefit the universities in the long run.

Talk of revamping financial aid policies among the nation's top universities is nothing new. In fact, Uncle Sam has been waiting a long time to see a little competitive action from the Ivy League.

In 1991, the federal government first tried to promote competitive pricing within the Ivy League with a much publicized anti-trust suit challenging the annual meetings of the so-called Ivy League Overlay group as collusive price-setting.

By the time Princeton University made the first move with its financial aid reforms last January, the controversy surrounding the anti-trust suit had long disappeared from college campuses.

So why the recent changes?

After the demise of the Ivy Overlap Group, Yale and

other institutions began to focus on how changes in financial aid policy could benefit their individual needs.

So while Princeton's surprise policy change immediately set off the flurry of changes at universities nationwide, financial aid reform was already in the works at Yale.

And with financial gains from the stock market boom boosting university endowments to unprecedented highs, wealthy schools like Harvard, Yale and Princeton can now afford to fund increased financial aid programs.

But schools with smaller endowments will face greater pressure to respond to the recent changes.

"What you will see is that the schools with the greatest resources, primarily drawn from their endowments, can be the most creative with their initiatives," said David Warren, president of the National Association of Independent Colleges and Universities.

Warren predicted that schools with smaller endowments, like Cornell and Duke, will launch major fund-raising campaigns to gain the cash necessary for their own reforms.

That's the move Cornell announced last week. ∎

Housing

For all that money you're putting out, can you expect to live in fancy digs once you arrive at Prestigious U? Probably not. A dorm by any other name would still smell like sweatsocks, and housing at highly competitive colleges is no different. What you may find on the campuses of prestigious universities, however, are alternatives to single-sex dormitories. At Stanford University, you can live in Naranja, the Entrepreneurial Spirit theme dorm, where psych majors and computer science majors (who live on "Yahoo Hall") focus on pursuing their career passions and sharing them with the world. There are commons and co-ops, and you can probably live off campus. The *Vanderbilt Hustler* reports here on its recently instituted coed dormitories.

VANDY GIVES GO AHEAD ON COED DORMS

By Joanna Pluta

VANDERBILT HUSTLER (Nashville, Tenn.) 09/01/1998

To the upper classmen, it's odd to see men running around the Hemingway dorm. But to the class of 2002, freshman housing that is coed by floor is just a way of life. It's the only thing they know.

But it is not a way of life that Vanderbilt considered lightly. After a year of debate by Dean Mark Bandas and Interhall, the choice between coed by floor or single-sex housing was added to the freshman housing application.

"We examined the top 10 schools, which is where we want to be," said Interhall President Nathan Moore. "Some of them have dorms that are coed by room, which is way too liberal for our clientele, but most of the top 10 schools are coed by floor."

"It weighed on my mind that if I was a student looking for a balanced place, segregated housing might indicate a school that wasn't with the times," said Steve Caldwell, Associate Dean of Housing.

"I like coed housing, though I never knew that it wasn't coed before this year," said Anne Clasen, a freshman living in Hemingway Hall. "It wasn't a plus when I made my list of pros and cons when choosing schools. I looked at Emory and Wake Forest, too, and housing didn't play a role in my decision." Clasen can't compare living in a coed dorm to a single-sex dorm, because she hasn't had the other experience.

After collecting all of the housing applications, enough women chose the single-sex option to fill approximately 65 percent of a building, so Interhall and Bandas decided to create a building that would serve the greater good. For the men, slightly over half of one building wanted to be in a men-only building, and so one was created for them as well. "My guess is that it will be similar in the future, and my humble opinion is that guys will lose their building over time," said Moore.

In observing other schools, Vanderbilt seemed to be the only one with single-sex housing for freshmen. "And the reports were good," said Caldwell. "There didn't seem to be as much dorm damage. Interaction between males and females was good, more lively, more engaging.

There were very few negatives. The only thing was that a number of schools felt compelled to offer single-gender buildings, and they weren't filled."

But the change in environment has not greatly altered the housing policy. As for the escort system, males must still be escorted in female halls, and vice versa, though Moore has not seen much concern about violations of the escort policy.

But while the administrative decision to change housing involved a lot of discussion and research, students do not seem to feel the same impact.

"I don't think anyone pays attention when they walk straight to their door," said Ethan McDaniel, a freshman living in Dyer. "You see more women outside than you do in the dorm. If you want to see women, you might as well go outside." McDaniel looked at things like scholastics when he was looking at colleges, not where he was going to put his head at night. "I don't think the dorms are a big deal."

The Office of Undergraduate Admissions has heard little about the housing at Vanderbilt, coed or not.

"There is no direct admissions issue, but it is an indirect issue," said Bill Shain, Dean of Admissions. "Nationally, coed housing is a popular issue. And anytime we have happier students, it helps admissions. Coed floors result in solid interactions and living environments, though I can't predict a definite bottom line change."

"I don't think we can attach the way we house our freshmen to a lessening conservative attitude at Vanderbilt. It's just that times have changed," said Moore. ∎

Diversity

Whatever type of dorm you decide to live in, don't expect to be surrounded only by smart, rich, white kids looking for careers in investment banking. (Okay, so everybody *will* be smart.) This is a common misconception of highly competitive schools. Since they're privately controlled and funded, highly competitive schools can pick and choose those to whom they want to offer admission. While on paper this could spell disaster for minority students, highly competitive colleges are actually quite proud of the fact that their students are a super-diverse lot.

Some claim, however, that highly competitive colleges worry *too* much about enrolling minorities, to the detriment of the schools themselves and perhaps in violation of the law. Earlier this year, the Center for Individual Rights (CIR) accused fifteen colleges, many of them highly competitive universities, of reverse discrimination, claiming that minority status is used as a deciding factor for admissions in far too many cases. "We think that almost every elite school is in violation of the law," a CIR rep said. Dartmouth President James Wright came to the defense of that school's admissions policy, asserting his school's ongoing commitment to diversity and affirmative action.

All of this affects life at prestigious schools in noticeable ways. Diversity in and of itself does not guarantee harmony, and many students claim that there is little interaction between different groups of students at these schools. Minority students struggle to get their concerns heard and to be accepted by the mainstream. Organizations tend to be homogeneous, not mixed, which perpetuates the separateness minority students feel. These problems are not unlike those at other types of schools. What is different is the overwhelming concern for minority issues at highly competitive schools. Prestigious schools are more likely to address problems head-on and work for solutions quickly, as you'll read in this section.

Because of their emphasis on diversity, highly competitive schools find it necessary to consider the needs of many different racial and ethnic groups. One group you don't usually find represented in large numbers is Native Americans. Yale has welcomed these students, however, and is working hard to accommodate their needs and attract more Native Americans to campus.

NATIVE AMERICAN YALE STUDENTS MAKE VOICES HEARD

By Adrienne Lo

DAILY HERALD (New Haven, Conn.) 10/23/1998

"You're standing on Indian land." Last week, chalked messages on Cross Campus called attention to an increasingly vocal and integral group of Yale students: Native Americans.

Over the past few years, the number of Native American students at Yale College has risen steadily. This fall, 51 Native American undergraduate students are enrolled at Yale, as opposed to 42 in the fall of 1996 and 44 in the fall of 1997. Now, along with the student-run Association of Native Americans at Yale (ANAAY), the University is taking steps to accommodate the needs of Native American students and to attract more Native Americans to Yale.

This year, Yale is providing a senior peer advisor to offer guidance to Native American freshmen and sophomores. Ross-Alan Tisdale, '99, this year's peer advisor, also serves as ANAAY moderator. "I believe deeply that the Native experience at Yale is one of constant struggle both in our classrooms and in our colleges," Tisdale, who is affiliated with the Osage tribe, said. "Few outsiders are able to grasp the complexity of our diverse backgrounds."

Yale's Native American students appreciate measures like these. "Involvement in cultural activities is very important to me," Nelvan Cerventes, '02, said. Cervantes, born and raised on a Native American reservation, said the vibrancy of Yale's Native American community led her to select Yale." I hoped to be able to continue to be a part of an active and supportive Native American community," she said. "ANAAY has made this possible." Founded in 1991 by three Native American students, ANAAY's aim is to unite Yale's Native American community.

Although Yale's Native American population is small relative to other minority groups, ANAAY is an increasing presence on campus, and Native American undergraduates and graduate students from many backgrounds and tribes are active in its activities.

ANAAY plays a role in a major annual Native American Conference held at Yale. Last year's conference featured such distinguished Native American scholars as N. Scott Momaday, Elizabeth Cook-Lynn, and Vine Deloria. This spring will mark the second year of the conference. At the end of the conference, ANAAY will host its first pow-wow, a traditional Native American festival that includes dance, drumming, singing, crafts, and food.

ANAAY is trying to make prospective students aware of its presence as well. The association is pressuring the Undergraduate Admissions Office to begin recruiting students on Native American reservations to increase the small number of students who have made the transition from a reservation to Yale.

ANAAY Political Action Co-Chair Amanda De Zutter, '01, serves as a student recruitment coordinator focusing on Native Americans in the Minority Recruitment Program. "It's very important to inform minorities of the opportunities at Yale," she said. "It's a way to diversify Yale even more. Some [students] have no idea they could go to an Ivy League school."

Outside of ANAAY's activities, Yale has other resources available for Native American students. The Native American Cultural Center, which shares a house on Crown Street with the Asian-American and Chicano Cultural Centers, is a place for students to meet, study, and relax. The Administration is also implementing a chapter of the American Indian Science and Engineering Society (AISES), a nationwide organization.

ANNAY's and Yale's recent efforts to bring together Yale's Native American community—and to increase its numbers through recruitment—are making progress in addressing an important concern: the retention rate of Native American undergraduates at Yale.

Of the 42 enrolled Native American students at Yale in the fall of 1996, only 33 stayed for the spring semester. Last year, however, showed a significant increase, with 41 out of 44 Native American undergraduates remaining in the second semester. ∎

You may think from the comments made earlier in "Brown U. deemed 'too liberal to donate money' " that homosexuality is not looked on favorably on the campuses of highly competitive schools. Keep in mind that those comments were made by older alumni who left campus nearly 50 years ago. The prevailing attitude today at prestigious schools is one of acceptance. These schools pride themselves on their liberalism and on the power of education to promote understanding. At Northwestern, straight and gay students united to keep discussions of sexual awareness alive in light of the tragic death of Matthew Shepard.

NORTHWESTERN U. ALLIES TRIES TO INCREASE SEXUAL ORIENTATION AWARENESS THROUGH UNITY

By Michael Hope

DAILY NORTHWESTERN (Evanston, Ill.) 02/02/1999

Following the murder of University of Wyoming student Matthew Shepard last year, several Northwestern students worked toward organizing a new satellite of the Bisexual, Gay and Lesbian Alliance (BGALA).

Its name? NU Allies.

Its purpose? To serve as an educational outreach program to inspire discussion about sexual orientation in a relaxed setting.

The group has been operating since an October

vigil in memory of Matthew Shepard, the University of Wyoming student who was beaten to death, allegedly because he was gay.

For a time, hate crimes related to sexual orientation had the media spotlight and became the talk of college campuses across the nation.

But some students at NU didn't want the discussion to stop.

"Whenever you have a big event, you have a couple days where everyone thinks about it, and then the interest fades away," said Kate Pietsch, NU Allies education outreach chairwoman. "I didn't want that to happen."

As a result of the desire to continue discussions about sexual awareness among gay and straight people, students on campus wanted to create a satellite of BGALA that would serve as an intermediary for people interested in gay issues, whether gay or straight.

"NU Allies tries to provide a model for how straight people can be allies with gay people," said Karen Sheley, chairwoman for the executive board of NU Allies.

Many of the people who started NU Allies are straight but have friends who are gay and are concerned about gay issues and awareness. The group is focused on improving relations among gays and straights, and there are gay and straight members in the group.

"The problem about sexual orientation is it's about sex, and people don't like to talk about sex." Pietsch said. "People on campus are more comfortable talking about sexuality if it isn't all about the sex."

Instead of addressing controversial political issues or gay rights in America, students in NU Allies hope to focus on sexual orientation in a laid-back manner. To raise awareness, students plan to hold firesides in dorms and in Greek houses.

"You can be the most openly liberal person on campus, but if a group is in your face, people might get uncomfortable," Pietsch said.

While some students at NU assume that members of BGALA are gay, NU Allies leaders want to debunk that stereotype.

"My goal would be that there would be fewer assumptions made about a member of this group," said Sheley, a senior.

Student groups that address sexual orientation sometimes face a negative association by being politically active and overtly aggressive, and NU Allies wants to avoid that image, Pietsch said.

"NU Allies is organized by many straight people with gay friends, who wanted to educate people about gay issues, but didn't want to deal with the stigma that was associated with BGALA," said Amanda Johnson, president of BGALA. ∎

You'll find diverse religious influences on the campuses of highly competitive schools. Many of these schools were affiliated with religions when they were founded, some still are today, and others incorporate religion into ceremonies and other campus traditions. Organizations representing all religions exist alongside atheist groups. While private schools are free to do what they like in terms of religion, the fact that religion—and overwhelmingly, Christianity—is incorporated into the tradition of education bothers some students, especially this columnist from Yale.

COLUMN: KEEP RELIGION OUT OF YALE'S FRESHMAN ASSEMBLY

By Christopher Mooney

YALE DAILY NEWS (New Haven, Conn.) 09/08/1998

Three years back, I remember being quite moved by the Freshman Assembly at Woolsey Hall. The way I felt had much to do with the solemn formality of the event: the heraldic banners, the deans and masters in gowns, the seals involving symbolic acorns and just

generally the feeling of traditions arching back hundreds of years.

But the thing that really bothered me about Freshman Assembly was that huge Woolsey Hall organ. I'd only heard music like that once before, in St. John the Divine Cathedral in New York City during a Passion Play. I remember coming out of St. John's and saying, "Well, now I know I'm completely immune to religion. If that organ couldn't convert me, nothing ever will." And a friend said: "No, you're just lucky they didn't play Bach."

This year's Freshman Assembly started with Bach's 29th Cantana on the organ.

And, also rather Passion Play-like, the opening organ gonging was followed by an invocation by the Reverend Frederick Streets, the University chaplain. Streets asked everyone present to bow their heads, and then invoked a "Creator God." He then lead a hymn: "Oh God, beneath thy guiding hand."

There followed the dean's and president's addresses, which were appropriately secular. But then came another hymn: "We Gather Together" (short for "We Gather Together to Ask the Lord's Blessing"), and Streets' benediction, which included more prayer. And then, more organ.

Whether or not this Freshman Assembly made any converts, it certainly generated some grievances. The next day at the Bazaar, working the table for the Yale College Society for Humanists, Atheists and Agnostics, I heard so many tales of freshman woe about the religious content of the Woolsey Hall Assembly that I felt like a therapist.

Cheryl Conner '02 said that "it doesn't seem to me that the Freshman Assembly should have been that religious. I think it was basically Christian, and other people of other religions might have been uncomfortable with that."

Tom Stout '02 said something very similar: "While I was not completely offended by the Christian orientation, I was not entirely comfortable with it either and would much rather religion had been left out of it altogether. I think it sent a bad message for the first week, that Yale recognizes one student's beliefs over another's."

So not only did these freshmen find the assembly to have a religious flavor to it; they found it distinctly Christian in character! To be fair, the Yale Chaplain's Office does not officially embrace any particular faith. Its mission statement reads, "The Chaplain's Office has as its mission to foster an understanding of and appreciation for the diverse religious and spiritual life of the University community." And when informed of

these comments by freshmen, the Reverend Streets commented: "It is too bad that some students think there is only one religion represented on campus."

Nevertheless, the fact remains that the Chaplain's Office has no particular interest in those students without any "spiritual life." It is thus a distinct Yale institution, and an allocation of resources which serves only religious, or "spiritual" students. Non-religious students rightly perceive the licensing of such an organization to speak for the University as a whole as a slap in the face. Yet this is precisely what happened at the Freshman Assembly.

The Yale Chaplain's Office's outlook is quite typical of the supposedly "tolerant" approach to religion in the United States as a whole. We defend freedom of religion tooth and nail, but we really don't seem to care much about freedom from religion. In other words, we privilege those with religious beliefs over those without them, and constantly subject the minority of unbelievers to the tyranny of a religious majority.

Here's a particularly outrageous example. Currently, the state constitution of Mississippi proclaims that "no person who denies the existence of a Supreme Being shall hold any office in this state." The constitutions of Tennessee, Texas, Maryland, North Carolina, and Arkansas contain similar discriminatory clauses, but South Carolina takes the cake. Its constitution bars unbelievers from state office three separate times!

It's hard to imagine such blatantly unconstitutional and discriminatory offenses being directed toward any minority group, save unbelievers. The fact that phrases like this and like "In God We Trust" persist in our public documents and currency shows quite clearly that while we pride ourselves on tolerance, we truly tolerate only the religious. The rest can just squirm in their seats.

Yale's Chaplain's Office must overcome this pervasive American myopia, and the sooner the better. Of course, it is great and commendable that the Chaplain's Office aims to serve those of all faiths, but it is not good enough. The Office must also address its efforts to those without any religious faith at all, or else at the very least it must not headline at Freshman Assembly. Otherwise, Yale's atheists, agnostics, secular humanists, rationalists, and freethinkers have every right to feel slighted and insulted.

The solution to this problem is actually fairly

simple. First, the Yale Chaplain's office must appoint a humanist counselor or chaplain for students without religion. Secondly, it must desist from making any positive religious statements or endorsements when addressing Yale as a whole.

And above all, there must be absolutely no prayer at Yale assemblies. Some of us find prayer not only superfluous, but debasing.

Of course, many will say that the religious presence at Freshman Assembly is "just traditional." But traditions are like appendixes. Sometimes, true, they don't bother you. Other times, they explode. ■

Another topic that has garnered a good deal of attention recently is the role of women in academica, long considered a "boys club." There's a lot of truth to this. Far more men than women hold administrative positions, particularly top administrative positions, at colleges and universities nationwide. Because they are steeped in tradition and move more slowly to change "the way things have always been," highly competitive colleges have been slow to address this problem. Recently, in fact, Stanford faced serious accusations that it was hostile to women as well as minorities. In light of this, their move to appoint a women to the position of Dean of the Law School early this year may have raised some eyebrows, but the qualifications of this fabulous professor, who some say may be next to be named to the Supreme Court, speak for themselves.

STANFORD SELECTS FIRST FEMALE DEAN

By Patrick Bernhardt

THE STANFORD DAILY (Stanford, Calif.) 02/23/1999

On her final day at Stanford as a visiting professor during the spring of 1992, Law Prof. Kathleen Sullivan entered an eerily quiet classroom to deliver her last lecture before returning to Harvard.

"I scribbled all over the top chalkboard, until I finally ran out of space and rolled the board up from the bottom position to the top, and underneath [my class] had scrawled in giant letters 'Defect to Stanford.' "

A year later the renowned constitutional scholar stunned the legal world and answered her students' call, leaving Harvard for a third-floor office at Stanford Law School.

Monday the 43-year-old New York native accepted another call, this time from University President Gerhard Casper, when she agreed to become the school's dean.

In September Sullivan will become the first female dean of any school in the University's history when she replaces outgoing Law School Dean Paul Brest, who announced his retirement last fall.

Sullivan takes over at a time when students and former faculty are claiming the school fosters an environment hostile to women and minorities.

Two weeks ago former Prof. Linda Mabry spoke out on her reasons for leaving the Law School in December.

"I left Stanford because it is an institution that engages in a pattern of practicing intense bias, which devalues, discourages and marginalizes people of color," Mabry said.

Mabry, who is black, is one of a number of professors who filed complaints with the U.S. Department of Labor, alleging discrimination in the University's tenure practices.

Sullivan, who did not return phone calls yesterday, has repeatedly held that the Law School is a family-like community far ahead of its peer institutions in issues of diversity.

"Since [Law Prof.] Barbara Babcock pioneered the advent of women to the faculty, Stanford has done extraordinarily well attracting women to the faculty," Sullivan said soon after coming to Stanford in 1993. "Tokenism is just not an issue here."

When she left Cambridge for Palo Alto, many national newspapers speculated that she did so because she found Harvard a hostile environment for female faculty. Sullivan, though, has always downplayed that speculation, saying that she was not pushed from Harvard but drawn to Stanford.

"This place was too good to be true," she usually quips in response to questions about her motivations for moving. "I mean, who could resist a world-class law school in paradise?"

Emeritus Law Prof. Gerald Gunther, who for more than a decade was the school's longest-serving teacher and the highest rated by students, had always said he would retire when another faculty member bettered his evaluation scores.

"Then Kathleen comes along, and I had to amend that statement," he said. "I said, 'I'll quit as soon as I get poorer teaching ratings than anyone other than Kathleen.'"

According to Sullivan, "Teaching has always been the absolute center" of her career.

But her commitment to the classroom has not kept her out of other venues, such as the U.S. Supreme Court.

Sullivan has presented more than 10 written briefs to the nation's highest court and has twice argued cases herself. She has battled on behalf of abortion rights, against Colorado's 1992 anti-gay Amendment 2 and in favor of President Clinton's attempt to delay Paula Jones' civil lawsuit until after he left office.

Many legal pundits have suggested that Sullivan will eventually leave academia for the other side of the bench.

"USA Today," "The Washington Post" and "The New York Times" have all floated her name as a potential appointee to the Supreme Court. During the past six years all three have reported rumors that she was being considered for the job by President Clinton.

Sullivan even once called being a Supreme Court justice a "dream job" but quickly followed the thought with another pro-Stanford quip: "Who would ever want to leave paradise?"

Thanks to Casper, for the next five years she will be in charge of a small part of her paradise—or at least until she decides to answer someone else's call. ∎

Because there are fewer students on the campuses of highly competitive schools, the incidence of large-scale alcohol-related incidents like those described in the Large State Schools chapter is much lower. But don't think that students at these schools don't drink—or that administrators don't keep their eye on those who do. Of course there are parties with alcohol at these schools, but there are punishments for overindulging, too. Just like any other school, highly competitive schools want to keep liability insurance costs down, abide by the law, and, most importantly, keep students safe.

Highly competitive schools are joining in the national trend to reduce alcohol abuse on college campuses. Vanderbilt held numerous events during Alcohol Awareness Month last year. Brown trains students as party managers to enforce campus policy. Prestigious schools realize that being private doesn't mean being above the law, and you should, too. Attending a private school does not make you immune from the state and federal laws covering alcohol, as students as Washington University found. But because of the greater levels of communication between administration and students at highly competitive schools, the administration will in all likelihood work with you to support your right to party—responsibly—as *The Chronicle* from Duke reports.

WASHINGTON U. DRAFTS NEW ALCOHOL POLICY

By Liz Bower

THE STUDENT LIFE (St. Louis, Mo.) 04/13/1998

In the midst of a nationwide trend to address alcohol-related problems on college campuses, Washington University's All About Alcohol committee has drafted a new Drug and Alcohol Policy which would take effect next year.

The draft reiterates several current mandates and creates additional rules as well. The policy states at its beginning that WU must adhere to Missouri state laws concerning alcohol and drug use because the school receives federal funds.

Senior Daniel Freedberg, a member of the committee, said; "This committee was supposed to combine [the two listed policies] into one. The law is the law, and WU cannot have a policy that is in violation of Missouri State law."

Sophomore member of the committee Shashi Kara agreed that currently WU was violating state law.

"I think in a strange way, [the new policy] is a necessary evil at some point for the university to follow federal law. Right now, [WU's] breaking every federal law—that's not a good thing," Kara said.

Several students were concerned that new, strongly enforced sanctions against alcohol use would force students to binge drink in private before parties. These students felt people would be reluctant to call Emergency Support Team (EST) if they or their friends became ill, because they would fear the legal repercussions of their actions.

"The issue of emergency service is important. With a stricter alcohol policy, students may be afraid of sanctions, and maybe more hesitant to call EST in an alcohol-related emergency," Freedberg said. "This is an issue students are concerned with. . . . The policy should be clear about the results of calling EST."

Junior Mike Perlmutter, who helped type the proposal, agreed that students were concerned that the new policy could result in an increase of unreported alcohol-related health problems but felt WU would

not punish students for honesty in these cases. Perlmutter said that instead of referring students under the age of 21 who contact EST after experiencing alcohol-related illness to the court system, WU administrators would continue to refer the students to health professionals who will try to help students avoid alcoholism.

"The major concern I've heard voiced to me by students is about discipline from calling EST. They are afraid when students [are sick from excessive consumption of alcohol] they will try to sleep it off," Perlmutter said.

"You need medical attention, not discipline if you are sick. I hope [students] continue to [contact EST if they become ill from drinking]. They are there to help. It's never good to sleep it off—students should err on the side of safety."

Administrators involved in the drafting of the policy emphasized that it could foster more responsibility among students.

Director of the Campus Police Department Chief William Taylor pointed out that the draft featured only recommendations for improving the alcohol situation on campus.

"By and large, most students deal maturely with alcohol," he said. "When we took another look at the culture [on campus], we thought there was a more mature way to deal with alcohol." ∎

BEER TRUCKS EARN DUKE U. FUNDING SUPPORT
By Maureen Milligan

THE CHRONICLE (Durham, N.C.) 01/19/1999

The University has served students beer before, but this semester it will help pay for it too.

Through a $5,000 grant from the Department of Alumni Affairs and Development, student groups will only have to spend $100 to use the University-owned beer truck at their social functions this semester, a drop of about $500. A group of University administrators solicited the grant after meeting at the end of last semester to discuss the beer trucks.

Students will now be able to apply, on a first-come, first-served basis, to use the truck once at the reduced price. Two student groups must apply together to use the beer truck, splitting the new $200 rental fee. Only

10 beer truck events can be subsidized through the grant, said Shannon Bieter, coordinator of the Event Advising Center. The deadline for registering for the subsidized beer truck is Feb. 1.

Last semester student groups paid between $529 and $629 to rent the truck in addition to the $2 charged to individual students wishing to buy alcohol.

"We thought it was really high to pay for beer, because [the students] still have to pay for the beer on their own," Bieter said.

Bieter stressed that student groups are only eligible for the low rate once, and must still pay for the event if it is canceled less than a day in advance due to bad weather.

Administrators largely credit the beer trucks for encouraging students to attend and stage on-campus parties, Wasiolek explained.

"There was a sense that, at least to a certain extent, social life had returned or reemerged on campus," Wasiolek said. "I had talked to enough students and they felt [the beer truck] had worked for them but one main concern was that it was too expensive."

Several fraternities began using the beer truck last semester after its success at Campus Social Board events.

"I am very pleased that the administration has done this. It shows they are making an effort to keep social life on campus, which is good," said Interfraternity Council President Stephen Broderick, a senior.

Administrators decided to apply for funds from various University departments because there was no way to reduce labor costs, which constitute the truck's primary expenses.

According to University policy, three bartenders and two University police officers are needed whenever the truck is used at a party, Wasiolek said.

Bieter said administrators applied for money under University Life's Program Enhancement Fund and approached the office of Alumni Affairs for a grant. University Life denied the request because they would not sponsor alcohol-related events, but Alumni Affairs agreed to offer support.

"My gift was to help overcome the obstacles of bringing parties back to Duke," said Laney Funderburk, associate vice president for alumni affairs and development. "Students are alumni-in-residence." ∎

Besides alcohol consumption, another area that appears to be scaled-down at highly competitive schools is activism. Recently, only one highly competitive university (Brown) made it onto *Mother Jones* magazine's list of the top 10 activist campuses in the country; in striking contrast, 7 on the list were big state schools. There just doesn't seem to be that much that gets prestigious school students riled up. So focused are these students on their studies that they find little to protest about. They're secluded, in a sense, from the outside world, the trials and tribulations of which have little effect on them. One Tufts student longs for yesterday.

COLUMN: STUDENTS LOSE IDEALISM TO DREAMS OF POST-COLLEGE SUCCESS

By Lauren Heist

Tufts Daily (Medford, Mass.) 9/28/1998

"Johnny's in the basement, mixin' up the medicine/I'm on the pavement, thinkin' 'bout the government."—Bob Dylan, quoted in the 1968-69 Tufts yearbook.

1968. Students protested in the streets, they held signs in front of the Capitol building, they chanted in Chicago.

Students stood up to their parents by wearing their hair long and their skirts short. They stood up to the government by burning their draft cards and fleeing to Canada.

In 1968 students may have been rebellious, but they had ideas.

Fast forward exactly 30 years to 1998. Students are complaining more about dining hall food than government policy. We are trying desperately to fit into the mainstream world, not rebel against it.

What has happened in 30 years? Where has activism gone? What happened to our passion?

Sure, the student activists in the 1960s had a war to bring them together. But their activism was more than just anti-war sentiment; it was also about changing the status quo and altering a society which they felt was inherently wrong.

Today, the world is just as filled with problems and inequalities as it was 30 years ago, but for some reason students have stopped thinking that the world's problems have anything to do with them.

Why the change of heart? I think the answer lies in economics.

A college education used to be something only necessary for the upper class. For many jobs, all you needed was a high school diploma, or maybe some training at a technical school. But as time has passed, a college education has become more and more necessary to get even a mediocre job, and for many jobs you now need a master's degree.

And, not surprisingly, as more people demand a college education, the price tag on that diploma has skyrocketed. Simple supply and demand.

Because a college education has become more necessary, parents have begun looking at college as an investment in their children's future. For the amount of money that people spend to go to college, they feel that they ought to be learning something useful and marketable once they graduate. Students see college as a place to prepare for a career, not as a place to sit back and contemplate life.

This change in attitude is evident in the growing numbers of freshmen who plan to attend graduate school after college.

You can see the emphasis on the real world aspect of school even in the pre-frosh who come to visit. Every college tour guide emphasizes how many internships their students get every year, stressing the fact that their students are better prepared to enter the "real world" than those at another school.

This focus on the future and career has significantly altered what was traditionally seen as college life. We never sit around late at night and discuss philosophy or social issues. We never stand in front of the administration building with signs demanding change. And if we do sit around at all, we talk about what we are going to major in, or how we are going to get into med school. We've come to college to get somewhere in life, and we've forgotten how to think.

I am just as guilty as the next person of worrying too much about the future.

I have two friends from home that I sometimes refer to as my "hippie" friends. One of them volunteers for a group called Food Not Bombs, which distributes food to the homeless, and she is a member of Habitat for Humanity. The other worked for Women's International League for Peace and Freedom over the summer, attending an international women's conference in Baltimore and rallying in front of the Capitol

Nabarun Dasgupta/*The Daily Princetonian*

until the police came to break it up. Both are staunch vegetarians and both went to Washington, D.C., to support the freedom of Tibet.

I, on the other hand, spent my summer working six days a week in two different internships—three days at a newspaper and three days at a television station. I got great experience which will look good on a future resume, but did I do anything that will change the world? No. Did I follow my beliefs and fight for a greater cause? No.

I feel very guilty for being just like every other college student who has blown off social responsibilities to pursue their own personal goals. My "hippie"

friends are doing what they think is right. They are doing what I should be doing too.

Some people might claim that they are not apathetic, but they don't think there are any issues affecting the world right now that are important enough to merit protesting in the streets.

While I agree that it's stupid to protest for the sake of protesting, I disagree that there isn't anything worth fighting for. There are oceans that are polluted, and politicians that are corrupt and workers that are being exploited. There are thousands of causes that need young, idealistic college students to fight for them. Students' work isn't over; it is just beginning. ∎

Of course, we don't want to stereotype, and we really should give highly competitive college students their due. When they mount a protest, it's a big deal. Students from Stanford's Redwood Action Team took on The Gap recently in protest of its affiliation with a firm that employs unsafe logging practices. Duke Students Against Sweatshops attracted national media attention with a 31-hour sit-in protesting manufacturers of college apparel which inspired a series of similiar protests at schools across the country, including Georgetown University, where students fought long and hard for the cause on their campus. In the end, both groups influenced university policy regarding this controversial issue.

GEORGETOWN U. STUDENTS, OFFICIALS REACH SWEATSHOP COMPROMISE AFTER SIT-IN

By Andy Amend

THE HOYA (Washington, D.C.) 02/09/1999

Student activists signed an agreement with Student Affairs administrators shortly before 1 a.m. Tuesday, ending an 85-hour sit-in by approximately 25 students in the office of University President Leo J. O'Donovan, S.J. The details of the compromise will be announced at a rally scheduled for 4 p.m. Tuesday in Healy Circle.

The students had occupied O'Donovan's office since 11:50 a.m. Friday in an effort to force the university to negotiate with them about issues related to working conditions in the factories that make collegiate apparel. O'Donovan was out of town for the entire sit-in and is expected to return to campus Tuesday.

The solidarity committee had been attempting to persuade the university to reject a controversial code of conduct released in November for apparel manufacturers.

The committee maintained that the code, the

product of a task force made up of representatives from 14 member schools of the Collegiate Licensing Company, did not do enough to counteract sweatshop labor practices. The licensing company acts as a go-between for clothing manufacturers and approximately 170 colleges and universities.

The Georgetown activists' major concern this weekend was that the code did not require licensed companies to publicly disclose the locations of their factories. While the solidarity committee outlined other criticisms in a pamphlet distributed two weeks ago, disclosure became the students' primary demand because, they said, it was essential for achieving their other goals, which include improving wages and strictly enforcing compliance with the code.

Andrew Milmore, president of the solidarity committee said the students' goal was to ensure that companies who did not disclose their locations within a year would not have their contracts with Georgetown renewed. However, he said, the administration did not wish to be bound by an absolute commitment.

Former solidarity committee president, and one of the students' lead negotiators, Ben Smith concurred, "We got what we wanted."

Dean of Students James A. Donahue portrayed the discussion somewhat differently, saying the administration wanted to ensure that the entire university community would be included in a commitment to full disclosure. Meanwhile, he said, the students wanted to be sure the university's commitment to full disclosure would remain firm.

Solidarity committee leadership decided to stage the sit-in after Donahue failed to reach a compromise with

students last week and said the university intended to sign the code.

Both sides at Georgetown welcomed the agreement after three and a half days of negotiation. Applause accompanied the signing ceremony, in which Donahue, and student protesters, as well as those who helped manage outside communications during the sit-in, signed the accord.

"I have a profound sense of accomplishment. When you work hard for something and you reach a goal, it's a great feeling." Donahue said.

"I've never fought so hard for something," Smith said. ". . . It's been a life-changing experience." ■

Student Services

Highly competitive colleges have the money and other resources to provide students with top-notch campus services. Because of the quality and diversity of resources offered, it was hard to pick which to include. As you'll see from our sampling, highly competitive schools are concerned with helping students feel like they belong, investigate a career, face physical challenges, and stay healthy. These services and many, many more will help you navigate your way if you attend a prestigious university.

By now you probably get the hint that the stress of adjusting to life at a highly competitive university will be immense. Administrators are well aware of this, and helping students adapt is a major consideration on these campuses. Prestigious schools go out of their way to provide freshmen with the tools they'll need to stay sane while adjusting to their new way of life. At MIT, focus groups hone in on the particular problems of women students.

WOMEN SHOWN HOW TO ADJUST TO MIT

By Susan Buchman

THE TECH (Cambridge, Mass.) 09/02/1997

To help female freshmen adjust to the stress of MIT, students and staff held a series of informational forums directed at women during Residence and Orientation Week.

Activities like this have existed for many years, but two events were added this year "to present women with options and to expose them to all the resources available to them at MIT," said Loreto P. Ansaldo '00, an organizer of the events.

"While academics are immensely important, being a whole human being is just as important," said Lynn A. Roberson, a staff associate in counseling and support services and a program organizer.

On Monday, those attending the Chocolate Plus event dined on chocolate delights while listening to MIT professors, administrators, and students discuss various aspects of being female at MIT.

Wednesday's session, which was led by a panel of

students, presented information from a young woman's perspective. This meeting, called "How to Survive at MIT: A Woman's Guide," allowed freshmen to hear examples of how upperclassmen dealt with problems ranging from culture shock to roommate disagreements.

The Nature's Calling Tour, sponsored by the Association of MIT Alumni and Alumnae and the Women's R/O Committee, took place on Thursday and exposed women to MIT with a tour of the Institute's scarce women's rest rooms.

The health and well-being of women at MIT was given in-depth coverage on Tuesday when freshmen gathered for "The Best Kept Secrets about Women's Health and Fitness at MIT."

The afternoon started off with a welcome from Roberson during which she urged students to remember that "your well-being is most important. "That means intellectually; that means physically; that means emotionally."

Tracy A. Desovich, a health educator for students and a representative of MedLinks, a peer health advocacy service, was the first speaker. To start her

Campus Shapshot

MASSACHUSETTS INSTITUTE OF TECHNOLOGY
Cambridge, MA
The Tech

By Doug Heimburger, Editor

Students at MIT are usually too busy studying, playing on a sports team, or running an activity to have special traditions during the school year. But each fall when the freshmen arrive, the campus goes wild for a weekend as frosh choose their housing. Both Greek houses and dorms open their doors, serve food ranging from steak to lobster and plan events from paintball to water-skiing in the hopes of persuading freshmen to join. Starting in 2001, however, all freshmen will live in university housing, so the future of this tradition is uncertain.

presentation, she gave a definition of health: a state of complete physical, mental, and social well-being, and not merely the absence of disease or infirmity.

Citing an extreme example Desovich asked students, "Are you staying in the library twenty-four hours a day and never talking to another person?"

She also counseled those in attendance to be fully aware of the changes in their lives now that they are no longer under their parents' roofs, such as the lack of nourishing meals and the absence of the security provided by curfews and rules about dating. "You can be running marathons and still not feel healthy," she concluded.

Following up on Desouch's comments about nourishment was Anna Jasonides, a registered dietician and nutritionist with MITMedical. She announced that she is available for discussions on all dietary concerns, including weight loss or gain, eating disorders, and general good nutrition. "The number one thing students can do," says Jasonides, "is maintain their weight."

This can be done by watching fat intake and portion sizes and realizing that foods marked low fat or no fat can be high in calories, she said. She listed her five power foods, foods high in essential vitamins and minerals and simultaneously low in fat and calories: brown rice, wheat germ, nonfat yogurt, broccoli, and orange juice.

Ritu Gupta '99, a volunteer for MedLinks, spoke to the women about alcohol use and rape on campus. "Not everybody on campus is drinking," she said.

On the topic of rape, she told students to understand that rape is "not always someone jumping out of the bushes. That's the biggest and the most dangerous myth."

Wrapping up the afternoon was Sergeant Cheryl de Jong Vossmer of the Campus Police. She attempted to soften the image of police officers by saying, "Just because you come to me doesn't mean it's a formal report."

Vossmer warned that one of the most common mistakes a woman will make is not being aware of her surroundings. She then demonstrated the self-defense skills that women learn in the Rape Aggression Defense Course, which is not only a source of PEcredit, but an important prevention tool for college women. ∎

Making all aspects of college life accessible to those with physical challenges is another area where highly competitive schools work hard to meet the needs of their students. As the *Daily Free Press* of Boston University points out, creating wheelchair access for buildings that are over 100 years old—as is the case on many prestigious school campuses—is a costly endeavor. While not all facilities have been made accessible, BU works hard to provide solutions to problems.

HANDICAP ACCESS IS A PROBLEM FOR COLLEGES

By Amber Hansman

DAILY FREE PRESS (Boston, Mass.) 02/02/1998

The obstacles most students deal with on campus each day are limited to slippery sidewalks, dodging the T and maneuvering through crowds on Commonwealth Avenue.

But for Boston University's approximately 300 students with physical disabilities, simply gaining access to some academic buildings can be a challenge.

While the majority of buildings on campus are wheelchair accessible, there are exceptions. Most of the buildings on Bay State Road, including residential brownstones and the English and political science departments, do not have ramps. The Castle and the admissions office are also inaccessible to students confined to wheelchairs.

Massachusetts began requiring handicap access to any public building in 1975, long before the 1990 Americans with Disabilities Act took effect. Many of BU's buildings, however, predate the laws.

The ADA requires that buildings be made handicap accessible, but only if modifications won't be too costly or time consuming. A building's historical value can also prevent it from being renovated.

"There are exceptions within the rule that consider historical preservation," said Allan Macurdy, director of BU's Office of Disability Services.

Additions like ramps and automatic doors have been added where possible, but some buildings remain inaccessible. In these instances, students work with Macurdy's office to solve access problems.

Most often, Macurdy said, the conflicts involve class-

Daniel Rodrigues/*The Tufts Daily*

room assignments, which can be solved with a simple room change. In the case of inaccessible faculty offices, the faculty members are expected to make other meeting arrangements.

The ODS also provides disabled students with other services, including note-takers and parking permits, and it assists them in getting extra time on exams.

Alison Jones, a freshman in the School for the Arts, said that while most professors are understanding of the situations her wheelchair creates, there are some who aren't. That is when she calls ODS.

"You, along with the office, can educate the teacher so you can have a productive time in class," Jones said.

Jones uses the note-taking service, although she sometimes finds that other students seem disapproving.

"It doesn't have anything to do with wanting to get away with something. I really do need the accommodation. Once I have a writer I'm fine and I can get the work done," Jones said.

Jones lives at 1019 Commonwealth Ave., which along with Rich Hall make up the two housing areas specifically designed for wheelchair access. Her fourth-floor room is equipped with wide doors and a special bathroom.

Jones said she has seen improvements on campus since she came BU. Her biggest concern centers around Commonwealth Avenue.

"Some of the sidewalks are difficult," she said. "A lot of the time on Comm. Ave., cars will park in front of the curb cuts. I'll have to ask some stranger to lift up my chair. I guess it's a good way to meet people." ∎

The stress of life at a highly competitive school can manifest itself in many ways that compromise students' well-being. Medical facilities at prestigious schools take care of those who have made themselves physically ill with stress, but the damage can also go deeper, affecting students' mental health. While highly competitive schools offer services that help students work through psychological difficulties, it often takes a lot to get students to seek help there, especially students obsessed with perfection. Recognizing a recurring problem on their campus, two seniors at Northwestern have started a counseling program for those suffering from eating disorders.

NORTHWESTERN U. STUDENTS ESTABLISH SUPPORT NETWORK
By Ellie Phillips

DAILY NORTHWESTERN (Evanston, Ill.) 02/03/1999

Senior Lauren White didn't know what to say to her friend last year.

They got along well, but White said she didn't know how to handle her friend's eating disorder.

"My (friend) was anorexic and bulimic, and nobody could tell me what to do, what to say," White said. "I went to (Peer Health Educators), RAs, everyone."

Northwestern does not offer a support system for friends and roommates of people with eating disorders, she said.

White and Tamara Weil-Hearon, also a senior, have started a counseling network for people with eating disorders and their friends and roommates.

They hope to operate in conjunction with Counseling and Psychological Services, and have already contacted an eating disorders specialist at CAPS to get training advice, White said.

"Psych services is of paramount importance," she said. "This is meant to be a supplementary service, to help out."

Students typically have to wait two weeks for an intake appointment at CAPS, and NU health insurance only covers 10 on-campus visits, said John Dunkle of CAPS.

Eating disorders are widespread at NU, said Annann Hong, adviser for peer health educators. Current studies estimate that one in five college females suffers from an eating disorder.

At the busiest time of year, the beginning of Fall Quarter and Winter Quarter, a couple of students may have to be put on a waiting list, Dunkle said.

But if someone has an eating disorder, CAPS tries to accommodate them sooner, Dunkle said. In emergency situations, they can see someone immediately or refer them to services off campus.

White and Weil-Hearon said they plan to use personal counseling and phone call support.

Friends are not equipped to handle the situation, White said.

"My first reaction was to build her positive image, tell her how great she looked," White said. "I wish I had known then that was the wrong approach."

They also want to establish a one-on-one counseling service for people who do not feel comfortable going to CAPS or do not want to wait for an appointment, White said.

"Taking that first step through the door of CAPS is a huge step," she said. "This would just give people a number they can call, if they don't feel ready for a group."

The phone number will be for people to call when they need help, whether they have an eating disorder or know someone who does, White said. Callers would be paired with a volunteer who has faced a similar situation.

The relationship could be anonymous, or the pair could meet regularly, depending on what the counselors and callers want, White said.

"We don't expect this to be a cure," she said. "But it always helps to talk to someone who has lived through the same thing." ∎

Fun Stuff

Worry, worry, worry—you might think that's all you'll do at a highly competitive college. You've got to make mom and dad proud, you've got to keep up your GPA to renew your scholarship for next year, you've got to pull your resume together for summer internships and apply for that study abroad program in Germany next year. Who has the time, or the energy, for fun?

You do, that's who. You've got to blow off steam somehow, and at a prestigious school there will be plenty of opportunities to get funky, laugh, play dress-up, and even—dare we say it?—date.

FUNKY FATHER FIGURE: GEORGE CLINTON FUNKS UP CROWD

By Andrew Schinder

CORNELL DAILY SUN (Ithaca, N.Y.) 11/03/1997

Junior high school kids could have had a field day with all the "types" of people represented at last Saturday night's George Clinton concert.

Clinton's mass appeal (Who doesn't like to get funky?) and longevity in the music industry—he's been a staple since the late '60s—brought out a wide array of races, ages, and sexes (two sexes to be exact). On a

less biological basis, there were preppies, punks, hippies, frat boys, Deadheads, potheads, funkheads, peaceniks, jocks, dorks, nerds, thugs, high school kids, scruffy-looking nerfherders and, of course, people who didn't know who the hell Clinton is but just didn't have anything better to do that night. Oh yeah, the press was there, too.

The United Nations of the Social World, though, is

Danya Pincayage/*The Dartmouth*

what made the George Clinton and the P-Funk All Stars that much better, because, usually, you don't see that many groups party together very often. It's a low-fat day at Chinese Buffet when Phish and Bad Religion pay a double bill, and when was the last time you partied with your professor? But they were all out at last weekend's funk-festival, dancing, singing and having a blast together. Life is a beautiful thing.

The only aspect of the concert more incredible than the crowd was the music itself. There aren't too many musicians half Clinton's age who perform with the energy, animation and charisma of the master of funk himself. Nor do they play for the length of time as Clinton and Co., as the Parliament Funkadelic jammed for an amazing three and a half hours, despite the fact that the show actually began an hour late. It isn't often a man in his sixties wears out a large group of college kids.

Serving as musical director and vocalist, Clinton doesn't really act as much of a musician during the show. In fact, during the entire show, he played about three or four notes on a keyboard. That's it. Clinton is a figurehead, and his presence is more important than any bassist or hornplayer. Credited as basically the inventor of modern funk, and sampled heavily by hip-hop artists, Clinton is a legend in the music industry and is an inspiration and idol to his musicians. The audience members, be they familiar with his work or getting funked up for the first time, each showed admiration with their overwhelming enthusiasm.

Clinton didn't just stand on stage and look patriarchal, however. Like the emcee at a large party, he worked the crowd like none other. He got funky like a college student, dancing about, jumping and singing—totally ageless. Clinton's granddaughter, Shonda, even appeared herself and rapped a few verses—three generations of straight-up, old-school funk represented to the delight of a most enthusiastic crowd.

The concert lasted past midnight, everyone had been partying for quite a while and a good portion of the crowd had left. But the audience members who remained were still energized, dancing around like the concert had just started, as the Parliament Funkadelic, with its rhythms and stage show, made it simply impossible for anybody not to dance and simply have a blast. Truly powerful music, and an absolutely captivating stage show.

Like Clinton & Co. preached during the closing song, "Ain't no party like a P-Funk party 'cause a P-Funk party don't stop." ∎

CONAN O'BRIEN BRINGS LAUGHS TO COLUMBIA U. DORM
By Eli Lassman

Columbia Daily Spectator (New York, N.Y) 11/17/98

Conan O'Brien, host of the television show "Late Night with Conan O'Brien" and a favorite among college students, entertained a crowd of 80 people in Carman Lounge last night. After a spontaneous tour of Carman's eighth floor, which included a brief surprise stop in a student's room, O'Brien answered students' questions during a free-form discussion.

O'Brien is well known for his work writing for "The Simpsons" and "Saturday Night Live." His late-night show, "Late Night with Conan O'Brien," is in its fifth season on NBC, and its popularity and ratings have steadily climbed since he succeeded "David Letterman" in the 12:35 a.m. time slot.

When O'Brien arrived, Carman Lounge was already filled with students. He talked briefly with students and posed for pictures. O'Brien asked for a tour of the dorm, claiming that the line for food from the buffet was not getting any shorter.

Guided by eighth floor resident advisor Joel Daniels, '00, and a growing entourage of students, O'Brien toured the eighth floor of Carman. Stopping at a message board, he drew the familiar caricature of himself that appears on Late Night. O'Brien said he used to do the same to boards all over campus when he was in college.

O'Brien paid a visit to the eighth-floor lounge and paused to watch "Jeopardy" with a group of stunned students. He made several jibes at the quality of the competitors in celebrity "Jeopardy" and expressed his desire to appear on the show.

"Watching "Jeopardy" was more fun with Conan mocking the contestants," eighth-floor resident Eric Phillips, '02, said.

Before leaving the floor, he toured the room of Nia Jacobs, '02. After trying out the bed, O'Brien asked if he could stay there for the night. An excited Jacobs pointed out the picture of O'Brien that was hanging above her bed.

"I'm never washing my sheets again," Jacobs said after O'Brien's visit.

"My residents watch him every night, and when he went up there, they were really excited," Daniels said of the visit.

After the tour, O'Brien returned to Carman's lounge, where he spoke to a standing-room only crowd.

O'Brien spoke briefly about his work, then opened the floor for questions from the audience. Many students asked about his tenure as a writer for *The Simpsons*. When asked what *The Simpsons* were like, he responded, "Well, they're not real."

Students also asked many questions about O'Brien's college experience at Harvard University. He said the most important thing that happened to him at college was that he started taking comedy seriously. O'Brien fell in with "The Harvard Lampoon"" by accident and found out he had the ability to write satire.

One of the most well-received stories was about the craziest thing he did while in college. O'Brien told the audience that he tricked comedian Bill Cosby into appearing at Harvard by fabricating an award. Students laughed at his account of picking Mr. Cosby up in his father's 1980 Ford Limited station wagon.

Most audience members seemed to enjoy the event. Jennifer Kim, CC '01, said, "[O'Brien] was really honest, but he was still funny, naturally funny." She was quick to add, "But he's also smart."

Nick Singer, CC '02, said O'Brien's discussion motivated him to be creative.

"He made me want to go out and do things. He inspired me to go out and do something creative; to go and create something funny," Singer said. ∎

Small Liberal Arts Schools

Alabama
Talladega College

Arizona
Prescott College

California
Mills College
New College of California
Pitzer College
Whittier College

Connecticut
Connecticut College

Florida
Flagler College

Georgia
Morehouse College
Thomas College

Idaho
Albertson College of Idaho

Illinois
Illinois Wesleyan
Millikin University
Shimer College

Indiana
DePauw University
Martin University
Tri-State University
Wabash College

Kentucky
Alice Lloyd College
Berea College
Sullivan College

Maine
Bates College
Bowdoin College
Unity College

Maryland
Goucher College
St. John's College
Villa Julie College
Washington College
Western Maryland College

Massachusetts
Bay Path College
Bradford College
Endicott College
Hampshire College
Lasell College

Pine Manor College
Wheaton College

Mississippi
Belhaven College

Missouri
Stephens College

Nevada
Sierra Nevada College

New Hampshire
Colby-Sawyer College
New England College

IN THIS CHAPTER

Bates College
Belhaven College
Bowdoin College
Bryn Mawr College
Connecticut College
DePauw University
Drew University
Hamilton College
Illinois Wesleyan
Lawrence University
Linfield College
Millikin University
Susquehanna University
Vassar College
Wake Forest University

New Jersey
Drew University

New Mexico
College of Santa Fe
College of the Southwest
St. John's College

New York
Boricua College
Cazenovia College
College of Mount Saint Vincent
Daemen College
Dominican College of Blauvelt
Hamilton College
Hartwick College
Hilbert College
Hobart and William Smith Colleges

Manhattanville College
Marymount College
Marymount Manhattan College
Medaille College
Molloy College
St. Joseph's College, New York
St. Joseph's College, Suffolk Campus
St. Thomas Aquinas College
Utica College of Syracuse University
Vassar College
Wells College

North Carolina
Johnson C. Smith University
Wake Forest University

Ohio
Antioch College
Denison University
Marietta College
University of Rio Grande

Oregon
Linfield College

Pennsylvania
Bryn Mawr College
Chatham College
Delaware Valley College
Juniata College
Point Park College
Susquehanna University
Washington and Jefferson College

South Carolina
Coker College
Limestone College

Tennessee
Cumberland University

Vermont
Burlington College
Marlboro College
Southern Vermont College

Virginia
Hollins University
Sweet Briar College

West Virginia
The College of West Virginia
Salem-Teikyo University

Wisconsin
Lawrence University
Mount Senario College
Ripon College

Small Liberal Arts Schools

It's time to shift gears and talk about small liberal arts colleges. We've included in this chapter private four-year colleges with enrollments ranging from under 1,000 to a maximum of 6,000 students. Most of the schools in this section don't have post-graduate programs.

Many small liberal arts schools originally had a religious affiliation (most often Christian), so you may find that some still have religion requirements. More often than not, however, there is no overt religious emphasis on campus. Keep in mind that the difference between a small liberal arts college and a religious college, which we'll talk about in the next chapter, may be that you'll be able to take courses in any religion offered, whether it be B'hai or Buddhism in small liberal arts schools, whereas most colleges you'll find in the next chapter on religious schools require you to take courses in the faith with which the university is affiliated. Naturally, because of the small number of students, the campuses of small liberal arts schools will be small; oftentimes there will be just one cafeteria and only a handful of academic facilities and dormitories. You'll find a range of selectivity in admissions policies, from least difficult to most difficult, as well as a range of locales, from rural areas to suburban and city locations.

Two factors distinguish small liberal arts schools from the rest: the atmosphere created by their small size and their focus on a well-rounded education through small classes. There's a definite feeling of "community" at small liberal arts schools; students have the opportunity to get to know each other, the faculty, and the administrators very well. In a way, it's a very safe feeling knowing everyone around you. But small size means there'll be few secrets on campus; there's a tendency at these schools for everyone to know every last detail about each other's lives. Many small schools also have Honor Codes, which you'll read about in depth in this chapter. Basically, that means that there are certain rules you'll be honor-bound to live by for the good of your small community. It's a lot of responsibility, but the rewards you'll receive for living by your school's Honor Code will be worth it. Best of all, the small classes will really allow you to get the most out of your education. You'll get down to the nitty-gritty in classes that encourage discussion among faculty members and students. Expect to develop close relationships with your professors. Both in and out of class, you'll find that your professors are focused on you—not just academically, but as a person, too. Expect very small classes, even for your freshman survey courses. At the average small liberal arts college, only 5 percent of all classes have more than fifty students—now that's impressive. Expect to live on campus; unless you're married or live with your parents, you'll probably be required by the school to share a dorm room with one or two other kids, maybe even for the duration of your schooling.

Naturally, you'll need to combat some myths about small liberal arts schools should you decide to enroll:

- Small schools don't offer a wide range of academic programs.
- Small schools don't offer a wide range of extracurricular activities.
- Small schools don't offer a wide range of student services.

Wrong on all counts. It's a big mistake to think that just because a college is small it will offer fewer academic programs, extracurricular activities, or student services. Academically, you'll find all kinds of coursework in an amazing array of subjects, as well as honors programs, study abroad programs, internships, "Jan plan" and winter semester programs, independent study options, and much more. And don't forget those small classes— another asset to small class size is that you'll be able to travel off campus easily for field trips, so there will be plenty of opportunities to experience as you learn. As far as extracurricular activities are concerned, you'll find the full

gamut at small liberal arts colleges: fraternities and sororities, varsity and intramural sports, and as many clubs and organizations as you can imagine. Since the arts are promoted at small liberal arts schools, you'll be able to express yourself creatively in a ton of ways, from ballet troupes and jazz bands to modern theater groups and choral ensembles. Since these colleges have a strong focus on writing, the campus newspaper and yearbook will also be strong forces on campus. Finally, you'll find that

David Clucas/*The DePauw*

student services at small schools will be plentiful—and top-notch. These schools are focused on you, and the services they provide prove it. Because of the great relationship you'll have with your professors, you'll find that advising services are fantastic; the same is true for career services, medical facilities, campus security, and all the other services you'll encounter.

On a typical day at a small liberal arts college, you'll probably start your day with a shower in the shared bathroom on your floor

(enough said about that). You and your roommate will head to the cafeteria for breakfast—hey, you better take advantage of that meal program, since it's included in your tuition. Then it's off to Intro to Art History, a course you're taking to fulfill your fine arts requirement, followed by your favorite— Advanced English Composition, a course for your major. Today your class will be critiquing each other's essays on the poetry of T. S. Eliot. Talk about a challenge! Then back to the caf for lunch before you make your way to the Sciences Building for Biology 101, or "Baby Bio," as they call it. (Another required course under your belt.) At 3 on the dot you gather with friends in the dorm lounge for a little *General Hospital*—after all, the saga of Luke and Laura has been a staple for many a college student. Better run—it's time for band practice, followed by intramural volleyball. Then you're back to the caf for dinner (believe us, you'll spend a lot of time in the college cafeteria) before a few hours at the library; you need to brush up on Emily Dickinson for your next Advanced Comp paper. On your way back to your dorm, you stop by the Student Center for a little Monday Night Football and nachos. The same crowd as usual greets you when you walk through the door.

As time boes by your little slice of the world will really feel like home. You'll take comfort in the fact that you know everyone. You'll reap the benefits of the Honor Code, if your college has one, and you'll feel safe among the faces you see everyday. Completing all those core requirements will give you an appreciation for subjects you never thought you'd be interested in, and you can just imagine what you'll learn in small classes that encourage interaction and dialogue. You and the gang will lay claim to a "regular" table in the cafeteria, and you may even get a private bathroom—or at least one you only have to share with three or four others—by the time you hit senior year. But best of all, after you graduate, you'll feel a special thrill when you're asked where you went to college and someone actually knows where it is! ■

Academics

Because none of the schools in this chapter offer graduate degree programs, you'll find that the attention at small liberal arts colleges will be on you, the undergraduate. Teachers, not graduate students, will teach your classes. And your classes will be small—really, really small. At both Vassar and DePauw, only 1 percent of all classes have fifty or more students; at Connecticut College, 68 percent of all classes have fewer than twenty students; and the student-faculty ratios at Vassar, DePauw, and Connecticut College are 10:1, 12:1, and 11:1, respectively. These data are representative of small liberal arts colleges nationwide. The further you get into your studies, the smaller your classes will be. Of course, that means that you probably won't be able to blend into the woodwork in your classes. Your professors will know you by name and will note your absence if you're not there. Many small liberal arts colleges have policies whereby your grade could be lowered if you miss a certain number of classes. Because classes are so small, it will be easy to bust you if you oversleep or feel like pitching horseshoes instead of going to your Friday afternoon class. But look at the bright side—you won't need to sit in the front to get noticed.

Most small liberal arts colleges require that you take lots of core courses to make you a well-rounded student. You'll probably have to complete a certain number of science, math, foreign language, English, and social science courses. There will also be a big focus on writing in all of your classes; teachers can grade papers much more easily because of small class size (so prepare for a fair share of 20-pagers), and expect lots of essay tests. But that's beside the point—we're talking about academics here. In addition to core courses, you'll find that small colleges offer as many academic possibilities as you can imagine; from coursework on the Holocaust at DePauw, the Harlem Renaissance at Hamilton, and the Cuban experience at Wake Forest, classes at small liberal arts colleges provide you with once-in-a-lifetime experiential learning opportunities that can satisfy any area of interest.

With small class size comes a focus on teaching and individualized attention. At small liberal arts colleges, teaching is, for the most part, emphasized over research. Students who attend small liberal arts colleges consider this to be one of the most beneficial elements of the overall learning environment. In fact, small class size and a focus on teaching are two reasons why students pay higher tuition rates to attend private liberal arts schools. "Editorial: Students play critical role in tenure evaluation" raises the issue of tenure, a hotly debated topic on small liberal arts college campuses. As you'll see, students at small liberal arts schools take exception to the fact that their professors are often required to focus attention on outside scholarly research to get tenure.

Perhaps most controversial of all at small liberal arts colleges are Honor Codes. Most of these schools, particularly those with a religious background or traditions, have very strict Honor Codes that students must sign or agree to before matriculating. While it's hard to disagree that Honor Codes improve everyone's lives by promoting a campuswide attitude of trust and freedom, it's even harder to ensure that everyone is taking them as seriously as the administration and most of the student body would like. The series of articles we've included from *The College Voice* of Connecticut College show that their honor code, while considered laudable by almost everyone on campus, is understood—or even adhered to—by a smaller percentage of students.

Admissions

Many of the colleges and universities in this chapter also consider themselves "most difficult" or "very difficult" when it comes to admissions standards, according to Peterson's Annual Survey of Undergraduate Institutions. Why, then, are they included in this chapter? For one reason in particular: size. Because these schools are often quite small (sometimes their student bodies number fewer than 1,000), they exhibit several common characteristics—and face many of the same problems. Admissions is one such area. Small liberal arts schools have to fight to get their names out there and into the minds of prospective students, whose exposure to colleges may only be to the "biggies" you see in televised collegiate sports.

Because they are smaller and have less name recognition, small liberal arts colleges often use innovative procedures to pique student interest and generate inquiries and applications. *The Bates Student* describes how their school is making the most of off-campus interviews, using upperclassmen to assist admissions representatives with prospective students, getting the word out about Bates on the World Wide Web, and making it easy to apply with the Common Application.

COMMON APPLICATION NOW THE STANDARD FOR BATES

By Joanna Standley

THE BATES STUDENT (Lewiston, Maine) 10/13/1998

While the class of 2002 is still adjusting to life at Bates, the admissions office is already actively recruiting the class of 2003. Last week, 25,000 high school seniors across the country and abroad received applications from Bates—specifically, the Common Application.

In the past, Bates accepted both its own application and the Common Application, giving equal consideration to both. However, this practice created some confusion on behalf of students and guidance counselors who wondered if one application had an advantage over the other.

In an attempt to remove the ambiguity associated with accepting both applications, Bates has switched exclusively to the Common Application, in conjunction with the Bates Supplement to the Common Application.

Dean of Admissions Wylie Mitchell hopes that this move will simplify the admissions process. "We were constantly being asked by students, 'Which application should I use?' So we said, let's eliminate the confusion," Dean Mitchell explained.

"We want to make it easier for students to apply to Bates and potentially de-stress students who are in the process of applying," he said.

The Common Application, which is printed and distributed by the National Association of Secondary School Principals, is currently accepted by 191 selective colleges and universities across the country, many of which use the form exclusively.

The concept behind the Common Application is simplicity—students fill out just one application, photocopy it, and send it to as many of the participating colleges as they want. Collectively, the participating colleges decide on the content and format of the application.

As with most college applications, the Common Application consists of an application for admission, a school report, and two teacher evaluations. Applicants must also write a personal statement, either on a topic of their own choice or on one of the topics suggested on the application.

Bates also requires that applicants complete a supplement to the Common Application, which requests information that is of particular interest to the admissions staff at Bates. The supplement includes a midyear report form, optional arts and athletic forms, and a contract for students who are applying Early Decision. In addition to the Common Application essay, applicants must respond to the question, "Why, in particular, do you wish to attend Bates?" Applicants are also encouraged to send supporting materials, such as slides of art work, creative writing samples, or personal recommendations.

Karen Kothe, assistant dean of admissions, explained that the supplement requires that applicants are familiar with Bates. "We want applicants to have had an interview and to have seen the campus. This is not an easy way out," she said. Switching to the Common Application is part of a larger effort by Bates to reach out to prospective students and raise the visibility of the college. Another venue Bates is increasingly utilizing is the world wide web. The Bates Admissions web site, www.bates.edu/admissions/, enables prospective students to download the Common Application, as well as access on-line companies like Apply! and CollegeEdge. Through CollegeEdge, students can build a profile on the internet and can essentially get recruited by colleges. "We can get names of students who meet the Bates criteria and then contact them," explained Dean Mitchell. "I think in a couple of years, most students will use one of these companies."

Between now and mid-December, Bates is also offering off-campus interviews in over 24 U.S. cities, as well as several locations overseas. "We're emphasizing getting the deans out of the office and to other cities," said Dean Kothe. "The idea is to take Bates on the road to prospective students."

However, the fall is also the busiest time for on-campus interviews, so the admissions staff has selected eight seniors, called Admissions Fellows, to assist with interviewing and other related tasks. "With so many of the deans out of the office, we need to have people manning the shop," Dean Kothe said.

Both Dean Mitchell and Dean Kothe are very optimistic about the new direction in which admissions is heading. "This admissions office is very innovative," said Dean Mitchell. "We are looking to balance how to provide personalized assistance while working on the scale we are on, which is clearly both national and international." ■

As you can see, Bates's no-holds-barred approach is getting their school noticed. The same is true of Connecticut College, which spreads the word about the school's early admissions policy through special mailings and group sessions at high schools. All of this leads to increased awareness about the college's topflight programs.

CONNECTICUT COLLEGE'S EARLY DECISION POOL LARGEST EVER

By Tiffany Taber

THE COLLEGE VOICE (New London, Conn.) 12/04/1998

The early decision program at Connecticut College has greatly increased in popularity this year with a 12 percent increase in students applying to the College by the month of November. This is the largest early decision pool in the history of the College.

The advanced notice program was established in 1968 with the class of 1972. The initiation of the procedure was due, for the most part, to a national trend among colleges recruiting desirable and interested students.

Essentially, early decision at Connecticut College is an option open to any applicant who has selected this institution as his or her first choice college. Applications are due in early November, and the applicant is notified of his or her acceptance in January.

The advanced notice option has been slowly increasing in popularity for the last five years, this year reaching its largest proportion yet.

This steady rise in the number of prospective students applying early is due to a number of factors. One contributing element is that the Office of

Admissions has sent out a special mailing to all prospective students outlining the details of the program. This is the first year that such a mailing has been distributed, and, though it is not entirely the cause of the jump, it helped to bring about awareness of the option.

According to Martha Merrill '84, the Assistant Director of Admissions, there are two other very important reasons why early decision is so popular this year. Merrill attributes the rise to the fact that the selectivity of the College has gone up quite a bit, while the admittance rate has (accordingly) gone down. With this occurring, many more students wish to secure a place in Connecticut College by applying early.

Campus Snapshot

CONNECTICUT COLLEGE
New London, CT

Craziest Thing That Happened on Campus:
Senior Streak—At the end of the year, the senior classes marches (runs) naked from one end of the campus to the other

Best Place to Be Alone:
The Arboretum—700-acre nature preserve

Most Popular Study Abroad Location:
This year, Vietnam

Things You Love to Hate About Your School:
Skunks

Recreational Sports of Choice:
Ultimate Frisbee

Although early decision does not necessarily guarantee that a student will be accepted, Merrill notes that "these students express a strong interest in Conn, and this really says something to the admissions committee."

The admittance rate among early decision applicants is greater than that of regular decision applicants, but this does vary yearly. It is important to note that even though the rate of admittance is higher in the early decision pool, this group is much smaller than the regular decision cluster.

Merrill also commented that another reason for the jump in advanced notice applicants is because of the many "distinctive and innovative programs" currently being offered at the College. She enthusiastically stated, "Connecticut College is becoming a first choice college among many prospective students now . . . which is a very good thing."

Even though this increase is a very exciting and positive occurrence, the admissions department is quick to point out that Conn promotes early decision; it does not force or "push" the program on students. Connecticut College advertises the procedure as an option.

The College also promotes the program by keeping families and high school guidance counselors informed and sending representatives of the College to school to talk about it. Many representatives also schedule group sessions with students at different high schools in order to showcase more perspectives about the benefits of the option.

Merrill stated that even though early decision is a great way to get an edge when applying to schools, the program is not always for everyone. She commented, "Basically each student needs to come to his or her own conclusion about which college is right. . . . [College selection] is a thoughtful process, and some students are not ready to make [early] decision a valid option in the beginning of the selection period." ∎

Teaching

One of the hallmarks of a small liberal arts college education is high quality teaching. As a small liberal arts college student, you'll get a lot of one-on-one attention right from the start of your education and will have the opportunity to form personal relationships with faculty members throughout the course of your studies. In fact, the bond you create with your faculty adviser will be one of the most important of your college experience. At a small liberal arts college, the emphasis is on teaching over research, although that's not to say that professors at small colleges don't do important research in all kinds of fields. But many professors who teach at small liberal arts schools do so to because they want to avoid the academic rat race of "publish or perish." They are there, quite simply, because they want to teach—lucky you!

But since they do perform outside scholarly work less often, professors at liberal arts colleges often have to contend with tenure issues. In academia, tenure is a status granted to a professor that gives the professor protection from summary dismissal. And, since colleges and universities want their professors to be both teachers *and* scholars, the amount of outside scholarly work a professor does or doesn't do can seriously affect his or her chances of getting tenure. It's a Catch-22 that many small liberal arts professors face: They want to ensure their job stability but often find that commitments to research can take time away from teaching, which is supposed to be their primary focus. What often makes the difference in tenure decisions at small liberal arts colleges, however, is student opinion. This editorial from *The College Voice* points out that students have a say at small liberal arts colleges when it comes to faculty tenure. At these schools, your opinions regarding faculty members are taken seriously.

EDITORIAL: STUDENTS PLAY CRITICAL ROLE IN TENURE EVALUATION

Staff Editorial

THE COLLEGE VOICE (New London, Conn.) 02/26/1999

By the time we have arrived at Connecticut College, we, the 1600-plus students of this College, have collectively experienced thousands of different teaching styles. In one class period, we have the practical experience to determine who can teach and who cannot. After having experienced millions of hours of education, we are, in effect, experts in judging the effectiveness of a professor's ability to teach.

Granted, there are exceptions to this rule. As individuals, we may be biased toward particular educators. In addition, we may not always be immediately able to recognize good teaching. However, as a whole, we overcome these limitations. We see a professor's ability to teach everyday in the classroom. As was the case with Professor Borelli last year, when the administration couldn't see Borelli's obvious teaching ability, we, the students, brought it to light.

Of course, teaching is only one part of the tenure evaluation process. Professors going up for tenure are generally reviewed on three grounds: teaching, scholarship, and service. In terms of scholarship, that is where our role in the process decreases. The best qualified group then becomes a professor's peers (other professors). The faculty as a whole clearly sits in the best position to judge one of their member's scholarship.

Finally, in the category of service, the entire Conn community is best qualified to judge a professor's performance. What has that professor's involvement in life outside of the classroom been like? How has that professor contributed to the quality of life at Conn? How much does he or she care about our community?

In evaluating a professor for tenure, it is crucial that we exercise our combined expertise as a college. Professors do their part, but we need to make sure that the student voice is continually represented. When course evaluations come around at the end of the semester, take them seriously. As students, we are professional in our ability to evaluate teaching. Accordingly, we do and must play a fundamental role in the tenure evaluation process. ∎

Research

Because they're so focused on teaching, professors at small liberal arts colleges don't participate in the kind of large-scale scientific or technical studies you've read about at highly competitive colleges and large state schools, and the funds for their research aren't usually as big—compare the size of the grant given to Professor Hess at Illinois Wesleyan to some of the numbers we saw at highly competitive and large state schools. However, as Professor McNicol from Connecticut College points out, liberal arts professors try to make their research relevant to world in which we live. To that end, small liberal arts college professors who do conduct research often tackle pretty cool, if obscure, topics, and undergraduates often have the chance to study with them. In fact, both *The College Voice* and *The Argus* mention using undergraduates in research studies.

CONNECTICUT COLLEGE PROFESSOR FINDS SUCCESS IN BOOK ON RURAL RADICALS
By Jeanine Millard

THE COLLEGE VOICE (New London, Conn.) 11/13/1998

Connecticut College's Associate Professor of History and Director of the American Studies Program Catherine McNicol Stock is the author of Rural Radicals: From Bacon's Rebellion to the Oklahoma City Bombing, which was recently released in paperback. The book examines "rural political radicalism" in the United States.

Stock says she got the idea for her book from the history course she was teaching here at Conn at the time the bombing occurred. She wanted her students to pick current events in the United States and look at them through their historical context. She used the Oklahoma City bombing as an example of something that could be better understood if looked at in an historical context, by studying other anti-government attacks of the twentieth century. The class outlined possible paper ideas, and Stock developed one of the

ideas into her book, with the help of a few students who acted as research assistants. Stock referred to the development of her book as a "happy accident."

Professor Stock thinks her book has been fairly successful for an academic book. It has been adopted by large classes at major universities, but she says, "Success of a book is also judged by how it's reviewed and whether it's controversial or not." Stock has been invited to speak about her book on many occasions and has continued to gain attention as more and more militia related attacks occur. Presently, Stock is still interested in rural history and rural politics and is working on an anthology of essays about rural politics in the twentieth century.

With regard to her time here at Connecticut College, Stock thinks it has affected her in a positive way, because the "liberal arts teaches us to make our scholarship relevant." ∎

NASA GIVES ILLINOIS WESLEYAN PROF $33,000 GRANT
By John Vrakas

THE ARGUS (Bloomington, Ill.) 10/27/1998

Cynthia Hess, assistant professor of physics, received a $33,000 grant from NASA Oct. 5 for proposed research using a new satellite telescope to be launched in January.

The Advanced X-ray Astrophysics Facility Telescope (AXAF) is a new, 40-foot telescope that will read X-rays from stellar objects in the universe. Hess said that "the Hubble of X-rays" promises dramatic advances in stellar information because of its unique vantage point in space.

The AXAF facility at Harvard granted Hess six hours on the AXAF next year to study an X-ray binary system, a neutron star and an ordinary star orbiting each other, in a nearby galaxy.

"I was really surprised to get the AXAF satellite time," Hess said. "They had four times the number of applicants for AXAF time than they actually had available."

This is Hess' third NASA grant in two years. She received a $10,000 grant and permission to work at the NASA Goddard Space Flight Center in Greenbelt, Md. during the summer of 1997 and a $10,000 renewal of that grant in 1998.

"This is vital to the IWU community because it provides students the opportunity to do high-tech, cutting-edge research with someone on the forefront of their field," Gabe Spalding, assistant professor of physics, said. "It's a real validation of her work from some of the top scientists in the country, and it's wonderful to be able to make students here a vital part of such recognized research."

"I think it's fantastic that undergraduates get to play such an important part in this research," junior physics major Matthew Dearing said. "It's rare that undergraduates have the opportunity to work on professional research with professional scientists."

The extremely dense neutron star is several times the mass of the sun but is only about the size of Chicago. In the X-ray binary system Hess is studying, the neutron star is pulling off the outer layers of the ordinary star, which spiral toward the neutron star to form a disc-shaped cloud of X-ray emitting gas.

With the help of the AXAF, Hess hopes to learn what is producing the X-rays and the composition, shape and size of the gas cloud. This will lead to a better understanding of how an X-ray binary system works and could shed further light on the behavior of stellar objects. ∎

Funding

You've got to figure that small schools need less money to operate. Because there are fewer students, housing demands won't be as great, academic facilities don't have to be as big, and the need for other facilities won't be as pressing. For example, most small liberal arts colleges have one cafeteria—compare that to some of the large state schools, which have cafeterias in every dormitory. *The Bates Student* reports on the excitement generated by a new academic building, which will house 11 separate departments in *one* building—compare that to large state and highly competitive schools, which often dedicate entire buildings to one discipline alone.

But that doesn't mean that fundraising isn't an issue at small liberal arts colleges. Let's look at the flip side of having fewer students: fewer alumni to hit up for funds, smaller endowments, less money brought in by research. The importance of fundraising is therefore paramount at small liberal arts colleges. When ground is broken on new facilities funded by hard work and generous donations or capital campaign goals are reached, then, you can understand why excitement would run high, as it did recently at Bates College and Connecticut College.

NEW BATES BUILDING GETS NEW GRANTS

By Jennifer Merksamer

THE BATES STUDENT (Lewiston, Maine) 10/16/98

The new academic building, which will house eleven departments, including all of the social sciences, will be finished for the beginning of the 1998-99 academic year.

The building, which is composed of various sized classrooms and the resources for student lab research, will cost $18.5 million including the cost of maintaining the building. Funding was provided through a $6 million bond from the Kresse Foundation and $12 million from 130 individual donors.

The principle behind the building originated from the concept of uniting departments with common bonds whose offices and classrooms are currently scattered around campus, including anthropology, history, political science, education, psychology, economics, sociology, classical and medieval studies, women's studies, African American Studies and American Cultural Studies.

State-of-the-art classrooms will be provided which include outlets for laptop computers and the ability for flexible tele-conferences. There also is a kaleidoscope lecture hall which can seat 125 people. On each floor, lounges for faculty-student conferences, faculty offices, student research centers, and 25 and 60 person classrooms will be provided.

Space was allotted for an anthropology laboratory on the ground floor, three psychology labs on the third floor and an education workroom on the third floor as well. The three story atrium may be used as a gathering place, as well as for small events.

Fund-raising was accomplished by the Trustees, through the Development Office, and is almost complete. $1.8 million is still needed. Ursula Pettengill donated a wing with a contribution of $2.3 million in memory of her husband Frederick B. Pettengill '31 because she wanted to do something for the school. Ralph Perry provided the funding to build the atrium in his wife's name, Joan Holmes Perry '51. ∎

Academic Resources

You can see that everything's done on a much smaller scale at the colleges in this chapter. This also applies to library and computer facilities. At a small liberal arts college, the library won't be as huge, and there may only be one. This could work in your favor—you might find it far less intimidating to study and research in the more cozy digs that you'll find at small liberal arts colleges. With fewer students on campus, there's more of a chance that the book you absolutely need to review for the art history paper that's due tomorrow (how could you have waited so long?) will be on the shelves, and not checked out by some graduate student that's had it for two years while he works on his dissertation. But smaller libraries could have a down side, too; usually, it's less convenient hours. *The Miscellany News* reports here how Vassar students have had to fight for what most students at large state schools and highly competitive schools would take for granted—late library hours.

STUDENTS PROPOSE EXTENSION OF VASSAR COLLEGE LIBRARY HOURS

By Nicholas Loss-Eaton

THE MISCELLANY NEWS (Poughkeepsi, N.Y.) 02/19/99

Members of the Vassar Students Association Council and representatives from the Vassar College Libraries have been discussing the possibility of extending the library's hours into the night.

Class of '01 President Allison Berger met with Director of the Libraries Sabrina Pape to discuss the possibility of the main library increasing its night hours. Both Pape and Berger are in support of this change. However, financial, employment and logistical details remain unsolved for now.

"The library should be open as much as possible. Extending the library hours to 2 a.m. is a good idea, a good start. Ideally, I'd like to see the library open 24 hours," said VSA President Evan Greenstein '99. "Even the administration supports the concept. Now it's a matter of taking the concept and looking at the hard facts of how much it's going to cost."

Berger said that the current library hours are not adequate, since there are numerous students who have "meetings, activities and sports, many of which cause students to be unable to begin studying until 10 or 11 p.m."

According to Berger, the idea of extending library hours came up earlier this year while the VSA Council was examining the apparent success of the extended library hours during the past two study weeks (prior to final exams).

"We started [extending library hours during study and finals weeks] last year. I wanted to see how useful students found that," said Pape. "I haven't gotten a lot of feedback but the feedback I have gotten was [positive]."

Many believe that the library should be open later every night instead of merely during study week.

"I like to try to study later at night, but I cannot study in my room because my roommate wants to sleep," said Clarice Meadows '02. "I use the library a lot, but I would definitely use it more if it were open later."

The library committee considered the idea of opening the library later in the morning to keep it open later at night, which would not add extra hours, but shift those already in existence. However, this option did not prove viable because, while most students do not often use the library in the early morning, professors make heavy use of it during that time period.

One idea that was discussed was to keep the library open for students to study until 2 a.m., but to close the research desk and reserve room earlier. This would only require employees to check out books, which Berger said that she hoped would cut down the cost of extending the hours.

"I'm very supportive of extending library hours, but I am not supportive of trying to do it with [only] student assistant help," said Pape. "Their chief reason for being here is not to work in the library, and they are often not as reliable as we need them to be."

Nevertheless, Pape has looked into the hours of other colleges' libraries. "Fifty percent are open until midnight; the other 50 percent [remain open until] 1 a.m. That would be a more feasible time for us [than 2 a.m.], though I am open to looking at 2 a.m. as well. That extra hour would make a big difference in students' lives," she said.

"I think if we pushed for it, it could happen. If an hour's all we can get, an hour's all we can get, but even that would be well worth it," said Berger. ■

Keep in mind, though, that smaller can be better. This particularly applies to technology facilities at small liberal arts colleges. You probably won't have to sign up to get a spot at the PC lab at a small liberal arts college, since you won't be competing for space with 20,000 other students. Small liberal arts colleges like Wake Forest can also often afford to buy a manageable number of students their own laptops. Imagine the pandemonium that would ensue if a large state school tried to gather together its entire junior class to exchange laptops, which recently took place at Wake Forest.

WAKE JUNIORS EXCHANGE THINKPADS FOR UPGRADE

By Sarah Rackley

THE OLD GOLD & BLACK (Winston-Salem, N.C.) 08/28/1998

On Aug. 22 and 24, the junior class completed the first ThinkPad exchange as part of the Undergraduate Plan. The junior class, the first class to receive ThinkPads, returned the models they received upon entering the university in exchange for new ones. .

The exchange took place in Reynolds Gymnasium for the approximately 940 juniors. Each student reported with his ThinkPad and all accessories and basic functions were checked.

Fines were assessed for missing components or damage to hardware, and the students parted with the ThinkPads they had used for two years.

After numerous ID checks, juniors left the gym with new ThinkPads and few complaints about the process. Features of the new ThinkPads, which the freshman class also received, include Netscape Mail and hardware upgrades.

The juniors will take the computers with them when they graduate. The similarity of the new computer to the original ThinkPad used by the juniors has made transition between models only a minor inconvenience. "I was kind of getting used to the old one, and now I have to learn a new one," junior Stephanie Fulton said.

Microsoft Office '97 will be installed in 800 of the used ThinkPads, which will then be sold to the Winston-Salem/Forsyth County school system for classroom use. The computers, originally purchased by the university for approximately $2,800 each will be sold for $550 each to the school system. ■

Academic Opportunities

One thing that won't be smaller at a small liberal arts college will be the number of academic opportunities available to you. As a small college student, you'll be able to enroll in lots of great classes, just like at other schools. And you'll also benefit from the philosophy of a liberal arts education, which stresses interdisciplinary studies, writing and language skills, and critical thinking. Small, seminar-type classes will be built on student-faculty discussion and interaction. And because class size is small, you'll get all the attention you need. Small class size not only encourages more lively discussion; it also means that the entire class can go on field trips together or can meet at your professor's house for a study session (and some home cooking if you're really lucky).

Read on to find out more about the great academic opportunities you'll find at small liberal arts colleges across the country. At DePauw University, you can take advantage of its Winter Term trips and classes, which encourage nontraditional, experiential learning through coursework, both on campus and at other institutions; group travel/study, like the "Remember the Holocaust Tour" highlighted here; internships; and independent study projects. In 1999, Susquehanna University will graduate its first majors in writing, proving that if you want it, you can find it at a small liberal arts college.

DePAUW STUDENTS TAKE WINTER TERM TO EXPERIENCE THE LESSONS OF THE HOLOCAUST

By Emily Fox and Abby Lovett

THE DEPAUW (Greencastle, Ind.) 10/05/1998

Most DePauw students that go on Winter Term trips expect to change someone else's life. Students going on the "Remember the Holocaust" tour should expect to have their lives changed.

"Remember the Holocaust Tour" is a new Winter Term project designed and proposed by music professor Cleveland Johnson. For three weeks, the group will tour points of interest relating to the grim and appalling events of the Holocaust in the Netherlands, Austria, Hungary, Poland and Germany. In Amsterdam, the group will visit the famous Anne Frank House and the exceptional Jewish Historical Museum. In Vienna,

students will explore the Austrian Jewish Museum, another fine opportunity to examine the history of the Jewish people. In Vienna, there will be daytime excursions to Eisenstadt, the site of the Jewish Ghetto in the early 20th century, and to Mauthausen to tour a former Nazi concentration camp.

From Vienna, the group will proceed to Budapest where they will have the opportunity to see the Great Synagogue, which was reconstructed after being razed by Nazis. In Krakow and Lublin, the tour will include walks through pre-war Jewish sites such as the Old Jewish Quarter.

While in Poland, the group will also visit one of the

most haunting reminders of the Holocaust: the infamous Auschwitz concentration camp.

In Prague, students will tour more concentration camps and see such sites as the Old Jewish Cemetery. The tour concludes in Berlin with a five-day German Rail Youth Pass, which allows five days of travel through Germany by train.

Throughout the tour, Johnson plans to hold occasional reflection sessions in the evenings to allow students to share their intense personal reactions to such life-changing experiences as the trip to Auschwitz.

Johnson arrived at the idea last spring after Kitty Steele passed away. Steele was a member of the English Department and taught a literature course on the Holocaust. She was an integral part of Holocaust studies at DePauw and Johnson said he is "trying to pick up the ball where she left off." He considers the trip to be in memory of her influence.

He expects the trip to be more than just sight-seeing. "I want this to be a personally transforming experience."

Indeed, this is exactly what students are expecting. Sophomore Ian Winn hopes to gain a better understanding of just what happened there and good experience with travel abroad.

When Johnson first visited the sites on tour, it was "a turning point in my life. Actually seeing the sites made such an amazing impact." He said he hopes the trip will impact the students similarly.

Johnson encourages all students to consider the "Remember the Holocaust" project. He does not want money to be the deciding factor of a student' s interest. "Money is out there. I don't want financial concerns to prevent anyone from experiencing such an opportunity for personal growth." ■

FIRST WRITING MAJORS TO GRADUATE FROM SUSQUEHANNA U.

By Branden Pfefferkorn

THE CRUSADER (Selinsgrove, Penn.) 12/04/1998

"Ever since fourth grade, I've wanted to be a writer. I thought that I couldn't get a job or make money as a writer. But I discovered my passion. I'm going to do what I love and not worry."

Sandra Hrasdzira's words show the passion for writing that started early for her and Julie Danho, members of the first senior class of writing majors. Danho commented, "We're like the guinea pigs," referring to the new writing major.

Danho started her writing career with a poetry assignment in third grade. Both students said they began to write seriously after their first creative writing courses. This occurred for Danho in ninth grade and for Hrasdzira in eighth grade.

Writing about women's issues is one thing both students have in common. Hrasdzira said, "I think it's important that women realize that they aren't always going through things alone."

In addition to writing about women's issues, Hrasdzira also writes about her dreams, fears and religion. Hrasdzira added she does not like writing when she feels limited on a subject.

"I'd rather write what I want, in the way I want," she said.

Danho said she also writes about women's issues as well as her own life. She added she would like to move from this personal writing to writing based on research or interviews.

In either case, she said, "I like the finished product best—to have a work that I'm proud of . . . and I can be happy with it until I write the next thing."

Both students said they are looking forward to careers that will enable them to use their writing skills. Danho plans to attend graduate school and work for a magazine or a non-profit organization as a writer. Hrasdzira said she plans to work either for a women's magazine or in publishing.

"I just want to write," she added. ■

Outstanding Professors

What makes professors at small liberal arts schools great? First and foremost, their attention to teaching and their personal connection to students. Many professors choose to teach at small liberal arts schools because they want that connection with their students—notice here how Professor Dudley at DePauw comments that he found the fast pace of a big school unappealing and how Professor Wethli of Bowdoin says that teaching is integral to his art. Although both of these men enjoy recognition in their fields outside the college—one in book publishing and editing an important journal and the other through exhibiting his artwork around the country—both find that the experience of teaching is what gets them going. At small liberal arts schools like DePauw and Bowdoin, you can get to know great professors like these on a personal level and really find out what makes them tick.

DePAUW U. PROFESSOR AND HIS QUIRKY BOOKS EARN RECOGNITION

By Mary Anne Potts

THE DePAUW (Greencastle, Ind.) 02/09/1999

"Numbers are male and female. Now, I didn't say this; it goes back to the ancient Greeks," Professor Woody Dudley explained regarding "Numerology," one of his five books.

"See, odd numbers are male while even numbers are female because they can easily be divided—they are weaker," the 32-year fixture of the Mathematics Department said with a knowing smile, apparently aware of the offensive nature of the Greeks' numerical gender bias.

Dudley is a long-time math professor and writer whose books have even been cited in *The New York Times*. That paper cited Dudley and his book "Mathematical Cranks" earlier this month.

While Dudley's work made its way from Greencastle to New York, Dudley himself took a slow road from the Big Apple. A native of New York City, he studied mathematics at Carnegie Institute of Technology, now Carnegie Mellon University. After graduation, Dudley took a job at Metro Life Insurance as an actuary.

"I probably would be a big VP by now," Dudley confessed. But he chose to take his life in a different direction. "I remember it well, the crummy room, the dreary day. I thought, 'I can't spend my life like this,' " he said.

So, he then spent six years earning a doctorate in mathematics from the University of Michigan. After a brief stint teaching at Ohio State, Dudley said he found the fast pace of a big research university unappealing. He's been at DePauw ever since. He enjoys teaching and nurturing the 10 to 15 math majors each year.

"The hard part is that people think math is plugging numbers into formulas, but math is really thinking, not finding the right answer," he said.

Again, Dudley's books have brought him much recognition. Math is a hard topic to write about, which is why textbooks are revised every year. However, Dudley was proud that his textbook "Numerology," published in 1969, is still in print today. In fact, he teaches from it in his numerology class.

"I make the students buy my book but I refund the royalties. They get five bucks back," Dudley said. "You can't make a profit off of your students." Dudley wrote his books in his office in the science and math center, writing in the morning while caffeine still surged through his bloodstream. He admitted that writing a book is hard work.

"You scribble something down and then turn that into a first draft and then write it over again, then see that it's not very good and has to be done again," he said.

Dudley has also written journal articles and is currently serving a five-year term as editor of the College Mathematics Journal. The New York Times recently ran an article about mathematical phonies who used Dudley and his book as sources. "Mathematical Cranks," published in 1992, describes the cranks as "mathematical amateurs who don't know that much about mathematics but like to work on mathematical problems. Sometimes, when you can't convince them that they haven't done what they thought they've done, they turn into cranks; but they aren't nuts, they're just people who have a blind spot in one direction."

Dudley said he does not plan to write any more books. "There are easier ways to earn 50 cents an hour," he said. ∎

BOWDOIN ART PROFESSOR RECEIVES CHAIRED PROFESSORSHIP

By Stacy Humes-Schulz

THE BOWDOIN ORIENT (Brunswick, Maine) 02/17/1999

Professor of Art Mark Wethli was recently named the A. Leroy Greason Professor of Art, an endowment granted to professors in the creative arts.

A realist painter, Wethli has taught drawing, painting and printmaking at Bowdoin since 1985, when he joined the college as an associate professor of art and director of the studio art department. His own work focuses on small-scale realistic interior views. "I'm interested in the play of light on interior spaces," he said.

Wethli's work has been exhibited nationwide, and several of his paintings are included in the collections of major museums such as the Metropolitan Museum of Art and the Portland Museum of Art. The National Endowment for the Arts awarded Wethli a $20,000 endowment in 1995, selecting him and twenty other painters from a pool of over 2,600 artists.

According to Wethli, teaching art at Bowdoin is just as important as painting or preparing for exhibitions. "For many artists, to do what they do and then teach it is two sides of the same coin," he said. "I am most productive and most complete when I am teaching. It's a way of being public and social with my knowledge."

Wethli says he was attracted to teaching at Bowdoin because of the liberal arts atmosphere. "It is precisely the type of environment where teaching art is important, he explained. "Half of my students are majors in other fields, and this is yet another perspective of the world they can graduate with."

Ten of Wethli's newest works will be introduced this Saturday at the opening of a show in Los Angeles. The Alumni Club of Los Angeles is hosting a private preview of these pieces prior to the public opening. Wethli has also held individual shows at the Tatistcheff gallery in New York for the past eight years.

Before coming to Bowdoin, Wethli taught at the University of Northern Iowa, California State University at Long Beach and Barry College of Florida. He was also employed as an art director by several New York publishing companies after earning his bachelor's and master's degrees at the University of Miami.

The A. Leroy Greason Professorship was established in 1987 in the name of former Bowdoin College President Greason in 1987. Leon O. Gorman U56, who was greatly influenced by the president and former English professor, set up the endowment, with help from Wendy A. Gorman. "I probably consider the award the greatest honor one can receive," Wethli said. ∎

Advising

Need help choosing your courses or picking a major? Never fear—advising at small liberal arts colleges has a great reputation. Once you declare your major, you could be one of only a handful of advisees that your adviser has. And even before you declare your major, you'll be able to develop a personal relationship with your freshman adviser, who will do much more than just sign off on your proposed courseload for the semester.

Small liberal arts colleges also focus strongly on peer advising, which we've seen at other schools. Peer advising is great for both the advisee, who gets the help he needs, and the adviser, who gets valuable experience. Because writing is an important focus at small liberal arts colleges, students often need a little extra help to eliminate the wicked dangling modifier from their parallel constructions. For this reason, peer writing centers like the one at Vassar are big at small liberal arts colleges.

NEW VASSAR WRITING CENTER AIMS AT PEER ADVISING FOR ALL DISCIPLINES

By Kevin Aldridge

THE MISCELLANY NEWS (Poughkeepsie, N.Y.) 02/26/1999

The new Writing Center, a college-wide facility funded by College President Frances Fergusson, will have its own study room once the library is renovated, according to Associate Professor of Classics Rachel Kitzinger. In the meantime, study room 302 in the tower of the library serves as a center for peer writing help.

The focus of the program is to allow students to comment on and critique other students' work. "Students working with other students on writing is a very valuable thing," said Kitzinger.

An important aspect of the program is that it is not meant to replace the professors, but rather to supplement their input and tutelage. The center's hours are designed for times when professors are not typically available for office hours.

Sometimes when professors critique, their suggestions are taken as directives, and students feel as if they have to follow instructions. According to Kitzinger, with peers, students feel free to think on their own, plus they are more comfortable asking questions and admitting that they do not understand.

The senior interns are skilled writers who are able to communicate and offer advice. Their responsibility is to go over papers that are already corrected or critiqued. Students are deterred from showing up at the center with nothing written; there must be some

initial effort on their part. They can bring a sketch of a paper or a rough draft and use the intern's help to flesh out a paper or ideas.

The main goal is for the interns to help people think through what they want to write about, organize a paper and figure out how to support an argument.

The service was initially offered last semester, when the four senior interns were assigned to specific freshman English courses. The students made appointments with the interns to discuss their papers. Because of fewer freshman courses this semester, the interns had more time on their hands and less to do. Kitzinger decided to take advantage of the extra help and implement the Writing Center, a project she's wanted to start for several years.

A few years ago a committee devised an elaborate proposal which included two writing interns per freshman class. The project was too big to start out with. This semester there was the opportunity to start smaller.

Kitzinger stressed that the service is open to anyone who wants help with their writing. It is not discipline-specific, even though all four senior interns are English majors.

The center is still very much in the experimental stages, trying to figure out what to keep and what to change. Kitzinger is dedicated to keeping it going and would like any comments or suggestions that anyone may have to improve it. ∎

Academic Dishonesty

At small liberal arts colleges, academic dishonesty is a big deal. In fact, most small liberal arts colleges have Honor Codes that students must sign or otherwise agree to. At some small liberal arts schools, Honor Codes reach into other aspects of students' lives as well. In fact, Honor Codes can apply to areas from cheating and plagiarism to stealing and alcohol policy violations. Students who attend small liberal arts colleges willingly sign and agree to Honor Codes for many reasons, the biggest reason being the increased freedom it gives them. Students at schools that have Honor Codes can take self-scheduled or unproctored exams, don't have to worry about sensors on library books, and leave their bicycles unlocked in front of dormitories. They enjoy the trust that the faculty members and administrators have in them and don't want to lose the benefits gained from that trust. If you agree to abide by a school's Honor Code, however, you're committed to do so; violating your pledge can result in severe punishments. Students look down on those who don't uphold the code; with every infraction, everyone loses a little bit more freedom. Violators may be summoned before student-led courts that try violators and decide their fate; for this reason, proceedings of these courts are very discreet.

That Honor Codes are a big deal at small liberal arts colleges is brought home in this series of articles from *The College Voice* of Connecticut College. Connecticut College's Honor Code is one of a few of its kind left in the country. It covers all academic and social interactions of students, is governed completely by students nominated and elected from each class by their peers, and has no common religious point of view. *The College Voice*'s finding that a full 50 percent of students polled by the newspaper had broken the code and that 27 percent had signed the code knowing they would break it unleashed a firestorm of accusations and counteraccusations across campus. While most find the spirit of the Honor Code to be admirable, many find the tenets confusing, some question the way violations are handled, and some point out that faculty members are reluctant to bring offenders before the board. The articles point to the same problems with cheating that we found at other schools, even with an Honor Code in place.

HONOR CODE CONFUSES CONNECTICUT COLLEGE STUDENTS

By Kate Woodsome

THE COLLEGE VOICE (New London, Conn.) 10/23/1998

On Sunday September 6, this year's freshman class followed the tradition of previous years as they entered Palmer Auditoreum for their Matriculation. An integral part of this ceremony includes pledging to abide by the Honor Code. Although this code is unwritten, over 1,500 students have declared to uphold it. In a recent Voice survey, however, many students have expressed uncertainty about what the Honor Code actually is.

Survey results showed that of 106 participants, 97 of them believe the morality implied in the Honor Code is a noble concept. While taking the poll the majority of these students expressed ambiguity over the definition of the Honor Code. First year student Leslie Feinberg hesitated over her survey saying, "It's a nice idea but they didn't explain it clearly." Her friend, Alex

Band, chimed in "I don't even know exactly what the Honor Code is!" Feinberg and Band are not alone.

Despite the great number of students who believe in the Honor Code, 50 percent of them reported that they have broken it. Ninety-two percent of those students say they have breached the code for reasons other than cheating. Eight percent reported that they have cheated. Expecting to see a greater number of cheaters, students were surprised by the low percentage. Junior Tricia Auro believes that significantly more students cheat on tests than what the survey shows. "I think a lot of people come to this school because they can get away with everything. Come finals time, you hear a lot of stories about cheating. It's enough to make you mad," she declared.

Another student claimed the Honor Code "helps

Campus Snapshot

CONNECTICUT COLLEGE
New London, CT

Best Thing About On-campus Housing:
Coed bathrooms, singles for all sophomores and up

Phrase on Everyone's Lips:
"What's the TNE this week?" (Thursday Night Event)

Popular Social Causes:
Free Tibet, Free Burma, Save the Spotted Owl Society

Bands that Came to Campus:
Goo-Goo Dolls, Dave Matthews, Redman, Agents of Good Roots

Beverages/Cocktails of Choice:
Busch Light, fuzzy navels

cheaters graze in this school. [The administrators] don't care if students cheat. If they did, they'd have someone watch you." He also said he doesn't know many people who play by the rules. He does not have much faith in Conn's Honor Code, alleging that "[the administrators] don't want you to get in trouble because they don't want to hurt the school's image." In addition, he believes that the Judicial Board will not do anything to reprimand breaches in the Honor Code.

Judiciary Board Chair Matt Cipriano and Dean of Student Life Catherine Woodbrooks counter such accusations. They believe students can be reprimanded more severely at Conn than at other colleges because punishment is left up to the students' peers. Wood-Brooks feels students learn more about their moral values after facing their peers than after facing an external conduct office. She claims that institutions with self-scheduled exams and honor codes have fewer incidents of students cheating. She attributes this information to a 1990 survey of 30 undergraduate colleges and universities issued by Don McCabe. In addition, Woodbrooks says there are generally less than ten instances of academic dishonesty brought before the Judicial Board each year.

Cipriano admits that the Judicial Board can be hard on wrongdoers, but claims the council's purpose is not to make life miserable for students violating the unseen Honor Code. Also, despite student concerns about the Code's vagueness, Cipriano believes that the Honor Code can be followed without being set in stone. Glen Harnish disagrees with Cipriano concerning the severity of the Judicial Board's punishments and believes teachers are a lot more understanding of students. Harnish added, "The Honor Code's so unclear that it gives too much leeway to the Judicial Board. These kids [the members of Judicial Board] have something to prove." ∎

HONOR CODE SURVEYOR TO CONN STUDENTS: CODE ONLY AS POWERFUL AS STUDENTS MAKE IT

By Karen O'Donnell

THE COLLEGE VOICE (New London, Conn.) 12/04/1998

In response to shocking student responses in a College Voice Honor Code survey, members of the J-Board brought Honor Code surveyor Don McCabe to speak about the correlation between Honor Codes and academic honesty. In the October 23 issue, several students said that they were either unconcerned about adhering to the terms of the Honor Code or were simply unaware of its conditions.

McCabe, the Associate Provost for Campus Devel-opment and professor of organization management at Rutgers-Newark, is also the founding president of the Center for Academic Integrity. Over the years, McCabe has surveyed over 6000 students at 31 small to midsize selective colleges and universities, including Connecticut College, in an attempt to see if students attending schools with an Honor Code are less likely to cheat.

Comparative results gathered from 1962, 1990, 1993, and 1995 surveys show that cheating has increased over the years, with a higher rate of cheating occurring in schools without Honor Codes, especially larger universities. McCabe explained that students are more likely to cheat at larger, less selective schools "because it's easier to blend in and not get caught," whereas, with smaller schools, other students will notice Honor Code violations. If the student body largely supports the Honor Code, "it's difficult to survive and feel comfortable cheating," McCabe said.

According to McCabe, whether or not a school has an Honor Code, "there is a certain understanding the students come to as to what's permissible and what's not permissible" when it comes to cheating. McCabe calls understanding the "cheating culture," and it is "the single most important influence on new students as they arrive." New students observe others' work ethics and are very likely to adopt similar opinions and habits of academic integrity and cheating. If the majority of the school's student body doesn't support the Honor Code, incoming students are also unlikely to place value in the Code.

Aside from campus socialization, another factor

influencing students to either support or disregard the Honor Code is their perception of faculty enforcement of the Code. "If students perceive they aren't likely to be caught or punished, they will be more likely to cheat," McCabe said. "Faculty have issues in that they will lose some control" in adopting an Honor Code with a student-run judiciary board, but "students happen to be tougher on cheaters than teachers are."

Because a large portion of the audience consisted of members of the J-Board and SGA, several students asked McCabe how they could improve Conn's Honor Code. To this, McCabe referred to Bryn Mawr College's successful Honor Code that "focuses around caring rather than discipline." Students at Bryn Mawr are not permitted to discuss their GPA because it incites competition, and they have arguably one of the most strongly supported and successful Honor Codes among the schools surveyed. However, McCabe went on to say that the cheating culture remains the most important source of influence, and if the student body does not place value in their Honor Code, the Code will hold no power. ■

COLUMN: CHALLENGE TO STUDENT GOVERNMENT—GET RID OF CONFIDENTIALITY

By Brian Bieluch

THE COLLEGE VOICE (New London, Conn.) 02/19/1999

You receive a notice demanding that you appear at a secret location before an arguably elected tribunal. You are notified that you are being brought up on charges which you may not discuss with anyone, "even to the extent that" a case exists. If you do "violate" this "confidentiality," you can be prosecuted.

Is this a Turkish prison? Are you a political prisoner in Iraq? Has Martial Law been declared? Actually, no—you have just been "invited" to defend your "honor" in secret in front of Connecticut College's Student Judiciary Board.

J-Board as a whole is not a bad concept. On the other hand, so-called "confidentiality"—the requirement that no student discuss a current J-Board case, and after the case is resolved only the accused may report limited facts—is a horribly unjust concept. The

principle of habeas corpus has been fundamental to American democracy. The concept of "producing the body" (bringing the accused into a public forum to stand trial) is a fundamental protection against arbitrary and capricious use of power by authority.

For the accused, our school's version of "confidentiality" prevents them from having the best possible defense. Individual students, faculty, and staff, even when directly consulted, cannot offer their advice to the accused on a defense. In addition, witnesses with information on an incident may be unaware that an individual is being tried.

As a community, the implications are even scarier. Individuals "confidentially" J-Boarded for driving under the influence of alcohol will not have to face the local authorities. (Being shielded from the law is also bad for the accused. Rather than receiving a fair trial held in accordance with fundamental American rights, accused individuals have no such protection of their individual rights.)

In the broadest sense, "confidentiality" means that we cannot learn from our mistakes as a community. Rumors fly throughout the campus on J-Board trials, and no legitimate campus news organization is allowed to dispel them with a fact-based news story. In short, "confidentiality" guarantees that nothing good can come from our mistakes. Instead of an individual's

bad choice leading to a campus-wide discussion on how we can improve Conn, "confidentiality" dooms us to repeat our mistakes.

Where does this leave us? Connecticut College's honor code is a student honor code. Accordingly, the Student Government Association has the power to change it. We need to take a hard look at our school's "confidentiality." While there may be some aspects of "confidentiality" we want to keep, a lot of it clearly must go for J-Board to ever be just. ■

Grading

If you sign an Honor Code, chances are that you'll be living your life on the straight and narrow at a small liberal arts college. You'll have to work extra hard to get good grades. Remember how we said that nothing you do will escape the notice of your professors at a small liberal arts college? Because you'll be so close to your professors, their personal opinion of you could affect your grade. Many support blind review, where the professor grades your work without seeing your name. Of course, if your work is truly exemplary or stands out in any other way, the professor will probably know it's yours even without the name, but many, like the editors of *The Lawrentian*, still consider blind review to be a good thing.

EDITORIAL: A CASE FOR BLIND REVIEW AT LAWRENCE U.
Staff Editorial

THE LAWRENTIAN (Appleton, Wis.) 05/26/1998

Part of the duty of a professor is to grade student work fairly. While Lawrence professors generally make an effort to do so, subjective influences sometimes diminish that state of fairness. To combat such personal consideration, many professors grade student work without knowledge of who produced it. It would be beneficial for professors who currently do not use such a system to follow the lead of their colleagues.

Blind review would protect against conscious personal consideration of students. That the person reviewing a paper would intentionally consider his or her personal opinion of a student in figuring a grade seems unlikely, but it is a possibility. Blind review of work can safeguard against this possibility.

The problem with identification of a work with its

author lies mainly in subconscious, not conscious thought. It is possible that knowing the author of a work can have an unintentional effect upon the grade. Even something as trivial as remembering that the author related an amusing anecdote during office hours or does not attend class regularly can affect the person reviewing the work. It can change a professor's mood imperceptibly and thus influence the final grade. While some of these influences may seem too small to matter, the attempt should be made to remove any influences—whenever practical.

We do not, however, advocate a university policy that mandates blind review of all work. Such a mandate would be impractical at times.

Seminars or small classes are examples where blind review may not be applicable. In some cases, students' discussion in class is relevant to their work on a paper, so blind review would hinder a professor's ability to judge the students' understanding. Some classes are small and have projects that must be discussed with the instructor. There, blind review is impossible.

It is also not always necessary in classes with work that has definite right and wrong answers. The square root of nine is three, diamond is harder than quartz, and there are four quarter notes per bar in 4/4 time—no matter how annoying, beautiful, or totally unremarkable a test-taker is.

Blind review is more essential to those subjects with

essays graded on sophistication of reasoning and effectiveness in language, for example. Perfect objectivity in grading is impossible when reviewing work that has no fundamental right or wrong answer. Even employing blind review, both the atmosphere of a professor's room or a guess as to who produced the work can have an effect on the final grade. However, where it is applicable, it is the most objective means of grading. To safeguard against both intentional and unintentional subjectivity in grade determination, blind review should be implemented wherever there is not a compelling interest against it. ∎

Graduation Rate

According to *The Decaturian*, fewer than 41 percent of students who enroll in college (any college, not just small liberal arts colleges) get their bachelor's degree within six years. Why do students drop out of college? Some become discouraged if they get off to a poor start, some leave because of family problems or illness, others take off a semester to raise money to continue their studies but then don't return, some may not fit in at one particular school and then get put off of further studies, others leave to join the military, and many just decide that college isn't for them.

Retention is a hot issue at schools nationwide, and it's a problem that can affect small liberal arts colleges, which enroll fewer students to begin with, to a striking degree. A sampling of statistics reveals, however, that small liberal arts college students seem to be graduating at a higher rate than the norm. *U.S. News* quotes the following graduation rates for some small liberal arts colleges: Susquehanna University, 71 percent; Illinois Wesleyan University, 75 percent; Drew University, 76 percent; Wake Forest University, 85 percent; and Bryn Mawr College, 78 percent. Another small liberal arts college that's above the norm is Millikin University in Illinois.

COMPARING MILLIKIN'S RETENTION RATES TO NATIONAL STATISTICS

By Darren McGill

THE DECATURIAN (Decatur, Ill.) 12/09/1998

Fewer than 41 percent of students who enroll in college graduate with a bachelor's degree within six years, according to a national study of 28,000 students taken by the National Institute of Independent Colleges and Universities (NIICU).

In this survey, only 15 percent completed a bachelor's degree within four years. At private universities, 25 percent earned degrees within four years.

Millikin University has a significantly higher graduation rate, according to a study headed by Paul Folger, coordinator of institutional research and assessment.

Of students who enrolled in 1991, 60 percent graduated within four years, 64 percent within five years and 65 percent within six years.

However, over one-third of Millikin students never earned a bachelor's degree. What is causing these students, and students nationally, to abandon their college education without completing it?

Katie Welter, former Millikin University student, said she chose not to return after completing one year. Welter was not happy at this school and found it hard to stay focused on her studies. She said she is unsure of where she will go after dropping out of Millikin.

"Our goal for each student is that [he or she graduates]," Mauri Ditzler, dean of the College of Arts and Sciences, said. "Often, students leave Millikin because they cannot find a way to recover from a difficult start or a poor semester," he said.

Sophomore Brenna Ormond said dropping out has never been an option for her.

"A college education is too beneficial to me to consider not completing it," she said.

Ormond said she strongly believes that earning a bachelor's degree leads to more money and better jobs and that college in general is a valuable learning experience.

Sophomore Michelle Clements agreed that dropping out was never an option.

"I'll be the first one in my family to graduate from college with a bachelor's degree, and that is too important of a goal for me and my family to consider sacrificing," she said.

Millikin administrators assert that students must fit in at the University and feel a connection. Folger said that both the University and the administration are responsible for this.

"If students make connections to the institution early in their first semester, they are more likely to remain at the institution," Sherilyn Poole, dean of Student Life and Academic Development, said.

"It's important for students to make these connections, so that they will be assured of the feeling that someone cares and not be as overwhelmed by college adjustment," she said.

Reasons given by students who voluntarily left Millikin include the cost, discontent with school location and program disappointment, according to a survey conducted during the 1996/1997 academic year by Folger. ∎

BEYOND THE Classroom

A fantastic social life awaits you if you choose to attend a small liberal arts college. These schools are small only in the number of students they enroll. We've already seen how lots of academic opportunities are at your beck and call at small liberal arts colleges; the same, of course, holds true for extracurricular offerings. At small colleges, you'll find clubs and groups to suit your personality, from the College Republicans at Vassar to the alternative radio station WQSU at Susquehanna University. You can join a club that takes off-campus trips to local cultural sites, like the lucky students from Drew that you'll read about, or see the world as a college musician or a Model United Nations team member. If you want, you can get involved with officials from the city your school calls home; "Students represent BMC at Student Congress meeting in Philadelphia" reports how student government reps from Bryn Mawr are trying to find common ground with the city of Philadelphia. You can dance and act to your heart's content, and if you want to give to others, there will be plenty of opportunities to get involved with religious groups or volunteering.

You can also learn outside the classroom through fabulous lecture series that feature speakers from all walks of life. Just last year His Holiness the Dalai Lama spoke to students at American University. Other speakers at small liberal arts colleges over the past year have ranged from the former president of Costa Rica, who spoke at Illinois Wesleyan University; to Pulitzer Prize winner David Shipler, who lectured at Haverford College; to Jesse "The Body" Ventura, who visited Augsburg College before winning the gubernatorial race in Minnesota. Here you'll read about other great men and women who have brought their knowledge and experiences to the campuses of small liberal arts colleges.

Maybe you prefer activities that are a little more rough-and-tumble. If you're an athlete, you'll find plenty of ways to work off that pent-up energy at a small liberal arts college. From more popular sports—like football, baseball, and basketball—to sports with smaller followings—like badminton, skiing, or squash—you'll find it all at these schools. "Bowdoin Bears find competition on the slopes" recaps the ups and downs of a team the school fields in a lesser-known sport: alpine skiing. Small liberal arts schools have a little bit of something for everyone's tastes; if your school doesn't offer a varsity letter in a sport, chances are that they'll field a team at the intramural level. Or maybe they'll go all the way and start a brand-new team; "First season proves victorious for Belhaven Football" profiles the Belhaven Bears football team, that made quite a name for itself its very first year on the field. Want to participate in sports but aren't exactly the most coordinated kid on campus? At small liberal arts schools, as *The Decaturian* points out, everyone who contributes to the team is an all-star.

At small liberal arts colleges, you'll find a lot of difference between campuses when it comes to Greek organizations. Some small schools support fraternities and sororities; others have worked to eliminate them from campus. Here's a sampling: Of Vassar College, Drew University, Linfield College, and Connecticut College, only Linfield has Greeks on campus. But this proportion may not be indicative of Greek life at small liberal arts colleges as a whole. "Wake Forest rush attracts large numbers" attest to the fact that at least some small liberal arts schools support active and successful Greek organizations. DePauw University has a thriving Greek structure especially for minority students in addition to numerous other fraternities and sororities. The final word is this: If you think you want to go Greek, be sure to check on the status of Greek life if you plan to attend a small liberal arts school.

Student Groups

There seems to be a wealth of extracurricular opportunities at any college or university you'll go to, and small liberal arts colleges are no exception. Because the groups will be smaller, you'll really get to know people and make great friends with other students who share common interests. You'll also get to contribute to the groups in more noticeable ways. Face it—if there are only 15 members of the debate club, chances are you'll be able to run for an office, and win, if you really want to. Even if you're not a member of one of these fine clubs, you'll reap the benefits of your fellow students' involvement through plays, concerts, and even holiday cheer.

Student government is important at any college, but it's especially so at small colleges, where students may feel that their smaller numbers give them less of a voice in campus and community issues that concern them. At small colleges, student representatives play vital roles as go-betweens—between students and administrators and between students and community officials. At Bryn Mawr College, for example, students are working with Philadelphia officials toward greater cooperation and understanding between the city and the college.

STUDENT GOVERNMENT

STUDENTS REPRESENT BMC AT STUDENT CONGRESS MEETING IN PHILADELPHIA

By Carmen Jardeleza

THE BI-COLLEGE NEWS (Haverford, Penn.) 03/02/1999

Cameron Braswell '02 and Seba Kurian '00 represented Bryn Mawr College in the first Student Congress meeting held February 2 at City Hall in Philadelphia. They discussed issues regarding improvements in the quality of college life with forty other colleges in Philadelphia and the surrounding areas, including Haverford and Swarthmore.

The meeting is the result of collaborative efforts between officials of the City of Philadelphia and student leaders from these colleges. The mayor, senators and other officials have formed a Student Retention Committee in the hopes of encouraging students to stay after graduation and preventing a brain drain in the area.

"[They intend to] keep Philly young—keep it a college town," said Braswell. "They are meeting to sell us on the idea of helping them keep people in Philadelphia." Kurian says that a packet containing articles about Philadelphia was made available to them.

The Student Congress serves as a feedback committee to the Student Retention Committee by helping with ideas, such as improvements with the Southeast Pennsylvania Transit Authority (SEPTA) train service. The intention is for the student leaders to make their suggestions and comments heard about college life and be acquainted with the high government officials. Kurian says that this is the first time that a Student Congress meeting was called and that this should become a final committee.

SEPTA service and especially the Weekend Pass received a lot of attention in the meeting. SEPTA recently chose to stop providing Weekend Passes because it decided that most students don't use them. SEPTA also declined the suggestion of having extended train hours.

The student leaders also requested that more internships in the Philadelphia area be made available. Many also suggested that more college loans be offered. Other ideas included improvements in the entertainment scene, such as having more concerts.

A Fall Festival for Philly's college students will be held in Penn's Landing next semester, according to Braswell and Kurian. They are currently in the organizational and planning stages.

When asked about how Bryn Mawr would effectively contribute to this upcoming committee, Braswell says that "[colleges in the outlying suburbs] offer a different slant or opinions on how things should be working in the suburbs." ∎

Another force speaking loud and clear at small liberal arts colleges are campus radio stations. At a small colleges, radio stations are often the place to be. Student DJs are the voice of the college—they play the music you want to hear, keep you—and the community—informed about campus activities and news, and help a lot of students get through those inevitable all-night study sessions. Students at WQSU at Susquehanna University recently proved that they were responsive to their entire listening audience—not just students, either—by changing their format to alternative music.

MEDIA

SUSQUEHANNA'S WQSU CHANGES ITS TUNES: ALTERNATIVE IS IN

By Brian Ianieri

THE CRUSADER (Selinsgrove, Penn.) 02/26/1999

A disk jockey punches a button, which instantly transforms into a glowing red light. Twelve thousand watts of power jolt through the airwaves and arrive at any radio within a 76 mile radius that is tuned in to 88.9 FM.

However, the music emitted from the radio does not resemble the sounds that used be played on WQSU, Susquehanna's on-campus radio station.

Instead of the regular classic rock, the station is playing modern rock and alternative music.

What happened to "Led Zeppelin" and "Pink Floyd"? What happened to the source of "your rock and roll education"? It changed the curriculum.

After a student-based research team spent the fall semester analyzing the demographics and opinions of the audience that WQSU wanted to attract, the general consensus was for the station to change its format.

Instead of the previous programming of jazz in the morning, classic rock in the afternoon and a classic rock and alternative mix in the evening, the station switched to "modern rock with an alternative slant," according to junior Brian Renehan, music director.

This recently discovered identity means that bands like "311" and "Cake" will take priority in the station's daily musical rotation. Classic rock songs will still be played, but not as frequently as they had been during the past two semesters. Brown said that the radio station was already in possession of many modern songs, but in the past they were unable to play them often.

The decision to change formats was based on the research of several Susquehanna students, who concluded that a certain type of music was not being provided within the listening area while other types were overabundant.

"We didn't need to be classic rock," said sophomore Christine Allen, a researcher for the project. "We thought people wanted something different."

Part of the research project included the distribution of surveys to random people on the streets of Selinsgrove, Bloomsburg, Lewisburg and other areas that can receive WQSU's radio signal.

According to junior James Hand, assistant promotional director, the survey asked people about the kinds of music that appeals to them and the types that do not.

"The biggest percentage group we were dealing with felt they were being ignored," Brown added.

The final decision, Renehan said, was to gear the music toward a 15 to 35 age bracket. He continued that there has not been a radio station that targeted a young demographic because local radio listeners are "all very conservative."

Augustine noted, however, that he also expects the radio station to lose some of its older listeners due to the formatting change.

Brown said that a lot of people prefer to stick with music that is comfortable to them, such as top 40 or classic rock. He continued by saying that the new format will result in less repetition of the same songs.

A problem that WQSU encountered in the past was that DJs only played the classic rock songs that they knew, Brown stated. This lead to the redundancy of many of the more popular songs and the neglect of the lesser-known bands, he added.

"The DJs are now more excited about coming here," Hand said, "because they may have recently seen that band in concert."

"It's not your grandfather's music," Brown added.

"We're college-age people and we're dealing with the music we know," Hand said. "It makes it easier to ad-lib something on the mic if you're comfortable with the music . . . it will lead to a more exciting station."

The format may change, but as Led Zeppelin put it, "The Song Remains the Same." ■

Based on the story from *The Bi-College News*, you may think that small liberal arts students live in their own worlds. That may be the case to a certain extent, but that doesn't mean that they never venture off campus. In fact, small liberal arts schools are more able to mount events that take students off campus for activities in the local community. Because their numbers are smaller, it's easier to get transportation for great off-campus trips. In fact, small liberal arts students enjoy opportunities for field trips in classes as well as extracurricular activities. That's great news for Kuumba, the African-American student organization at Drew University, who took advantage of some of their area's great cultural resources.

CULTURAL

DREW AFRICAN-AMERICAN STUDENT GROUP CELEBRATES AFRICAN HISTORY

By Lara Shaljian

THE ACORN (Madison, N.J.)
11/20/98

Last weekend, Kuumba, Drew's African-American student group, celebrated African Emphasis Weekend, a three-day-long series of events focused on African heritage and culture.

"The purpose of African Emphasis Weekend," Kuumba Co-chair Ngina Wiltshire said, "is a concentrated weekend of events based on actual African culture instead of just African-American culture."

Kuumba sold tickets and arranged for buses to take Drew students each day to the scheduled events, all of which took place in Newark.

John C. Vrakas/*The Argus*

The first event was an evening at the New Jersey Performing Arts Center on Friday, Nov. 13, where the students attended Hannibal Lokumbe's "African Portraits," a combination of chorus and orchestra.

Kuumba Treasurer Melissa Vargas said the purpose of the performance was "to show the history of African-Americans through song and music."

The show opened with music by the Afro-American Symphony. Next was a performance by the Newark Community Chorus and the Jubilee Singers of West Minister Choir College.

The main portion of the evening consisted of the performances of several soloists who sang about the lives of African-Americans throughout history. The songs represented snapshots in time from life in Africa up to 20th century America.

The events depicted in song ranged from the Middle Passage to a slave auction to modern blues pieces. One of the soloists was Cissy Houston, mother of Whitney Houston, whose song portrayed a female slave who lost her daughter in a slave auction.

The students enjoyed the reception at the NJPAC that followed the show and then returned to Drew.

Saturday, Nov. 14, students went to Newark again for the Ghanaian Kinte Exhibit at the Newark Museum. Entitled "Wrapped in Pride," the exhibit focused on the cultural significance and uses of the Kinte cloth, a fabric which originated in the country of Ghana.

According to Wiltshire, the Kinte cloth was traditionally worn only by royalty in Africa, but it has now become devalued through its commercialization.

Today it is available throughout Africa and even in

the United States. Professor of History and African-American Studies Lillie Edwards moderated a discussion on the Kinte cloth following the exhibit.

Kuumba's final event of the weekend was Sunday services at Newark's New Hope Baptist Church. Following the services, the students had lunch at J.E.'s, a Soul Food restaurant in Newark.

African Emphasis Weekend represents just one of the many events Kuumba organizes throughout the year to promote the significance of African culture.

"Kuumba tries to educate the Drew community about the importance of African history in America and to have events on campus to create awareness among all Drew students," Vargas said.

The next event Kuumba plans is the pre-Kwaanza celebration scheduled for 6 p.m. Dec. 3 in University Center 107. This night of dinner and dancing is free and open to the entire Drew community. ∎

You can see that you'll have plenty of opportunities to see the outside world through different clubs at small liberal arts colleges. At some small schools, your talents could even help you visit another country. As a matter of fact, the world-class talent of the DePauw University Chamber Symphony took them all the way to the other side of the globe.

MUSIC

DEPAUW CHAMBER SYMPHONY KICKS OFF NINE-DAY CONCERT TOUR OF JAPAN

From Staff Reports

THE DEPAUW (Greencastle, Ind.) 01/04/1999

In a preview of a Goodwill Concert Tour of Japan during January, the 37-member DePauw University Chamber Symphony will present a pre-tour concert on Saturday, Jan. 9, at 7:30 p.m. in the Performing Arts Center, Moore Theatre.

The pre-tour concert, sponsored by Cinergy Corp., is open and free to the public. The performance will kick off the DePauw Chamber Symphony's nine-day concert tour of Japan. The tour is made possible by a significant gift from Fuji Heavy Industries, parent company of Subaru Automotive.

The Japan tour includes performances at the Ota City Concert Hall on Jan. 13, Minato Mirai in Yokohama on Jan. 14, Tsuruga Cultural Center on Jan. 16, Tochigi City Cultural Center on Jan. 17 and the Osaka International School on Jan. 18. The Ota City appearance will include performing a benefit concert for the Ota Arts School with the Ota Arts School Children's Orchestra.

The concert repertoire includes Bernstein's Candide Overture, Borodin's "In the Steppes of Central Asia," Beethoven's Symphony No. 1, Copland's Pieces from the Ballet Rodeo, and Gershwin's "Rhapsody in Blue."

Dave Rupp/*The Argus*

The Gershwin piece will feature DePauw junior Jeremy A. Rafal of Millilani, Hawaii.

Borrowing the namesake of the Japanese cultural holiday Seijin-no hi, "Coming of Age," the DePauw Chamber Symphony's tour in January is particularly timely. "Coming of Age" refers to the Japanese holiday on Jan. 15 that celebrates the point at which Japanese youth upon their 20th birthday go into the wider world. The DePauw Chamber Symphony will not perform on Jan. 15 in observance of this holiday.

"The phrase 'Coming of Age' has significance to the student musicians in the chamber symphony. The student musicians are all around 20 years of age, and this tour certainly takes them into the wider world and provides a different cultural experience," Conductor Smith said.

The Japan concert tour also is unusual, according to Smith, because each student will be required to complete an academic project related to an aspect of Japanese culture. "Although 'being there' and performing the music well are good experiences, each of the students will have the opportunity for a distinctive cultural immersion," Smith said. "The student musicians will pursue projects in secondary areas of academic interest that will help them understand cultural differences and similarities more thoroughly."

The DePauw Chamber Symphony is the elite core of the larger DePauw University Orchestra, and it has toured extensively since established in 1974 by Smith. The ensemble makes its concert tours as a part of the university's Winter Term in January. With more than 120 concerts to its credit, including performances in Austria, the Czech Republic, Great Britain, Canada, New York's Carnegie Recital Hall, Washington's Kennedy Center and Vienna's Musikverein Brahmssaal, the DePauw Chamber Symphony has garnered critical acclaim both in the United States and abroad. ■

The Acorn and *The DePauw* point out that small liberal arts college students often get involved in events off campus—often in locations around the globe—even though the campus community is somewhat insulated from the outside world. Small liberal arts college students are often very politically involved as well, on both the global and the national level. Students at Hamilton College took their love of world politics all the way to a national Model United Nations competition, where they proved their talents by winning an award. And the small group of Vassar College Republicans spotlighted here by *The Miscellany News* aren't afraid to voice political views that aren't necessarily those of the majority of students on their campus. It just goes to show you that there are all types of groups on the campuses of small liberal arts schools; just because these schools are small doesn't mean you'll be limited to just one point of view.

POLITICAL

HAMILTON MODEL UNITED NATIONS TRAVELS TO MONTREAL

By Suzanne Dougherty

THE SPECTATOR (Clinton, N.Y.) 02/19/1999

Similar to a debate club, Model United Nations seeks to simulate the United Nations as each group is responsible for representing the interests of various countries.

On January 28–31, twelve Hamilton students traveled to McGill University in Montreal, Canada where colleges from all around the country came to compete for awards. Hamilton College was responsible for representing Iraq and Greece.

Students participating in the conference must research and prepare a position paper that focuses on the issues currently facing the United Nations. Some of these issues include the eradication of poverty, nuclear weapons testing, International Monetary Fund currency and issues involving the elderly. The selection of the issue depends upon the specific interests and specialty of the student presenting the paper.

Hamilton was represented through various committees formed to discuss the issues surrounding Iraq and Greece. Jack Spangler '00 and Nicole Davidson '99 earned an honorable mention for their speech about the disarmament of national security in the United Sates in a proposed South Asian nuclear free zone.

Spangler feels his involvement in the Model UN group has provided him and others with a "great deal

of educational value that can be carried over into any other academic discipline. Model UN is trying to articulate learning in detail about other perspectives. The incorporation of these perspectives will allow insight into why these international problems occur."

Model UN is open to anyone on the Hamilton campus.

"It is a debate club brought to a higher level" says Darren Block '01. "It is a way for students to become more aware of the highly volatile issues of the world." ■

THE VASSAR COLLEGE REPUBLICANS: MINORITY LEADERSHIP TAKES SHAPE ON LIBERAL CAMPUS

By M. Tye Wolfe

THE MISCELLANY NEWS (Poughkeepsie, N.Y.) 02/26/1999

If you're a Vassar student who votes, Richard Lazio would seem like the perfect candidate. He's young, intelligent, handsome, articulate and, best of all, a Vassar graduate. In fact he is the first, and, to date, the only, Vassar grad to be elected to Congress.

One thing, though. He's a republican. The term "Vassar College Republican" indeed, seems like an oxymoron. However, many students would be surprised to learn that there is, in fact, a small, fledgling conservative movement within the bastion of liberalism that is Vassar.

The Vassar College Republicans have undergone so many incarnations that no one can really say how long they have been around. Those who have been at Vassar for a while may recall that in November 1994, the two (and only) members of what was then the newly-formed Vassar Conservative Society, could be seen outside Jewett, drunk out of their minds, howling "We won, we won!" after Newt Gingrich led the first republican sweep of Congress in 60 years. From there began the Contract with America, which subsequently launched vehement protests throughout the school.

Later, the group evolved to include libertarians, until being streamlined to its present form, as a nice counterpart to the Vassar College Democrats.

The Republicans are noticeably different from other campus organizations. For one thing, there aren't very many of them. Vassar College Republicans President

Thomas Conoscenti '02 estimates that there are around 10 members, who, at the very least, receive the group's e-mails.

Additionally, they are not as vociferous and opinionated as the members of other organizations. They don't hold demonstrations or get arrested, and members do not even draw a strict party line. There is none of the Bob Dornan bombast or the Rudy Giuliani bluntness. When interviewed about subjects like abortion and the death penalty—contentious issues for many republicans—they don't give the traditional conservative line. This may be due to a wariness about how their opinions are received on a campus like Vassar's, but it is also apparent that they are independent thinkers who want to reflect on their answers.

"I don't subscribe to the republican agenda as a big block," said Sally-Anne Moringello '99, who served as the group's secretary and treasurer last year. "It is not the issues per se that I identify with so much as the party ideals."

In fact, the Republicans mainly embrace the fiscal conservatism that is popular in the Northeast, where typically liberal states like Massachusetts and New York elected republican governors for their budget frugality.

Liberalism per se does not seem to bother Moringello or Conoscenti so much as the fact that, by default, most students at Vassar assume others think the same way.

However, the Republicans, just by virtue of existing,

bring attention to a disturbing amount of close-mindedness on the campus.

"There is a lot of hypocrisy on this campus" said Moringello. "People claim to be really tolerant, but, ironically, they are only tolerant of what they believe in." Moringello went on to note how it is par for the course at Vassar that slighting Republicans, pro-lifers, "jocks" and Christians is an OK thing to do.

After the Republicans applied for funding from the VSA, Conoscenti received an anonymous, curt letter in his box saying how republicans "sucked" and were too small to receive funding.

"Things like that make me rethink what this college is all about, but at the same time, I think it is known that [the republican view] is not the one that is really tolerated around here," said Conoscenti. "Still, the main thing about Vassar is that a lot of views are accepted here. I didn't come to change anything or make a difference, just, to be able to say my peace and know that that was all right."

"At a study break a girl was saying that when she went to D.C. for a semester, she thought it was 'so strange' to be around people who are right-to-life and have this or that conservative view, and I just started to laugh, because there are definitely people around here who have a conservative view," added Conoscenti. ∎

Students at small liberal arts colleges express themselves in varied ways; be it through music, politics, or religion. Since many small liberal arts colleges have religious origins, you'll find a religious presence on many of these campuses. But that doesn't mean that one religion will be promoted over all others. In fact, groups representing many religions can be found at small liberal arts campuses. Three such groups at Linfield College in Oregon join together each Christmas to keep the spirit of the season alive.

RELIGIOUS

CHRISTIAN HOLIDAY MESSAGE SPREAD BY CAMPUS GROUPS AT LINFIELD COLLEGE

By Mary Jo Monroe

THE LINFIELD REVIEW (McMinnville, Ore.) 12/04/1998

Your credit card bills are mounting, you have to fight your way to the mall and Toys 'R' Us has sold its last Furby. Yes, Christmas is fast approaching, and it's easy to forget why we celebrate this holiday at all. However, students who want a reminder of the deeper reason for the season can find the answers from three groups on campus.

Campus Crusade for Christ (CC4C), Chaplain's Team and Fellowship of Christian Athletes (FCA) all share a common goal—to spread the Christian message to non-believers that Jesus Christ is savior and Lord and to challenge believers to incorporate their religious beliefs in all facets of their lives.

"On Tuesday nights we have Real-Life meetings, which are geared toward everyday issues," junior Kelly Hopkins, who is a member of CC4C's leadership team, said. "We discuss issues like temptation and stress."

CC4C, an Associated Students of Linfield College (ASLC) chartered club, is a national organization that has had a chapter at Linfield since the late '70s.

The club is performing a Christmas musical written by senior Kris Horton Tuesday Dec. 8 in Jonasson Hall. Students will act out the story of the birth of Christ. Christmas carols will be sung throughout the play, and audience members will be encouraged to join in. The production is free and open to all community members.

Chaplain's Team, a co-curricular group, is also hosting Christmas festivities. With the help of the McMinnville Chamber of Commerce, they will hold a canned food drive the week of Dec. 7–11 to benefit Yamhill County Action Program (YCAP).

The team also organizes Linfield's annual Christmas service which will be held this year in Melrose Auditorium Dec. 13. Chaplain Jim Asparro will deliver the sermon.

Samantha Goldstein/*The Harvard Crimson*

In addition to these holiday events, Chaplain's Team hosts chapel on Wednesday afternoons, evening fellowship on Sundays and special services for Easter and Thanksgiving.

"At Sunday evening fellowship there is prayer, songs, games, a short message, announcements, snacks and fellowship," senior and Chaplains' Team member Matt Fischer said. "Wednesday chapel is more serious and organized. There's hymns, prayers and a speaker."

"You don't have to consider yourself a Christian to come, and you don't have to be an athlete, either," Tara Lepp, associate professor of health and human performance and FCA faculty adviser, said. "Quite a few non-athletes come because they want the fellowship."

Unlike the other two groups, however, FCA is not planning any holiday festivities.

"We try to keep it low-key for Christmas because we're [the students] so busy in December," FCA member and senior Matt Dyment said.

Whatever the groups' holiday plans are, one thing is for sure—with various fellowship and worship meetings held four times a week by FCA, CC4C and Chaplain's Team, there is a lot of prayer and praise taking place around campus.

"Linfield offers a lot of opportunity [for students] to get in touch with [their spiritual side] if they want to," Dyment said. "College makes for a good time [to explore your spiritual beliefs] because you're trying to decide your mission in life, who you are and what you're going to do." ■

Volunteerism

Each year, students at Linfield College spread joy to their fellow students through religious messages. At other small liberal arts campuses, students spread joy through volunteering. You probably wouldn't think that a small college would have a separate office for volunteering, but Connecticut College does. In fact, at Connecticut College, students, faculty members, and alumni all got involved to help the war-torn country of Liberia. And you definitely wouldn't think that any college students—not just small liberal arts college students—would prefer hard labor over spring break. But the dedicated students of DePauw sacrificed their vacations to come to the rescue of families in the South whose lives were devastated by tornadoes.

CONNECTICUT COLLEGE ALUMNA SPURS CAMPUS BOOK DRIVE FOR LIBERIA

By Abby Carlen

THE COLLEGE VOICE (New London, Conn.) 02/19/1999

Forty boxes of donated books began their journey across the globe from Connecticut College to the University of Liberia two weeks ago. Helen Granskog, from the Office of Volunteers for Community Service (OVCS), organized the drive and recruited students from Umoja to help.

Students contributed over 100 books during the book buy-back period of last semester. The drive was better publicized to faculty, who donated several hundred books. The bookstore also participated by providing books that were destined for the recycle bin.

Class of 1973 alumna Karyn Trader-Leigh, who now resides in Liberia, instigated the project. She returned to campus for her 25th reunion last May, where she first suggested the idea to President Gaudiani at an event at Unity House.

Trader-Leigh submitted a formal proposal to President Gaudiani at the beginning of last semester. The Connecticut College Source quotes Trader-Leigh's letter describing the desolation she and her husband have witnessed in Liberia.

"Working here, we have seen first-hand the devastation of civil war," Trader-Leigh wrote. "Peace is still in a very fragile state. People here are trying to put their lives together again and desperately want to return to normal life. The need is tremendous."

Trader-Leigh also sites the intense impact of the war on Liberia's education system. The donated books will help university students returning to the classroom after seven years of civil war. ■

SOME DePAUW U. STUDENTS SERVING ON SPRING BREAK

By Emily Lowe

THE DEPAUW (Greencastle, Ind.) 03/16/1999

Everyone is anticipating spring break.

It will be a week away from classes, DePauw food, and our schedules. While many will retreat to either a week's worth of home-cooking or spring break madness, not everyone will spend late nights clubbing and early afternoons sleeping.

Groups of students, sponsored by the Hartman Center and the Religious Life Center, have organized alternative spring break trips to Birmingham, Ala.; Dallas, Texas; and Myrtle Beach, S.C.

Eight DePauw students will drive down to Midfield, a suburb of Birmingham, where they will repair houses damaged by last year's tornadoes.

The students are freshmen Carmeleta Rouse, Jessica Thompson, Michael Mitchell, Jennifer Barsema and Aaron Hackman, sophomore Julie Doan, junior Becca Holdzkom, and senior Junko Hozumi, The students will be under the supervision of faculty sponsor Bryan Brooks, a graduate assistant for the Religious Life Center.

The Birmingham in-service trip differs from the South Carolina and Texas trips DePauw offers because of the religious factor. The trip is arranged with UNCOR, an organization founded by the United Methodist Church. Thompson described UNCOR as a mixture of Habitat for Humanity and Red Cross centered on the Methodist Church.

The group has been paired up with a Methodist church in the small community of Midfield. The students will stay at the Walnut Grove Methodist church where the congregation will supply them with homemade meals and give them access to a kitchen, bathrooms and other utilities.

The satisfaction of helping the less fortunate coupled with religious contentment attracted Carmeleta Rouse to this program.

"I always went to church camps when I was little, and I felt like [this trip] was the reflection I needed," she said.

Senior Jen Coomes is a student organizer of the Birmingham trip. She participated in last year's in-service trip to Leesburg, Florida.

"The religious focus attracts students because it allows them to help the less fortunate with similar religious backgrounds and also provides Bible study and readings in the evening [after working all day]," Coomes said.

Although the religious aspect is part of the program, it was the basic idea of the trip that appealed to Aaron Hackman.

"It sounded interesting, helping those houses damaged in last year's tornadoes," Hackman said. "Plus I have wanted to get re-involved with community service, especially away from just my hometown."

Thompson was also drawn more toward the community service idea of the program, although it was the opportunity to build stronger bonds with her friends that really made her decide to go.

"I found out about the program through a friend, checked it out, and we got a group of people together," Thompson said. "We decided to go down south where it was warm, but we wanted to have a different [spring break] experience and thought this would be fun. The religious aspect didn't necessarily make or break my decision, but I am looking forward to participating in the religious-based activities."

The trip will definitely be an experience none of the members will forget. "I want to help people without expecting anything materialistic in return," Rouse said. "I just want the experience of going."

Thompson also has hopes for the trip.

"First of all, [I want to] help people that have been devastated, but also become closer to the friends of mine that are going and the others that will be there."

The group will be in Birmingham from Saturday evening to the following Saturday morning. They will join up with other schools associated with UNCOR. All groups will work together to repair the damage in Midfield. ■

Sports

You'll find that all kinds of sports thrive on the campuses of small liberal arts colleges. And they're very important to the people who play—as well as to their loyal fans. What's different at small liberal arts colleges is that they're played on a smaller level. You won't find a national sportscaster giving the play-by-play or the Fox television network camped out in the endzone. At these schools, sports and money aren't married; they don't generate the massive dollars that sports at large state schools do. And while athletic scholarships are awarded at small liberal arts schools, the numbers aren't as big as at large state schools. This could be considered a good thing, since students at small liberal arts schools often don't resent the importance placed on sports, like we saw at large state schools.

What's great is that you'll also find plenty of venues for less-talked-about sports at small liberal arts colleges. In fact, lesser-known sports thrive on the campuses of small colleges. The Vassar women's squash team brought home the Howe Cup last season, awarded to them for being the best in the nation in their division. Bryn Mawr's badminton team performs admirably each year. The Horned Toads Women's Football Club (rugby, in other words) is big news at Bryn Mawr/Haverford; the men of Bates also rough it up on the rugby field. And the Bowdoin Bears alpine ski team gets a lot of respect from the students of Bowdoin, and the *Bowdoin Orient*, for their fine forays on the slopes.

BOWDOIN BEARS FIND COMPETITION ON THE SLOPES
By C.W. Estoff

BOWDOIN ORIENT (Brunswick, Maine) 02/26/1999

Last week, captain Ryan Hurley summarized the state of the alpine team best: "We'll try our best with what we have."

Injury has taken a toll on the team roster. Unfortunately, the Polar Bears could only carry a squad of four men and two women, half the size of a normal team, to last weekend's Williams Carnival.

The University of Vermont Catamounts once again dominated the weekend with a fifth straight win. Out of the eleven competing schools, Bowdoin still finished tenth, managing to beat out Harvard.

The Giant Slalom was held on Friday under cloudy skies and moderate temperatures. The courses held up well this week on the moderately hard snow conditions. The race was won by UVM's Willy Booker, who finished a full 1.37 seconds ahead of the pack. This margin of victory is nearly unheard of in the ski racing world. This accomplishment is comparable to winning a football game by ten touchdowns.

In the face of the intimidating competition, the men's squad tried to rally. The top finisher for Bowdoin in the G.S. was Mike Lieser, who started 53rd and finished 39th. Michael Prendergast started 54th and finished

44th. Ryan Hurley started 49th and finished 46th. Jason Kim crashed and did not finish the first run.

Lieser continued to have a good weekend as he was the top Bowdoin skier again in the Slalom on Saturday. He finished 32nd from a start position of 51. Hurley started 53rd and finished 35th. Prendergast fell and did not finish the second run. Kim managed to put together two runs and finished 39th from a start of 57th.

On the women's side in the G.S. on Friday, Captain Shalyn Yamanaka started 50th and finished 33rd. Kat Crowley fell and did not finish the second run.

The only women's start on Saturday was Yamanaka, as Crowley decided not to race because of a recurring ankle injury. Yamanaka started at 38th and finished 41st after falling and hiking to make a gate in the first run. The team is looking forward to next weekend's New England Championships held at Middlebury College's Snow Bowl.

Team slalom specialist Nate Vinton will return for this last regular season competition. Middlebury will be the last chance for the team members to shoot for a required top-twenty finish to gain points to qualify for the NCAA Championships. Vinton is the team's best hope for representation at NCAA's with one twentieth place finish this year. ■

McClure/*The Bradley Scout*

Don't think that only the out-of-the-ordinary sports get recognition and inspire pride at small liberal arts colleges. Judging from *The Quarter Tone*, the Belhaven Blazers football team generated enough enthusiasm in its fans in their first year on the field to rival any large state school. And they even made it to The Mississippi Sports Hall of Fame.

FIRST SEASON PROVES VICTORIOUS FOR BELHAVEN FOOTBALL

By Haley Rice

THE QUARTER TONE (Jackson, Miss.) 12/16/1998

As the semester draws to a close, it's time to take a last look at the Belhaven Blazer Football season. Under the leadership of Coach Norman Joseph, and the entire Belhaven Blazers Coaching staff, Belhaven football has a first season to be proud of. The Blazers won four games and lost six. The schedule of games was a tough one, with five out of the six teams that

Belhaven lost to being ranked nationally. Belhaven's team members represented the school very well on a national level, with four players receiving recognition in the Mid-South Conference.

Cedric Killings was named to the 1998 All Conference Team as a First Team Defensive Player and Jeremy Clark was named to the Second Defensive Team. Nick Helms and Johnnie Horne were named First Team Offensive Players, and Jeremy Waldrip was named to Second Team Offense. Quarterback Ricky Fremin finished the season within six yards of having two thousand yards passing. Coach Joseph is pleased with these achievements from his first year team. "I am real proud of those guys and the accomplishments that they have made and what they did to add leadership to this program. We are the only school in the NAIA to be able to say that we have a one thousand yard rusher and a one thousand yard receiver."

Belhaven hasn't just added a football team this semester; it's made history. The original team will not be forgotten. A team picture and first victory ball signed by all the team members will be placed in the Mississippi Sports Hall of Fame to commemorate this beginning. "No one can take away what this first team did, because they are the original crew. There is a place in the Mississippi Sports Hall of Fame for them. They called and wanted the team picture and all," said Coach Joseph.

Megan DeMarco/*The Towerlight*

If you've been at any of the football games, you've probably noticed that the student section is almost as much fun to watch as the football game. Coach Joseph says that the Belhaven Blazer fans have made this season what it has been. As we've suspected all along, Belhaven as a definite edge as far as enthusiasm goes. In Coach Joseph's words: " We went to several road games, and I can say that our fans were the best. We went up to play the number four team in the country and their fans sat on their hands the whole time. There

was no noise, no clapping, nothing. We came home the next week and our fans were going crazy. That's the kind of enthusiasm we need and I love it."

With this season behind the team, Coach Joseph is looking forward to next year, and laying the groundwork for another great season. Recruiting is already taking place for next year's team. Coach Joseph is presenting Belhaven College as a whole to the recruits. "The thing I have been saying to our recruits for over a year now is that Belhaven College has a lot to offer. I can't think of a better place to come in and get your education, to play the quality of football we are playing here in the Mid-South Conference and then to be in the environment and great Christian atmosphere that Belhaven has. I am selling all aspects of the school. I think we are attracting a quality football player and a quality young man to come to school here."

Looking back on the season, Coach Joseph seems to have no regrets and is looking forward to next year. "To be where we are now as opposed to where we were this time last year is like night and day. I could tell from the first game that this is a group of players that has the potential to be something really special, and they've proved that as the season went on." His promise to the campus: "We will coach hard, play hard and perform to the best of our ability. Hopefully we have given the campus something to rally around and a chance to be a part of something very special, because it's been special for me. It's been good. It's been real good." ∎

Greek Life

You'll find lots of Greek activity at some small liberal arts colleges, less at others, and none at still others—kind of like we saw at highly competitive colleges. On some small liberal arts campuses, fraternities and sororities provide most of the social life and are famous for weekend parties. One good aspect of these schools' smallness and the part that Greeks play in campus life is that since most students usually live on campus—including Greeks—worries about drinking and driving are alleviated. But Greeks at small liberal arts colleges are not immune to some of the other problems we pointed out in the chapters on large state schools and highly competitive colleges. DePauw recently had to tighten its regulations on hazing, and Greeks and drinking are still problems on many campuses. Despite the problems, Greeks have managed to find success on some small liberal arts campuses, like Susquehanna University. In fact, at Susquehanna, Greeks recently distinguished themselves with a higher average GPA than the rest of the student body. Greeks are also alive and well—and growing—on the campus of Wake Forest.

OVERALL GREEK G.P.A. RISES ABOVE INDEPENDENTS' AT SUSQUEHANNA U.

By Rebecca Lee

THE CRUSADER (Selinsgrove, Penn.) 02/12/1999

The overall grade point average of Susquehanna's fraternity and sorority members was greater than the overall G.P.A. for all Susquehanna students last semester.

During the 1998 fall semester the fraternity and sorority members obtained an average GPA of 3.19. Compared to the average GPA of 3.04 for all of the student body combined, that is almost five percent higher.

"My hope is for the Greeks to capitalize on this," Director of Campus Activities Gail Ferlazzo said. She said she feels some professors think all the Greeks do is party and hopes this achievement would help break down that stereotype.

Junior Sigma Kappa Scholarship Chairperson Lisa Swanhart said that members of fraternities and sororities are showing Susquehanna another side by achieving this.

"It's a really big achievement because of the stereotypical view," Swanhart said. It shows freshmen there is more to being a Greek than partying, she added.

Ferlazzo said she believes the Greek infrastructure, which encourages members to be dedicated to scholar-

Kimberely Barnhart/*The Bradley Scout*

ship, was what caused the high GPA. Some fraternities and sororities also have a system by which members are required to attend and record study hours if their averages fall below a certain point.

"Having the built-in organization is better than what a normal person can encounter," Ferlazzo said of the infrastructure.

Swanhart said a program that may have helped Sigma Kappa was Scholarship Olympics, which was organized last semester. The program divided the sorority into small groups that would compete with one another. Based on an individual's grade, he or she would get a certain number of points that would contribute to a group total. The group to get the most points would receive a gift. Swanhart said the program was "very successful."

A Phi Sigma Kappa brother, senior Neil Popovich, said he doesn't believe the high GPA can be attributed to any specific thing. "Usually, it's brothers who are good friends in the same major who get together and study," Popovich stated. ■

WAKE FOREST RUSH ATTRACTS LARGE NUMBERS
By Brad Gunton

THE OLD GOLD & BLACK (Winston-Salem, N.C.)
01/14/1999

Women wishing to rush this semester had a new sorority to consider, as Phi Mu joined the university's Greek community and recently participated in its first formal Rush.

Sophomore Ryann Galganowicz, the Phi Mu standards chairwoman, said that she was excited to be a part of the chapter's formation.

"It was an opportunity to make something that we wanted it to be, and not to conform to something that already existed," Galganowicz said. "It was a big risk, but it was worth it."

Phi Mu's officers seem to agree that Rush was successful for them.

"We've had an incredible amount of energy and enthusiasm, and we think it showed in every party we had," Barr said.

Formal Rush began Jan. 8 when the 333 women who had registered for Rush attended parties at each sorority, which were meant to give the rushee a feel for the different sororities.

The rushees then attended five parties on the second day, three parties on the third day and finally two on preference night, when they decided which sorority they wanted to join.

The rushees received bids from the sororities that invited them to become a member Jan. 12.

Senior Julie Harmon, the Rush counselor coordinator on the Executive Rush Committee of the Panhellenic Council, said the social aspects of Greek life were what drew so many women to rush.

"Greek life is extremely important around this campus," Harmon said. "Most of the social life is fraternity parties. They see fraternity boys with sorority girls, and they want to be a part of that."

Many of the rushees echoed Harmon's sentiments that the social life was an important factor in their choice to rush.

"(Rushing) is something I wanted to do for a long time," freshman Bethany Turner said. "I have a lot of older friends who've done it, and it's a good way to meet people."

Freshman Eleah Gamble agreed with Turner that Rush was an important way to make new friends.

"I wanted to learn more about the sororities and meet new people," Gamble said of her decision to rush.

Senior Whitney Montague, Chi Omega's Rush chairwoman, said the Panhellenic Council is responsible for the large number of women who decided to rush this year.

Phi Mu officially became a chapter Oct. 25, with 28 women being initiated into the sorority. Its officers consist of sophomores Catherine Barr as president, Ellen Burger as vice president, Melissa Newman as secretary and Anne Haith as treasurer.

The Panhellenic Council decided to add a sorority because of the growing number of women interested in the Greek system. After gathering information about 13 national sororities, women from the university's sororities narrowed down the possible choices to three and eventually decided on Phi Mu. ■

Although Greeks are thriving on the campuses of small colleges like Susquehanna and Wake Forest, other small liberal arts colleges seem to be at the forefront of shutting down Greeks. Early this year, Hamilton College settled a lawsuit with fraternity members who didn't want to sell their houses to the school; that battle had raged since 1995, when Hamilton did away with "society houses" by requiring that all students live in college-owned facilities. Bowdoin College has abolished fraternities on its campus and is presently in negotiations to buy their houses and turn them into campus facilities. Marietta College has seen six of its Greek organizations shut down; none have been started to take their place.

Remember the uproar in the highly competitive college chapter about Dartmouth administration's plans to eliminate single-sex Greek life on their campus? *The Dartmouth* points out here how Greeks and administrators at highly competitive colleges can take some pointers and learn a few valuable lessons from Greeks at small liberal arts colleges. Dartmouth would be wise to take heed of the stories of six small liberal arts colleges that, with varying degrees of success, eliminated single-sex Greek life on their campuses.

FIVE SCHOOLS SHOW OPTIONS FOR DARTMOUTH'S TRANSITION FROM SINGLE-SEX GREEK SYSTEM

By Jen Taylor

THE DARTMOUTH (Hanover, N.H.) 02/22/1999

As members of the Dartmouth community try to imagine what the next few years will be like as the College's social system undergoes what is expected to be a near complete transformation, they may look to a handful of northeastern colleges who also eliminated single-sex Greek systems from their campuses.

The colleges—Williams, Middlebury, Bowdoin, Colby, Amherst and Hamilton—all had fraternity-oriented systems at one point in time, but their reasons for change and current systems are quite different and demonstrate the wide range of possibilities for the future of Dartmouth's social system.

The chief complaint against the single-sex fraternity system at other colleges has mirrored the Trustees' criticism of Dartmouth's system—selectivity and exclusion, and in particular, exclusion by gender.

In the 1980s, the Middlebury College Greek system was entirely male, consisting of about eight fraternities—sororities voted themselves out of existence 20 years prior to the decision to terminate Greek life at Middlebury, according to Elizabeth Burns '99, former president of the Inter-house Council which oversees the small Vermont college's five current coed social houses.

In 1991, former Middlebury President John McCardell issued a report prohibiting single-sex organizations—fraternities could stay, but they would have to admit women.

At Williams, the small college located in northwestern Massachusetts, exclusivity of the fraternity system was also an issue, but the 1962 decision to move away from fraternities came before coeducation at the school, Dean of the College Peter Murphy said.

The most recent college to disband their Greek system, Bowdoin College of Maine, voted in 1997 to eliminate fraternities by May 2000. An announcement by the Board of Trustees in 1988 first called for all fraternities to be open to all students regardless of race and gender in keeping with college legislation, Dean of the College Scott Hood said.

The increased need for social space and the poor conditions of the fraternity houses also necessitated the college takeover of the houses at Bowdoin, Hood said.

The 90-percent membership enjoyed at one time by the fraternity system in its "Golden Age" dropped dramatically, dwindling to about 25 percent—meaning one-quarter of the students were in control of all the social space.

"The buildings suffered," Hood said. With financial pressure to provide social opportunities the fraternities could not maintain their houses.

The Middlebury plan involved the conversion of single-sex fraternities into five coed houses whose membership varies from 15 to 100 students. The change has been largely a language game. According to Burns, The houses still have rush, called "open house" and pledge periods, known as "new member education."

It is rumored that there is still a single-sex fraternity at Middlebury, although it operates underground—in secret and without recognition from the college. The house of one fraternity, Delta Kappa Epsilon (Deke), sits empty since it refused to go coed or sell the house to the college.

Alumni of the fraternity use the house for parties during Homecoming weekend, and the top floor of the house has been converted to office space used by the college's faculty.

Under the Bowdoin plan the fraternity houses will be bought and restored by the college. Each residential hall will have an association with a particular house, and living in a dorm will mean automatic membership in a house. Students will still be able to hold parties and have money in the bank to fund them, Hood said.

Although one of the goals of the Middlebury administration's plan was to eliminate exclusion in residences, the exclusivity of the social houses is still a debate.

"We give out bids, and it's always a question of—'what criteria do you base it on?'" Burns said, a member of the coed house Omega Alpha, known on campus as Tavern.

The new Middlebury social system only incorporates seven percent of the student body.

As a Williams administrator, however, Murphy said he has encountered an alumnus "maybe once in four years" who was not pleased with the elimination of the fraternities.

"I never talked to anyone who liked fraternities," he said. Murphy said in the field of admissions where Dartmouth and Williams are very competitive, "one of the advantages we have is the absence of fraternities."

The student body at Hamilton has changed to meet the changes in the social atmosphere of the college, Zoll said.

Younger students are happier with the environment and tend to be "more academically oriented than socially oriented."

The controversy at Hamilton seems only now to be calming—after holding out for years and refusing to

Kimberely Barnhart/*The Bradley Souct*

sell their houses to the college even after administrators forbid students from living in them, the fraternities have finally caved under the weight of legal fees resulting from the battle and agreed to sell their houses to the college.

Hamilton administrators decreed that only seniors can live in off-campus housing and seem to be moving toward mandating that all students live in on-campus housing for all four years of college.

Some of the fraternity houses have sat empty, entered only for maintenance purposes as fraternity alumni held out and refused to sell the houses to the college. Some could not sell the houses to anyone other than the college because although the houses are privately owned, they are built on college owned land.

Of the houses already sold to the college, three have already been turned into college dorms.

Although students are increasingly accepting of the new system at Hamilton, local residents have complained about the increase in drunk driving and public drunkenness since the loss of the fraternity system, according to Phil Allogramento '00.

The success of the Bowdoin social system, which most students there have embraced, is largely due to the comprehensiveness of the report issued by the Trustees, Hood said. Open forums on the issue—both residential and dining space debates—were held on-campus and with alumni in New York, Boston, and Washington, D.C., mostly with former fraternity members.

"The reaction was probably less volcanic than it could have been," he said.

"The new system embraces what the fraternities do well," Hood said, such as hosting social gatherings—something they couldn't do prior to the change because of a lack of resources. ■

Interesting Speakers

Small liberal arts colleges are able to attract their fair share of fabulous speakers. In fact, small college lecture series are considered to be an important part of students' education at these schools. Most schools have well-established speakers series that can garner national attention. Although cost may be an issue, the colleges still feel the experience is worth the money. In a nice twist, Drew charges admissions to cover fees but uses profits toward student scholarships. Above all, small liberal arts colleges use speakers to promote the philosophies of a liberal arts education—creating well-rounded students who are aware of what's going on in the world around them, even in small countries like Timor.

JOURNALIST COKIE ROBERTS AND LAWYER JAN SCHLICTMANN WILL KICK OFF DREW U. SPRING LECTURES
By Shannon Gould

THE ACORN (Madison, N.J.) 02/05/1999

The Drew community has had the opportunity to hear several speeches from prestigious individuals over the last five years, thanks to The Drew Forum.

This program, designed to provide the Drew community and the general public with the opportunity to hear speakers such as Colin Powell, Leah Rabin, George and Barbara Bush, and many others, continues this semester with speakers Jan Schlictmann and Cokie Roberts.

Schlictmann's personal struggle as a lawyer has been recently portrayed by actor John Travolta in the film "A Civil Action."

Currently a lawyer and advocate for the Environmental Protection Agency (EPA), Schlictmann's career began as a personal injury lawyer. He and a few partners ran a successful firm that prided itself on large settlements.

His career took a drastic turn, however, when he accepted a case that was contingent upon environmental issues. Although he initially saw the case as an opportunity to gain multi-million dollar settlements from huge corporations, he would lose everything fighting for the cause of his clients.

Schlictmann will discuss these experiences at Drew.

Cokie Roberts, who will speak on April 6, is a 54-year-old wife and mother of two who serves a plethora of public roles.

She published a book last May entitled 'We are our Mothers' Daughters,' in which she explores women's issues such as the balance between work and family, the diverse roles of women in our society, and the connection and distinction between different generations of women.

In addition to her talent as an author, she has been the co-anchor of the ABC Sunday morning talk show with Sam Donaldson, "This week with Sam and Cokie," since November of 1996.

She is also a special correspondent for ABC news and a substitute anchor on "Nightline," covering politics, Congress and public policy issues.

Roberts was the recipient of the Edward R. Murrow award, the highest honor in radio broadcasting, for her Monday morning news analysis on National Public Radio. She was the first broadcast journalist to receive the Everett McKinley Dirksen Award for coverage of Congress.

Deputy Chief of Staff Jeff Cromarty plays a large role in bringing these prestigious speakers to the Drew campus. "I basically act as a sounding board for ideas from the Drew community," Cromarty said. He surveyed the campus last fall, asking students whom they would like to hear speak.

"A lot of students want to hear Maya Angelou, but unfortunately she is very expensive," he said. Although Cromarty wasn't permitted to disclose the cost of the spring speakers, he admitted that they weren't cheap, probably ranging between $20,000 and $60,000 per speech.

This cost is defrayed through ticket sales and sponsorship from large corporations, Cromarty explained. "Most corporations don't know who Angelou is and wouldn't sponsor her speech, making it financially impossible to bring her to campus," he said.

With a speaker like Schlictmann, there are several local law firms that may be willing to cover a significant chunk of the cost, he added.

Students not only benefit from the Drew Forum Speakers Series by having the opportunity to hear famous individuals share their thoughts but also reap any profit that is made in the form of scholarship assistance.

Cromarty said that a plan is underway to continue the series with a third spring speaker and another speaker next fall. He encourages students to attend the speeches and welcomes any student who wants to help with the series. ■

STUDENT ACTIVIST FROM EAST TIMOR SPEAKS AT BRYN MAWR

By Janet Bunde

THE BI-COLLEGE NEWS (Haverford, Penn.) 03/02/1999

Nearly 25 years of foreign invasion, settlement and subjugation have plagued the small country of Timor. One-third of the population has been decimated through torture, massacre and starvation. And behind it all, a people small in number but enormous in their determination to have their own country—this was the topic of a talk given by Luciano Valentin da Conceicao, a student activist from East Timor. The talk, sponsored by the Bryn Mawr chapter of Amnesty International, took place February 25.

Timor, an island located approximately 300 miles off the northern coast of Australia, has been long been contested territory. From 1614, when the Portuguese first claimed the Massachusetts-sized piece of land as a colony, the island has passed through the hands of Portugal, the Netherlands and Indonesia, with a brief week of independence in between.

A line, determined by a conference of European powers in 1914, divides the island roughly in half; both halves are ruled by Indonesia, but West Timor is satisfied with a more independent status. East Timor desires self-sufficiency—and the subsequent clash between the Indonesian government and native activists is tearing the country apart.

Conceicao described the arrests and deaths of his parents, over 20 uncles and even a 13-year-old nephew, who was gunned down at school. As he spoke, he seemed inured to the brutality of the crimes committed—what bothered him most was the lack of knowledge about the issue in other countries.

"You can see yourselves how the blood is, how the killing is in the other parts of the world," said Conceicao. "But because there is no report on the television about East Timor—no evidence—no one believes."

The latest instance of violence in East Timor that received any coverage from international news media was the murder of 271 nonviolent student protesters by the Indonesian army. This single instance cannot, according to Conceicao, convey the reality of life under the Indonesian regime.

"For me, it is only one of the thousands and thousands of massacres in East Timor," he said.

However, it is not only the threat to life that forces Conceicao to speak out—freedom of expression has all but been stifled among the East Timorese. In order to attend an Indonesian university, for example, one must sign a card stating that no matter what circumstances may occur, one will not protest against the Indonesian government or military. Students cannot register for classes without signing the card.

A declaration of religion was also required for any official identification card issued by the Indonesian government; if any East Timorean chose any religion aside from Catholicism, Protestantism or Islam, he or she would be executed. According to Conceicao, over 95 percent of East Timoreans are Catholic because fear of execution prompted conversion.

Yet despite all the violations of human rights, the East Timoreans still have hope.

"Our independence is inevitable," said Conceicao.

This hope helps them continue the fight against the Indonesians—and against the world as a whole. According to Garrick Ruiz, a member of the East Timor Action Network, a national organization devoted to the issue of East Timorean independence, the United States played a huge role in Indonesia's subjugation of East Timor.

"Indonesia could not, without U.S. help, have done what it did and continues to do," said Ruiz.

From 1975, the year of the first invasion, United States presidents from Ford through Clinton have tacitly condoned East Timor's invasion, according to Conceicao and Ruiz. At the time of the invasion, 90 percent of the weapons belonging to the Indonesian army were supplied by the United States. In 1979, then-President Jimmy Carter authorized the sale of Bronco fighter planes to Indonesia—planes that were subsequently used to "strafe the countryside and mountain regions, looking for people," said Conceicao. The United States also continues to train Indonesian military officers both here and abroad in such tactics as sniper techniques and urban warfare—tactics that, according to Ruiz, are only used to control a group of people—not to wage a defensive war.

Finally, one audience member asked the pivotal question of the evening: Why would the United States choose to aid Indonesia rather than East Timor?

Ruiz attributed the choice to economics. According to him, many American firms have plants in Indonesia, and the government is hesitant to alienate such a source of income.

Ultimately, however, the question could not be answered by the people in the room.

"Who can respond to this question?" said Conceicao. "You are American. Ask your president, ask your representatives." ■

LIFE ON Campus

"Where everybody knows your name . . ."

"It's a small world after all; it's a small, small world . . ." These refrains could be sung by small liberal arts college students across the country. At a small liberal arts school, you live on campus and eat on campus. You take classes in a few buildings that aren't spread out over hundreds of acres. And you see the same people all the time—it's amazing how quickly you can get to know 2000 faces. But remember, one of the great things about a small school is that you'll become a part of a community that's fostered by your closeness to everyone else on campus. The whole school is kind of like one big clique, and that's a great feeling. There's also a safe feeling on small college campuses; since everybody knows everybody else, it's unlikely that any intruders with bad intentions could make their way onto campus without someone alerting security. You'll also find that small colleges instill fierce loyalty in their alumni. Think of it as one gigantic club—in which you've got exclusive membership.

At small schools, everyone is involved in all kinds of activities. Because of their schools' liberal arts focus, students enjoy tons of opportunities for artistic pursuits in particular. The liberal arts philosophy, which promotes well-rounded students with myriad interests and abilities, is staunchly defended by these schools. "Are we forgetting the value of a liberal arts education?" notes that, even with all the talk of training students in science and technology fields, the knowledge gained from a liberal arts curriculum still has great merit in today's society.

One thing you should know about small liberal arts colleges right from the start: You'll probably have to live on campus. Only a very small percentage of students, those who are married or live with their parents, are not required to live in campus dormitories. This policy, administrators say, promotes unity and strengthens the campus community. It can also be fun. And, especially when you're a freshman, you'll benefit from living on campus, where you're in on all the action at all times—just ask the students interviewed for "First impressions from Milliken House at Bates College."

Your life on campus will also be influenced by the fact that you'll undoubtedly be spending four years with a fairly homogeneous group of students. The truth is that there's not a lot of diversity in the student body at small liberal arts schools. This can lead to anything from hurt feelings and exclusion at one end of the spectrum to blatant acts of bigotry on the other end. "Race issues still plague Hamilton students, administrators" discusses one small school's battles with racism. But problems with diversity aren't just about race, however; "Coming Out weekend returns to Bates, old issues revisited" reports on that college's attempts to integrate gay and lesbian curriculums and students into life on campus, and *The Crusader* points out some students' complaints that religions other than Christianity aren't getting proper recognition at Susquehanna University.

Moreover, you'll find that much is the same at small liberal arts schools as it is at large state schools and highly competitive colleges. Drinking seems to be a problem no matter where you go; this is reinforced in "Alcohol abuse alive and well at Conn." You'll also read how DePauw and Susquehanna are, much like other schools we've read about so far, experimenting with different policies to curb student alcohol abuse. Just like at other schools, students at small liberal arts colleges are prone to activism; "American U. students defy Burmese government" and "Bowdoin College holds Sexual Assault Awareness Week Activities" report on those who fight for causes on the other side of the globe and right here at home. You'll find student services to help you get the most out of your college experience. And of course, there will be plenty of chances to have fun.

The Liberal Arts

What exactly is a liberal arts education, and why is it so important? As we saw in the chapter on highly competitive colleges, the emphasis at schools with a liberal arts focus is on producing students who can think critically, express themselves both in words and in writing, and are well-rounded through interdisciplinary studies. Education and participation in the fine arts is also given importance. At a school with a liberal arts focus, you are encouraged to explore various areas of interest and express yourself creatively. The emphasis is not on preparing you for a career but on giving you the tools to understand and appreciate diverse subjects.

But what is a liberal arts education worth in today's world, where technology seems to rule the day? Despite a drive to educate students in science and technology, this editorial from *The Argus* clearly expresses the value of a liberal arts education.

EDITORIAL: ARE WE FORGETTING THE VALUE OF A LIBERAL ARTS EDUCATION?

Staff Editorial

THE ARGUS (Bloomington, Ill.) 02/05/1998

Struggling against the recent avalanche of accusations and criticisms regarding his personal life, President Clinton attempted to turn the spotlight on other issues of national concerns in his State of the Union address last week.

In his speech, Clinton stated that improving the quality and the funding of the United States educational system was one of his top priorities.

Clinton unveiled a plan to increase education spending by $20 billion over the next 10 years, and, in a speech at the University of Illinois on the day after the State of the Union address, he stated that his goal is to make college education as universal as a high school education is today.

Despite recent speculations, President Clinton's statements suggest that his interest in America's colleges does go beyond their ability to produce future interns for the White House. However, his proposals also imply that his vision of the future of America's colleges is rather narrow.

In his speech at U of I, Clinton emphasized the importance of scientific research and praised the university as a leader in technological developments that are key to the progress of human life.

But the President also stated that the University of Illinois embodies what we're trying to build for the future of America, which suggests that the ultimate goal of education should be to prepare students for careers that will position the United States as the international leader of technological developments.

So where does Illinois Wesleyan, an institution committed to providing its students with a liberal arts education, fit into Clinton's plans for the future of American colleges? Is a liberal arts education still valuable to us as a society?

Clinton's focus on science and technology is not uncommon, but rather it corresponds to a broader system of American values. We respond in surprise and horror when they hear reports that American students test lower in subjects like math and sciences than students of other nations, but would we have the same reaction if studies revealed that our students have a below-average level of knowledge in subjects like literature, art, music or drama?

Have we, as a society focused on improving the condition of human life, lost sight of the importance of appreciating and celebrating the things that communicate our basic humanity?

As we chase after the American dream, we use our brain power to obtain faster cars, more intelligent computers and more dangerous weapons than our neighboring countries. Unfortunately, these material goals, which seem to be based on the assumption that someone who can quote Shakespeare cannot balance a chemical equation, limit the potential growth of students.

The leaders of our nation must recognize that the people who are most qualified to search for ways to improve human life through science and technology are people who also have a broader understanding of human beings. But funding for education in the arts is sadly lacking in the United States. In fact, art and music programs are often the first to be cut when public schools face financial difficulties.

The administration, faculty and students of IWU need to remind the rest of the nation of the value of a liberal arts education.

IWU must continue to provide courses that offer a liberal breadth of knowledge and constitute the intellectual home where students critically examine the implications of what they learn, as promised in the university's catalog. This university must remain committed to this promise because it must demonstrate the value of the education it offers to the rest of society.

Further, students need to take full advantage of IWU's commitment to a liberal arts education while they are here. Preoccupied with reading assignments, tests and papers, we often forget how fortunate they are to be surrounded by such a culturally rich and creative environment. We need to expose ourselves to the world around us, to attend a production of the theater department, to listen to a music recital or to walk through the Merwin and Wakeley Galleries.

If students gather this larger sense of things in their education here, they can then go out into the world and provide an example of the benefits of a liberal arts education. We can prove to our nation's leaders and to the rest of the world that our education has provided us with a unique knowledge that gives us an edge that will allows us to guide the future of humanity in the right direction. ∎

Exactly how far a small school decides to take its focus on a liberal arts education will be up to them, so you'll find that different schools define "liberal arts education" in different ways. If liberal arts schools aren't keen on providing venues for technical training, where do computer science and business programs fit in? Surely no one doubts the important place that these programs, and others that provide traditionally "career-oriented" curriculums, have at our nation's colleges and universities. Additionally, programs in business and computer science are in great demand these days, and very few administrators would want to turn away students seeking this kind of an education. Finding a definition of "liberal arts" has therefore left many confused, as this editorial from *The DePauw* points out.

EDITORIAL: DePAUW UNIVERSITY MUST DEFINE 'LIBERAL ARTS'

Staff Editorial

THE DEPAUW (Greencastle, Ind.) 12/08/1998

For the past several months, the Committee on Academic Policy and Planning has been reviewing the merits of DePauw's Health and Physical Performance major. After examining the curriculum, talking to students and faculty in the department and discussing the issue, the committee voted to recommend to the faculty that the department be phased out.

According to the committee, the HPP major doesn't coincide with the liberal arts curriculum that DePauw strives to maintain.

Student Body President Ryan Danks, a member of CAPP, expressed concern that not enough time had been spent discussing what that phrase "liberal arts" truly means.

Danks' concern is a valid one. If the committee is recommending sacrificing the HPP department in the name of liberal arts, we had better spend some time discussing exactly what that entails. More importantly, we should discuss what it means for DePauw.

Without a definite, agreed-upon definition to use as a guideline, many other departments could be subject to the same attacks that the HPP department is under. Does computer science fit in with a "liberal arts" curriculum? What about biological sciences? Both could be criticized for being specialized, technical training programs and straying from the University's general curriculum. It's a slippery slope that could lead to a university with little more than philosophy, English and political science majors.

The concept of a liberal arts education should be more than just a definition. It should be a guiding principle that is used to justify many of the decisions made on a day-to-day basis. It should be a statement of purpose for the University, not just an admissions tool.

Defining what it means to be a liberal arts school is

a significant matter. It should come from a discussion among faculty, administrators and students. DePauw's tradition as a liberal arts institution is a proud one, but it's healthy to re-examine what it means from time to time. Now, with the validity of an entire department called into question, a lot of questions are being asked. Those questions are of significance to the entire University community and should not just be answered by nine committee members.

Before the faculty votes on the future of the HPP department, it needs to seek answers to some of these questions. Eliminating a department is a significant action, and it sets a precedent for what is expected from a DePauw education.

The only way we can continue DePauw's liberal arts tradition is to actively understand what that tradition means. ■

Single-Sex Colleges

A small subset of liberal arts colleges that merits mention here is single-sex colleges. Keep in mind that the single-sex college is not unique to small liberal arts universities; some military colleges, like Virginia Military Institute, or religious universities, like Divine Word College, also feature single-sex enrollments. For the most part, however, single-sex institutions are small liberal arts schools like Bryn Mawr College, Barnard College, and Spelman College for women and Wabash College, Morehouse College, and Hampden-Sydney College for men.

Why do students enroll in single-sex colleges? For the most part, students who attend these colleges do so because they find it less competitive and more liberating. You don't have to worry about how you look when you go to class, so your time isn't consumed with the latest "be beautiful" regimens. Your academic life, not your dating or social life, is your top priority. Some research studies have also proven that both men and women gain from single-sex academic environments, where they feel more comfortable and more able to express themselves without the fear of looking awkward in front of students of the opposite sex.

Why are single-sex colleges important? The editorial from *The Bi-College News* suggests that women's unequal status in society necessitates it, and until equality is achieved, they urge the college to remain single-sex.

EDITORIAL: IN PLANNING PROCESS, BRYN MAWR MUST BE PRACTICAL

Staff Editorial

THE BI-COLLEGE NEWS (Bryn Mawr, Penn.) 03/02/1999

Bryn Mawr's strategic planning process could not have come at a more opportune time than now. To welcome the 21st century knowing what we as a liberal arts institution and as a community want will help Bryn Mawr gear up and get ready for the challenges that the new millennium brings.

The list of initiatives, in the words of President Vickers, should serve "as criteria for ways to assess the channeling of resources for institutional support." The immediacy of this list comes with the upcoming capital campaign to raise funds. If Bryn Mawr intends to win the race for grants and donations, she should know what exactly she wants and how to allocate resources as such.

While it may sound as if everything is being reduced to matters of economics, there is no doubt in saying that what Bryn Mawr needs to keep in mind throughout this process is the practicality of any initiatives or plans that she intends to make. What seems to be the greatest challenge Bryn Mawr is facing is that of the struggle between keeping her traditional liberal arts thrust and keeping up with the advancements in technology and education. The landlocked college that we are and with our being a David compared to UPenn's Goliath, it is crucial for Bryn Mawr to search for the most practicable ways of resource allocation.

One of the hotly contested issues raised in the first open college meeting was that of the creation of a separate ethnic studies department. If Bryn Mawr intends to be in keeping with the traditional liberal arts focus, she does not need a separate Ethnic Studies department. What she needs is a more diverse community, from the administration to the maintenance staff, and more diverse, culturally sensitive menu of courses to choose from. The idea of a liberal arts education is to have a well-rounded education in the different fields of learning. One can benefit from an increased awareness of culture-sensitivity if a reorganization or addition of courses were to take place in departments such as Anthropology or Sociology, without having a separate Ethnic Studies department. The complaints about having to go to UPenn or Berkeley make the point obvious: in the same way that one does not come to Bryn Mawr to study business, engineering or architecture, one should also not expect to have an ethnic studies major.

Some have commented that the most practical way for Bryn Mawr is go to coed. Others are skeptical about Bryn Mawr remaining as a separate institution from the tri-college system and UPenn. If women have been elevated to such a status 30 years from now that the need for a single-sex college would disappear, Bryn Mawr's entire purpose is claimed to cease also.

Bryn Mawr should stay single-sex and as a separate institution from Haverford, Swarthmore, and UPenn. She can benefit from increased cooperation with these colleges, but she does not have to go to coed. A purely economic reason would be that donors would just simply stop giving, and this would undermine the whole point of the planning process. Many, especially alumnae, presumably donate to Bryn Mawr foremost as a single-sex, liberal arts institution.

Thirty years is a long way to go; we do not know what or where the next thirty years will bring us. If ever women do attain the societal status that they deserve, this does not mean Bryn Mawr should stop being single-sex. It just means a reorganization of focus and priorities. If Bryn Mawr in the past century was for women's empowerment, then the next one should be Bryn Mawr for the preservation, affirmation and upholding of this elevation of status. ■

The last editorialists needn't worry; single-sex colleges don't seem to be losing any favor. In fact, enrollments in all-women's colleges are on the rise as study after study confirms that women in particular excel in single-sex environments. Barnard is one such single-sex school that's enjoying increased enrollments.

APPLICATION, SELECTIVITY UP AT BARNARD

By Lisa Szymanski

COLUMBIA DAILY SPECTATOR (New York, N.Y.) 02/11/1998

Following on the heels of a dramatic seven-year rise in applications, Barnard College is now the nation's hottest women's school, according to Barnard Admissions Deans.

Since 1991, applications for Early and Regular Decision have each skyrocketed by 117 percent. Growing interest in Barnard can be attributed to the school's small size, its ideal location in New York City, and growing awareness of the benefits of women's colleges, admissions officials noted.

This year, 43 percent of the 272 Early Decision applicants to Barnard were accepted. Median SAT scores of the Early Decision Group exceeded 1,300.

Currently, 3,810 applications for first-year admission have been submitted. Last year, the admissions office received 3,554 first-year applications. Together, Early and Regular Decision applications have increased by seven percent overall from last year.

Dorothy Denburg, dean of Barnard College, explained that the growing interest in Barnard has allowed the college to become more selective in the admissions process.

"We are absolutely committed to maintaining the size of the college at its present enrollment of 2,200. That means an increase in applications—in this case, several years of sharply increasing applications—enables us to be more selective, and we have been, and we will continue to be," Denburg said.

Barnard receives more admissions applications than any of the other Sister colleges, which include Bryn Mawr, Mount Holyoke, Smith and Wellesley, said Doris Davis, dean of admissions. Among the Sister colleges, Barnard's dramatic increase in applications is unprecedented, Davis said.

Davis cited the hard work of the admissions staff and assistance from Barnard alumnae as reasons for Barnard's appeal. However, she also noted that the school itself—its location, its size, its faculty and students-are its most attractive attributes. "The most important reason for [admissions] success is Barnard itself. Barnard is a premier liberal arts college that pays attention to its students. Our faculty serve as mentors, advisers and friends, and the support Barnard students receive allows them to grow both academically and personally," Davis said.

Denburg noted that New York City's many opportunities also draw students to the school.

According to Davis, Barnard's search for independent, individualistic women has made acceptance to the College increasingly difficult. "Barnard women know that they will make a difference and they come to a women's college to better understand how to make that possible. Our students are smart, savvy and sophisticated. They are the women who will lead our world into the next century. We expect no less of them," Davis said. ∎

What about the guys? It turns out that more than half of the nation's single-sex schools are all male. And men who attend all-male colleges feel just as strongly about the values of a single-sex college. At least this next columnist does.

COLUMN: WABASH IS A SINGLE-SEX COLLEGE FOR MALE STUDENTS . . . DUH

By Chris Cotterill

THE BACHLEOR (Crawfordsville, Ind.) 02/18/1999

Faculty and various members of the community seem to think that The Bachelor asked the faculty to commit to Wabash remaining a single-sex college for male students. We didn't. That's a non-issue—the decision has recently been made. We're not asking the faculty to say that single-sex education is better than co-education. We're not stupid, we already know the faculty answer to that.

We're sorry if last week's staff editorial irritated some old wounds by talking about young women in our classrooms, but we're not asking you to tell us why Wabash men should gain from female students in the classroom. We concede this loss and take what we gain.

When the co-ed debate comes around again, then we will all enjoy that conversation. For now, Wabash is a single-sex college for male students. We're asking the faculty to make a commitment to what we do have. Surely all of you can recognize some benefit to the all-male student classroom.

Since there are good reasons for the all-male student classroom, we're asking that its strengths not be undermined. Yes, undermined. When non-faculty females are regularly in the class they become students and change the atmosphere of the class in such a way to undermine the strengths of all-male student classrooms. If it's going to be undermined, what's the point?

And, for those faculty that argue that a professor has the right to allow guests into his classroom, I say yes and no. At some point, a guest becomes a student when they attend many classes. Admissions ultimately accepts students—male students—not faculty.

Some have labeled us sexists for supporting single-sex education. We didn't say that women should not get an education. We never argued not to have female faculty. We never argued that guests shouldn't be allowed into our classrooms—there is an obvious difference between a guest and a person who attends and participates so regularly that they effectively become a student.

If you really want regular non-faculty females in our classrooms, then make a decision on it. Make a statement that you're committed to that. It's much too easy to sit quietly or to argue tangential points and never address the issue head on.

This "challenge" was meant to be an invitation to commit to a fundamental part of the uniqueness of Wabash. I know full well that we don't need the faculty to make this happen; the Board can surely do it well enough on its own.

Admissions sold us on this type of education—at $2000 per course. Many of us came here seeking this type of education, and virtually all of us want it to stay this way. We have a right for what we ask. ∎

Paying for College

Small liberal arts colleges are, in a word, pricey. Here's the lowdown on tuition and room and board fees at some of the schools you'll find in this chapter: Per year, tuition and room and board at Hamilton College is $28,350; Susquehanna University, $24,420; American University, $24,040; and Illinois Wesleyan University, $23,200. That's an average of over $25,000 per year. Note that these fees include room and board; that's because you'll probably be required to live on campus if you attend a small liberal arts school, at least for the first few years. So forget about saving money by eliminating room and board fees. And because the financial aid offices at small liberal arts colleges usually aren't as big as those at highly competitive colleges or large state schools, students need to take the initiative to get financial aid. But don't fear. If you really want to attend a small liberal arts college, you'll find plenty of kind financial aid representatives ready and willing to help you. Small liberal arts colleges like Wake Forest are also finding that, to keep enrollment numbers steady, they need to provide more financial aid options. That spells good news for you.

STUDENT AID MAY SOON SEE INCREASE AT WAKE FOREST

By Jared Klose

THE GOLD AND BLACK (Winston-Salem, N.C.) 12/07/1998

A task force on admissions and financial aid is in the final stage of preparing its report that it will submit to university president Thomas K. Hearn Jr.

According to Samuel Gladding, the associate provost, the committee has held frequent meetings throughout the semester to work on the report and expects to have it ready for Hearn sometime next week.

William Wells, the director of financial aid, said the task force will convene for a final meeting on the proposal Dec. 8.

Although he was hesitant to reveal the contents of the report before the president has had a chance to examine it, associate provost Samuel Gladding did confirm that it calls for an increase in the amount of scholarship money available to students.

"In general, we are going to be making some recommendations as (Hearn) has asked us in regards to making more money available for scholarships," Gladding said.

At the time of publication, Gladding was unable to disclose how much more money would be available for student financial assistance.

"One proposal has to do with the amount of the scholarships given out," Wells said. He said that need-based awards were also reviewed and might increase in some instances.

"There are a wide array of proposals designed to make the financial aid process more comprehensive, but proposals are all they are at this point," Wells said.

Deciding where the money will come from and how it will be distributed is also undetermined. Gladding said that if the changes are adopted, the school would have to rely heavily on outside contributions to support the additional costs of the scholarships.

"We will be looking at re-allocation and at the next capitol campaign in terms of how much our alumni base could contribute to our effort," Gladding said.

"Any changes we make and when we make them are directly related to what additional resources we have," Wells said.

As far as the rest of the report is concerned, Gladding said that it is up to Hearn whether or not he implements any policy changes. "There are going to be a number of recommendations and they will be positive for the most part and he'll have to weigh what he thinks is most important," Gladding said. ∎

Housing

As we mentioned before, the large majority of small liberal arts college students live on campus unless they're married or live with their parents; at most small schools, they're required to do so. It's not that small liberal arts schools have any malicious intentions in mind when they require you to live on campus; they just know that their small size gives them the unique opportunity to create a community-like environment that benefits everyone. The variety of living situations you'll find at small schools makes living on campus fun, too. There are single-sex dorms, coed dorms, fraternities and sororities with houses on campus, fraternity and sorority houses that have been turned into dorms, and, sometimes, dorms for upperclassmen that have private bathrooms. Because they make students live on campus, small liberal arts colleges like Wake Forest, which lets students pick themes and live together by common interests, really try to make living on campus interesting and fun. And most students, like those from Milliken House at Bates College, agree that dorm life isn't that bad after all; what better way to get the "real" college experience?

THEME HOUSES UNITE WAKE FOREST STUDENTS

By Brad Gunton

THE GOLD AND BLACK (Winston-Salem, N.C.) 10/14/1998

For students wishing to pursue an interest that they share with their peers, theme houses offer the opportunity for a group of students with a common bond to live together.

According to Connie Carson, the director of Residence Life and Housing, the theme houses were established with the purpose of promoting interests that developed among students.

"The idea behind the theme houses was to connect students' residential and social lives with an interest area," Carson said. "In some cases the interest area is academic and in others it is a special interest."

Carson said that the theme houses offer students a way to meet people who have something in common.

"The themes provide another option for students looking for a close-knit community," Carson said.

The number of themes varies from year to year,

John C. Vrakas/*The Argus*

with some years featuring several language theme houses and other years having special-interest themes. The current themes are fine arts; Nia, which is named after a principle of Kwanzaa meaning "purpose;" Students Housed In Substance-Free Theme (SHIFT); the German house; and Huffman Residence Hall for students who have a high academic interest.

Sophomore Paige Arrington, a member of SHIFT, said that she decided to join the theme because she wanted to live with students who shared her standards.

"It's an environment where I could be with other people who hold similar morals," Arrington said. "We've got a unique setting where we can get to know everyone on the hall because we all have something in common, whereas a normal hall probably wouldn't have that bond."

There are four theme houses, each located on Polo Road. SHIFT, because it has 65 members, is housed in the second floor of Luter Residence Hall.

A group of student athletes on the baseball team has applied to become a theme for the next school year.

According to sophomore Adam Heaps, living in the theme house would benefit them because their sport demands that they keep difficult hours, with practices and away games, and non-athletes have trouble adjusting to that.

He said he thinks that if they live together, their schedules will not conflict with each other and they can help each other study.

"We wanted to have a theme house because the seven of us guys have become pretty close, and we're all interested in academics, so we wanted to have a place to hang out together," Heaps said.

Applications for theme houses were due Feb. 1. Among other questions they needed to answer, applicants had to establish a purpose for their theme, set goals and say how their theme will benefit the university community.

The final decision about who will live in the theme houses will be made sometime in February. ■

FIRST IMPRESSIONS FROM MILLIKEN HOUSE AT BATES COLLEGE

By Jennifer Giblin

THE BATES STUDENT (Lewiston, Maine) 09/19/1998

Anticipating a week of community service, socializing with new friends, and adjusting to college life, Maura Kelly arrived on the Bates campus a week before classes began to participate in the volunteering program offered to first-year students. That same week, Dan Neumann hiked through Baxter State park with the other members of his Annual Entering Student Outdoor Program (AESOP) trip. Eric Kaviar opted to come to Bates several days later, forgoing the pre-orientation activities to spend more time with his girlfriend. All three students, members of the Class of 2002, live in Milliken House, a first-year residence that houses twenty-eight students and two Junior Advisors.

If anyone has walked by Milliken House recently, he or she is sure to have recognized some changes. Most prominent is the fuzzy beige welcome mat that adorns the front pathway. She may also notice that residents often congregate on the front porch or leave in large packs as they head to Commons for dinner (okay, so maybe that isn't a change). This is a group of students who, in only two weeks, have bonded in such a way that each considers him or herself a member of a "big family." Most Milliken residents agree with Eric, who believes, "Kids in the dorms seem more isolated, there's not as much mingling. Milliken is a closer environment—everyone gets along and respects each other."

The strong opinions of these first-year students is not limited merely to housing life. Having been on campus for several weeks, they have already formed their own perspectives of Bates life, from the effectiveness of Orientation programs to the hassle of getting into classes.

Students in Milliken House enjoyed the college's pre- orientation activities, AESOP and the community service program. They considered both to be great experiences, offering the opportunity to meet other first-years in a close environment. Dan's group, for example, still hangs out together, often meeting for lunch at Commons. The itinerary offered during Orientation Weekend, however, was not as well-liked. With the exception of the speech on date rape, programs were viewed as boring and redundant. Still, the students did acknowledge them to be helpful.

In general, the students were happy with their classes. Katie Zutter states that while some of her introductory courses seem "ridiculously easy," they are nonetheless interesting. She characterizes her other classes as "absolutely amazing." All agreed that their professors seem brilliant. On the negative side, students thought that classes might be smaller and more discussion-oriented and were disappointed that most 100-level courses are quite large and primarily lecture.

The residents of Milliken House were unanimous in

their praise of the social scene. Most have joined a variety of sports and clubs or plan to do so. From crew to community service, these students plan to be active and involved. On the weekends they find that numerous opportunities exist to kick back and have a good time. Many appreciated that with no fraternities, the social scene is more open, with no pressure to drink. Eric, who prefers smaller gatherings, observes, "Some people seem like they're really adjusting well but

others are just trying to go out, get drunk, and get laid. I don't have a problem with either but it just seems like a waste if that's all you're trying to get out of college. It's about socializing not animalizing."

The first-year students from Milliken House are a friendly, optimistic group who have quickly adjusted to life at Bates. Largely satisfied with their experiences thus far, all have a positive outlook for the upcoming year. ■

Don't think that everyone who attends a small liberal arts school is thrilled about living on campus, however. As we've already mentioned, room and board fees are not cheap at small liberal arts schools; some students find it unfair that these colleges wouldn't let them take advantage of less expensive housing facilities off campus. And some students, like this next columnist from Hamilton College, claim that an enforced separation from the "real world" can do them harm.

COLUMN: HAMILTON COLLEGE RESIDENTIAL POLICIES HURT OUR FUTURE

By Tait Svenson

THE SPECTATOR (Clinton, N.Y.) 02/19/1999

A month into the spring semester of junior year, and the pressures of signing a lease for off-campus housing are already upon all of us who wish to get our own apartment. The main problem here is that we are not guaranteed a spot in Hamilton's off-campus housing lottery. My friends at other universities and small colleges have had this opportunity when they became sophomores. They have the luxury of their own bedroom, a semi-private bathroom, a living room, a functional kitchen and the chance to choose who they live with. If Hamilton refused to allow us the freedom to live off-campus because of financial reasons, that would be an acceptable reason. However, it seems that this is not the case.

I understand Hamilton's goal is to have a residential community where all students live in 'harmony' together, and that is a nice idealistic goal. Residential Life provides options that are supposed to replace the need to live in your own apartment, such as Rogers or TDX. Living in TDX this semester, I have realized this does not adequately replace the experience of living on your own. Speciality housing requires you to sign on to the 21 meal plan, spending heaps of money

for next to nothing in return. Despite being on this plan, I had to haggle with a lady in Commons just to get a cup of coffee in the morning.

There is something wrong with housing at Hamilton. What if you don't enjoy being pampered by Hamilton or if you do not need a custodian to baby you? What if when you ask to move and attend numerous appointments with Res-Life, they do not consider your situation a priority? It seems reasonable that one should be able to live off campus if it is less financially crippling than living on the hill, is nicer in general, and enables you to prepare for the real world. Upon graduating from Hamilton, does Res-Life expect all students to have randomly learned to cook for themselves and be comfortable with living in their own place?

Although the academic rigors of Hamilton may be slightly stressful, I don't think they can compare to the first couple of years after graduation. I don't want to try to miraculously juggle a 9 to 5 job, my first apartment without Hamilton looking after everything, and at the same time trying to find the time to cook something besides Ramen noodles or resorting to take-out.

I write this because there have been rumors floating

around that Hamilton is attempting to open enough housing so that off-campus would no longer be necessary. I think the values and lessons learned from having your own apartment far outweigh this false vision of a "community" on the hill. This could never actually happen, as people form separate cliques by nature and as a result, tend to stay within their most inner social circles. ∎

The policies at small liberal arts colleges encourage students from all walks of life to apply. But small liberal arts colleges, although they're generally forward-thinking and liberal-minded in their policies, more often than not enroll student populations that aren't extremely diverse. We've stated that small liberal arts colleges are expensive and that financial aid opportunities may be a little harder to find there. For this reason, these schools tend to enroll students from upper-middle-class and upper-class socioeconomic backgrounds. The campuses of small liberal arts colleges, for the most part, are also fairly homogeneous when it comes to race, religion, and sexual orientation. And surprisingly, you'll find more women than men at most small liberal arts colleges.

Unfortunately, small liberal arts schools experience their share of problems based on race. If a school with a small student body only enrolls a minority population of about ten percent, which is the norm at small liberal arts schools, students of other races may feel extremely uncomfortable with the overwhelmingly white face of their school. Moreover, white students may single out minority students because of their differences. It's also been said at institutions like Hamilton College that the administration turns a blind eye to the problems of race on their campus. *The Spectator* from Hamilton describes that school's ongoing battle with race.

RACE ISSUES STILL PLAGUE HAMILTON STUDENTS, ADMINISTRATORS

By Matthew Brand

THE SPECTATOR (Clinton, N.Y.) 02/02/1998

February is Black History Month, a time dedicated to the recognition and celebration of Black culture, particularly the great social advances made throughout history. The observance is intended to influence people—black, white, or otherwise—to think about race issues from the past to the present.

How far have we come? What problems still remain?

These questions are being asked more frequently at Hamilton College, where minorities comprise only 8.3 percent of the entire student body. On this small and largely white campus, February is always a time when students, faculty, and administrators wonder both why there are not more minorities at the school, and if this lack is harmful in some way.

A recent study indicated that even at a school with such few minority students, those few are often victims of racism. Jessica Johnson '00, Kristen Ward '99, Angela Walker '00, Lourdes Valverde '00 and Kelly Pavese '01 asked the student body via e-mail to share any stories where they experienced racism of some kind. They sent out the question three times, and by the second they were receiving masses of responses, some of which were distributed on a flyer in early December.

On the flyer, students of many different races recalled instances where they over heard racist remarks or were the victims of such remarks themselves.

One such account recalled: "A white car drove by us, (there were, I think, three white guys in the car), and they hung out of the window and screamed, 'White power!' They also made jeering noises at us."

To Pavese, the study was proof that racism is a big problem at Hamilton—a problem that is met with apathy among students and administrators alike. Pavese and many others wonder if the school ignores its racial dilemmas.

"No one knows if the administration even realizes that they have racial problems here," she said.

Dean of Faculty Bobby Fong, himself of Chinese descent, acknowledged strains in campus race relations, and the need to bridge the gap between white and minority students.

"Race relations have to be worked out in particular channels," he said. "We need to strengthen programs that bring different people together, and find common points of interest."

Rafael Arias '01 is one minority student who feels that Hamilton's racial problems can only be solved by increasing the number of minority students. By engaging with racially diverse people on a daily basis, he said, people will be forced to question their own prejudices.

"People will naturally have misconceptions about those whom they don't engage with," he said.

He added that another danger of Hamilton's one-sided racial environment is its ability to reinforce problematic social conventions. That is, a good education and prestigious job opportunities are restricted to privileged white kids and a very select few minorities. He felt that Hamilton is part of a system that dedicates itself to the perpetuation of the white upper class and cares little about the advancement of other racial groups.

"Hamilton's purpose is and always has been to educate the white elite," he said. "Diversity is not a means to those ends."

Many minorities here are unhappy with the College's seeming disinterestedness in racial issues. For example, a mere 50 students attended the Dr. Martin Luther King celebration in the Chapel last Monday night. The ratio of black students to white students was largely disproportionate.

Most obvious, however, is the lack of interaction that takes place between minority and white students. The social groupings in the dining hall mirror the split—minorities sit at certain tables, and whites, others—and rarely does one see interchange.

Margo Anderson '00 links the tension to a general apprehension among white students about approaching and talking with minority students, at least in the Hamilton sphere. Whites know little about blacks, she said, causing an unease that prevents normal discourse.

"White people are afraid of sounding racist to blacks, so they just won't talk to us," she said.

Most people agree that communication between races will only come when more minorities make up the student body. Until then, racial isolation and "fear of the other" will remain the norm.

"We need to take down the barriers and talk to each other," said Susan Gittens '99. ∎

The problems at Hamilton College may not be representative of the racial situation at every small liberal arts school, but it goes without saying that schools with student populations that are not diverse are going to have problems, especially when the administration chooses not to confront the situation. The same applies to issues of sexuality. Because of their size, it's likely that small liberal arts colleges do not enroll large percentages of gay, lesbian, bisexual, or transgendered students (although we should add that statistics on the sexual orientation of students at small liberal arts colleges were not available). But many small universities, like Bates College, for example, are reaching out to these students. As the article from *The Bates Student* reports, however, it may be tough to get recognition and respect for this minority population on campus.

COMING OUT WEEKEND RETURNS TO BATES, OLD ISSUES REVISITED
By Shawn P. O'Leary

THE BATES STUDENT (Lewiston, Maine) 10/09/1998

Roughly a year ago a number of students chalked messages, slogans and images on the walkways along the quad in recognition of Coming Out Weekend. A late night decision to remove the markings sparked a sit-in of Lane Hall, where nearly 100 students witnessed the signing of a contract ensuring sensitivity training for Bates students, faculty and staff; funds for renowned speakers on queer issues; the recognition of queer students and Alumni and Admissions reports; as well as the institution of a gay/lesbian/bisexual/trans (GLBTA) studies curriculum at Bates.

In accordance with these demands the Committee on Homophobia and Institutional Change (CHIC) was convened. The CHIC is charged with supporting Coming Out Weekend activities and has acted in that capacity this year.

"Some activities are planned for Coming Out Weekend, including transportation to participate in the civil rights march in Orono/Bangor on Saturday," said Erica Rand, associate professor of art and a member of CHIC. "Other events include a campus march and chalking, and a panel on Sunday," she continued.

Daniel Ludden, assistant dean of students and also a CHIC member, outlined the role of CHIC in its first full year of existence. "We are trying to assemble a queer studies program and have GLBT issues more visible in college and alumni publications," he said. "There is a sense of a dedicated effort by the dean of students office to support this."

Laura Sundstrom, co-coordinator of the Gay-Lesbian-BisexualTrans Alliance (GLBTA) and a member of CHIC, said that the administration "has been very willing to listen to what we have to say, but action does take time."

"Both the students and the administrative people are working to get things going but the process is slow," Sundstrom added.

Ludden also noted that College Relations, Admissions and alumni groups are in agreement to incorporate GLBTA issues and activities into their literature. In addition, the activities surrounding Coming Out Weekend have been incorporated into this year's Parents and Families Weekend handbook, and rainbow-colored lapel pins will be available for parents at the registration.

Both Ludden and Rand acknowledged that CHIC's task is not an easy one. "Conquering a queer studies program is huge," said Ludden. He said that the task is not nearly as simple as hiring new faculty members.

Ludden said that because money is limited that the college must first find individuals within the college qualified to start such a program. In addition, those faculty which are hired must not only be an expert in GLBT issues but also qualified to teach in existing disciplines of the college. One such example would be a psychology professor who teaches one or more courses within the psychology department which relate to GLBT issues.

Ludden also noted that a large pool of qualified applicants doesn't exist. He said that while some have experience in these issues, very few are experts and therefore the recruitment and selection of applicants will be daunting.

Ludden also noted that there is a growing demand for such people. "We certainly aren't the only college without a queer studies program," he said.

Rand cited means by which social resistance to CHIC's work may also come into play, such as "homophobia and transphobia, including a tendency to minimize that there is a problem."

"People often view Bates as an inclusive environment, but the fact is that Bates is a site for acts of violence, harassment and intimidation, along with the daily acts of prejudice, misunderstanding and discrimination," she added.

Rand's remarks were echoed by the actions of at least a few Bates students Thursday night when several of the GLBTA posters promoting the Coming Out Weekend posters were torn down.

Sundstrom was informed of the hate crime by a custodian who found the posters. "This is definitely evidence of the resistance to what is going on," said Sundstrom. ■

Religion, too, seems to be an area of concern at small liberal arts colleges. As we mentioned before, many small liberal arts colleges started out with religious affiliations or still have religious affiliations to this day. Most of these affiliations are with Christian faiths. And while small liberal arts colleges do not consider religion a factor in admissions decisions, the vestiges of religious influence remain on the campuses of many small schools. *The Crusader* from Susquehanna University reports on this problems at their school and calls for more awareness of religion and race on their campus.

EDITORIAL: SUSQUEHANNA U.'S ADMINISTRATION FAILS TO ACKNOWLEDGE ALL HOLIDAYS

Staff Editorial

THE CRUSADER (Sellinsgrove, Penn.) 12/07/1998

The holiday season is upon us. Thanksgiving slipped past last week, prompting people everywhere to festoon their houses in lights, put up trees in their living rooms and descend on the shopping malls in hordes.

At Susquehanna, the Christmas holiday is being observed in a traditional way. Christmas trees decorate every residence hall lounge and other public place on campus.

Only one thing has been overlooked: Christmas is not the only celebration of faith and culture observed by Susquehanna students at this time of year.

Hanukkah and Kwanzaa are observed by members of the Susquehanna community, yet very little in the way of recognition of these celebrations is visible on campus. To make matters worse, a display on Kwanzaa in the window of the campus bookstore is badly flawed.

Kwanzaa is a relatively new non-religious African American celebration. The display contains, among other things, a book about the Kwanzaa and a kinara, a type of candle holder used in the celebration. The kinara should hold seven candles, each representing a distinct principle of Kwanzaa.

Senior Kamika Cooper pointed out that the center candle which should be black is actually white in the store display. The color black is meant to represent the people. To substitute a white candle is, in Cooper's words, insulting.

While the misplacement of the candle was almost certainly an innocent mistake, it represents a lack of knowledge about other cultures on this predominantly white and Christian campus. When paired with the fact that very little has been done to represent Kwanzaa or Hanukkah here, this mistake points to the need for students to take notice of the many religions and cultures represented here.

Part of living in a multicultural environment is understanding separate and distinct cultures other than the one you most closely identify with.

At this time of year, many students are celebrating the birth of Jesus, a man who taught acceptance and understanding of others. It is in the spirit of the season to take the time to recognize and learn about the many cultures and religions that are represented by the students at Susquehanna. ■

While gender equality may not be as big of a concern on the campuses of small liberal arts colleges as race, sexuality, and religion are, *The DePauw* points out that, by and large, small liberal arts colleges enroll more women than men. DePauw, for one, isn't worrying about the numbers right now, but some small liberal arts colleges are. Does a liberal arts curriculum by its nature attract more women than men, or are the greater numbers of women at these schools simply representative of the population at large? The answer isn't that easy, but this topic is sure to be one that generates a lot of attention.

MISSING MEN: FEWER MEN THAN WOMEN ATTEND LIBERAL ARTS SCHOOLS

By Jessica Mccuan

THE DEPAUW (Greencastle, Ind.) 11/11/1997

The recent push by some Midwestern liberal arts colleges to enroll more men doesn't scare DePauw.

Because of increases in female enrollment, liberal arts colleges like Beloit College in Wisconsin are developing recruiting strategies and admissions policies that encourage male enrollment. But although DePauw's student body is 55 percent female, DePauw's Office of Admission will not follow suit.

Director of Admission Larry West said DePauw has enrolled more women than men for quite some time. West said he doesn't see the disparity as a problem.

"If the numbers were something like 80 percent females and 20 percent males, we might start looking into it and considering it," West said. "But seeing this situation as a problem seems almost like a throwback to the 'good-old-boys' days."

West said the surge in female enrollment at other schools similar to DePauw hasn't affected DePauw's numbers at all.

In his June 1997 article in the Chronicle of Higher Education, writer Ben Gose investigated the national increase in female enrollment at liberal arts schools and asked administrators how they were dealing with it.

Gose told of administrators at Whitman College in Washington State who—after their ratios increased to 60 percent women in 1995—were recruiting men by mailing information cards to more men than women. Gose reported that the mailing plan angered some women on the campus, but was effective in recruiting 40 more applications from men, thus preventing the gender gap in Whitman's 1997 entering freshman class from widening.

Some schools, Gose said, are even willing to break the Title IX Education Amendment in order to recruit more men.

The Title IX amendment requires that schools have roughly the same proportion of female athletes as female undergraduates. This means that, in a school whose enrollment is 60 percent female, roughly 60 percent of the athletes in that school should be females.

Recent studies show that schools with increased female enrollment find it difficult to meet this standard. Schools like Lebanon Valley in Pennsylvania, wrote Gose, will start an intercollegiate hockey team in 1998 in order to recruit more men—whether this violates Title IX or not.

Gose also reported on a group called the Associated Colleges of the Midwest, a consortium of 14 liberal arts colleges which includes schools like Beloit, Carleton and Knox colleges. The ACM recently conducted a study that tried to determine why so many of its member schools were experiencing gender disparities.

ACM President Elizabeth Hayford said the study showed men tend to express preferences for "big sports" and "frat life," as well as majors like business, agriculture and science—things liberal arts colleges sometimes can't offer.

Researchers also found that gender imbalances lead to problems in areas like athletics, social life and curriculum. The study showed that men's athletics programs and male-dominated majors would suffer because of a jump in female enrollment, and that females would be socially unsatisfied because they couldn't find enough dating partners.

Hayford said that, based on the study, the ACM is recommending that its constituent schools should "try to better convey the strengths of liberal arts colleges to men."

In the Great Lakes College Association, which includes DePauw, Hope College, Oberlin College and nine other schools, GLCA president Jo Ellen Parker said not a single school is attempting to tinker with its gender ratios.

Parker said even administrators of GLCA schools whose female enrollment has increased to nearly 60 percent this year "just aren't that excited about it."

Parker said she thinks it's "silly" for liberal arts schools to see increased female enrollment as a problem, and she refuses to recommend that the GLCA do similar research. The new recruiting strategies and the ideology behind them, she said, are "just a hoot."

"It seems absurd that anything that's majority female is seen as a problem," Parker said.

Curriculum problems also seem absurd, Parker said. In her speech she suggested that if a curriculum like math or science is losing students, administrators

should make the class more attractive to both sexes instead of recruiting more men.

Parker also said that there actually should be more women than men in colleges nationwide.

"We all know that the population isn't really half male: males are slightly less than half the population—49 percent—to begin with," Parker said to her radio audience. "Add in the fact that young men are more likely than young women to go to work directly after high school, to be incarcerated, to choose military service or to have been killed by accident or violence, and the population of potential college attendees is a majority female group."

Parker said she isn't planning on looking into gender disparities as a problem that needs correcting until GLCA schools begin to lose appeal to everyone— and she doesn't think there's evidence for that.

"It'll be an interesting thing to watch," she said, "but it's not a problem until we have evidence that it's a real problem. There are schools that take pride in having a lot of female students. I think that's a step forward in correcting their own sexist tendencies." ■

Drinking

Different chapter, same story. It seems that problems with alcohol know no boundaries. At all types of colleges—large state schools, highly competitive colleges, even, as you'll see later, religious schools and two-year schools—drinking is a serious problem. Because most small liberal arts students live on campus, the problem is often intensified at these schools. While the fact that students won't be traveling to off-campus residences for parties alleviates concerns with students drinking and driving, this just means that problems with alcohol will be more concentrated on campus. Connecticut College, as *The College Voice* reports, is not immune to the havoc that alcohol can wreak on college campuses.

ALCOHOL ABUSE ALIVE AND WELL AT CONN
By Kate Woodsome

THE COLLEGE VOICE (New London, Conn.) 09/28/1998

The class of 2002 has only been on campus four weeks, and if they didn't get the hint when they saw the first senior with a 30-pack walk by, then surely the parade of ambulances has told them that drinking is a large part of the Conn social scene.

In a random survey of 124 Connecticut College stu-

dents, 50 percent claimed that they do indeed drink to get drunk. Of the remaining respondents, 46 replied that they drink socially but do not aim to become intoxicated, while the other 16 do not drink at all. These results closely tie in to a Harvard School of Public Health report stating that 44 percent of college students engaged in binge drinking in 1993.

Contrary to what one might assume from the weekend chorus of ambulance sirens, there are only two confirmed reports of Conn students going to the hospital for drinking-related illnesses. In an effort to avert the freshman class from taking a ride in the big white bus, administrators make annual attempts to educate incoming freshmen about the risks of alcohol consumption.

Despite attending the alcohol awareness seminar and signing the Honor Code, however, it is evident that Conn freshmen are still drinking. One freshman, Alison, said she drinks because she feels "it's payback." She explained, "I feel I owe it to myself to party at the end of working hard all week. I wouldn't want to start a Monday without having fun during the weekend." Many students agreed with Alison and added "Everybody else is doing it."

Terry, another freshman, said "Dances are a lot more fun when you're drunk. It helps you loosen up and it makes you do crazy things."

Not all students feel the same way, however. Will, a volunteer EMT, chooses not to drink for obvious reasons. He said, "You couldn't exactly walk into a fire drunk." Concurrently, Tyler said that if he drinks at all he does so to relax his muscles: "One or two and I'm set."

There was not a major difference in drinking attitudes between males and females. More girls admitted that they don't enjoy the taste of beer but often drink anyway. Karen claimed that although "The psychological experience is cool," she doesn't like what it does to her body.

Many students were not fazed by the idea of seeing a friend going to the hospital for excessive drinking. Mike said, "I'd send him flowers and a bottle of wine." At the same time, Meg asserted "I'd be more cautious the next couple of times, and then I'd forget about it." In all, students seemed detached from the possibility of getting sick.

Although the alcohol seminars may be less than stellar, Dean of Freshmen Theresa Ammirati feels that it is important that students realize "how little alcohol it takes to alter their judgment." She believes that the majority of students abide by the Honor Code, but she is always looking for ways to improve alcohol awareness on campus. Simply telling students not to drink has not proven to be effective. Ammirati would like students to contact her and voice their concerns and suggestions about the orientation programs and methods of raising awareness of campus alcohol abuse. Ammirati said, "Kids that drink too much aren't bad people, they've just made some bad decisions."

This year, freshman orientation included a seminar called "After the Party," a workshop presented by Niantic Bay Counseling Services. Presenter Duff Chambers utilized an overhead projector to display and read statistics to students for more than a half hour. Subsequently, students listened to the story of a college graduate who had killed his best friend in a drunk driving accident.

Unfortunately, the seminar did not impress the audience as much as Conn administrators would have liked. Jacqui Pirie attended the seminar and explained "all the presenter did was read facts off a sheet of paper. I listened to the information but was emotionally detached from it. It didn't sink in." Several freshmen agreed that the orientation program was not an effective means of alcohol education.

"Statistics don't teach you anything," said Matt Turcott. "You never think you're going to be another number."

Even Dean of Freshmen Theresa Ammirati was apprehensive about the results of the alcohol seminar, acknowledging that the workshop "didn't do everything" they hoped it would do. Despite the bad reviews of Niantic Bay's presentation, Ammirati feels the seminars are somewhat successful, stating, "this year has been quieter than previous years. There have been fewer students sent to the hospital."

Numbers from the Dean of Student Life office supports Ammirati's assessment. Linda Van Doren, Dean Woodbrooks' assistant, reports that six students were sent to the hospital last year for alcohol-related cases. Though two students have already gone to the hospital during the past four weeks, Van Doren says that it is typical to have about two students go to the hospital by the end of September. ∎

Just as problems with alcohol are evident on the campus of any college you'll go to, so too are programs, rules, and regulations designed to keep student drinking in check. Bates College's new Choices program offers intramural sports as an alternative to partying and has enlisted student-athletes to challenge student perceptions of drinking. They've also changed the rules so that only a caterer can serve alcohol on campus and have enacted a new "three strikes" policy concerning alcohol violations. Other small liberal arts colleges, too, are enacting new rules regarding alcohol. *The DePauw* reports that hefty fines, parental notification, and even expulsion are part of that school's revised alcohol policy.

DRINKING IN DePAUW U. DORMS BRINGS NEW FINES

By Michelle Geary

THE DEPAUW (Greencastle, Ind.) 09/01/1998

With the revision of the new Student Handbook, the University is implementing a stricter disciplinary policy for all violations for the 1998-99 school year.

Formal warnings and level-one violations involve fines beginning at $100 and other measures such as parent notification and attending educational classes. Students will face these punishments if they are caught with a beer in their hands or caught doing something else on that level.

Level-two violations include property destruction and personal injuries. Fines for infringements on this level are $200, and the extreme penalties include suspension and expulsion.

Depending on the circumstances, serious violations will go on the student's record. Graduate schools and other institutions will then receive this information.

"[The freshmen's] faces completely dropped and went pale white," said sophomore and new-student mentor Meghan Duke about the reaction of her group after she informed them of the change. "No one has $100 just sitting around. My group asked if this policy was really going to be enforced. Some of the freshmen did say that it's not going to stop them from drinking, but they are definitely planning on being careful and staying under control."

The money that the University receives from these fines will go into an awareness and prevention fund. This account supports education, forums and speakers on alcohol. Instead of coming from the tuition of the general student body, alcohol prevention events are now supported by those who are violating the rules.

A selected group of students from the judicial board and student cabinet helped certain student affairs and

student services administrators write this policy. Every year, there is a review of the handbook and changes are constantly made.

"In the past, students who violated DePauw's alcohol policy received a mere slap on the wrist. Therefore, there were many repeat violations," said Dean of Students Alan Hill. "Now they have to decide if being caught is worth it. One hundred dollars is a pretty expensive beer."

According to Hill, one of the reasons behind this change is because of a study that showed 70 percent of students who aren't drinking are still affected by those who are. This includes having to pay for floor damage, dealing with harassment and not being able to sleep because of drinking students' rowdiness.

Although students living in the dorms are aware of the consequences, resident assistants have already been at work, writing people up for disobeying the rules.

"It's not my choice. I wish I didn't have to write people up, but I accepted doing it as my job. And as an RA, I think the fine will make my job easier though because students will think before they drink. I know if I was under 21, a $100 fine would really make me think," said Kendall Noyes.

"It's about making the right decision," Hill said. "Students have to make better choices. There are plenty of things to do on the weekends besides drink. But people don't come to dances, sporting events, plays and other activities sponsored by the University because they can't drink. Besides one time, I have never told a fraternity that they can not have a party. They can have a party. They can laugh and talk and dance and have a band. They just can't provide alcohol."

Some students do not view the University's new

policy in the same light as those who formed it.

"It's caused a lot of grief in our dorm," said freshman Alex Lainfield who lives in Anderson Street Hall. "The University's a little out of control, all up in your business. It's one thing if you're loud, but the RAs just walk in. This is a violation of individual rights."

As soon as this year's handbook is distributed, students are required to sign a contract stating that they have read it and agree to abide by its rules. ■

Activism

Because their campus becomes their community for many liberal arts college students, you may not think that students at small schools would be very involved in activism. Quite the contrary. Read on to find out how courageous students from American University defied anti-democratic Burmese officials in an extraordinary move that landed them in a foreign jail for days. And closer to home, *The Bowdoin Orient* reports on a campus organization, Safe Space, that fights for awareness of the problem of sexual misconduct and violence in our society.

AMERICAN U. STUDENTS DEFY BURMESE GOVERNMENT

By Jeremy Feilera

THE EAGLE (Washington, D.C.) 08/19/1998

Four AU students who were detained in Burma August 9 discussed the uncertainty of their first few days of captivity and their defiance in the face of police interrogators last Thursday.

Anjanette Hamilton, a College of Arts and Sciences and School of International Service sophomore, Sapna Chhatpar, an SIS junior, Michelle Keegan, a CAS sophomore, and Nisha Anand, an SIS graduate student, were the detained members of AU's chapter of the Free Burma Coalition.

The students said that their mission in Burma, officially known as Myanmar, was thoroughly planned, with most contingencies mapped out.

They traveled to Burma with 14 others and distributed pro-democracy leaflets to the Burmese on August 9. This was the day after the 10-year anniversary of the military crackdown in the capital city of Rangoon, now called Yangon, during which more than 3,000 Burmese students were killed in a coup that overthrew the democratically elected National League of Democracy and its president, Aung San Suu Kyi.

The demonstrators planned to hand out fliers and catch a flight back home later in the afternoon, although they had tickets for August 13 in the event of their arrest.

"We had contingency plans," Anand said. "We had contacts in Bangkok who called the (American) embassies on August 9, and who knew who to contact in the media and government."

"The embassy was ready and prepared," Anand added. "Burmese citizens don't have that."

The activists did not realize they would be detained for six days. "When you're working with a military dictatorship, nothing's assured." Keegan conceded. "But we did have a calculated risk."

When the 18 demonstrators were arrested, Burmese police brought them to police headquarters in Rangoon, Keegan said.

The building was crumbling, filthy, and the prisoners shared their quarters with scurrying mice and insects, Hamilton said. The demonstrators were divided into groups of three and jailed in six offices while armed guards stood outside.

"We thought we'd be interrogated for a few hours and released," Chhatpar said. "We knew we might be stopped . . . but we didn't expect to be detained for six days."

All four students said that they and the other 14 prisoners were treated decently, even though they were not fed until late on the day of their arrest and were unable to bathe for the first four days of their captivity. They said that during their captivity they subsisted on Chinese take-out food. Anand was the only one of the four students struck by a Burmese police officer.

"I think because I look like a Burmese citizen of Indian descent, he mistook me for a Burmese citizen," Anand said. "He slapped me in the face but didn't do it again when he found out I was an American... but the first thing he did was physical violence. It was just a little glimpse into it, but I thought, what would he do if I was Burmese?"

Anand said that she "tried hard not to be fearful. I said 'No, I'm not answering questions. You violated my human rights.'"

"I kept repeating that I was protected by the Fifth Amendment. It was a useful tool to use against my captors," she said.

After the first four days the 18 prisoners were moved to the more accommodating conditions of the Police Guest House. The main problems confronting the prisoners were boredom and a lack of information, Chhatpar added.

A trial was held on the AU activists' sixth and final day of captivity. At a Burmese court located within Insein Prison, they were sentenced to five-years imprisonment.

But the activists said they knew that the sentences would not stand.

The trial lasted late into the night, but all 18 prisoners were deported the next morning. They were later told by Burmese activists that pro-democracy demonstrators never survive the standard five-year prison sentence due to isolation and torture or the alternative—and just as fatal—punishment of being cast into general population with violent offenders.

After the trial, Burmese police officers threatened to take away several activists' shirts that said, "8/8/88 Don't Forget, Don't Give Up" on the front and had the Burmese translation on the back.

"The people we met—Burmese exiles—told us what was going on," Anand said. "Being up there . . . people told us what we had done that worked and what we could do for them." Hamilton agreed.

"It was heartening that people had heard of something like Massachusetts passing sanctions against Burma," Hamilton said. "Even our interrogators heard about it."

Hamilton said that their efforts are only a small part of the Free Burma Coalition's efforts to press nations to divest their economic interests in Burma.

"Sanctions aren't only economic. They're symbolic," Hamilton said. "We're the leading democracy interested in human rights. Saying 'we don't support this' sends a message to Burma and sets the stage for other governments to follow suit."

Keegan then acknowledged that the Burmese military regime actually helped them get their message out within Burma, not just outside of it.

"The regime printed the goodwill message we were handing out in their newspapers, our pictures and explained what we did," Keegan said. In the end, they helped us deliver our message." ∎

BOWDOIN COLLEGE HOLDS SEXUAL ASSAULT AWARENESS WEEK ACTIVITIES
By Kathleen Parker

THE BOWDOIN ORIENT (Brunswick, Maine) 02/26/1999

Next week the College will hold Sexual Assault Awareness Week activities, sponsored by Safe Space, to promote awareness and support survivors of sexual assault. According to one of the event organizers,

Annie Powell '01, Safe Space wants to heighten the awareness of sexual assault on campus.

Powell explains that Safe Space feels there is a general lack of awareness of sexual assault that is not unique to the College but is a problem on all college campuses. "We're hoping our events will be well attended and show support for people who are survivors," she said.

Safe Space has organized several events throughout the week. According to another of the event organizers, Sean McClead '99, "We wanted to get a chance to send the message out to people who might not normally be inclined to listen."

With that purpose in mind, Safe Space invited speakers whose talks might reach more of the Bowdoin community. On Monday, Jackson Katz will give a talk entitled 'More Than A Few Good Men' that focuses on sexual assault and surrounding issues from the male perspective. In the past, Katz has spoken to professional sports teams, and he places emphasis on helping men become activists. According to Powell, Katz aims to make men into protectors instead of perpetrators.

Tuesday features an open panel discussion with Sexual Assault Services of Midcoast Maine, Robin Beltramini from Dudley Coe Health Center, and all of Safe Space. On Wednesday there is a presentation by Maria Falzone, a former comedienne, entitled 'Sex Rules!'

Falzone speaks on how sexual assault support groups are often perceived as anti-sex coalitions, but points out instead that while sexual assault is bad, sex is healthy. "We're really trying to emphasize the difference between sexuality and violence . . . that sex is to be celebrated but violence is unacceptable," said McClead.

Falzone talks about how society discusses sexually transmitted diseases and sexual assault in the same context, but she wishes instead to separate sexual violence from sexuality.

Friday there will be a candlelight vigil and speak-out along with a showing of the film 'The Accused,' starring Jody Foster, which is sponsored by Safe Space and the Bowdoin Film Society. Throughout the week, Safe Space will have a table in Smith Union offering pamphlets and answering questions. All of the speakers

Campus Snapshot

BOWDOIN COLLEGE
Brunswick, ME

Popular Campus Myths or Legends:
Mel Gibson tearing into fried chicken (bones strewn all over the place) on the quad while filming "The Man Without a Face" on campus; the "Ana gravestones" on campus where students burned and buried their books and notes from the formerly required Analytical Geometry course

One Event of the Year That Everyone Attends:
Bowdoin/Colby hockey game

Most Cherished Alumni:
George Mitchell, Bill Cohen, Nathaniel Hawthorne, Henry Wadsworth Longfellow, Joshua Chamberlain, Robert Perry

Least Popular Move by Administration:
Banning Fraternities

Campus Protests:
Silent protest during Trustees Weekend

are well-respected and have been well-reviewed, and Safe Space encourages attendance.

Safe Space was originally founded by a small group of concerned friends and is now a student organization that offers support to survivors of sexual harassment and sexual assault. McClead pointed out that each year Safe Space is becoming more diverse.

The activities during Sexual Assault Awareness Week are just a few of the efforts put forth by the group to help make people more aware of the presence and effect of sexual misconduct in every community. ■

Student Services

Small liberal arts colleges do a great job of providing for all of their students. Because of their focus on you, small colleges have excellent facilities to address all kinds of concerns. Because they're dealing with a smaller number of students, student service offices on campus can give you more individualized attention than you'd find at a larger school.

Even on a small campus, problems are bound to arise. And while most colleges have avenues through which students, faculty members, and administrators can resolve conflicts, few have a special officer for just that task. Bryn Mawr College is one of the few schools in the nation to office this service to its campus community.

BRYN MAWR HIRES FIRST COLLEGE 'OMBUDSPERSON'
By Christine McCluskey

THE BI-COLLEGE NEWS (Bryn Mawr, Penn.) 02/02/1999

Eleanor Funk has been hired by Bryn Mawr College to be the College's first Ombudsperson. She started working Jan. 18 in the part-time position as a resource for "staff, faculty, and students seeking to resolve conflicts in the College community," according to a Jan. 15 letter to the community from President Vickers.

According to the Mission Statement of the Ombuds Office, Funk will be acting as "an independent, impartial and confidential resource to facilitate conflict resolution within the College, able to supplement any level of the College's existing conflict resolution procedures."

Funk comes to Bryn Mawr with much experience in conflict resolution, having worked with schools, businesses, and other communities. She was most recently at Rutgers, where she started a peer mediation program. She has also worked at companies such as AT&T, Lucent Technologies, and Nabisco; has been a mediator for divorce and custody cases in the New Jersey court system; and has served as community Ombudsperson with the Division of Senior Services. She is a Certified Mediator, a Certified Ombudsperson, and a Licensed Clinical Psychologist in New Jersey.

The Ombudsperson's specific responsibilities include the education of the community on conflict management and resolution, confidential assistance to individuals or groups in conflict, working with groups such as the Honor Board who currently facilitate conflict resolution on campus, training people to be mediators, referral to off-campus sources for help in resolving problems, and making periodic evaluations of the entire program of conflict resolution at Bryn Mawr.

"The position is funded to help everyone, including faculty, staff, and students; I especially want to welcome students to come to me for help with stressful situations they are in," said Funk.

With the Social Honor Code, students in conflict with each other first discuss the problem in the nonhostile confrontation, and then seek outside help from their Housing Assistant (HA) if they can't resolve the problem on their own. If formal mediation from a third party is needed beyond what the HA can do, students can go to the Mediation Intake Coordinator, a Dorm President, an Honor Board member, an appointed undergraduate or McBride mediator, or, now, the Ombudsperson.

Since the Honor Code does not apply to faculty and staff members, they used to have few options for formal mediation. Now, the Ombudsperson fills this need, as well as working with students as described above.

An example of a case Funk might work with is that of a staff member who has worked with Housekeeping for a long time and is upset with her new supervisor. The supervisor has made some drastic changes in Housekeeping without consulting her or any of her co-workers. According to Funk, an Ombudsperson would "help [her] look at all the options—help her weigh each option and decide on a course of action." The Ombudsperson might talk with the supervisor on the woman's behalf or facilitate a meeting between the woman and her supervisor.

Funk might also work with cases involving issues of faculty and staff promotion and tenure, discipline, termination or academic dismissal, grades, wages/benefits, sexual harassment, discrimination, financial aid, and many other areas of conflict. ∎

Unlike large state schools or two-year colleges, small liberal arts schools have very few commuters. This is largely because students are required to live on campus unless they're married or live with their parents. A commuter population does exist, however; what's problematic is getting them involved in the campus community. As the *Decaturian* reports, small schools like Millikin University in Illinois are tackling this problem and are working toward getting commuters involved in campus life.

INSPIRING COMMUTER INVOLVEMENT DIFFICULT AT MILLIKIN

By Alyssa Sherman

DECATURIAN (Decatur, Ill.) 03/11/1998

Getting involved with campus activities is easy for most students who live within walking distance, but involvement for commuter students is a slightly harder endeavor.

Some commuters cited the distance they travel to get to campus and the time it takes, along with a lack of information, as major reasons why they don't get involved in campus activities.

Freshman computer science major Jesse Gray, who is a commuter, said he is not involved with campus activities.

"I don't even know what's going on," Gray said. "That's why I don't get involved." Other commuters agreed.

"Everything is advertised in the dorms," said sophomore biology major Jill Franquelli. "If the groups advertised a little better for us, and if the events were held a little earlier, it would be easier for me."

Some groups, including the Black Student Union, make an effort to reach out to commuters.

"We have commuter legislators in our legislative body," said Danielle Gittens, BSU recording secretary. "We have Commuter Wednesday when we hand out flyers in the Union. Many commuters do come to our social events."

Things on campus don't start until late, even movies at the Hoff Theater, Franquelli said.

"We really don't hear about activities as much as on-campus students," said commuter Jen Rice, a sophomore kinesiology major.

Rice and Franquelli said they are as involved as they can be, given their commute.

"We go to things we hear about by e-mail," said commuter Angela Newby, a sophomore biology major. "They are usually departmental and once a month or

Campus Snapshot

MILLIKIN UNIVERSITY
Decatur, IL

The Decaturian

By Adrienne Puyear, Editor

Millikin University has a unique tradition unlike any other: the annual Bun Run. This long-standing event occurs at midnight on the day of the first snow after holiday break. The men of Mills Hall then take their annual jog around three girls' dorms (Blackburn, Walker, and Aston Halls), completely naked except for their shoes. Most participants, however, wear bags or masks over their faces. For good reason, the Bun Run has become both an attraction and a legend.

week." Some commuters said they do make time to get involved.

Senior biology major Kelly Orzechowski said she joined student groups because it was hard to meet people in her classes.

"Commuting makes it hard to meet people," Orzechowski said. "I joined several activities, like the eating disorder task force, Best Buddies and a sorority to get more involved."

Commuter Joy Freeman, a junior journalism major, said she frequently gets herself in over her head.

"I'm involved because I want to be," Freeman said. "I tend to overload myself and involve myself in more activities than I have time for. I realize how some commuters can be under-involved, though. Many things are geared for those who live on campus." ∎

You may think, since small liberal arts colleges are committed to the philosophy of a liberal arts education and not to career preparation, that they wouldn't go out of their way to make sure you get a great job after graduation. This is hardly the case. In fact, most small liberal arts colleges regularly host career fairs, where prospective employers converge upon the school to talk with students, review resumes, and, sometimes, offer positions. As *The Argus* reports, Illinois Wesleyan University is one of many small schools that benefit from career fairs.

JOB FAIRS OFFER CAREER CONNECTIONS FOR ILLINOIS WESLEYAN U. STUDENTS

By Diane Tasic

THE ARGUS (Bloomington, Ill.) 02/03/1999

The first week of February will be busy for the Career Center. With the Senior Job Fair and the Career Fest, students will have opportunities to explore both potential career options and internships.

IWU co-hosts the Senior Job Fair with Illinois State University.

"The reason [IWU] established this relationship with ISU is because it made sense to pool our resources so the businesses could come once to Bloomington-Normal and see both institutions' students," IWU Career Center director Warren Kistner said.

Approximately 225 organizations and businesses will be in attendance. This fair focuses primarily on seniors who will be ready to enter the work force soon after graduation.

"Students fared well at last year's job fair. It lead to opportunities in terms of follow-up and on-site or arranged campus interviews," Kistner said.

Kistner expects approximately 100 seniors from IWU to attend the job fair, but he still hopes for more people to come than last year.

"There are opportunities for students of all majors, and it helps to establish an initial contact with companies," he said, stressing the importance of bringing several copies of a resume to the fair.

The Career Fest, unlike the Senior Job Fair, offers both internship and job opportunities for all interested upper-class students.

"IWU is a member of the Illinois Small College Placement Association, which consists of 32 small colleges including Augustana, Knox, Wheaton and North Central," Kistner said.

According to Kistner, the ISCPA holds this yearly event in order to provide assistance in job and internship searches to students from several small colleges. "More can be done in the way of help by linking with other schools," he said.

Kistner hopes that there will be an increase in IWU attendance at this year's fest. Last year, 94 IWU students attended, which was an increase from the 64 students in 1997. Currently, IWU has the largest number of pre-registered students for the fest.

"I believe part of the increase in numbers at these fairs is due to word-of-mouth from friends and advice from peers," he said.

The Drury Lane accommodates space for 150 businesses to represent themselves at the Career Fest. "Companies come out to the event because they recognize the profile of a student from a school such as IWU, and they value the liberal arts education these students are obtaining," Kistner said.

Kistner also added that employers tend to find the students at this ISCPA-sponsored fest to be more articulate and professional than at other job fairs. In general, he strongly encourages students to consider visiting this fair.

"It's always good practice doing interviews and presenting oneself," he said.

Senior Stacy Cornelius agrees with Kistner about the benefits of attending the fair.

"A lot of people get interviews set up while they're there. If you're not going there to get direct contacts, at least go for the experience," Cornelius said. ■

Since the overwhelming majority of small liberal arts college students live on campus, quarters can get pretty close, so they need to have lots of space to get away from it all and relax, enjoy themselves, and socialize. Small liberal arts colleges are known for their great recreational facilities—from campus cafes, movie theaters, and art galleries to small concert spaces and lounges for studying and just plain kickin' back. Students at small colleges like Haverford are never at a loss for things to do—so why would you ever want to leave campus?

NEW STUDENT LOUNGE OPENS IN HAVERFORD CAMPUS CENTER

By Janet Bunde

THE BI-COLLEGE NEWS (Haverford, Penn.) 01/26/1999

Over the past several months, the inside of the Whitehead Campus Center has been under construction in order to create a new student center and several offices. Now that the construction is complete, Haverford's Campus Center finally has what it has lacked since it's initial construction—a place where students can socialize and study, the new student lounge.

The lounge is the result of nearly three years of planning by a committee comprised of faculty, staff and students.

The Campus Center Task Force, as it was called, "was created with the mission of making the Campus Center a more usable space," said Students Council Co-President Ellie Brown, '00.

Erected in 1993, the current Campus Center filled many of the community's needs, according to Dean Robin Doan, chair of the task force. But the admissions office overflowed its space in Hilles, and the bookstore, snack bar, post office and game room suffered in their location beneath the Dining Center. The new building allowed these organizations to move as well as opening up space for a formal art gallery.

Despite the center's usefulness, students still found something lacking in the building.

"There was no social space for students," said Doan. "The building contained fine materials and craftsmanship, and it served many of our needs, but the social space in the building was minimal."

In January of 1997, former Students Council President Kevin Joseph, approached Dean Randy Milden about the possibility of reevaluating the allotment of space in the Campus Center. Milden took Joseph's recommendation to the senior staff, who agreed the proposal merited a second look. Out of this student-fueled request, the new task force was born.

"Originally we wanted to create a larger room, but in the logical places to put such a room, such as the office space and foyer outside the bookstore, we ran into a wall that contained a lot of important ductwork and electrical wiring," said Doan. "Eventually we realized that we couldn't move the bookstore or the post office, and we couldn't knock down any walls."

Given these criteria, the task force recommended several small improvements to the Campus Center.

Lighting was increased 400 percent in the hallways and atrium, making some areas more conducive to studying or chatting and providing a more "welcoming" atmosphere, according to Facilities Coordinator Kathy DiJoseph, a liaison between the task force and the physical plant. The activities room on the third floor was cleared of stored items and lockers, making it easier to use. The information desk and manager's office were moved to the ground floor, and the new student lounge was built at the location of the old information desk.

"We decided that the Coop was the most well-used existing space in the Campus Center," said Brown. "An expansion of the type of hang-out space found there would be a good use of our limited resources."

Doan cited a second reason for locating the lounge between the Coop and Cantor Gallery.

"We were looking for a space that people would naturally pass," said Doan.

The most basic components of the lounge were designed with students in mind, explained DiJoseph. Transparent walls allow students to see who is inside with minimal trouble. Dimmable track lighting allows students to choose an appropriate atmosphere for their activities. The furniture, described by several students as "eclectic," was a portion of the plan from the beginning.

In addition to privacy and soft-stuffed chairs, five Internet connections were added so that students could bring their laptops and work in comfort. Because the lounge was designed primarily as a study or social room, a television was deliberately left out of the plans.

"All additional lighting will be switchable, allowing students to have a party without breaking fire regulations," said Diaz. Previously, to darken the campus center for dances and concerts, dark paper had been used to cover the fixtures, an action that violates the fire code of the building. ■

Fun Stuff

Not to be outdone by their larger school counterparts, small liberal arts college students can party and have a good time with the best of them. Just because you go to a small school doesn't mean you can't have big fun—now, that's the attitude! College life is college life, after all, so whether you go to a big school or a small school, you'll spend your share of time at campus hotspots, enjoy great festivals, rock on at college-sponsored concerts, and even, despite English 101, come to speak your own language.

COLUMN: SENIOR ENCOURAGES COMPLETE ENJOYMENT OF THE MUG BY ALL

By Charles Pugliese

THE MISCELLANY NEWS (Poughkeepsie, N.Y.) 03/23/1999

Two lines of chairs, parallel and seemingly unending. I sit on one of these chairs, waiting. On both sides of me, drunk people are talking, waiting, pushing. From beneath me, a thumping beat emanates; I can feel it through the floor. I sit and wait as another typical night at the Mug (or at least in the line) passes.

Now that I'm a second-semester (read: terminal) senior, I find myself going to the Mug more and more often, and I don't really know why. I'm not particularly enchanted with the music, the $2 beer isn't especially smooth going down and I usually have to wash the smell out of my clothes.

Yet, this past weekend, I made the journey into our basement bar no fewer than three times. I sat on those maroon Retreat chairs for long periods of time and endured harassment by a member of Vassar's newly-formed Cheerleading Squad (some accounts of the story may say I harassed her, but that's not how I remember it), just to get into the Mug. I even found myself fighting to get in, arguing, (or yelling, as my friends recount it), with a security guard who let people in ahead of me. I can't remember the last time I displayed such passion towards anything—and I just finished my thesis.

Maybe it's because I am done with my thesis and one of my hardest classes is tennis, but I really think the reason behind my numerous pilgrimages to the Mug is more simple. I realize that I've only got three months left before I won't be able to get into the Mug without a guest pass.

That's right, I'll say it: I am graduating and leaving Vassar. It's a harsh reality, and I'm trying, I'm desperately trying, not to face it. But I can't get past the fact

Kimbereley Barnhart/*The Bradley Scout*

that in three months the kind of social venue I enjoy here at Vassar will disappear forever.

No more trudging out to the THs to enjoy some free lemon-laced Saranac (supposedly, I was told, a "summer beer"). No more $5-all-you-can-drink nights at the Dutch. But most of all, no more Mug. I mean, how can you beat a bar that, for some people, is actually inside your dorm (I lived in Main for three glorious years), never charges a cover and always has some sort of dance music? At what other bar can you can always be sure that even when you go alone, you'll always find a few of your friends?

On Tuesdays, I have an internship in the real world. I work with a couple of recent Vassar graduates whose eyes glimmer with a kind of pathetic nostalgia every time I mention I'm going to the Mug. "Drink one for me," they say; then they pack up their briefcases and head home to their cramped apartments.

I really never thought that I would be an advertisement for the Mug, but every time I see my co-workers,

I'm invigorated with a sense of energy (and urgency) to go out and enjoy Vassar and its unique social scene. Maybe that's why every Thursday night I try to make the triangular journey from the Pub to the Dutch to the Mug.

As graduation, a.k.a. the apocalypse, approaches, I'm comforted by the thought that I probably will make it in the real world, even though I may not have as much fun. And that's why I'm going to make these last three months count, even if I spend most of my time in the Mug line.

There is no time like now. So come on, put those half-finished-and-due-tomorrow theses down. Shut the boring textbooks. Put on your black tank top and head out to the Mug. Or go to the Dutch, or the Pub or even the THs. Go to a dorm party, for Christ's sake, because no matter who you are, you've only got a limited time left here. After all, what good is sitting alone in your room? ■

ANI ANI ANI

By Anne McConnell

THE ARGUS (Bloomington, Ill.) 04/16/1998

A really fast version of the Indigo Girls, or a cross between Henry Rollins and Patty Larkin.

These are just two attempts to describe the emerging music star who seems to be indescribable.

Ani DiFranco continues to take listeners by surprise with a style and intensity that has never been heard before. DiFranco is to music what the Impressionists were to painting and the Beat generation was to literature—she is an artist willing to lose fame and fortune simply to express herself.

DiFranco's childhood and musical beginnings are rooted in Buffalo, New York. Today Buffalo is the home of her personal record label, Righteous Babe Records. At 15, DiFranco was writing songs and performing locally.

At age 20 she produced her first album and went on the road. She made her first engagement with Illinois Wesleyan, which was actually her first concert west of the Appalachian Mountains.

Associate Dean of Student Affairs Darcy Greder started the Blue Moon Coffeehouse at Illinois Wesleyan in 1990 and invited DiFranco to perform in the first year of the annual music series. Greder remembers DiFranco as "someone the students could relate to because she was only 20 years old at the time."

The first appearance at Blue Moon Coffeehouse not only started Wesleyan students' love for DiFranco's raw talent and confrontational style, but also induced the loyalty that DiFranco now has to both Greder and the school. DiFranco will be making her sixth appearance at Illinois Wesleyan this spring.

After a successful road trip in 1990, DiFranco got mainstream offers to market her into music production. Although she considered the possibility at first, she turned away after reading the contract from a small indie label.

"It made me realize that the music business is a business like any other, and the focus is profit," DiFranco told Advocate magazine.

This realization encouraged DiFranco to create Righteous Babe Records. With her own record label,

DiFranco could make every decision about the production and marketing of her albums.

In a statement about Righteous Babe Records, she describes it as "a people-friendly, sub-corporate, woman-informed, queer-happy small business that puts music before rock stardom and ideology before profit."

Righteous Babe was started in Buffalo because DiFranco wanted to support her hometown's business and grassroots culture workers. The label relied greatly on DiFranco's "on the road" marketing of new music. With each concert, she won over a new handful of fans who now make up her broad fan base. DiFranco's independence, unique style, honesty and incredible talent generated interest across the country and soon attracted attention from the media.

So how was a self-promoted, hard-nosed folk singer from Buffalo ever noticed by the world? The simple answer is that DiFranco is a performer. Her stage performance is both a drama and a concert, peppered by comical and light-hearted monologues to the crowd. If she broke a string, DiFranco would captivate the room of people with a spoken word piece while someone from the crowd was stringing her guitar.

Each song is played with an unmatchable passion that lures in listeners with both the music and her words. DiFranco, who has recorded 11 albums, never runs out of things to say or ways in which to express them.

DiFranco's recent accomplishments include work on soundtracks, benefit albums and also the release of her latest album, Little Plastic Castle, which was preceded by a summer tour with musical legend Bob Dylan.

"Bob Dylan is the greatest poet of his generation, a legend and [an] icon, she said in Billboard magazine. But when I met him, I realized he is just a folk singer who loves playing music, a folk singer like me," DiFranco said.

With her rising popularity, DiFranco has seen both the difficulties and benefits of being a music star. As an independent artist with new-found fame, she is under the scrutiny of the media and is misrepresented constantly. For a self-promoted artist, bashings by the media can be extremely damaging.

DiFranco's popularity has made way for other independent artists, though, and has salvaged the idea that a musician can succeed without succumbing to the music industry. Furthermore, Righteous Babe Records has expanded and produced the albums of other musicians not wishing to sign with large labels.

DiFrancos accomplishments are endless, but her simple devotion to music, humanity, and her own beliefs make her an easy person to admire.

When asked what separated DiFranco from other musicians, Greder summed it up perfectly.

"Music crystallizes time, and Ani attaches words to these times." ∎

STUDENTS BRING THEIR OWN VERNACULAR TO DePAUW U.
By Emily Fox

THE DEPAUW (Greencastle, Ind.) 09/04/1998

"That hoser just skiefed my CD and then he had the nerve to invade my ish!"

"Oh my God, that's so random. Sounds like he has some major issues."

"Yeah, I heard he got in a fight with his HTH after she found out that he hooked up with some girl last weekend."

Are any of these terms foreign to you? Don't worry, you haven't entered the twilight zone. You have entered the great melting pot of DePauw slang. You may be in need of a crash course in Slang 101, since slang is an integral part of any sound liberal arts education.

One of the best parts of coming to college is meeting new people from all over the country. It can also be one of the most interesting and confusing parts. Everyone brings their own idiosyncrasies from home: accents, mannerisms, expressions and, best of all, slang.

Some slang terms are funny, some are cool (or shall I say "money"?) and some are just plain strange. I am here to explain them, or perhaps break them down.

The slang terms mentioned most often in my interviews were "mash 'n dash," "hooking up" and "random." Many incoming freshmen never heard of these terms before coming to DePauw.

Here at school, we have our own special uses for "random," all of them very dear to our hearts. One of my favorite examples of this term was given by junior Laura Bennett when she said, "That dinner at Longden was so random."

It seems that some of the most memorable slang terms were first heard in students' freshman year. When senior Brian Hersh was a freshman, he had some concerns about his bubble sheet and was a little confused. That's when his new student mentor told him, "It's all good."

Freshman Meridith Christman remembers the term "tool" from her freshman year. This is used in a sentence like, "He's such a tool," meaning that he is such a dork or loser. A variation on this term is "toolbox."

Sophomore Todd Rainer has many fond memories of the unusual expressions used by his Michigander floormate freshman year. One of his favorites is "hoser," which has a fairly open-ended definition. Its most useful definition seems to mean a really annoying person. Rainer thought that perhaps "hoser" was his friend's attempt to pronounce Hoosier.

Sophomore Tracy Charleton remembers surprising people by using the expression "cop a squat;" it means "have a seat." She also remembers being confused the first time she heard the acronym "HTH," which stands for "Hometown Honey," or a significant other from home.

Sophomores Joel Hruska and Anna Haisley remember hearing the word "money" used in a different way when they came to DePauw. The phrase "he's money" means "he's really cool." Another term for a person with an awesome personality is "madfly," as in "She's a madfly." This term hails from Boston.

Andy Carroll, a sophomore, was very enthusiastic about some of his favorite slang terms. One of them is "skief," as in, "he skiefed [stole] my CD." The other one is "called out." Carroll explained that "called out" comes into play in a three-person conversation. When a person accuses one of the others of doing something that they would rather not admit to, the third person would then say, "You were called out!"

Junior Matt Clifford had never heard the word "erickader" before meeting classmate Nick Parcell. Apparently it is a term Parcell used to mean "duh"

when he was in middle school.

Last, but not least, my favorite new slang of them all: "ish." Sophomore Chuck Queen learned this melodious expression from his RA freshman year, junior David Johnson. "Ish" is a word which means personal space. Some examples: "Why are you in my ish?" and "Get out of my ish!"

If you ask me, the term is so . . . random. ■

CAMEL CONNECTION BRINGS TOGETHER CONNECTICUT COLLEGE COMMUNITY

By Jennifer DeLeon & Nicole Mancevice

THE COLLEGE VOICE (New London, Conn.) 12/11/1998

Two hundred Connecticut College faculty, staff, and students ate ice cream sundaes and rode on horse-drawn hayrides together last Sunday afternoon. The third annual Camel Connection, an afternoon of fun and festivity, took place in the 1941 Room and Alice Johnson Room in the Crozier-Williams Student Center.

The event began three years ago when students and faculty felt that they would benefit from coming together in a non-academic environment. The event was sponsored by the Board of House Governors and the Office of the President in hopes of increasing informal relationships within the community.

Some of the highlights of the Camel Connection included a jazz band, performances from student a cappella groups, hayrides with a sing-a-long banjo player, and raffles of donated prizes. Businesses have been generous with their donations to the event and, in turn, students support those establishments.

The 1941 room bustled with people enjoying a Make-Your-Own Sundae Bar and musical entertain-

ment. In the Alice Johnson room, Governors and House Fellows joined children to make crafts from beaded necklaces to glittery holiday decorations. At small tables, children and volunteers played with Play-doh and sung along to holiday favorites and classic oldies.

The event was successful in bridging the gap between faculty and students. According to Jenny Marchick '99, "It's nice to see faculty and staff coming together with their children and interacting with students."

The event was successful due to the careful planning of the Board of Governors, he Housefellows, the Chair of Residential Life Sara Burns, Bridget Bernard from the President's Office, Assistant Director of Residential Life Conway Campbell and Assistant Dean of Student Life Kristine Cyr Goodwin.

Conway Campbell agrees, "This is an event that needs the entire campus community's help to be successful . . . it's amazing that offices and students can work together to pull off such a fun event." ■

DePAUW LITTLE 5 COMMITTEE LINING UP EVENTS

By Jen Nielsen

THE DEPAUW (Greencastle, Ind) 03/16/1999

With about a month to go, plans are underway for the biggest race of the year.

Senior Kim Paradise, co-chair for the Little 5 Steering Committee, has been planning for the big race. "[Planning] is going really well. We're totally on schedule," Paradise said. "We've had meetings with all the riders and handed out all the rules."

Senior Debbie Perez, chairman of special events, is in charge of activities during special events week. Events will be numerous and will take place every night during the week. "We're going to have a lot of the same events as last year with a few less things since there were so many things last year," Perez said.

Some of the special events planned include mud volleyball and tug of war, tomato dodge ball, turkey bowling, a Jell-O toss, a Subway eating contest, a four-square tournament and Mini 500.

"Mini 500 is a relay race where each team is on trikes," Perez said. "They have to go to different stations, which are usually pretty messy." Past stations have included eggs, chocolate and other messy foods.

A blood drive will also take place during special events week, sponsored by both the Little 5 committee and the Student Union Board.

The activities for the opening ceremony haven't been planned yet. "We're still trying to figure out what to do with the opening ceremonies to get lots of people to come out and participate," Perez said. In past years, Union Board has sponsored a band or other event the Friday before race day. Again this year, they are looking at providing some entertainment on Friday night, but so far no plans have been set in stone.

As far as the race goes, Little 5 riders are currently training for the big day.

"Things are moving along," said junior Jake Sommer, race chair for the Little 5 Steering Committee. "The track opened up to rookies [Monday], and it will open up to everyone after spring break."

The eight sororities with houses on campus are each boasting a team this year, which will increase competition.

"The women's race is shaping up to be very competitive," Sommer said.

According to Paradise, all houses will be allowed to participate this year. Last year, Kappa Kappa Gamma was not allowed to have a team due to social probation. But this year, Kappa is sponsoring a team, and Paradise believes this will only increase the women's competition.

The men's competition may not be as fierce as in previous years. A few teams are competing for the first time. The women will ride first in Little 5, which starts at noon. The men's race will begin one hour after the completion of the women's race. ■

Alabama
Concordia College
Samford University
Spring Hill College
University of Mobile

Arkansas
Central Baptist College
Harding University

California
Azusa Pacific University
Bethany College of the Assemblies of God
Biola University
California Lutheran University
Chapman University
College of Notre Dame
Fresno Pacific University
Holy Names College
Hope International University
La Sierra University
LIFE Bible College
Loma Linda University
Loyola Marymount University
Mount St. Mary's College
Patten College
Point Loma Nazarene College
Saint Mary's College of California
San Jose Christian College
Santa Clara University
University of San Diego
University of San Francisco

Colorado
Colorado Christian University
Nazarene Bible College
Regis University

Connecticut
Fairfield University
Sacred Heart University
Saint Joseph College

District of Columbia
American University
The Catholic University of America
Trinity College

Florida
Barry University
Florida Baptist Theological College
St. Thomas University
Southeastern College of the Assemblies of God
Trinity Baptist College
Trinity College of Florida

Georgia
Atlanta Christian College
Beulah Heights Bible College
Clark Atlanta University
Georgia Baptist College of Nursing
Luther Rice Bible College and Seminary
Mercer University
Reinhardt College

Hawaii
Chaminade University of Honolulu

Illinois
Benedictine University
Concordia University
DePaul University

Dominican University
Lewis University
Lincoln Christian College
Loyola University Chicago
Moody Bible Institute
North Central College
Olivet Nazarene University
Saint Xavier University
University of St. Francis

Indiana
Indiana Wesleyan University
University of Evansville
University of Indianapolis
University of Saint Francis
Valparaiso University

Iowa
Emmaus Bible College
Faith Baptist Bible College and Theological Seminary
St. Ambrose University
University of Dubuque

IN THIS CHAPTER

Baylor University
Boston College
Brigham Young University
Creighton University
DePaul University
Loyola University
Luther College
Marquette University
Notre Dame University
St. Bonaventure University
St. Michael's University
Texas Christian University
University of Dayton
Villanova University
Yeshiva University

Kansas
Baker University
Manhattan Christian College
MidAmerica Nazarene University

Kentucky
Bellarmine College
Cumberland College
Kentucky Christian College
Spalding University
Union College

Louisiana
Centenary College of Louisiana
Loyola University New Orleans
Xavier University of Louisiana

Maine
Saint Joseph's College

Maryland
College of Notre Dame of Maryland
Griggs University
Hood College
Loyola College in Maryland

Mount Saint Mary's College and Seminary
Washington Bible College

Massachusetts
Anna Maria College
Assumption College
Eastern Nazarene College
Emmanuel College

Michigan
Andrews University
Aquinas College
Calvin College
Cornerstone College
Madonna University
Marygrove College
Reformed Bible College
Rochester College
Sacred Heart Major Seminary
University of Detroit Mercy
William Tyndale College

Minnesota
College of St. Catherine
College of St. Scholastica
Martin Luther College
North Central University
Saint Mary's University of Minnesota
University of St. Thomas

Mississippi
Mississippi College

Missouri
Avila College
Berean University of the Assemblies of God
Calvary Bible College and Theological Seminary
Central Bible College
Columbia College
Fontbonne College
Lindenwood University
Ozark Christian College
Park College
Rockhurst University
Saint Louis University
Southwest Baptist University

Nebraska
Clarkson College
Creighton University
Grace University
York College

New Hampshire
Notre Dame College
Rivier College

New Jersey
Beth Medrash Govoha
Georgian Court College
Rabbinical College of America
Saint Peter's College
Seton Hall University
Talmudical Academy of New Jersey

New York
Canisius College
Iona College

Continued on page 305

Religious Schools

O ur definition of religious schools is pretty much what you'd think it would be: These are private colleges with no enrollment limitation that are affiliated with a specific religion. At religious colleges and universities, courses in religion are part of the required curriculum for all students.

Furthermore, we categorized all Catholic colleges and universities as religious institutions because certain mandates from the Catholic Church dictate how many faculty members at these schools must be priests, lay clergy members, and so on. As with highly competitive colleges, religious colleges can be found in rural, suburban, and urban locations, in places as different as Decoran, Iowa (where Luther College students hang their hats), and New York City (home to Yeshiva University). While the student body at religious schools usually hovers around 4,000, you'll find religious school campuses with as few as 200 and as many as 25,000 undergraduate students. Many, but not all, religious schools have advanced degree programs.

If you decide to attend a religious college or university, just what should you expect as you begin your studies? Obviously, expect religion to be a topic everyone's talking about. Practically every aspect of college life will be viewed through the lens of religion. Not only will you be required to fulfill religious requirements, but religion will enter into extracurricular and social arenas as well. Expect small classes with incredibly low student-teacher ratios; the average is about 15:1. It will be a fluke if any of your classes exceed fifty students. Expect to be the lucky beneficiary of religious schools' focus on teaching and out-of-classroom attention. While faculty members at many religious schools conduct brilliant research in diverse areas, the overwhelming emphasis at religious colleges and universities is on teaching and learning. Expect to live in single-sex housing, at least for the first year; not many religious colleges have made coed dorms a reality on their campus. And expect a fairly homogeneous student body—religious schools aren't exactly known for their diversity.

What are the two factors that set religious colleges apart from the rest? You guessed the first one—religion. We've already mentioned that you'll be required to take courses in religion; the number will vary from school to school. You may need to master another language in order to better pursue religious studies—Hebrew, for example. You may probably be expected to attend church or synagogue services weekly (in some cases, more than that). School policies—ranging from rules concerning alcohol to the types of exhibits you'll find in the campus art museum—will have their basis in religion. There will likely be an emphasis on service, and you'll find many students committed to charitable causes. Your professors, for the most part, will be vocal proponents of the school's religious philosophies. But most importantly, you will be free to practice your religion in an environment that promotes it. Many students attend religious schools for just this reason.

The second factor that distinguishes religious colleges is their focus on teaching. Colleges and universities of all faiths take great pride in the fact that they emphasize teaching and learning over research. Professors at religious schools lavish students with attention both in and out of the classroom. Hands-on, interactive learning in the liberal arts tradition is strongly emphasized.

You can only imagine the myths that have cropped up surrounding life at a religious college. Let's deal with three biggies:

- Religious requirements will consume your time academically—you won't have much choice in choosing classes
- Religious requirements will consume your time extracurricularly—you won't be able to pursue other interests, and outside activities will be extremely limited in scope
- If you're a member of a minority population, there is no place for you at a religious school

First, although you *will* need to complete coursework in religion, these requirements will be just a small part of your overall academic experience. Religious schools offer the same courses, majors, and minors that other colleges do—the religious classes you take are the icing on the cake. You'll find a great variety of subject matter to explore; courses will be far from limited to religious topics. If you

want to major in it, chances are you'll find it at a religious school.

You should also plan to enjoy an active social life if you attend a religious school, and it won't revolve solely around religion. On the campuses of religious schools, students participate in sports, fraternities and sororities, and every club and organization imaginable. Granted, you may need to attend a weekly devotional service, but other than that, you time will be your own.

Finally, we've already made the point that religious schools are, for the most part, homogeneous. (We'll

Alisha Bellene/*The Bison*

get into the stats later.) But that doesn't mean that those from other backgrounds aren't welcome to apply and enroll at religious schools. Most religious schools go out of their way to accommodate a diverse mix of students. What you may confront, however, are your fellow students' stereotypes. This is where minority students find the most resistance to their presence on campus. Look at it this way—this could be your chance to educate them and make the world a better place.

It's hard to describe what a typical day might be like if you attend a reli-

gious school. Because it will vary based on the amount of religious influence you'll find, you may or may not be rising for morning devotionals in the chapel. You could head off first thing for a required course in Hebrew or the history of Christianity. On your way, students could be chatting about how the students in Israel are faring, about the subject of this week's Campus Ministry lecture, or about the school missionaries entering their second year in South America. At lunch everyone's buzzing about the next great campus service project—this semester you'll be raising money for a local AIDS hospice. Back to the dorm for *Oprah* (required viewing for every college student), then off to afternoon classes. Before dinner, you spend an hour with your adviser reviewing the courses you plan to take next year. Dinner in the cafeteria, hit the books at the library, a quick stop at intramural basketball practice, then you're back to the dorms for a good night's sleep.

As you finish your freshman year and move into further studies, you may decide to get more or less involved with the religious life on your campus. That will be your choice. Once you've completed your religious requirements, how you divide your time between secular and religious pursuits will be up to you. You'll try out all those clubs that caught your eye when you first enrolled, and who knows? Maybe you'll even live in a coed dorm by senior year. ■

Academics

If you attend a religious college, two factors will be sure to impress you when it comes to the academic program: small class size and an emphasis on teaching. For example, Marquette University in Wisconsin boasts a student-faculty ratio of 15:1. Even one of the larger religious schools, Boston College (with an undergraduate student body numbering 8,900), has a student-faculty ratio of 13:1. The numbers for Creighton University in Nebraska are equally astounding: Only 4 percent of their classes have more than fifty students. Those who attend religious schools look at small class size as giving them a great advantage over students who attend larger schools with much larger class sizes. In fact, when class sizes begin to grow at a religious schools, students are sure to notice. "Proposed curriculum changes aim to keep class size small at Luther College" points out the problems created by enrollment growth and faculty departures. Judging from these two articles, however, it appears that the administrators at religious schools recognize the importance of small class size and work hard to avoid the large, lecture-type classes that are a given at big schools.

Hand-in-hand with small class size is the emphasis on teaching rather than research that you'll see at religious colleges. Students at religious schools expect and get lots of individualized attention both in the classroom and out of the classroom. For this reason, many students look at faculty time spent on research in a negative light. But while most religious colleges and universities feel that their priority is education over research, there's no doubt that faculty members at religious universities perform valuable research in many fields. In fact, *U.S. News and World Report* recently named Yeshiva University one of the nation's top fifty research institutions.

Of course, you'll find the same great academic offerings at religious schools that you will on secular campuses. Imagine managing $1 million in a finance class and being able to put it on your resume—if you attend the University of Dayton, you can. In Brigham Young's Capstone Program, an engineering and design course for seniors, students help corporate sponsors solve real world problems and may even see their products reach the marketplace.

Keep in mind that you'll probably need to fulfill certain religious requirements as part of your academic studies. Luther College requires that students complete three 3- to 4-hour courses in religion/philosophy; one course must be in Bible studies, and one must be in religion. Yeshiva University students must complete a Jewish studies component that includes courses in Hebrew language, literature, and culture. Texas Christian University requires its students to take one religion studies course to fulfill its Cultural Heritage requirement, although we should note that in addition to courses in Christiany, TCU offers religion studies classes in Hindu and East Asian religious perspectives, Buddhism, Islam, and mysticism.

Admissions

At any institution of higher education—big, small, private, or otherwise—keeping admissions numbers steady or, better yet, growing over the years is of great importance. More new admissions equal more tuition dollars for the school, which in turn means more professors, more classes, and better facilities for students.

Religious schools are keeping pace with other colleges and universities in their quest to enroll more students. Because these schools are smaller, their name recognition may not be high, so some have used innovative techniques to get the word out. Marquette University in Milwaukee, for example, spread the word about their excellent school through television, radio, and print ads. The ads got potential freshmen interested, and now the school is faced with the welcome dilemma of having to cap its admissions for 1999.

ADS, VALUE ATTRACT LARGE FRESHMAN CLASS TO MARQUETTE U.

By Ann Hanson

THE MARQUETTE TRIBUNE (Milwaukee, Wis.) 09/01/1998

Marquette is making history with this year's freshman class enrollment, a nine-year high of 1,735 students and the university's largest two-year increase. Students of the class of 2002 represent 48 states and about 20 countries.

Dean of Admissions Ray Brown attributes this rise to a variety of factors.

"We are an institution that has not gotten a lot of negative press," Brown said. "We have a good spokesman in university president Father Wild, who is leading us down the path of a positive university image."

Brown said being able to keep a tuition increase at 3 percent for the past two years has also contributed to more inquiries and ultimately more freshmen.

An extensive advertising campaign launched two years ago, originally as an experiment, has been another important factor in the increasing enrollment. Marquette advertised on the radio, in print and on television in the Milwaukee area. Radio and print advertisements also ran in the Fox Valley of Wisconsin.

According to Brown, the print and television ads were "very effective," but the radio ads were a "flop." Television and print ads are now the only means through which Marquette advertises.

As a result of those ads, Brown said the greatest increase is in students from Wisconsin.

Brown also said summer visits to the university by prospective students have increased dramatically.

"Summer visits hit the ceiling," Brown said.

In August 1997, 382 prospective students visited Marquette. This July, 490 prospective students came to the university and over 400 came in August.

"We are going to continue working on new things and continue experiments," Brown said. "We want to increase inquiries to increase applications."

For the future, Brown says if enrollment continues to increase as it has, the freshman class for 1999 may be capped.

"We are considering capping freshman enrollment at 1,800," Brown said. "There is nothing to suggest that we won't have it."

Brown said there were no plans to change admission standards to increase selectivity.

"I think that might happen by default. When (you cap enrollment), you automatically become more selective."

Ultimately, Brown said the Office of Admissions cannot take full credit for the increased amount of freshmen.

"It is truly a campus-wide mobilization of resources," he said. "It is the interaction the (prospective students) have with students and faculty that will sway them towards (attending) Marquette." ∎

While Marquette is looking at the largest freshmen class in years, Stern College of Yeshiva University is facing just the opposite problem. Their on-campus freshman year enrollment numbers are down, as many incoming students have chosen to spend their first year abroad in Israel. Not everyone at the college sees this as a disadvantage, as *The Observer* points out.

MOST FIRST-YEAR STUDENTS SATISFIED WITH YESHIVA U. DESPITE LOW ENROLLMENT

By Sara Kostant

THE OBSERVER (New York) 03/15/1999

Maybe you have met her in one of your classes, or bumped into her in the cafeteria. She is the rare Stern College freshman, or rather, freshwoman. The 155 freshman are the smallest class in Stern College for Women, because many students who would have been in this class boarded planes to Israel in August. At most universities, the freshman class consists of approximately a quarter of the student body, but at Stern College the freshman proportion is much less. The class population swells when students on the Joint Israel program return to SCW from their Israeli seminaries, but how does the freshman class fare until then?

Most freshman do not consider their small size a disadvantage. Rashka Balarsky, SCW '02, and Susanne Goldstone, SCW '02, said that they both knew before they came to SCW that their incoming class would be small. This fact did not deter them from enrollment. They still don't mind. Balarsky, who is president of the freshman class, says that she thinks that there is "a lot of spirit" in her year because it is smaller. "Even though we all have different cliques, we get along" she said. "Many freshmen hang out with other freshmen." Balarsky emphasized that her goal as the freshman class president is to "get as many freshmen as I can to meet each other." Goldstone, who is majoring in Political Science, noted that the low number of incoming students made it easier for her to obtain a position as Vice-president on the freshman class student council. "I knew it wouldn't be as difficult to get a position," she said, "because I have to talk to less people" during elections.

The Jewish atmosphere is a major factor in the choice to enter SCW as a freshman. "I live in Texas, and I really wanted a Jewish environment," said Rashka Balarsky. "I wanted Jewish friends." Goldstone said that knowing people who were already in SCW and the school's Manhattan location played a part in her

decision. The Jewish setting, however, was the primary reason she enrolled at SCW. She said that while other colleges organize Jewish programming, SCW possesses a "pretty highly rated" Judaic studies program. This program includes the beginner's level Hebrew classes that are essential to her since she did not come to SCW with a strong religious background. Chana Batko-Taylor, SCW '02 and a Philosophy major, said that she chose SCW for its "Jewish environment and Jewish curriculum. That's what makes Stern stand out."

All of the freshmen interviewed for this article pointed out that most of their friends are scattered throughout the sophomore, junior, and senior classes at SCW, because their courses included students from all four years. Although most freshmen seemed satisfied with their experience in SCW thus far, one student pointed out that the freshmen receive the lowest priority when it comes to registration. "You see freshmen in the office crying and complaining," she said. "I only got into the classes that no one else wants."

The freshman class will gain a lot from their decision to spend four years at Stern College, said Rachel Katz, SCW '00. She came to Stern from Hamilton, Ontario, and didn't know a single person. Katz attended a public high school, and wanted to attend college in a Jewish atmosphere to make up for the Jewish education she had missed out on. She describes herself when she arrived at SCW as a shy, "small town girl in the big city" who was terrified of Manhattan. Katz is now a resident advisor in the Schottenstein Residence Hall, and is majoring in education. "I think I'd be stunting my growth if I were here for only two years," she said. "I've grown so much in this time. So many internal changes happen in your college years, and if you skip them, they [the changes] won't happen." ■

Class Size

You can tell from the last article from Yeshiva University's *Observer* that many students who attend religious schools do so for the closeness that a small student body encourages. As a whole, student populations at religious schools are small, numbering anywhere between 2000 and 5000 (although there are big religious schools like Brigham Young that enroll over 28,000 full-time undergraduate students). Because the student population isn't as big, young men and women who attend religious schools generally enjoy smaller class sizes and more one-on-one attention.

In their desire to bulk enrollments, however, some religious schools have found themselves with more students than they had anticipated and are now working on ways to ensure that incoming students get the attention they expected when they enrolled at the school. Luther College in Iowa has recently reexamined the way its required *Paideia* curriculum—in which students focus on interdisciplinary studies through historical and literary texts, lectures, and essays designed to provide a foundation liberal arts education—is taught. As you'll read, of prime importance to the administrators at Luther was avoiding large lecture hall–type classes for which large state schools are known.

PROPOSED CURRICULUM CHANGES AIM TO KEEP CLASS SIZE SMALL AT LUTHER COLLEGE

By Matt Becker

CHIPS (Decoran, Iowa) 05/01/1998

Members of the Curriculum Review Task Force recently unveiled an outline of proposed curriculum changes that could drastically redefine scholastic requirements such as Paideia, physical education, religion and foreign language proficiency.

One of the most significant and controversial proposed changes concerns the first-year Paideia course. Under the working model, faculty from all disciplines, not just English and history, would be eligible to teach Paideia courses. There would be significantly fewer large lectures, perhaps only one lecture for each text. Instead, classes would meet regularly in discussion groups.

"Students get discouraged that they come to a small liberal arts school and end up doing maybe 50 percent of their first-year learning in a large lecture setting," said John Moeller, chairperson of the task force. "Why pay $20,000 a year to come to a smaller college and learn in that large lecture setting?"

According to David Faldet, professor of English, also a member of the task force, some faculty see advantages in keeping the lectures. They feel the lectures allow for a more interdisciplinary approach to

the course and give students more varied exposure to faculty, said Faldet. Also, lectures appeal to students with auditory learning orientation.

During the fall semester in Paideia, all students would study between five and seven common texts, but during the spring semester different interdisciplinary courses would be offered. Teams of two or three professors from different departments would create courses on a variety of topics. The model explains that a chemist and a biologist might offer a class that examines biochemical ideas.

This proposed change has also generated concern among faculty, said Faldet. Some worry that students could graduate without learning about historical perspective. Others have different objections.

"I feel Paideia accomplishes quite a bit. It ensures students are exposed to Western civilization, global studies and American diversity," said Faldet. "On the English side it is a coordinated writing program. There is a benefit to having a common intellectual experience that goes throughout the first year. Those strengths are worth keeping."

The writing component of Paideia would not significantly change. Students would write thesis-driven essays in the fall and research papers in the spring.

Both Moeller and Faldet feel that professors in fields besides English and history can effectively teach students to write.

"It's not what department teaches writing," said Faldet, "but whether or not people are committed to teaching writing. I think a biologist can teach writing." ■

Teaching & Research

Along with small class size, religious schools place great value on the amount of individualized attention their professors can give to students. Traditionally, importance is placed on teaching over research at religious colleges and universities. Students who choose to attend religious schools consider this facet of the overall learning environment to be highly beneficial to their education. In fact, small class size and a focus on teaching are two reasons why students pay higher tuition rates to attend private religious schools rather than larger, less expensive, state schools. For the most part, students at religious schools like Brigham Young University, as our next article from *The Daily Universe* points out, benefit from outstanding professors who practice interactive methods of teaching.

BUSINESS PROFESSORS ENLIVEN THE CLASSROOM AT BYU
By Misti Pincock

THE DAILY UNIVERSE (Provo, Utah) 09/05/1997

Teaching at a university used to mean standing at the front of a large lecture hall, with hundreds of eyes gazing down at the all-knowing professor, who used a very non-interactive style of teaching.

The professors of the Marriott School of Management, however, are working on getting rid of one-way communication in the classroom. They are trying out new and creative ways to teach the same concepts of business and accounting.

For Bob Daines, professor of business policy and finance, and Burke Jackson, professor of business policy and operations, written final exams are a thing of the past. The objectives of their finals are, among other things, to allow the students to review the concepts of the course and to present those concepts in a creative manner. One group of MBA students, for example, created a magazine for their final exam, while other students have written poems, produced videos and written games.

Mark Hansen, an assistant professor of organizational leadership and strategy, brings out the creativity of his students throughout the semester. After assign-

ing his class to read two case studies of how two CEOs managed a similar situation, three students draw their interpretations of the different approaches on the chalkboard. Hansen said this exercise is one of the most thought-provoking he has used in his teaching.

"We often see things that we would not have thought of otherwise," Hansen said. "It unleashes creativity in some fun ways." Hansen said the concepts taught in this exercise are not easily forgotten.

James Stice of the Accounting Department says his students retain course concepts better when they are placed in the "hot seat." At the beginning of each class, the names of six students are written on the board. Each time a question is asked in class, those students take the role of teacher and must answer the question.

Stice acts as a ricochet and said he is there to rescue the six students when they need help. He feels students and teachers should understand each other in order for this to work. "Before you can do anything with your students, they have to be able to trust you," Stice said. "Students think it's us against them. You have to let them know that there isn't that kind of division." Other teachers take advantage of everyday life to teach the students.

Hal Gregersen, an associate professor of organizational leadership and strategy, has his students work in local soup kitchens. The students write about their experience and how it has taught them the concept of individual identity.

Stice said the reason is that students are willing to allow their teachers to change their curriculum. "The secret to good teaching is to create an environment of trust and learning," he said. "Be excited about your subject and the students will let you do whatever you want with them." ∎

Professors at religious schools don't live in a professional vacuum, however, and pressure to perform research and to publish articles on their findings affects them, too. This is not always met favorably by the student body. Students who attend religious schools enjoy the fact that their professors know them by name. If faculty members are given the edict to "publish or perish," many students, like the editors of Baylor University's *Lariat*, fear that the extra time many professors have traditionally taken for personal attention outside the classroom will be lost in the shuffle.

EDITORIAL: FACULTY SHOULDN'T BE FORCED INTO PUBLISHING, RESEARCH

Staff Editorial

THE LARIAT (Waco, Texas) 10/30/1997

In September, a letter was sent to members of the Baylor faculty entitled "Statement on scholarly activity at Baylor University." The letter was approved by the Council of the Deans, Dr. Donald Schmeltekopf and President Robert B. Sloan Jr. Expectations for an increase in publishing and research by Baylor faculty members were spelled out in the letter.

In the past, Baylor has encouraged research and publishing by faculty members, but never expected it. This letter might change this attitude.

Baylor has a reputation of professors who know and care about their students. With less emphasis placed on publishing, professors had more time to spend with their students. Instead of having graduate students teach their classes, Baylor faculty members were able to put more effort into teaching without the added pressure of publishing or perishing.

Research and publishing by faculty members can be very positive for a university's reputation. Many professors have published work and improved Baylor's image. However, if too much importance is placed on researching and publishing, the students are going to suffer. Most students at Baylor chose this university because of the reputed faculty attention given to students. Most faculty members currently know their

students by name and provide them with necessary assistance to improve their educational experiences.

If faculty members are going to be pressured into doing additional research and publishing, they won't have time to write letters of recommendation, answer questions and help students outside of class.

Students keep Baylor University in business. We deserve professors who will devote their time and energy to teaching, not publishing. Taking time away from students will lower the quality of education students receive from Baylor University. This will then lower the value of a degree from Baylor University.

If Baylor students wanted to be taught by graduate students on a regular basis, they would have attended a state university. Small class size and strong teacher-student educational relationships are important factors that make Baylor appealing to students.

Research and quality teaching can go hand in hand. Research by faculty can bring new ideas into the classroom which, in effect, benefit students. However, at state universities, most faculty members are only responsible for teaching six to nine credit hours. At Baylor, expected classroom time is generally 12 credit hours. Because Baylor professors generally teach more classes, this leaves less time for research.

Once research is expected from them, they will have to balance classroom time, research and hours spent helping students outside of class. Which area do you think will be first to suffer? Faculty must teach class and they will be expected to publish. That doesn't leave much time for helping students in their free time. There won't be any free time.

Baylor needs to weigh the importance of education of students against publishing by faculty members. If a balance between the two can be managed without giving Baylor a state school atmosphere, then Baylor should pursue scholarly activity on the part of the faculty. If students begin to suffer because of the added responsibilities, then Baylor should realize that the purpose of the university is to educate tuition-paying students, not faculty members. ■

Funding

Other than funds gathered from tuition, how do religious colleges raise the money to finance their superior faculties and facilities? One way these schools stay in operation is with funding from the churches and synagogues with which they're affiliated. This money comes from the religious community in the form of tithes, donations, and other contributions.

Although a significant amount of the money generated for religious schools comes from religious sources, these schools are still like other colleges and universities in that they depend on endowments and corporate dollars to keep their doors open. In 1998, Luther College sought to increase its endowment to $100 million by calling on alumni and others to beef up the number of scholarships, professorships, and lectureships their school could offer; renovate campus buildings; and update campus technology.

US WEST BENEFACTOR IN LUTHER COLLEGE NETWORKING PROJECT

By Sean M. Helle

CHIPS (Decoran, Iowa) 10/15/1998

After months of ambiguous announcements by Luther College officials, a Luther administrator confirmed this week that US West, one of the nation's largest telecommunications companies, is responsible for the college receipt of what President Jeffrey Baker described as "the largest single telecommunications donation in Iowa's history."

David Roslien, vice president for college advancement, confirmed that US West is the donor of more than $4 million worth of networking equipment.

President Baker, in a July letter to all returning students, acknowledged Luther had received the monumental grant, but preserved the anonymity of the benefactor. The nature of the gift was also withheld, though Baker acknowledged what the donation would provide for the college.

"The grant will allow us to extend Ethernet connectivity to as many as 2000 student residence hall rooms and faculty locations throughout the Luther campus," the letter explained.

David Ranum, executive director of library and information services, explained the donor was reluctant to announce the gift at this time. Though he said he was not certain, Ranum predicted an official release during Luther's homecoming celebration.

Roslien was not positive when US West would publicly acknowledge the donation, although he believed the announcement would come out of the corporation's Denver headquarters.

"This gift is highly secretive," said Roslien, "they want to announce it themselves."

The technology to be used in the installation is revolutionary, according to Luther administration.

"This advanced equipment will permit students, faculty and staff to carry on a phone conversation while simultaneously accessing school computers or the Internet at high speeds," Baker's July letter explained.

College officials were unwilling to elaborate on the specifics of the network. Ranum said only that the technology was unlike anything else currently in use. He emphasized the dorm rooms themselves will not be wired for direct Ethernet connections, although Ethernet connectivity is being brought to each residence hall.

A Luther student affiliated with the project stated that the network connections will likely be achieved over already existing phone lines. Though such connections operate at speeds slower than direct Ethernet connec-

tions, the achieved communication rates are many times that of current modem technology.

The student reinforced Baker's claim that traditional phone use would be preserved, even while using the same phone line to communicate with the network.

Roslien said he believed that the installation would include a connection port for each bed in the dorm rooms, but he was not certain.

With US West's donation, Luther will be able to offer students capabilities available at other Iowa schools. Iowa State University first wired their dorms for Ethernet in 1986. The University of Iowa offers one dorm with network capabilities, while the University of Northern Iowa established an extensive dorm network this fall. ∎

Academic Resources

With the money that they raise from the many sources described in the last section, religious schools are able to provide their students with high-tech computing and other resources. At Villanova University, technological advances have taken the hassle out of a dreaded college task—registering for classes.

VILLANOVA UNDERCLASSMEN TO REGISTER ONLINE
By Gary Grochmal

THE VILLANOVAN (Villanova, Penn.) 10/02/1998

Registering for classes has typically meant missing class to stand in a long line outside the registrar's office, then finally reaching the front of the line and discovering that most classes are already filled.

Registrar Catherine Connor hopes to make students' frustration over registration a thing of the past. After a series of pilot programs open to engineering, nursing and commerce and finance students, all students will be able to register via the Internet for this year's spring semester, with web registration mandatory for half the school.

"What we've decided to do is [give] juniors and seniors the option for traditional registration or registration over the web. Freshmen and sophomores are going to register exclusively over the web," said Connor.

Connor outlined the following procedure for online registration, which begins for seniors on Nov. 2: students will first take their schedules to their advisors, as in the past, but once advisors have approved the schedules they will give students their web registering passwords.

"We are thrilled and anxious to offer something new to the students and hope everything goes as smooth as possible," Connor said.

One issue surrounding University-wide online registration is the availability of computers for students to use at the designated times. Connor said her office and University Information Technologies (UNIT) are trying to work out all of the logistics before spring registration begins. "I think that there will be plenty of computers," said Connor.

Students experiencing problems while registering online will be able to seek help at the registrar's office, where five computers will be available for registration. The registrar will also set up a telephone help line for students experiencing difficulties.

UNIT has increased the size of the University server so that it can handle more simultaneous hits from students using the site for registration.

Reactions from many students to the new registra-

tion system has been positive. "I did it over the Internet last semester, and there were no lines. It was really easy," said sophomore Ryan Siegfried.

Other students, however, expressed concern that they would feel uncomfortable depending on a computer to register for their classes.

"I don't want to register online. I would rather deal with a person than a computer," said Andrea Agalloco. ■

Enabling students to register for classes online is a great technological feat, and the students at Villanova appear to be benefiting from it. Some religious schools, like the University of Dayton in Ohio, have used another technological advance—Web site blocking—to prohibit students from viewing "inappropriate" sites. Because it's a private school, they can do that, and deciding what's appropriate is solely in the hands of the administration. Keep in mind if you attend a private religious school that your school may use technology in more subtle ways.

U. DAYTON INSTALLS WEB SITE BLOCKING DEVICE ON LAB COMPUTERS

By Dan Ketterick

THE FLYER NEWS (Dayton, Ohio) 09/16/1998

Internet access in many campus computer labs has recently been modified to give more control to administrators and to block certain objectionable web sites.

Labs in Miriam Hall, St. Joseph's Hall and the Humanities Building have been upgraded to use Microsoft's browser, Internet Explorer, a program which contains a content advisor able to block sites that are considered inappropriate.

"We want to have the lab set up so that if any student wants to go in there and do a particular assignment for their class then they are able to do that," said Chris Keck, computer systems coordinator for the College of Arts and Sciences. "We can't come back there and be security guards and say 'hey, you can't do that on the web because that is inappropriate.' That would take too much time to do that."

Keck chose Internet Explorer because it offered more control over how the students use the lab terminals. With the new program it will be harder for mischievous students to modify the settings of the computer.

"A lot of the flack that we got from the faculty was

that they were getting other people's mail when they sat down to their computer and they were coming up to these lovely web sites which were inappropriate," Keck said. "And they [lab users] were changing the overall Internet options."

Jackie Plaska, a Miriam lab monitor, said that the upgraded security offered by Internet Explorer has made her job easier by reducing the amount of supervision she needs to exercise.

"It's awful to have to bust someone for looking at pornography and it's embarrassing to have to call them out, as I'm sure it's embarrassing to be called out, for looking at pornography," she said.

The content advisor, sometimes referred to as a parental control, uses the Recreational Software Advisory Council's (RSAC) rating system which blocks unwanted content in four areas: language, nudity, sex and violence.

Sites rate themselves on a five point scale, from those sites with no violence or sex to those with gratuitous violence, frontal nudity, explicit sexual acts or extreme hate speech.

Keck said the content advisor does not block sites that have not rated themselves, nor does it target specific sites that some, including faculty, might want blocked, such as www.schoolsucks.com.

"The content advisor is a generic program that makes Microsoft look good," Keck said. "With it, you have limited blocking capabilities."

The limited blocking ability of the content advisor raises two points.

"Because UD is a private university, it's not subject to the First Amendment," said Charles Hallinan, UD law professor. "In the same way that it can say 'no distribution of condoms on campus,' it can say 'no distribution of pornography on campus.'"

Since the university is religious, Hallinan suggested that using content advisors could help characterize what the university believes.

"As a private university with a mission that is at least partially religious in orientation, it has, in some sense, not only the ability but even perhaps an obligation to define the culture of the campus in a way that is consistent with its mission," Hallinan said.

However, the limited blocking capabilities of

Internet Explorer's content advisors concerns Hallinan.

"Inevitably, screening software tends to screen out things that aren't offensive," Hallinan said. "And at the same time, it tends to be under-inclusive and over-inclusive—so that you still have access to things that are offensive.

Screening access sometimes winds up being used as if it were the solution to something that really ought to be dealt with more broadly by establishing a culture—by working to establish a university culture, a campus culture in which those things just simply aren't popular."

Monitors in the business computing labs in the Anderson Center also watch where students surf on the Internet.

"If a lab monitor sees objectionable material, students will be asked to stop looking," said Laura McManamon, administrator of business computing facilities. "We're telling people in the classes that they should not be going to those [inappropriate] sites." ■

Academic Opportunities

We've already described how religious schools are not unlike larger state schools and highly competitive schools when it comes to attracting admissions, battling with the problems of large class sizes, balancing teaching and research, raising funds, and providing top-notch resources. It seems, therefore, that no matter what kind of institution of higher learning you attend, the concerns will be strikingly similar.

But what will really be important to you no matter what kind of school you attend will be the quality of its academic offerings. You'll be glad to hear that religious schools provide just as many interesting classes as large state schools and highly competitive colleges. And because the focus at religious schools is on small class size and individualized attention, you'll be able to make the most out of innovative offerings—from managing a cool $1 million at the University of Dayton to working with corporations at Brigham Young.

U. DAYTON STUDENTS TEST FINANCIAL SKILLS

By Karaline Jackson

THE FLYER NEWS (Dayton, Ohio) 11/20/1998

For many UD finance students, the gap between simulated classroom experience and the reality of the volatile world of Wall Street is becoming more and more narrow.

Sam Gould, dean of the school of business, recently

asked UD's board of trustees for $1 million to invest. By a unanimous vote, the board approved the $1 million investment.

In January, upperclass finance students taking "Seminar in Investments" will have the chance to use the finance skills they have obtained in class to manage this large sum of UD's assets. The investment program, entitled Flyer Investments, is part of the new finance curriculum which will be adopted in the upcoming semester, according to the School of Business.

Faculty and students of the school of business are looking forward to the new challenge as a way of experiencing the reality of finance management while continuing to develop valuable and necessary skills in the classroom.

"The new finance curriculum should help the UD finance students to gain a competitive edge in the business market while earning increased respect from the finance industry," Gould said.

According to the School of Business, the students who are working for Flyer Investments will have the same responsibilities as the other investment managers that handle the school's finances, including quarterly reports to the board's investment committee.

The creation of Flyer Investments as a way to help finance students better prepare for their careers is the final part of a redesigned curriculum called the Vertically Integrated Investment Program.

The students working for Flyer Investments will be aided throughout the semester by professionals from the finance industry who will provide advice and feedback for the students. A finance executive will also be available to the students throughout the semester. This individual will serve as a mentor and will help create internship opportunities in addition to developing strong ties with the business community.

The renovation of Miriam Hall will also contribute to the anticipated success of the new finance curriculum. Once completed, Miriam Hall will house a Center for Portfolio Management and Security Analysis. Under the direction of David Sauer, the center will serve as a laboratory for students to develop strategies in security selection as well as become acquainted with sophisticated investment management software. Sauer, who is on sabbatical this semester, was unavailable for comment.

Students who participate in Flyer Investments can include on their resume their contribution to a team that managed $1 million. In the current job market, experience is a necessity and the finance students at UD are diving into the reality of today's financial world head first. ■

SENIORS AT BYU HELP DOLE CO. 'GET THE BUGS OUT'

By Janette Jeffress

THE DAILY UNIVERSE (Provo, Utah) 04/17/1998

Seniors in the Capstone Program never know exactly what they are getting into as they register for this two-semester course. This is because each project in the program depends on what problems corporate sponsors need solved at that time. This year, some of the many projects included developing a lettuce-washing system, creating a knee brace and improving a company's production process.

Dole Fresh Vegetable Company was looking for a system to help get insects out of lettuce, said Lance Larsen, a member of the team Clean Leaf Technologies, who tackled this problem.

Larsen, 25, a senior from Idaho Falls, Idaho majoring in mechanical engineering, said he liked doing a real project and that it was a valuable experience.

"No one was an expert; it was just us putting it together," said Larsen.

The team designed and built a prototype of a machine that would improve the process of cleaning lettuce. The team's machine involved a channel of water to float the lettuce in. As the lettuce was in the water, the insects and dirt would float to the top, and would be separated from the lettuce, Larsen said.

Doug Roberts, 25, a senior from Preston, Idaho majoring in industrial design, agreed it was a valuable class.

"It was a good experience geared toward learning the design process, and it ended up being a lot of fun because it looks like our project will be produced and manufactured," said Roberts.

The project Roberts helped to design was a knee brace that would prevent injuries.

"Since most braces, the better ones, are available only through a doctor, they are usually for after an injury, but this one is designed to be preventative."

The knee brace is made out of carbon fibers and Kevlar, and it wraps around the thigh and calf part way, in an "s" shape. It only has one hinge, which makes it much more lightweight and comfortable and less restrictive. Each brace is meant to be custom-built, because this provides better protection and comfort for the wearer of the brace.

"We built one for John Tait on the football team. We molded his leg, and he'll wear it in practices to try it out for us," said Roberts.

Roberts said the brace will probably be mainly for athletes, football teams in particular.

"We feel that this will open up a new market for a new type of brace," said Roberts.

Another Capstone team worked with a company that produces fruit rolls. This company wanted to change the way they produced the fruit rolls to reduce the amount of waste.

The company currently uses a plastic sheet on top of the fruit to keep it contained, and after the fruit is pressed, the plastic sheet is then thrown away.

"We changed the way they put the fruit on the plastic. We used an extrusion process, where the sheet of fruit was already formed as it was put on the plastic," said Doug Corbett, 25, a senior in manufacturing engineering technologies.

The team built a prototype for each of the two solutions and then tested them at the company's site. The extrusion method tested out better and the company may implement their developed process.

"The way that we narrowed solutions down was new, and was what the Capstone program was trying to teach us. The quality of solutions is better because we can compare all of the crazy ideas we come up with, and then narrow it down to the best one," said Corbett. ∎

In addition to exceptional course offerings, at religious colleges and universities you'll find fabulous faculty members that take great pride in the attention they lavish on their students. They not only teach but also act as mentors and role models for young men and women making their way through their college years. Amazingly, these professors also find time to extend their love of learning outside the classroom into research in their fields. Mark Fernandez at Loyola University is one such outstanding professor.

FERNANDEZ INVOLVED IN HISTORY PROGRESS

By Katie Vieceli

THE MAROON (New Orleans) 01/22/1999

Mark Fernandez, associate history professor, is passionate about the past, but far from living in it. His excitement about the subject is contagious, mostly because of his pleasant personality and his commitment to merging the future and past on the Internet. Although he still believes in the importance of primary sources and class participation, he is very excited about the potential applications of the Internet.

His office reflects this. The shelves are filled with books about American history, some of them inches thick. However, the computer also has a prominent place, right next to his desk. He has created his own home page and also helped compile the preliminary index to the Original Suit Records of the Superior Court of the Territory of Orleans, 1804-1809.

Fernandez called the project "a monumental undertaking." He unfolded the originally bundled documents, filed them in folders, and wrote file names and suit numbers on each folder.

"This index would not be possible without Dr. Fernandez," the web page states.

Now, people wishing to view court archives don't have to search through dusty basement offices, but can simply turn on their computers. This is the sort of thing that makes Fernandez so excited about the Internet.

"The format of the Internet makes the inaccessible accessible," he says.

Along with his work on the Internet, he has

published in various journals, including The Historian and The American Journal of History. His entire education has focused on merging the past and the future. Fernandez completed his doctorate at the prestigious College of William and Mary, where he was involved in the Omohundro Institute of Early American History.

"This was a real community of scholars. There were a lot of people doing cutting-edge things," Fernandez says.

After his move to Loyola in 1992, he taught two workshops for history teachers, in 1993 and 1997. As impressive as his knowledge and work on his subject is, he also has a good relationship with his students. He is usually accessible and his door is literally open.

"I think he really has it together. He knows what his students need and teaches according to that," Scott McLetchie, history instructor, says. Fernandez's students agree.

"He's one of my mentors," Mary Mees, history senior, says. "He knows his students' capabilities and is able to bring that out of them. In turn, he also respects his students."

"The Loyola Historical Journal has taken a real step forward this year," Fernandez says. "I was very proud of how professional it looked. It was a product of student activity."

Fernandez, along with David Moore, history department chairman, advise The Loyola Historical Journal.

"The Journal wouldn't have gotten off the ground if it weren't for Dr. Fernandez. He was involved in every aspect," said David Pipes, history senior and Journal contributor.

Perhaps the best testimony to Fernandez's character is the award he received last year, a commendation from the American Association of State and Local History. This honor is awarded to history instructors who have performed their duties with intelligence, competence and compassion. ■

Another way you can get a taste of the real world while attending a religious school is by interning for a semester or a summer. Students at religious schools find that their education has left them well-prepared for interning at huge organizations such as NBC and ABC. It's interesting to compare this next article from *The Daily Universe* from Brigham Young University with what we saw at highly competitive schools, where students bemoaned their lack of professional training when it came to internships.

BYU INTERNS WORK THEIR WAY INTO THE 'REAL WORLD'

By Pamela Jo Grundvig

THE DAILY UNIVERSE (Provo, Utah) 08/06/1998

From Washington, D.C., to Los Angeles, BYU students have expanded their horizons and are entering what some call the "real world" through prestigious internships all over the United States.

Imagine working first-hand with Peter Jennings on World News Tonight, Primetime Live with Diane Sawyer or Dateline NBC. This is just where a few BYU students have been this summer.

"It was neat to see how the real world is," said Deon Youd, a 23-year-old senior from Spanish Fork majoring in broadcast.

Youd interned at Primetime Live with Diane Sawyer, assisting in researching and consolidating stories.

After her internship Youd was hired as a 10 p.m. news producer of ABC's affiliate station KIFI in Idaho Falls.

Youd said her education at BYU has qualified her for the job experience she has now.

"My education can't show me the real world, but it can prepare me for the real world," she said. "It is neat to know that what I learned at BYU is not just fluff. It taught me what I need to know to be a better journalist and news producer."

Kathryn McKim, a 24-year-old senior from Englewood, Colo., majoring in broadcast, worked as an assistant producer for a few features on NBC's Dateline. She helped produce stories on why people love the dogs they do. She also produced a story on Texas cadet David Graham's murder trial.

McKim said the internship was the best possible learning experience for the career she wants to pursue.

"The whole thing was an amazing experience," McKim said. "Going to New York and working with Emmy award-winning producers and watching them do their work was a great experience for me. Once you work for the number-one market in broadcast you see how it really works."

Ashley Baker, a senior from Orem double majoring in political science and journalism, has been offered a full-time position as an associate for Jack Anderson, a syndicated columnist in Washington, D.C., after doing research and writing columns for him this summer.

"This is a journalist's dream come true," he said. "I show up when I want and do what I want. You don't need someone holding your hand to get real investigative journalism experience."

Baker said Anderson's column is well-respected and well-known around the area. It is sent to syndicates in New York and then circulated to about 250 and 300 papers.

Matt Karpowitz from Lawrence, Kan., majoring in broadcast, interned with World News Tonight on a "Closer Look" segment. He worked with Peter Jennings on the Belmont Stakes horse race in New York and investigated the state of horse racing and gambling in the nation.

Later he talked with Jennings about BYU, President Hinckley, the church and missionary work. ■

Advising

Even though they're smaller and focus largely on teaching and undergraduate education, religious schools still have their fair share of advising problems. As we've seen in other chapters in this book, advising seems to be a common student complaint on college campuses nationwide, especially in light of past years' increasing enrollments and, on many campuses, decreasing numbers of faculty members and class offerings. Changing the advising process is taking top priority at many religious schools. Religious schools realize that their focus on the teacher-student relationship must extend beyond the classroom into a comparable focus in the area of advising. Boston College's *The Heights* reports on their school's giant steps toward decreasing complaints about advising.

TASK FORCE TO RESTRUCTURE ADVISING AT BOSTON COLLEGE

By Ann Chaglassian

THE HEIGHTS (Chestnut Hill, Mass.) 10/06/1998

The recent implementation of an Academic Advising Task Force will permanently change the advising process for all undergraduate students at Boston College.

In a new development this week, the Office of the Academic Vice President agreed to sponsor the creation of the Advising Task Force.

UGBC [Undergraduate Government of Boston College] Chief of University Affairs Jay Turillo, A&S '99, described the creation of the task force as an important accomplishment for UGBC.

"This is the biggest step taken in fixing this problem in the past 11 years," Turillo said.

The preliminary goals of the task force include the creation of an Advising Center, which would focus on pre-major advising.

Students would be advised on the core curriculum before ultimately choosing their major.

The center would also use a combination of peer advisors and professional advisors to help students plan their curriculums.

"The addition of professional advisors will serve as a valuable tool for the students who have not been satisfied with their academic advising," Turillo said.

While the plans of the task force are preliminary in nature, current sophomores and freshmen will most likely benefit from the new advising program proposed by the task force.

Students in the College of Arts and Sciences rely on faculty advisors. The School of Education, School of Nursing, and the Carroll School of Management rely on faculty advisors, along with peer advisors.

Turillo described the ongoing problems with academic advising.

"This task force won't focus on what does not work at BC, but instead will focus on new programs we can create to solve this problem," Turillo said.

Turillo praised the actions of the BC administration in addressing the advising system.

"Dr. Burgess made it clear to me that he felt this problem has gone on too long and would like this task force to come up with a solution before the end of this academic school year," Turillo said.

"This task force is going to solve the biggest problem in academic life at BC," Turillo said. He added, "This is a sign that the administration is willing to do what needs to be done to make Boston College a more prestigious university." ■

On college campuses, advising needn't be solely between student and teacher. The mentoring relationship can take on many faces. At some universities, like St. Michael's in Vermont, upperclassmen act as advisers, mentors, and, most importantly, friends, to incoming freshmen.

NEW FRESHMAN BUDDY PROGRAM LAUNCHED AT ST. MICHAEL'S

By Kim McCray

THE DEFENDER (Colchester, Vt.) 09/23/1998

A new program at St. Michael's has helped bridge the gap between upperclassman and the class of 2002.

The Freshman Buddy Program matched 118 upperclassman with incoming freshmen in an attempt to make their transition to college life easier.

"It's another set of eyes and ears for our first-year students," says Jennie Cernosia, director of student activities. "It's another great way to enhance our community."

Senior Erin Lowery, the program coordinator, supervised the Buddy Program. Its structure was meant to provide freshmen with a multi-structured support system, she says.

Freshman Shannon Sullivan felt the program was beneficial from the moment she arrived on campus.

"I was the only person who came from my school so it was nice to know someone when I came here," Sullivan says. "I was very impressed."

Sullivan knew her big buddy, sophomore Laura Zavigin, before she came to St. Michael's. This was because Lowery organized the program so the big buddies were in contact with the incoming freshman throughout the summer.

The idea for the program came about last spring during family weekend. During the parent/student discussion groups, one mother suggested that her son might have been more successful at school had he had support and motivation from an upperclassman.

With that conversation in mind, Lowery started promoting the Freshman Buddy Program by having interested upperclassman fill out applications. From the applications, Lowery matched each freshman with a big buddy who shared common interests.

Junior Cheryl Messier approved with the matching process. "I liked the way they grouped us with common interests," she says.

The 118 big buddies, 30 seniors, 50 juniors and 30 sophomores, were divided in 11 teams, Lowery says. The 11 team leaders worked with their own separate group of about 11 big buddies. Each big buddy was given four or five freshmen to watch over. They were then asked to correspond with the freshmen before returning to school, Lowery says.

Senior Jamie Hughes says many big buddies want to develop strong relationships with their assigned freshmen.

"Basically, if she has any questions, I'm supposed to be there 24-7," Hughes says of his responsibility to freshman buddy Andrea Haines.

Haines says she felt fortunate to have a buddy like Hughes. "I have someone to talk to," she says.

Aside from the pen pal relationship between the freshmen and the big buddies this past summer, the first official event of the new program, The Freshman Buddy Picnic, was held on Sunday, Sept. 13.

Lowery says that 400 freshmen, about half the class, turned out for the event. She says that the main goal of the picnic was for the freshmen and big buddies to get more acquainted.

Lowery says that the future of the program depended on student reaction.

"Hopefully the little buddies will want to become big buddies," she says.

Freshman Stephanie Crawford says she has every intention on participating in the future.

"I want to do it when I'm an upperclassman," she says. ∎

Academic Dishonesty

Think that, by nature, students who attend religious schools wouldn't be prone to cheat? Well, think again. Academic dishonesty appears to know no boundaries. We've seen it raised as an issue at large state schools and at highly competitive schools, so it shouldn't be surprising that smaller, private—even religious—schools are not immune to problems caused by cheating.

There's no denying that the technological revolution has created exciting opportunities for academic research. But what you may not realize is that with this revolution have come increased avenues for cheating. For example, how much information can you "get" from the Internet before it's considered plagiarism? *The Creightonian* reports on students who buy prewritten term papers and use translator programs on the Internet, two practices that have set off an epidemic of cheating on college campuses.

TECHNOLOGY MAKES CHEATING EASIER

By Heidi Juersivich

THE CREIGHTONIAN (Omaha, Neb.) 11/02/1998

Click. Drag. Paste and print. Living in the computer age, it's never been easier to be a cheater.

Students have been stealing papers for as long as teachers have been assigning them. But the growth of the Internet is making this age-old temptation quicker and more convenient.

With a little know-how and a decent web browser, any computer literate can find an ample selection of web pages targeted to the unscrupulous student.

Pre-written term papers are out there on the Internet, and it doesn't take a genius to find them. Simply typing the words "term paper" and "price" will yield more than 24 million hits using the Infoseek search engine.

For as low as $7 a page, these sites promise selections of several thousands of term papers from any number of academic disciplines. Although they stipulate that the papers are to be used for "research purposes only," what the student does with the paper after he or she pays for it is left to the discretion of the buyer.

A student who spoke on a condition of anonymity said he turned to the Internet last year when he ran out of time to write a paper for his Rhetoric and Composition class.

"It was down to crunch time, and I didn't have time to do anything else," he said.

After pulling an all-nighter to work on papers for other classes, he had only three hours left to prepare his paper for the class. That's when he started looking up term papers on the net.

Alisha Bellene/*The Bison*

He said it wasn't all that difficult to find a paper. He wasn't caught and received a "B" for the course.

"I feel absolutely horrible. I had serious issues with myself for a week and a half after I turned in the paper," he said.

Web-based cheating goes beyond term papers. Students can even use it for translating assignments for their language classes.

An anonymous foreign language student estimated about one-third of her class uses an Internet translator to speed up homework assignments.

"It only takes a half-hour to write a composition instead of the three hours it would take to write it myself," she said.

She said she knows she is cheating, but she's never been caught.

Dr. Enrique Rodrigo, assistant professor of Spanish, said he isn't aware of any instances where students have used a computer program to translate assignments for his classes and that the subject has not come up at departmental meetings.

He said he suspects that because computer programs are not perfect, assignments in which they were used would not be difficult to detect.

The student who uses the translator program said it does make mistakes with tenses and that she has to check the computer's results. Despite the flaws, the program is helping her maintain a 'B' average in the course.

Dr. Graham Ramsden, assistant professor of political science, said he has suspected students of downloading papers from the Internet, but he has never been able to actually catch anyone.

"If I suspect it's from the web, I can usually flunk them for other reasons," Ramsden said.

Ramsden said two signs that a paper came from the web are if it strays too far from the assigned topic and if it is poorly written.

Dr. Bob Whipple, associate professor of English, said he has explored some of the sites that boast cheap term papers.

"Some of the papers were pretty mediocre—if not bad," Whipple said. ∎

Grade Inflation

As on large state and highly competitive college campuses, students at religious schools are seeing their grades rise not just through cheating but through grade inflation. From what you've read so far, this problem is apparently becoming a trend at universities nation-wide—regardless of size, funding, or affiliation. Religious schools also have their fair share of accusations of grade inflation, as the Baylor *Lariat* points out:

GRADE INFLATION SWEEPS COLLEGES NATIONALLY, AT BAYLOR

By Angie Tello

THE LARIAT (Waco, Texas) 03/05/1998

Many major colleges and universities are feeling the effects of the latest academic trend: grade inflation. According to some professors, Baylor has not escaped this trend.

A Feb. 18 front-page article in The New York Times reported that grade inflation is on the rise at such prestigious schools as Princeton, Harvard, Stanford, Columbia, Dartmouth and the University of Pennsylvania.

The article stated that "A's and B's still account for about 80 percent of the grades at Stanford," while at Princeton "83 percent of the grades given between 1992 and 1997 fell between A+ and B-, compared with 69 percent between 1973 and 1977."

Baylor's Office of Institutional Research and Testing said information concerning grades and grade point averages was not available.

Some professors, however, feel that grade inflation is definitely present at the university.

"When you look at the grades and see that two-thirds of them are A's and B's, then I think that really indicates grade inflation," Dr. Howard Rolf, professor of mathematics, said. "I think an A doesn't have the same value as it used to."

Dr. Rena Bonem, professor of geology, said that grades have inflated across the U.S. and Baylor.

"We see this especially now that people are applying for graduate programs here," she said. "It's hard to see if they've really learned and accomplished all that their grades reflect, and vice versa."

Rolf said the trend can be attributed to several different factors. One factor he sees is the changing culture.

"Our society used to be an agricultural one, with people doing work and chores everyday," Rolf said. "There is really not much of a work ethic."

Rolf also said that professors may not be demanding as much from students as they should be.

The value of grades is also debatable, Rolf said.

"A grade is a crude estimate of what a person knows," he said.

Student evaluations of professors can also play a role in grading, some professors said.

"Non-tenured instructors do feel the pressure to try to make students like them better," Bonem said. "However, now I think that the most constructive thing that could be done would be to change the format of the evaluations."

While professors might see this trend at Baylor, some students believe that it is not evident here.

"I have never really noticed it," Kerri Flanagin, an Austin junior, said. "I don't see it as grade inflation—I just think that expectations are raised and people step up to the challenge."

Some professors still believe that some things should be changed at the university to combat this trend.

"I think there needs to be uniformity between departments," Dr. Timothy Johnson, assistant professor of classics, said. "The grades need to be deflated simultaneously."

Rolf said that grade point average is not the only factor important in job and graduate school selections.

"It may suggest the better employee," he said. "However, the GPA doesn't tell the whole story." ∎

BEYOND THE Classroom

Your life beyond the classroom at a religious school need not be conservative. Hundreds of clubs at religious schools provide myriad opportunities for students with all kinds of interests to pursue a subject they love or find out about something new. For example, there's the Eco-Response Club and the Sports and Entertainment Law Society at Brigham Young University; the Chinese Friendship Association and the Martial Arts Institute at Notre Dame; and the TCU Community Action Network and Women in Communications at Texas Christian University. If you think that all religious school students are politically conservative, you might be surprised by what you read in "U. Dayton to host College Democrats regional conference."

"Texas Christian U. Catholic group fosters identity" tells you how groups of all faiths are represented on the campuses of religious schools. Speakers that have appeared at religious schools have included a scholar who challenged Catholic universities' ways of teaching, outspoken rap star Chuck D, and HIV/AIDS activist Greg Louganis. It just goes to show you: There's more at religious schools than you probably think.

What you probably do expect to find on the campuses of religious schools are students interested in helping humankind. On that count, you won't be disappointed. Student groups at religious schools practice acts of kindness and charity as the norm. You'll read here how students at Villanova reached out to help a young boy with a dream. "Creighton U. leadership program honored" describes the rightful accolades this community-minded, caring group has received. From Boston College in Massachusetts to Brigham Young University in Utah, students at religious schools put themselves to work for great causes close to home and in distant lands.

You might be surprised to find out about the importance of sports at some religious schools. Bigger religious schools like Villanova field varsity teams in 10 men's and 11 women's sports. Smaller ones, like St. Bonaventure and Yeshiva University, also field a number of athletic teams, 14 and 10 total, respectively. What's constant are the loyalty and devotion that students feel toward their teams—as you'll see here, only a loyal fan could wax so rhapsodic when talking about the horned frog, Texas Christian University's mascot. What's different about athletics at religious schools is how religious beliefs fit into the picture. At Brigham Young, athletes returning from missionary work must train hard to regain their strength and skills. You'll also read in "Reversal of 'BYU Rule' leaves many disappointed" how Brigham Young may miss championship games because they do not compete on Sundays. You'll see, however, that much is universal when it comes to athletics at any school, religious schools included. All schools must work hard to ensure that women get equal representation in athletics, and, more importantly, all schools have to know how to celebrate when their team wins. Think religious school students have what it takes to commemorate a big win? "Baylor students drag goal post to President's front yard" speaks for itself.

Similarly, the presence of Greeks at religious schools is interesting in both its similarities and its differences with other schools. Some religious schools support many Greek organizations, and fraternities and sororities are a big part of life. Some religious schools have no Greek structure whatsoever. Where there are Greeks, however, both the administration and the students have to tackle the same problems we've seen at other colleges. "Baylor fraternities take closer look into own actions" examines the problems with Greeks and alcohol at one religious school. One school's attempts to solve the problem of waning interest in traditional Greek organizations is described in "Deferred rush's future uncertain for Marquette," and "Rush means stress for would-be sisters at Creighton U." enumerates the differences between rushing a sorority and rushing a fraternity.

Student Groups

It's a mistake to think that, as a religious school student, your life beyond the classroom will be restricted to religious pursuits. Of course these colleges and universities emphasize religion outside the classroom, so if you'd like to join an organization or club with a focus on religion, you'll have more than ample opportunity to do so. But if you attend a religious school, you'll be far from limited when it comes to secular extracurricular activities.

As at other colleges and universities, student government takes on a large role on the campuses of religious schools. Because their schools have traditionally been more conservative than other schools and less willing to change with the times, student leaders with a more liberal agenda must exhibit the strength and ingenuity needed to go up against the "powers that be." Student leaders at Villanova University, who found themselves challenging their school's administration over access to teacher evaluations, took matters into their own hands.

STUDENT GOVERNMENT

VILLANOVA STUDENT GOVERNMENT PROPOSES ALTERNATIVE TEACHER EVALUATIONS

By Kelly Blevins

THE VILLANOVAN (Villanova, Penn.) 11/13/1998

Prompted by the lack of student access to the current Course and Teacher Evaluation Surveys (CATS), the Student Government Association will introduce a new series of professor evaluations designed specifically for students' use beginning Nov. 16.

SGA President Nicole Douglas, Vice President Brian Atkinson and Project Director Ken Racowski developed Student's VOICE (Villanova Offers Inclusive Course Evaluations) after the University Senate limited the availability of the results of CATS by making the posting of the surveys on the Internet optional, said Douglas.

"[The new surveys] were something Brian and I decided was necessary," Douglas said. "We wanted students to have access to them so they could make an informative decision on what professors to take."

Unlike CATS, which are administered in class by the Office of Institutional Planning and Research, VOICE surveys will be distributed by student volunteers before class begins and collected at the next meeting. About 355 midlevel courses, representing the majority of professors, have been targeted to partici-

pate in the first round of surveying, which will take place over the next three weeks.

After the surveys have been distributed, SGA will release the results to students next semester.

"The plan is to compile them and put them into a booklet which will be available when students pick up their registration information next semester," Douglas said.

According to Racowski, SGA began developing a student-oriented survey three years ago, but was invited by the Office of Academic Affairs to work with them on the universal survey they were developing to replace the non-standard departmental evaluations.

The result was CATS, which had as its purposes "faculty development, used as evaluation for promotion, tenure and salary, and used by students during course selection," said Atkinson.

SGA brought a motion before the Senate in October 1997 to make the evaluations available on the Internet. The Faculty Affairs Committee responded with a motion that read, "under no circumstances will the CATS results be made available . . . on electronic media."

The Senate finally agreed to make the posting of the surveys on the Web voluntarily, but, since few teachers actually released their results because of security concerns, SGA felt that students were denied their right to see the evaluations and decided to develop its own survey.

John Johannes, vice president for academic affairs, expressed satisfaction with the new CATS surveys. "I think it's a fitting response to the issues that were raised in the University Senate a year ago and a fitting response to student concerns," he said. "I also think it's a positive reflection on SGA initiative. They've identified a need and have gone through the proper process to take care of it." ■

As you can see from the last article from *The Villanovan*, students at one religious school challenged tradition by creating their own professor evaluations and making them accessible to everyone. Oftentimes, this is just what student groups on the campuses of religious schools do—shake things up, make life different. This needn't always be controversial. Sometimes, challenging tradition just means breathing new life into an established way of getting things done. At Loyola University, the editors of the school yearbook switched from a traditional, once-yearly format to a magazine format to generate renewed interest in their publication.

STUDENT MEDIA

LOYOLA U. MAGAZINE REPLACES ANNUAL WITH NEW FORMAT, MANAGEMENT

By Danny Layne

THE MAROON (New Orleans) 01/22/1999

Loyola's annual yearbook is now a multi-issue magazine. The first issue of The Wolf Magazine turned up on stands around campus early last week.

Three more issues will be released this semester. In May all four will be combined into a hardcover volume complete with headshots. Free copies will be distributed to seniors, but non-seniors must request a copy.

Michael Giusti, communications junior and Wolf editor in chief, said the new direction is a good one.

"We were very excited that we were able to turn the yearbook around because the last few years have been less than a success," he said. The switch from yearbook to magazine took a lot of cooperation from its sister publication, The Maroon.

Members of both publications said it was time for a change.

"Honestly, I'm really glad The Wolf is here. I hope it brings some healthy competition. . . . Friendly rivalry will help both publications become more creative," said Sarah Sparks, communications junior and Maroon editor in chief.

Giusti said he and former co-editor Adéle Furin created it to be an alternative news source for Loyola that will teach students magazine writing, layout and design.

"People will read The Maroon for news and The Wolf for trends," Giusti said.

Liz Scott, Wolf adviser, said she's glad Loyola has a general interest magazine.

"I'm really excited and proud of how it turned out. It showcases good writing, photography and layout," she said.

Students agreed. "I thought it looked nice and professional," said Shaun Garrett, drama/communications sophomore. But some students have concerns.

"I don't feel it represents the student body," said Erin Garland, drama/business sophomore. "I'm curious about what the yearbook fee is going to be . . . I don't think it's worth it." ■

You can see, then, that students at religious schools are not beyond challenging traditional ways of doing things if they think it will benefit their cause. Would you be surprised to find out that religious school students are not necessarily politically conservative? Traditionally, religion and conservatism have been tied together in the minds of many. You may be surprised by this next article from *The Flyer News*.

POLITICAL GROUPS

U. DAYTON TO HOST COLLEGE DEMOCRATS REGIONAL CONFERENCE

By Mary Beth Luna

THE FLYER NEWS (Dayton, Ohio) 02/19/1999

The University of Dayton will be hosting the annual College Democrats regional conference Saturday in Virginia W. Kettering Hall.

Approximately 150 college students from Ohio, Michigan and Indiana will be participating in the one-day conference featuring politicians, authors and trainers from the Democratic National Committee speaking about how to deal with running campaigns and media training.

Some of the schools attending include Ohio University, Indiana University, Michigan State University and Wittenberg University.

"There is one conference a year," said Julia Bordner, junior dietetics major and president of College Democrats. "Last year it was at Michigan State University and the year before it was at Notre Dame so it is a big deal to have it here."

According to Bordner, the conference is a way for College Democrats all over to get together, learn about their responsibility as Democrats and find out about possible internships.

"Everyone should have an idea what is going on," Bordner said. "People vote and sometimes don't realize what they are voting for."

Activities begin on Friday night with a party at the College Democrats' house. On Saturday, speakers will include Harrold Powell, president of the College Democrats of America; Michele Mitchell, author of A New Kind of Party Animal; David Leland, chair of the Ohio Democratic Party and Ted Strickland, U.S. Representative of Ohio's 6th District.

Following the conference will be a party at Flanagan's Pub featuring a political humorist.

"We're looking to bring people to UD, the campus, and show how active UD is in politics and show that young people can make a difference," Bordner said.

Russ Joseph, senior political science and sociology double major and co-chairman of the conference, said they have been working on organizing this event since October and have worked hard to raise $5,000 to fund it.

As a result of all the money raised, the price to attend is only $5.

The event is primarily for College Democrat members; however, all UD students are welcome to attend.

"It should be a good time and we are really excited about it," Joseph said. ∎

We've just seen an example of political diversity at a religious school. At Texas Christian University, a school affiliated with the Disciples of Christ, Catholic students work to promote unity and understanding among the various Christian denominations represented on campus.

RELIGIOUS GROUPS   TEXAS CHRISTIAN U. CATHOLIC GROUP FOSTERS IDENTITY

By Katy Graham

DAILY SKIFF (Fort Worth, Texas) 01/28/1998

Being part of the Catholic Community organization at Texas Christian University means more than attending Mass to a certain fellowship of students. This fellowship aims to promote a sense of community among Catholic students through worship and service to others.

Kathryn Kozlowski, a junior nursing major and publications chairwoman for the group, said the Catholic Community provides a chance for students to share a common identity.

"We all share an identity by being Catholic," she said. "We learn more about our faith and bond with one another because we share that faith."

Led by the Rev. Charlie Calabrese, TCU Catholic Community provides students a chance to deepen their faith through Bible studies, retreats and community service.

"My hope for Catholic students is that they grow into mature adults, understanding what it means to be Catholic," Calabrese said. "One hopeful outcome is that they will make a difference as a Catholic, since they are the future of the Church."

Weekly Mass, which takes place at 7:30 p.m. Sundays in the Student Center, is the most popular Catholic event on campus with about 80 students and faculty in attendance every week.

"I like Mass because it is aimed at students," Kozlowski said. "I can relate well to Father Charlie's homilies."

In addition to Sunday Mass, the group meets on Thursdays at 5 p.m. for a shorter Mass, supper and discussion. This program is a way for students to come together and share thoughts about contemporary and often controversial issues, Kozlowski said.

"We don't always agree on things, but the discussions are important because these divisions exist between Catholics," Kozlowski said.

Modern issues ranging from abortion to euthanasia are also discussed at the Catholic Community's overnight retreats, which take place twice a semester at Camp El Tereso.

"The Catholic Church writes doctrines based on tradition and Scripture, but most students don't just passively accept things," Kozlowski said. "We want to know why things are the way they are."

At discussions and retreats, Calabrese shares with students the standard Catholic teachings on various issues.

"It is important for students to have the chance to get in touch with a living tradition that has been proven over time to help people interpret life in a meaningful way," Calabrese said.

Students in Catholic Community also participate in service activities throughout the semester. On the first Sunday of every month, members of the group go to the Presbyterian Night Shelter and prepare 450 sandwiches for the people who stay there

Amanda Carroll, a junior biology major, student coordinator and service chairwoman, said she is in the process of organizing a service project involving children.

"Everyone who has expressed an interest in service wants to do something with children, like volunteering at a hospital with children or providing tutoring services," Carroll said. "So I'm looking into various options for this semester."

As part of Uniting Campus Ministries, Catholic Community welcomes all student and faculty participation. Its members work with other denominations to encourage the unity of the church while maintaining their unique Catholic identity.

"I think through prayer, service and study, there's the opportunity to grow in the understanding that life is good, and we're invited into that understanding of life and to live that way," Calabrese said. ∎

We've seen that organizations at religious schools work hard to challenge our ideas about what life at a religious school is like, but there's one preconceived notion that you probably have about religious schools that *won't* be dispelled: Students at religious colleges and universities truly are dedicated to helping campus, local, and international communities in many, many ways.

Even through small kindnesses—like building a treehouse for a young boy in Tennessee—religious school students come to the aid of their fellow humans. And Brigham Young University is so dedicated to service that they operate their own Campus Involvement Center.

VOLUNTEERISM

VILLANOVA U. STUDENTS DESIGN DREAM TREE HOUSE FOR YOUNG BOY

By Irene Burgo

THE VILLANOVAN (Villanova, Penn.) 02/19/1999

Villanova University students are always willing to lend a hand. In this case, two senior civil and environmental engineering majors, Rich Tamagno and A.J. Fritsch, who are members of the Villanova student chapter of the American Society of Civil Engineers (ASCE), recently put their engineering skills to work on a unique hands-on project.

The students helped design and build a tree house in response to a request from Matthew Draper, an 11-year-old boy from Cordova, Tenn., who wanted to build a tree fort in his backyard.

Matthew had contacted the University via email requesting help obtaining blueprints for a tree fort.

The initial request came to the attention of Frank Falcone, director of the Institute for Environmental Engineering Research and faculty advisor of ASCE, who directed the student project.

Tamagno and Fritsch both served as officers in the ASCE from December 1997 to December 1998. Tamagno served as president and Fritsch as treasurer.

"Rich and A.J. enthusiastically volunteered their time, talents and efforts for this ASCE extracurricular undertaking," remarked Falcone.

"They developed an unusual design, which was different from a standard tree house," continued Falcone. After several meetings to discuss the possibilities, Tamagno and Fritsch spent about six hours designing the specs. The students created a set of blueprints that illustrated a structure positioned

Linn Benton CC/*The Commuter*

between four 8-foot trees for support, as opposed to the traditional type of tree house which is built upon one tree. The plans included dimensions and directions for materials.

"The project was significant from an engineering standpoint because it contained all the aspects that would be involved in a larger project, including planning, design, procurement, construction, inspection and acceptance," explained Falcone.

The students enjoyed doing the project because it demanded ingenuity and reflected the challenges they would encounter in a real-life engineering enterprise. They worked from only tentative measurements supplied from the boy himself.

"This was more difficult than the type of tree house that sits atop one tree because this was positioned between four trees," said Tamagno.

"We explored several options for construction that would make it safe, easy and reasonably affordable, including specifications for structures that could be made in either concrete and or in wood with support beams," said Fritsch.

Both students said that they enjoyed working on the project. "It was a great opportunity to help someone because it incorporated all the skills we learned at Villanova, and it was fun to do," they commented.

When they completed their design last November, the student engineers mailed the blueprint to Matthew for his approval. ∎

SERVICE ENHANCES EDUCATIONAL EXPERIENCE AT BYU

By Mali Hegdahl

THE DAILY UNIVERSE (Provo, Utah) 06/24/1998

At a university where admission is partly dependent on volunteer service and leadership experience, many students come to BYU with a rich background in church and community involvement.

To them, "Enter to learn, go forth to serve" is not just a phrase they glance at when driving onto campus for the first time. It is their goal.

Many students, old and new, question how to get involved on campus and make the most of their "BYU experience." Fortunately, there are many opportunities for service around campus. The only problem is choosing where to roll up your sleeves and get involved.

The easiest way to find out about involvement opportunities is to go to the Campus Involvement Center. Yes, that's right, there is a place specifically designed to help students get involved on campus.

"Here at BYU, which is different than at a lot of campuses, there' s just a desire among the students to do service and give something of themselves," said Ann Marie Lambert, coordinator of the Campus Involvement Center.

Roxane Olsen, 1997-98 Student Alumni Association president, said it is important for students to look at their options and find an organization that will match their desire to serve. Olsen said students should start by deciding what exactly they want to do.

"When students choose to serve in organizations they really believe in, their commitment and feeling of fulfillment will be greater than if they choose one randomly," Olsen said.

Lambert said there are many benefits of becoming involved in activities outside of school. One strange effect of becoming active in an organization is improved grades, Lambert said.

"I often hear students say that they get more done when their schedule is full," Lambert said.

Lambert said many studies have shown that students who are involved outside of the classroom, actually do better academically. By working outside of the classroom, students get practical experience using the knowledge they gained in school, Lambert said.

"Their learning is definitely enhanced," Lambert said.

Olsen said the opportunity to serve also enhances individual skills that students may not be able to develop in a normal classroom setting.

Another benefit of getting involved in a campus-wide organization is the chance to meet new people, Olsen said.

Brian Bowers, BYU Student Association president, said being involved in an organization is important because it allows students to feel like they belong.

"When you come to BYU, it seems like such a big place, but by getting involved you feel like you're part of something. It helps the campus feel like a smaller place, more like home," Bowers said.

He said that serving on campus is also a way to give back and contribute to the university.

Bowers said, "Being involved in service prepares students to go into the world and build up their communities and the Kingdom."

He said being involved on campus and in student wards establishes a lifelong habit of service.

Bowers said, "It's what the BYU experience is all about." ∎

So far, we've seen both the unexpected and the expected when it comes to life beyond the classroom at religious schools. When it comes to sports on these campuses, what you'll find is a mixed bag. Brigham Young University fields teams in over 20 sports, yet they don't compete on Sundays. Until 1998, this wasn't a problem. Then the NCAA voted to eliminate the "BYU rule" for postseason play, probably to generate more money through televising games on Sunday. What would you expect Brigham Young to do? Surprisingly to the outside world—but not to the student body and administration of BYU—the school stood by its religious beliefs and still refuses to compete in athletics on Sundays.

REVERSAL OF 'BYU RULE' LEAVES MANY DISAPPOINTED

By Esther Yu

THE DAILY UNIVERSE (Provo, Utah) 04/29/1998

Many BYU faculty members expressed disappointment over the NCAA decision eliminating the 35-year-old rule known as the "BYU rule." The decision made last Wednesday lifts the ban on Sunday play in most postseason tournaments.

This means BYU teams will be eliminated prematurely from tournaments because it is against LDS church policy to play on Sunday.

Though there used to be other schools opposed to playing on Sundays, Campbell University, a Baptist school in Buies Creek, N.C., is now the only other school that has a Sunday policy affected by this decision.

President Merrill J. Bateman issued an official response to the decision. "We are disappointed that the NCAA Division I Board was not willing to continue with its long-standing policy that allowed some flexibility with regard to Sunday play. The discouraging aspect of this is that BYU will have teams that will qualify for postseason competition and may not be able to play. It's unfortunate the NCAA is not willing to continue with a program that has worked well the last 35 years."

BYU baseball coach Gary Pullins doesn't think the ruling will greatly affect baseball because so many other baseball games continue throughout the week. However, he said there is still that chance.

"It is disappointing to everybody. I have had coaches at different universities say that they don't know why they play on Sunday because it should be a day to let their players off. They end up using Monday as a travel day and missing classes," Pullins said.

Other faculty members in the BYU athletics department also believe the Sunday ruling could be a disappointment to teams outside of BYU.

"(Having Sunday off) gives them time to come home and prepare for the week. . . . [F]urthermore, coaches are already under pressure with travel and competition that Sundays are the only day that they can be at home with their families," said BYU Athletic Director Rondo Fehlberg.

Kelly Egan/*The Campus Times*

Brett Fagan/*The Bona Venture*

The Sunday ruling may not even have much of an impact on increasing publicity for many sports.

"Its nonsense," said BYU men's track coach Willard Hirschi. "There is no reason to be holding competition on a Sunday. There is no money to be made in track and field as a television sport."

Besides preventing BYU teams from playing in postseason tournament, the decision could affect BYU's ability to recruit. The non-member athletes that BYU has recruited in the past may choose to attend another school where they can compete with other teams where this decision is not made by the school.

BYU's golf team has had several non-member teammates on its squad who may choose to go to another school where they will be allowed to compete for the national championship.

In an official BYU statement, Fehlberg stated, "While we expect this ruling to have little immediate impact on football and men's basketball, we are worried that a number of our Olympic sports could be immediately affected. This decision, although disappointing, will have no effect on BYU's policies against Sunday competition."

BYU has the right to appeal the rule change and is considering its options. ∎

Note: BYU Rule is back in effect as of August 17, 1998. Ninety-eight schools joined BYU in protesting the NCAA's April decision. Under the new rule, colleges and universities that have policies against competition on any day—not just Sunday—for religious reasons can file for an exemption and change the scheduling of a championship event.

Brigham Young stands by its religious beliefs even in the face of losing prospective team members to other schools, surely a rarity in the world of college athletics. In this instance, the school chose not to "go along" with other schools. One area where college teams nationwide are *required* to go along is in their enforcement of Title IX of the Education Amendment, passed in 1972. By this law, women are guaranteed equality in athletic opportunities at institutions of higher learning. As you can see from the next article from *The Lariat*, Baylor University is working hard toward total compliance with Title IX.

BAYLOR WOMEN'S ATHLETIC PROGRAMS, FUNDING ON RISE

By Patricia Demchak

THE LARIAT (Waco, Texas) 05/05/1998

The percentage of female athletes and funding for women's athletic programs at Baylor is on the rise, according to the most recent figures released by Paul Bradshaw, assistant athletic director for compliance.

The proportion of female athletes in 1996–97 rose 6 percent from the previous year's figures, while aid for the athletes rose 4 percent. Bradshaw attributes the increase to the addition of the women's varsity soccer program and says that Baylor will probably experience another increase with the possible addition of a women's crew team.

"The University is looking at preliminary budgets for women's crew," he said.

The increase in proportions mirrors a nationwide trend in collegiate athletics. According to an article in the Chronicle of Higher Education, participation in and funding for women's sports is slowly creeping upward to approach men's levels. Thirty-eight percent of Division I athletes were women in 1996–7, up 6 percent from the previous year, the article said.

However, many schools, including Baylor, still fall short of achieving "substantial proportionality" in their athletic programs. Title IX of the Education Amendments of 1972 requires that institutions level the playing field for men and women, and one way of achieving equality is through substantial proportionality, or adjusting the proportion of female athletes to reflect the proportion of total female undergraduates by within five percentage points.

Although women constitute 57 percent of the Baylor population, they make up only 36 percent of Baylor's athletes, according to the 1996–97 figures. However, this does not necessarily imply that Baylor does not comply with the Title IX requirements, Bradshaw said.

"The university takes the position that it is in Title IX compliance based upon the fact that it provides programs that effectively account for the interest on campus," Bradshaw said.

Head Track Coach Clyde Hart said the inequality between men's and women's proportions in sports is not be as dramatic as it may appear and is due largely to the high expenses, recruitment, and numbers of team members involved in the men's football program.

"They're trying to make up for the large number of football scholarships because there's no women's sport out there that matches up to men's football," he said.

Baylor awarded 85 scholarships for football this year, more than the total of scholarships for all women's sports combined, according to numbers released by Associate Athletic Director for Business David Taylor. Baylor awarded a total of 83 scholarships to women's sports programs and 46.3 to men's non-football sports programs. NCAA standards require that Division I colleges and universities limit the number of men's scholarships in an attempt to balance the inequality between proportions of men and women in collegiate sports.

Because football programs involve so many players, Baylor must limit scholarships in other men's sports programs to tip the scales toward a more equal representation for both sexes. Bradshaw said this initially caused an "outcry," especially when the NCAA enforced cuts to men's basketball scholarships, but since then few complaints have been raised.

"If you're trying to go by the legal guidelines, this is what you've got to do," Taylor said.

Soccer player and Plano junior Julie Larson said she did not think the difference in proportions had any negative affect on other programs.

"Most people assume that most of the money goes toward guys and football, but it's never come across as a problem to me," she said. ■

The true test of real college football fans has got to be the number of times they tear down the school goal posts after a big win. As the following article from Baylor College proves, students at religious schools show just as much passion for the sport as fans at any large state school.

BAYLOR STUDENTS DRAG GOAL POST TO PRESIDENT'S FRONT YARD
By Luke McElmurry

THE LARIAT (Waco, Texas) 11/04/1997

As the saying goes, history repeats itself, and it finally did Saturday when students carried out the ultimate expression of fan support and attacked the goalpost for the second time in Baylor's history.

Following the final possession that clinched the victory against the University of Texas, Baylor fans rushed chaotically out onto the field. After a little bit of hesitation, a mob of fans, led primarily by members of the Baylor Line (a student spirit group), swarmed the goalpost and tore the helpless steel uprights from their welds.

The goalpost hit the ground and applause rang throughout the stadium, but that was only the tip of the celebratory iceberg. Members of the Baylor Line proceeded to heave the structure out of the stadium and march it to the Bill Daniel Student Center. After a brief interlude at the BDSC, members of the Baylor Line reconvened and carried their trophy to President Robert B. Sloan Jr.'s front yard. Fearing it would possibly get damaged, campus security had the goalpost put in storage at Waco Construction. However, following many fan and student requests, Sloan had it removed from storage and placed where it still sits in front of the Bill Daniel Student Center.

Sloan said he and his wife were excited to find the figure in their yard late Saturday night.

"I considered it a complement that students carried the goalpost to my house," Sloan said.

Sloan said he has seen no condemnation of the act and he is proud of the students for their support of the team.

"You cannot plan for something this spontaneous and it was really great to see it come about," Sloan said. "Everybody where I was sitting was cheering and clapping and crying in excitement."

According to Baylor Police Chief Jim Doak even the occupants of the stadium command center were cheering and celebrating with high fives as well when the goal post was toppled.

At the beginning of the fourth quarter, Doak had a meeting with personnel to anticipate the possible goal post tumbling and how to deal with it. While working within the athletic department's wishes to preserve at least one goal post the police department decided to concentrate more on U.T.'s head coach John Mackovic's safety rather than playing the grinch who saved the goal post.

"We had no intentions of putting a damper on the fans' emotion and spirit," Doak said. "It was a great time, nobody got hurt and the whole event turned out beautifully."

The Baylor police went so far as to escort the goal post victors safely through intersections.

Now on display, the goal post sits smothered in multicolored ink with an array of messages. Writings on the goal post range from "I love you A.J. love Brett" to signatures to the phrase pictured in The Waco Tribune-Herald, "It took 5 years and 50,000 dollars for me to see this finally happen. Thank God."

Stan Madden, vice president of student marketing, said that administration is considering several options concerning the fate of the goal post, and repairing and returning it to the stadium is not one of them. Preserving the goal post art in a clear lacquer and then hanging it in the bear pit is the top idea on the list.

"We want it to be something people can visit and remember and say, 'I was there,'" Sloan said. ∎

Greek Life

As with sports, Greek life has many faces at religious schools. At some, like Baylor, which has 16 fraternities and 12 sororities, Greek organizations are an important part of college life and a huge force on campus. At other religious schools, like Yeshiva University, fraternities and sororities are nonexistent. For the most part, what you're more likely to find at religious schools are smaller, local chapters of Greek organizations with a greater emphasis on service.

When fraternities and sororities do exist at religious schools, however, the same problems and concerns that we've seen at other schools tend to crop up—keeping Greeks from getting a bad rap, violations of alcohol policies, generating interest in fraternities and sororities, and the stresses of pledging a Greek organization and maintaining grades.

BAYLOR FRATERNITIES TAKE CLOSER LOOK INTO OWN ACTIONS
By Brittney Partridge

THE LARIAT (Waco, Texas) 02/12/1999

In the wake of recent tragic events surrounding the deaths of two students at Southwest Texas State University, some Baylor fraternities are taking a close look at the responsibility of their own actions.

"This and a number of events have happened in the last couple of years, and it has to make you step up and think that this could happen to any of us at any time," said Jason Zafereo, a Victoria senior and rush chairman of Tau Kappa Epsilon. "When people come to college, I think that they do a lot of things that they don't really think about. This should be a wake-up call to all of us, honestly, to think before we take action."

Zafereo also said after discussing this situation at a fraternity meeting Monday night, he and his brothers believe that this was an isolated incident.

"We really don't know the whole story behind this, but in opening yourself up by having parties, you take risks like that," Zafereo said. "I know that Baylor has taken steps in the last several years, and they have come down hard on parties. I think that's good, but maybe more education is the answer instead of just dealing with it after the fact."

Since the incident occurred at a TKE fraternity house at Southwest Texas State, Zafereo and others are concerned that it may give fraternities a negative image.

"It just happened to happen at a fraternity house at a party," Zafereo said. "It was really unfortunate, but it's going to give fraternities a bad name. I'm concerned that people have a negative image of fraternities to begin with. They'll hear 'fraternity pledge killed,' and that's all they'll hear from this story. It puts a different light on it, and I just think that people won't bother following up on the story."

Matt Murph, a Houston senior and a member of Sigma Nu, said his fraternity is also concerned with this situation.

"We are concerned about it because it is a bad situation," Murph said. "Those things are generally freak accidents, but a lot of irresponsibility is involved. I feel comfortable that this kind of thing wouldn't go on in the Sigma Nu chapter down there."

Zafereo said that this situation has alarmed many students who are involved in fraternities.

"I think people are stepping back and saying, 'whoa, this guy had a lot in common with us,'" he said.

Chief Jim Doak of the Baylor Department of Public Safety agreed that this was an isolated event, but he believes it should raise the level of awareness among college students.

"Alcohol is a killer, and it kills in many forms," Doak said. "People need to be alert and vigilant."

Doak said he is very alarmed with what he is seeing around the Baylor campus because students are consuming a vast amount of alcohol.

"We've issued just over 100 minor in possession

citations this year," Doak said. "We're very alarmed. That's the tip of the iceberg of what we could have issued if we had enough man power. We do not go looking for parties, but rather we respond when we are summoned due to the disorderly nature of parties and loud noise complaints."

Baylor is in a different situation since there are no "official" fraternity or sorority houses allowed on or nearby campus. Doak said he sees this as a blessing.

"We are delighted not to have officially sanctioned fraternity houses on campus or in close proximity,"

Doak said. "Other Big 12 schools can tell you horror stories. There are unofficial locations, but that's a huge difference, and we deal quite often with those unofficial locations."

Doak said that the volume of alcohol consumption among college students is spinning out of control.

"People need to be very concerned about the increased use of alcohol by college students," Doak said. "All we can do is continue to try to educate people, and hopefully, they will make good decisions." ■

RUSH MEANS STRESS FOR WOULD-BE SISTERS AT CREIGHTON U.

By Kamahria Hopkins

THE CREIGHTONIAN (Omaha, Neb.) 01/22/1999

Rush is an exciting introduction to Greek life filled with numerous activities, parties, food and friendly faces.

However, the experience and structure of rush week for men and women is very different.

The rush period for the five sororities at Creighton includes two informational gatherings, a skit day, preference parties and bid acceptance.

On skit day, each sorority puts together a performance that illustrates what Greek life is like. Preference parties allow each rushee to get to know their top choices better. The week concludes with a guaranteed bid for each rushee who wants to join a sorority.

The five fraternities on campus have a more relaxed rush.

The fraternities hold a two-week rush period including two "smokers" and three to four less formal off-campus activities.

The smokers are comprised of basic information and speakers. Each fraternity also organizes activities such as bowling and dinner at a variety of restaurants.

Dan Wientzen, President of the Phi Delta Theta Fraternity, said the main difference between women's and men's rush is the stress level.

"I think [women's rush] could be more fun and less stressful," Wientzen said. "Rush is one of the times I look forward to most each year and I wish for [women] it could be the same."

Jennifer Wallace, rush co-chair for Pi Beta Phi, said that the difference in the rush procedure is the structure, not the stress level.

"It's a big decision. Women's rush is more structured than men's rush, therefore, it is more uncomfortable for women," Wallace said. "Men don't have to go to every fraternity's party, so it's easier for them to enjoy themselves."

Unlike sorority rush participants, men are not guaranteed a bid to one of the five fraternities.

"At the end of the second week if we have decided to invite someone back, we'll go to their room and give them a bid," Wientzen said. "If they accept, we have a ceremony, go to dinner and throw a party."

The cost to rush for women is ten dollars more than men. Wallace said paperwork and costs for renting rooms is probably the reason for the slight difference is cost.

There is a strict rule about sororities offering food, drink or gifts to rushees.

"The rushees are allowed to eat and drink while at the parties, they are just not allowed to take it with them because it would be considered a gift," Wallace said.

The food and drink policy is more flexible within the fraternities. Many of the off-campus activities are held at such places as Old Chicago.

"We buy food like pizza and tacos for the rushees at no additional cost to them," Wientzen said.

Despite the differences in structure between men's and women's rush, both allow for students to become familiar with Greek life.

"I think their system works for them and our system works for us." Wientzen said. "What matters is that people are enjoying themselves." ∎

Interesting Speakers

Expect the unexpected—that should probably be the moral of this section. At religious schools you'll find all kinds of extracurricular activities to fit all kinds of needs. As we've seen, religious schools are far from conservative when it comes to the array of organizations and clubs they feature on their campuses. It's interesting to see how the religious schools in this section resist giving students one-sided views of life and the college experience. From the articles we found, this seems to be no different when lining up speakers for campus visits. *The Creightonian* reports how one speaker there challenged the way that Catholic colleges and universities exclude social theory from discussions of theology. Chuck D lectured Marquette University students about his radical views on race. And, Boston College welcomed Greg Louganis, an openly gay Olympic athlete, to its campus during its first ever pride week.

SPEAKER RELATES 'RADICAL' CATHOLIC IDEAS AT CREIGHTON U.

By Andre Nathaniel

THE CREIGHTONIAN (Omaha, Neb.) 02/05/1999

One theologian says many Catholic scholars today fail to appreciate the integration of theology and social theory because they work under an assumed separation between the two, a separation that gives special privileges to the agenda of the nation-state and marginalizes the radical vision of the Catholic worker.

In a speech entitled "Blowing the Dynamite of the Church: Catholic Radicalism from a Catholic Perspective," Rev. Michael Baxter of the University of Notre Dame addressed a group of about 120 faculty members, students and visitors in the Union Pacific Room on Tuesday.

Baxter said the theoretical paradigms and institutional structures shaping Catholic colleges and universities continue to separate theology from social theory.

"It is by no means a coincidence, therefore, that these Catholic schools all too often function as production sites of capitalist culture as to lead one to conclude, in darker moments, that the shepherding

being done at these schools is the kind that raises sheep not for the church, but for the market," Baxter said.

Baxter said Catholic radicals such as Dorothy Day and Peter Maurin did not separate theology from social theory in the 1930s, but instead espoused a social theory infused with theology.

Baxter said the social theory to which Maurin referred to was dynamic because it possessed Jesus Christ.

"The image of dynamite jolts the reader or listener into imagining Christ and the Church in temporal rather than in purely spiritual terms," Baxter said.

Baxter said Day envisioned society not as enclosed within an autonomous realm of human activity, but as radically open and dynamically oriented toward supernatural theology.

Baxter said Day's descriptions of feeding the hungry, clothing the naked and instructing the ignorant showed Maurin's "new society within the old" was thoroughly realizable here and now, through the power of the Holy Spirit. ∎

CHUCK D SPEAKS OUT, DISPELS MYTHS IN SPEECH AT MARQUETTE U.

By Pamela Williams

THE MARQUETTE TRIBUNE (Milwaukee, Wis.) 02/06/1998

Rap, race and reality. How do those three words fit together? Rap artist and political commentator Chuck D attempted to correlate the three when he spoke Wednesday night at the Weasler Auditorium.

"I'm not here to lecture you," he said upon stepping on the stage. "This is actually a conversation about things that are on my mind and possibly yours."

Chuck D is the lead rapper for the music group Public Enemy, one of the most publicized rap groups in the music industry. Since the inception of Public Enemy in 1987, the group has visited 38 countries and produced three multi-platinum albums, which have won numerous national and international music awards.

Chuck D has traveled the college speaker circuit for the past seven years, speaking at over 200 schools nationwide. Chuck D spoke about rap music and how he feels it has been exploited and manipulated ever since he broke into the business in 1977. People thought rap would die since its inception in 1979, but it's still around as strong as ever, and it exists in many different forms, Chuck D said.

Chuck D said rap is only criticized because it comes from a black's mouth talking with a brain behind it, and he strongly believes society opposes that. He said rap has brought many black males to the forefront of intellectual society. Chuck D also spoke about the "dumbing down" of society, where society gives people the impression that it's okay to be ignorant. Chuck D said he believes intelligence will save everybody in the coming century.

Anonymous students responded to Chuck D's appearance on campus with contempt toward his message of individualism by making 30 flyers that circulated around campus Wednesday, depicting Chuck D's message as supporting white racism. However, Chuck D handled the potentially embarrassing incident with relative ease.

"Chuck D is a pioneer in so many ways," freshman Michael Phillips said. "It was really an honor to hear him speak about topics from his point of view."

"A lot of people thought he was being racist, but he was just talking about the hype about race and our need to open our eyes to so many issues," Phillips added. Chuck D urged not only African Americans but everyone to keep themselves from becoming "sheep" to the "super-media" and "super-corporations," which he says "pimp" our minds and make it hard for us to distinguish what is reality and what is not.

Chuck D said African Americans in particular let themselves become sheep because they are not really in control of their lives. Chuck D said African Americans are in a "plantation state," because they have no control over their actions and resources.

"As far as gaining that determination, that's all in how you live your life," Chuck D said. "People need to give themselves the right mix of culture, reality and a little bit of fantasy."

Chuck D discusses these issues at deeper length in his current book, "Fight the Power: Chuck D on Rap, Race and Reality." First published in fall 1997, the book can be purchased at various local bookstores. ∎

LOUGANIS SHARES LIFETIME OF SECRETS AT BOSTON COLLEGE

By Brian M. Cohen

THE HEIGHTS (Chestnut Hill, Mass.) 04/22/1998

Four-time Olympic gold medal winner in diving, Greg Louganis, discussed the trials and tribulations of being a homosexual man living with HIV in St. Ignatius Church on Tuesday, April 14. The lecture was the first event of Boston College's first ever Pride Week.

Chris Goff, Undergraduate Government of Boston College director of AIDS Awareness, said, "This event is a long time in the making. It is our hope that the lecture will influence both this audience tonight and the community as a whole."

Goff introduced Louganis saying, "Greg Louganis is so much more than an Olympic champion, he is an extraordinary human being."

Louganis talked about secrets, and the importance of letting them go.

Louganis said, "When I was little, I just knew I was different. When I went to college, that's when I realized I was gay."

He spoke of bringing his mother to a gay bar when he was at the University of Miami.

"I remember the next day my mom turned to me and said, 'Greg, can we go back to one of those fun places?'" he said. "A couple of years after that I told her that I was gay."

He then told the audience the story of coming out to his mother about his sexuality.

"After having a fight with my then partner, Kevin, I called my mother to help me pack my things, which we mixed up with some of Kevin's things," Louganis said. "I turned to my mother and said Kevin and I are more than just roommates, we're lovers."

He said, "My mother turned to me and said, 'I know, Greg, what's for dinner?'"

He added, "She probably knew longer than I did, you know how mothers are."

Louganis also discussed his experiences with homophobia in US diving.

"When I was diving, I wasn't sure whether it was homophobia or jealousy," he said. "I was winning, and I was a 'sissy.'"

He told a story of abuse at the 1985 Olympic Festival in Louisiana.

"People wrote fag with a line through it all over the showers. The 'fag buster' campaign surrounded the festival," Louganis said, adding, "I always wanted my diving to speak for itself. I didn't want to have to speak for my diving." Later in the competition, Louganis was able to have his diving speak for him.

"Before my last dive, Ronny Meyers, who was the most vocal in the campaign, was winning," he said. "I felt like everyone was cheering against me."

"I found a fellow American swimmer, Lisa Tremble, in the crowd, who had always been quietly supportive of me, and she gave me the thumbs up. I ended up nailing the 3 1/2 reverse and won the competition."

He added, "When I went up to receive my medal, I stuck out my hand [to the losing diver], and he turned his back on me. No one wanted to win with the fag."

He then discussed how he came out to the public.

"Three weeks [after the Olympic games] I was to receive an award," he said. "I showed up to the event and there were 1000 people there. I was real nervous because I knew what I was going to say."

"I got the award and proceeded with the speech. I commended the Olympic committee for recognizing an openly gay athlete."

Louganis spoke of the reaction. "It was a brunch, so I heard knives and forks hitting the plate," he said. "Only about 12 people stood up, and the rest either politely applauded, or just sat there."

Louganis then talked of his other secret.

"I kind of suspected my partner at that time was HIV positive," he said. "My cousin, John, who is a doctor, wanted to treat me very aggressively. The prescription for AZT at that time was two pills every four hours."

He spoke of telling his coach. "I wanted to tell my coach, but I didn't want him to take it easy on me," he said. "Secrets really imprison you, so I had to share it."

"My coach turned to me and said, 'Greg, I'm not going to let you off the hook that easy,'" Louganis said.

He then discussed his relationship with his dad, and how he came out about his HIV status.

"In 1990 my dad was diagnosed with cancer," he said. "That's when I came out to my dad about my HIV status."

"I took care of him the last six weeks of his life," he said. "It was difficult, but I was there for him. We had a lot of very important conversations."

He then told about sharing his secret with his mother.

"When I told her about my HIV status she started sobbing," Louganis said. "She told me that mothers aren't supposed to outlive their sons."

He closed by saying, "I'm Greg Louganis. I'm a gay man living with AIDS. More importantly, I'm looking forward to the day I am just seen as a man."

Following the speech, Louganis entertained questions from the audience. One question asked was whether or not he would do anything differently.

"I wouldn't do anything differently," he said. "All the things I did made me who I am today, and I kind of like that person."

At the age of 24, Louganis was the first man in 56 years to win two Olympic gold medals in diving by winning both the platform and springboard events. He went on to become the first man to win double gold medals for diving in two consecutive Olympics.

The recent release of his autobiography, *Breaking the Surface*, has become one of the best-selling books ever written by an athlete. ■

LIFE ON Campus

What characterizes life on the campus of a religious school? Obviously, it's religion, but just how *religious* a religious school is varies widely from institution to institution. Brigham Young and Yeshiva University students, for example, enroll in those schools because they know that practicing their faith will be an important part of life there, both inside and outside the classroom—and that's how they want it to be. At other religious schools, like Villanova and Marquette, for example, religion is more of a tradition that need not play a part in the daily lives of students. At these schools, students may not even consider their religious affiliations a factor when deciding to enroll.

First and foremost, the *attitudes* of administrators, faculty members and students toward your religious place in the scheme of your school affect campus life greatly. The emphasis placed on religion will make the difference between a religious school with an obvious religious feel and a religious school that promotes, but does not prescribe, faith. Some students who attend religious schools value the way their particular schools place equal emphasis on both education and religion; the columnist from Yeshiva University makes this point eloquently. Other students find the religious emphasis at their schools to be not strong enough. A religious school's focus on religion—while it will always be in evidence—will vary depending on administrative policies and faculty and student attitudes.

Religious schools don't always exhibit the ethnic diversity that you'll find at large state schools and highly competitive colleges. "Knowledge of what is right better voiced than pondered," written by an African-American student, raises the unique problems facing ethnic minorities at Brigham Young. As you'd expect, there won't be a lot of religious diversity, either. While they do not deny admission to those of other faiths, and often welcome them, some religious school students may question just how far accommodations for those of other religions should go; "Student opinion divided over Luther inter-faith room" brings to light such student reluctance.

Otherwise, life at a religious college won't be all that different from life at other colleges. "Alcohol problems abound at Baylor U." points out that drinking is also a problem at some religious schools; "Spilling drinks for community service at Boston College" describes that school's innovative attempts to deter alcohol policy violations. Religious school students exhibit varying degrees of activism, just like on other college campuses; two religious universities—Marquette and Brigham Young—are spotlighted here for their activist efforts. Opinion will vary about student services at religious schools, just like it does on other college campuses. But best of all, you'll find opportunities to have a good time no matter where you go.

Religion

The number and variety of religious requirements you'll need to fulfill should you choose to enroll at one of the schools in this chapter will greatly affect your life on campus. Obviously, focusing at least some of your studies on religion and participating in out-of-classroom religious pursuits will be what separates your college experience from that of students attending other types of schools.

But there's more to the story than just academic and extracurricular requirements. The attitudes of school administrators, professors, and your fellow students toward religion will in large part determine the religious environment of the school. In other words, just because a school is religiously affiliated doesn't mean that its atmosphere will necessarily be overtly religious. For one, how rigidly each school adheres to and interprets the philosophies of the religion with which they're affiliated will be up to them. Some religious schools will choose to promote the views of their religion above all others. Other religious schools welcome the discussion of other points of view.

Another way that religious influence can affect life on campus is in the emphasis that the school places on religious education versus the emphasis it places on secular education. How important are both in the overall philosophy of the school and, more particularly, in the minds of the students themselves? In large part, students who attend religious schools do so because of their desire to keep a religious emphasis in their lives. Just how great this emphasis should be is a subject of great debate among the students themselves. One young woman writing for Stern College for Women of Yeshiva University's *Observer* admires her college's emphasis on both religious and secular education:

COLUMN: RELIGIOUS, SECULAR EDUCATION MIX WELL AT YESHIVA U.

By Susan Jacobs

THE OBSERVER (New York) 03/15/1999

Lately I've heard a lot of people complaining that Stern is not a "real college." Such complaints are not new, and, as usual, they often pass unchallenged. The problem is, whether they are meant to be taken seriously or not, such comments undermine the seriousness of this school and the self-concept students have about going to school here.

It would be foolish not to admit that Stern has its shortcomings. Stern is definitely limited in its ability to offer certain classes and majors. And we miss out on an important part of the American college experience by isolating ourselves from coeducation and from society's diversity. And it is no secret that Yeshiva University is often an inefficient bureaucracy, sometimes creating more harm than help. (It is worth noting that almost all universities have their share of inefficiency and red tape.) But we have to ask ourselves if acquiring a college education at Stern is worth these pitfalls.

When I was deciding where I would attend college, one factor I weighed heavily was the sort of life I would have in college, both intellectually and socially. I wanted to go to a college where I would have the opportunity to study the essentials of a liberal arts education, and where I would feel comfortable expressing my opinions with my fellow students. I also wanted to be in a school that would not only provide opportunities to experience Jewish life with other Jewish students, but would foster that involvement.

Quite honestly, I was afraid I would be sacrificing the quality of my secular education for these ends. As a student here, I have taken classes that bored or frustrated me. But most of my classes have been interesting and intellectually stimulating. I think that students at most colleges have similar experiences. Even the best schools have classes that are poorly taught or that are not challenging.

Some students insist that the better education is on the men's campus but they rarely cite grounds for this belief. I challenge them to ask any professor who teaches on both campuses for his/her comparison of the academic rigors of both schools. Most will tell you that the two schools are comparable, and that Stern is superior to Yeshiva College in some subjects, and vice versa.

Being in an isolated environment does breed a certain amount of insecurity. We are never quite sure how we measure up. Do we enjoy feeling inferior? Are we afraid that Stern just might be a pretty darn good school? Whether we like to admit it or not, a lot of us are still insecure about how we measure up to men. Statistics say that women tend to thrive in all-female environments because they are less intimidated to express themselves when men are not present. If anything, we should feel better about the education we receive here, knowing that, for all its limitations, Stern can also be a liberating place. We are only limited here by the limits we place upon ourselves.

I believe that is the real crux of the situation in this school. No, Stern does not have all the opportunities we would like it to have, and we should continue to press for improvements in the school's academics. But at the same time, there is so much to be gained from being a student here. Maybe in their rush to fill all their requirements in an average 2.5 years, students don't stop to take advantage of the many opportunities available to them. Maybe their experience here doesn't feel like a "real" college experience as a result, but that is their own fault, not the fault of the school.

Stern is not an Ivy League institution. If that's what you're looking for, then this is not the place. But that is not to say that Stern doesn't have some of the advantages of an Ivy League school or that it won't ever be taken as seriously as those schools. Stern has improved markedly in the four years I've been here and will continue to improve. ∎

The young woman from Stern is pleased with the balance between religious opportunities and secular education that her school has managed to strike. Other students, however, would prefer that more religious influence be exhibited by their schools. In fact, some—like the following columnist writing for *The Bona Venture*—feel that academic freedom should be secondary to spiritual goals.

COLUMN: CATHOLICISM INTEGRAL TO ST. BONAVENTURE UNIVERSITY

By Michael Bigos

THE BONA VENTURE (St. Bonaventure, N.Y.) 02/12/1999

Non-Catholic professors and university staff should not fear a radical inquisition resulting from the Pope's and the American Bishops' call for Catholic universities to honor their identity.

Attempting to portray a true Catholic identity on a university campus is extremely difficult because of the critical tension between academic freedom and spiritual identity.

Any university requires the freedom to search actively for truth in order to form students with the wisdom and knowledge to survive in a hostile world.

For a Catholic university, student formation in the faith and teachings of the church provide an additional tool for that survival package. As a result, though academic freedom remains important, it should be considered secondary to the spiritual goals of the university.

St. Bonaventure University should strive for a greater Christian unity while encouraging the essentials of the faith. Reasonable goals include encouraging a common prayerfulness and promoting active religious dialogue within the entire university community.

But to hear some faculty members refer to themselves as "heathens" unless they "convert" shows that great misunderstanding and disrespect exist for the seemingly sincere efforts of this institution to supplement its quality academics with quality moral and religious formation.

The papal document "Ex Corde Ecclesiae," released on Aug. 15, 1990, declares that "a model Catholic university informs and carries out its research, teachings and all other activities with Catholic ideals, principles and attitudes."

For example, professors could not actively support abortion or euthanasia in class—or at least the Catholic perspective would have to be clearly presented and discussed.

At the same time, universities must maintain the freedom of conscience and religious liberty of each person while respecting its Catholic character and the moral and doctrinal teaching of the church.

"Ex Corde Ecclesiae" stated that specific regions should develop their own specific norms from the Pope's guidelines. The U.S. Bishops' Conference committee published a November 1998 draft of the specific implementation planned.

Professors should not fear losing their jobs except in cases where they openly challenge Catholic doctrine: on the teachings of the Eucharist, abortion or papal authority, for example.

Our faculty members, especially those who are Protestant, represent a tremendous asset to this

community and should be encouraged to share their own beliefs provided they do not conflict with university mission.

Granted, some professors simply may not concur with the church and the university's attempt to follow its teaching. There should be no shame in their voluntary departure to seek an atmosphere conducive to their conception of truth.

Likewise, if the university actively chooses not to follow the teachings of the Holy Father and the church, it would be better for it not to bear the name "Catholic" and disappoint those students and professors seeking a vibrant religious community.

The university should take faith in other institutions, such as the Franciscan University of Steubenville or Grove City College, which have successfully braved the tension involved in maintaining a religious identity.

I pray that the university community trusts in the wisdom of God and the work of the Holy Spirit to guide this university to a dynamic religious faithfulness supportive and beneficial to all. ■

Because religious schools are private institutions, for the most part their tuition rates will be much higher than those you'll see at large state schools (although not nearly as high as those at highly competitive colleges). For a quick reference, here are some 1998 tuition figures for some religious schools: Notre Dame University, $20,900; Creighton, $18,048; Luther College, $20,175; and, on the low side, Texas Christian University, $11,090. Average those out, and you've got a whopping $16,875 yearly tuition fee (and that's not counting other costs, like fees for campus services, student activities, technology, or books!). When increased tuition rates are slated for campus improvements, it's hard for some students and parents to complain; but some, like those at the University of Dayton, question the logic of tuition hikes.

U. DAYTON TUITION INCREASE IRRITATES CURRENT STUDENTS, JUSTIFIED BY SOME

By Lisa Calendine

THE FLYER NEWS (Dayton, Ohio) 10/27/1998

The 5.86 percent tuition increase and technological requirements worry current UD students, but incoming students and parents welcome the new policy.

"Everybody likes it," said Emily Trick, sophomore

fine arts major who gives tours to prospective students and parents. "I haven't heard one complaint (from prospectives)."

Even the extra $600 annually for the university's computer requirement is a value to incoming parents and students. Trick said parents are saying the $600 is a very reasonable price for a computer for their child.

The new computer policy requires every incoming freshman to purchase or lease a computer from UD. They will have four choices of computers, including two laptop models.

The tuition increase and the computer requirement for incoming freshmen are all part of the technology-enhanced learning environment UD wants to create. The extra funds are to be used in wiring the student housing and providing other technology learning facilities. The tuition increase will also allow a 10 percent increase in financial aid.

Current students are doubtful about the need for such a high tuition increase.

"Maybe I'm the only one who thinks this, but if you don't increase tuition you won't need more financial aid," said Christina Rossetti, sophomore English major.

"I, as a student, want to know where all of this money is going."

Space constraints on incoming freshmen has been an issue that has arisen. Students who already own a computer will be forced to purchase one from UD.

"I think it is absolutely ridiculous that you can't bring your own computer, that you have to buy or lease one from the university," Rossetti said.

With the tuition increase as well as the room and board increase, students will pay approximately $20,400 to attend UD. Freshmen will add $600 annually to pay $21,000. According to a survey by the College Board, the current national average cost at private schools is $20,273.

In a UD press release on Oct. 16, the university stated some of the money from this tuition increase will go to faculty and staff raises, initiatives in the 2005 vision plan to attract more minority engineers, and scholarships for women athletes. ■

Housing

In housing, as in other areas of campus life, you'll find that a lot is different and a lot is similar when you compare religious colleges and universities with other schools. One area of difference is how housing is assigned based on gender. At the extreme end of the housing situation, Yeshiva University divides male and female students entirely into two separate colleges. Most religious schools, however, are coeducational, but in a stance that you may find extremely traditional, many have said "no way" to coed dormitories. Notre Dame University just recently considered allowing coed dorms on campus, and then only on an experimental basis.

FACULTY PANEL ADVOCATES CO-ED DORMS ON NOTRE DAME CAMPUS

By Christopher Shipley

THE OBSERVER (South Bend, Ind.) 03/27/1998

A panel of faculty addressed the issue of bringing co-ed dorms to campus Wednesday, overwhelmingly supporting a move toward co-residency.

Co-residential living would foster closer friendships and help students adjust to the social patterns of the University with greater ease, according to the panel. Co-ed dorms would also challenge students to gain a working relationship with peers of the opposite sex.

Eileen Kolman, dean of the First Year of Studies, addressed the topic of co-residency with respect to tradition, morality, social patterns and diversity at Notre Dame.

Kolman noted that the college experience is in many ways a maturing process and that the University must give students options in the choices they make. Co-residential, as well as alcohol and drug-free dorms, should be options for students coming to Notre Dame, according to the dean of the First Year of Studies.

The panel also discussed the moral implications of co-resident living. Many of the same rules students adhere to under the current system would remain in place under the new living arrangements.

"To say that single-sex housing is the only stance to take for a Catholic university is going out on a limb," Kolman told the group.

John Borkowski, Andrew J. McKenna chair of the psychology department, pointed out that the University already has examples of successful co-residential living in its study abroad programs. Borkowski, who taught and observed Notre Dame students in London last semester, expressed his belief that co-residency would also help some of the other issues, including alcoholism and diversity, currently being debated in the Notre Dame community.

The panel indicated that a five-year experiment consisting of two co-residential dorms would prove the success of such an idea, and could be implemented as early as 1999.

Dorms would have partitions by wings, floors or sections depending on the layout of the building.

Student government is putting together a proposal for the Board of Trustees, spearheaded by off-campus

senior and panelist Katie Beirne, which would attempt to answer the question of why a rising number of students are either moving off-campus or studying abroad.

In addition, the proposal will make a recommendation for co-residential housing.

This is not the first time that members of the Notre Dame community have addressed the idea of co-residency. An advisory committee to the provost made the first proposal for co-ed dorms in 1971. Recent proposals have included statistics that show tremendous support for such an initiative. A 1989 report showed that 70% of students would favor having co-residency as an option.

Panel members expressed the necessity to try co-residential living on an experimental basis first, before passing judgment on the future of such an initiative.

"I don't think it's wise to propose changing half the campus all at once, because it is important to try this experiment," a panel member said.

Student government and the University Committee on Women and Students sponsored the panel. ∎

Regardless of whether students live in single-sex or same-sex dorms, overcrowding appears to be just as big a problem at religious schools as it is at the other schools we've looked at thus far. Overenrolling freshmen seems to be a trend nationwide these days—at large state schools, highly competitive schools, and small private and religious schools. If you thought that only large state schools like the University of Minnesota would have numbers large enough to warrant housing incoming freshmen in local hotels, read on about a similar situation occurring at St. Michael's, a small college whose student body numbers only 1,700. As this report from *The Defender* points out, religious school students don't take this disturbing trend any better than other students seem to.

BIG ROOM, SMALL ROOM? SAME PRICE AT ST. MICHAEL'S

By Ben Murray

THE DEFENDER (Colchester, Vt.) 02/12/99

Due to rising enrollment numbers in recent years, Saint Michael's has been forced to seek new options for housing students on campus.

To maintain its ideal of being a residential campus, the college has leased rooms in the Day's Inn across the street and converted dorm lounges into four person rooms.

Sophomores Oscar Havens and Eric Eliason are

roommates that are experiencing the effects of the housing crunch. Living in a room that had been used as a single in previous years, they have stacked both their beds over their desks and a bureau to make room for a television and a futon.

"We live vertically, not horizontally," Havens says. "It's possible to live in [the room], but it's not comfortable. We had to give away a foot stool and our table. If they were in here you couldn't walk."

Around the corner, Ryan Hogan and Jay King live in a room close to twice the size of Havens and Eliason's room, where they are able to fit three couches around their television.

Havens questions the fairness of paying the same amount for his room that Hogan and King pay for theirs.

"I went and complained after Christmas and asked for a lower fee but they wouldn't do it," says Havens.

The answer for why Saint Michael's charges a flat fee for all doubles is that the cost is not just for the living space, but includes the cost of a residential life experience, says Mike Samara, vice president of student affairs and dean of students.

The student is also paying for the availability and proximity of such student resources as fire and rescue, security, physical plant services, phone and Internet services and fitness facilities, Samara says.

"Your best shot at learning is to have these personalized services in the proximity of the campus," Samara says.

"Being a residential campus means that we value learning in all aspects and that includes the value of growing and living in the residence halls," says Lou DiMasi, assistant dean of students and director of residence life.

Samara also says that some students remain in their housing conditions partly because of location preference. He says that to some students living in a certain area or building is more important than the actual room they live in.

"I'd still rather be up here in a small room than a big one on main campus," Havens says.

The reason some students are placed in undesirable housing situations is mainly due to rising enrollment, says DiMasi.

"In the fall there is a real crunch for beds," Kenney says. "We have an enrollment size that pushes our housing capacity."

Sheryl Fleury, executive assistant of student life, says that the rooms were technically doubles and were originally used that way because they contained two closets and two phone jacks. But Fleury acknowledges that the rooms were small.

"I wouldn't want to live there and I wouldn't want my kids to live in those rooms if they were all converted to doubles," Fleury says.

"You can stick two closets and two phone jacks into a two-foot box and call it a double," Havens says.

DiMasi also explains that the college does not make money by converting singles to doubles because of how housing allocations work.

He says that the college fills all possible beds in the spring, fitting students with compatible roommates.

DiMasi says that lottery numbers decide who lives in the converted rooms and that no students were forced to occupy them.

Only volunteers who were informed of the rooms size were taken to live in the rooms, he says.

In upcoming years a break on the fall housing crunch may be possible. Kenney says that with the graduation of this year's large senior class and more exclusive management of admissions, the college would help free up more beds for next semester.

"The direction we're anticipating is to expect a bit of a decline [in incoming students] by being a little more exclusive in our [admissions] offers," Kenney says. ∎

Diversity

Diversity is a hot issue at religious schools. By their very definition, religious schools are *not* diverse—they are affiliated with one religion over all others and the majority of students practice one faith—but that's not to say that religious schools are closed to those who practice other religions. Religious schools do not, and cannot by law, exclude any group based on their race, sexual orientation, gender, or socioeconomic background. But it's simply a matter of statistics, like those noted in the introduction to this section, that most students at all the religious schools in this book are white.

That said, it must be noted that religious schools do not discriminate based on race. And religious schools are by no means exclusively white. But because their numbers are so low at religious schools, students who are not white often note that it's difficult to fit in on campus. In fact, while they may feel welcomed by the administration, some—like this columnist from BYU's *Daily Universe*—claim that the problem is with other students, who don't know quite how to react to those who are "different."

COLUMN: KNOWLEDGE OF WHAT IS RIGHT BETTER VOICED THAN PONDERED

By Mark Morris

THE DAILY UNIVERSE (Provo, Utah) 06/19/1998

Are you on the football team at BYU? No. Do you play basketball? No. What sport do you play? I like basketball, football and volleyball, but I don't play for the Y. Then why are you here?

It's a conversation I have about three times a week. Could it be that I am here to get an education? Or to get married like every one else? Kidding, only kidding.

When I came to BYU, I saw "Enter to learn, go forth to serve" and "The world is our campus."

I didn't see the motto "Everyone enter to learn except for minorities, they need to enter to play a sport." But, sometimes I wonder if that is what people are thinking.

I'm Mark Morris. I am an African-American student on campus and these are some of the things that make me go hmmmmmm . . .

Between classes, as you follow a river of students to your next class, you look up. You look all around you and realize you're the only minority in sight.

For some reason this "realization" makes you uncomfortable. No, Toto, we're not in Kansas any more. We are at BYU where minorities are scarce.

But, does this "realization" only happen to minorities? NO!

My former roommate Matt, who is not a minority on campus, had a similar "realization."

He said the thought made him uncomfortable because the cultural diversity in Provo is so different from the diversity of his home in California; it's almost unnatural.

Now, don't get me wrong—I love BYU, and my experience here has been nothing short of extraordinary. But still I wonder, what is our problem?

It's as if we don't know how to treat people who have a different shade of skin or different shaped eyes or a different color of hair. Sometimes I wonder how we can be so ignorant.

But being ignorant is not all bad. At least most mistakes are made because people are trying too hard to make others comfortable. This would be an entirely different article if I saw people maliciously being racist bigots.

But that is not what I have seen. Again, people just try too hard.

You don't have to prove to me that you are hip, cool, down, tight or any other slang Ebonics term to be my friend.

I guess people try so hard because they fear they don't know how to treat minorities, when they really do. Let me give you the formula, or even better let President Gordon B. Hinckley give you the formula.

When President Hinckley became the prophet he gave a lot of direction to the membership of the church. In one of his addresses, he said we must always remember, as leaders, to be concerned with the individual.

That is how everyone deserves and wants to be treated. Although there are many different groups to which all of us belong, we all are individuals, and it's important that we treat each other as individuals with special wants, special needs and special talents to share.

In dealing with people, any kind of people, if you miss the importance of the individual you miss the point.

Throughout the history of America, there have been many calls to action that ask us to give a little more of what we have to advance the common good.

To me that is what this article is about, bettering the common good. Our treatment of all races of people is a matter of doing what is right.

Here are some calls of action to think about:

In the Gettysburg Address, President Abraham Lincoln invited us to give increased devotion to that cause for which the soldiers gave their last full measure of devotion.

Martin Luther King Jr. once said the greatest damage to the cause of racial freedom and equality was not done by those who wear white masks and burn crosses, but by those who knew what was right and said nothing.

Recently, President Merrill J. Bateman asked everyone to do their part in making BYU a Zion-like community.

So all of us must ask the question, "What can I do to give increased devotion? When will I speak out against racial stereotypes? How will I help make BYU a Zion-like community?"

I would just like to suggest two things.

First, we can focus on the individual, especially those individuals who are on the margins.

So many of my friends have left the university because they lack true friends. True friends, you know. Not the kind that just smile or ask how are you doing superficially. Those people are too concerned about appearing instead of being.

There are so many around us of every race that feel like no one really cares about them because they don't have a close network of friends.

I invite people to remember that it is possible to be lonely in a crowd.

Second, I invite people to open their mouths and stand up for what is right.

There are so many people who need a kind word. There are so many situations where your knowledge of what's right would be better voiced than pondered.

I hope this opinion is taken with the right spirit and no one sends me hate e-mail.

Theodore Roosevelt admonished, "Do what you can, with what you have, where you are." ∎

Simply by their nature, religious schools are not religiously diverse. If you attend a Catholic university, the students there will be mostly Catholic; the same is true for other religiously affiliated colleges. Students affiliated with particular religions choose to attend religious colleges because they desire an environment that will support and promote the practice of their faith. They go there because they feel that a university associated with their religion will best help them express themselves religiously. Of course, not everyone at a Christian university will be Christian. This is far from the truth. A percentage of students at any religious university will practice other religions—or no religion at all. What's important to note, however, is how welcome those from other faiths or those who choose not to practice religion feel at the religious school they attend and how accommodating the school is to the practice of other religions. Luther College is working on ways to accommodate non-Christian students on its campus.

The problem at Luther arose not with the administration, but with members of the student body, which brings us back to the first point we raised regarding diversity at religious colleges and universities: Just because the administration takes measures to support diversity doesn't mean that the entire student body will exhibit the same support or understanding.

STUDENT OPINION DIVIDED OVER LUTHER INTER-FAITH ROOM
By Matt Becker

CHIPS (Decoran, Iowa) 03/11/98

A proposed inter-faith room in Larsen Hall has raised many questions and triggered debate among the Luther community.

As explained in a written proposal from President of the Church Council Jenise Chalfant ('98) and Student Body President Sarah Tofte ('99), the inter-faith room would be a bare dorm room that could be used for worship, prayer or meditation by Christian or non-Christian students.

As written in the proposal, the special needs of non-Christian worshipers include a clean, quiet room where shoes cannot be worn and where food and drink are not allowed. Currently such a worship space is not available.

According to Student Senate Vice President Saqib Nadeem ('98), the room is needed to accommodate Luther's non-Christian students, many of whom are international students like himself.

More than 40 students from non-Christian backgrounds attend Luther this year.

"We have needs that aren't being fulfilled," said Nadeem. "I'm a Muslim and it's not really possible to worship anyplace else."

Nadeem also stressed the importance of accepting all the different aspects of diversity in international students.

"When prospective students come to our schools and recruit they say, "We welcome diversity." If you want to have diversity you have to accept all the diversity, not just someone's color," said Nadeem.

Student Senate voted on the proposal Wednesday. Community Assembly will discuss the issue March 10 and vote on the proposal April 14.

Even if Community Assembly passes the plan, President Jeffrey Baker and Dean of the College David Anderson will make the final approval decision.

The cost of the room would be equal to the room and board fees lost by using a dorm room, either $7400 for a double or $4300 for a single room.

Opposition to the room has developed.

"The room would be a welcoming act to international students, but it goes too far," said junior Doug Carlson. "Students know this is a Christian college when they come here. I wouldn't expect a college of another faith to provide me with a place to worship."

An inter-faith room is not in agreement with Luther's purpose as a college affiliated with the Lutheran church, said Carlson.

"It goes too far when we're sanctioning it, providing space for it, money for it. Will candles and incense be allowed? Also, will pagan or occult ceremonies be allowed in the room?"

That remains to be seen, said Chalfant.

"The room was designed with major world religions in mind," said Chalfant, "but I don't know how we could say you can use the room for this, this and this. That's one we're going to have to deal with."

It is also not clear who would be in charge of maintaining the room, said Martinsen.

An open forum will take place April 2 to discuss concerns and questions about the inter-faith, said Chalfant. Also, a group of students may be assembled to gather student opinion on the subject to bring before the church council and congregation, said Chalfant.

The issue raises many questions, said junior Johnna Hayward, such as how do Lutheran beliefs coincide with an interfaith room?

"If we believe that all gods are equal, where does Jesus Christ fit in?" asked Hayward. "Are we a good Christian college because we accept all people, or because we teach Christ?" ■

As we mentioned before, much of academia is still considered to be an " 'ole boys" network, and religious universities fair no better in this analysis. Although in the student body the number of women and men are equal, some women—like those at Marquette—decry a lack of equal treatment when it comes to hiring and promotion. The statistics given in the next article seem to support this claim.

AFTER 90 YEARS, MARQUETTE U. TREATMENT OF WOMEN LAGS

By Dave Young

THE MARQUETTE TRIBUNE (Milwaukee, Wis.) 03/03/1999

March is Women's History Month, and since Marquette was the first Jesuit university to admit women, women have a unusual history at the school.

In 1909, Daisy Grace Wolcott became the first woman to receive a degree from Marquette.

In 1982, Marquette's then-Dean of Students, Linda Kuk, said the university was and always will be male-dominated. Kuk told the Marquette Tribune at the time about her perception of the place of women at Marquette.

"(Marquette's) emphasis has been predominately male for 100 years, and it will continue to be like that," she said. "We have been here for a long time, but we haven't made our mark."

While more women now attend Marquette than men, many feel there is still much room to improve women's lots at the university.

Cathleen Morris, associate dean of students, said Marquette is still male-dominated.

Morris said the biggest problem is that only four of the 25 members of the Board of Trustees are women. The board deals with many issues affecting students, including tuition and other policy changes such as Campus Beautification.

"Since, in the general student population, there are more women than men," Morris said, "there is a representation problem (in the board)."

Male domination is also reflected in the faculty population. "Like many institutions around the country, Marquette has fewer women administrators and faculty," said Diane Hoeveler, professor of English and coordinator of the Women's Studies program.

"It has been very difficult for women to move up through the ranks here. For instance, not until 1999 was there a female full professor in the English department." Hoeveler was just promoted to full professor.

There are 386 male full-time professors and 167 female full-time professors. There are 241 male part-time professors and 169 female part-time professors. "There are a relatively smaller number of women on the College of Business Administration staff than comparable universities," Smiley said.

As of fall 1998, there were 5,512 females and 5,242 male undergraduate, graduate and pre-professional program students. Female/male ratios are being compiled for the spring 1999 semester.

Female students said the male/female faculty ratio has not negatively affected their experiences at Marquette.

"I've never been discriminated against in a class by my professors because I'm female," said Becky Cointin, a senior majoring in mathematics. "Even though I'm in a male-dominated major, there are still more women than men in my classes."

"I hadn't really noticed anything like that (male domination)," junior Patrick Van Dyke said. "Women are doing fine here at Marquette."

Caroline Goyette, an English graduate student, said that while she thinks more women than men are in the English programs, she would not consider it dominated by a particular sex.

"I haven't really noticed an unequal distribution," Goyette said. "I think it would be nice if it were more split down the middle. I think it would be nice to get (more of) both perspectives. I don't think it presents itself as a problem." ∎

Can you imagine a topic more controversial than homosexuality at a religious school? There probably isn't one. While many religious colleges are making efforts to promote tolerance and understanding—the Pride Week during which Greg Louganis spoke at Boston College is a case in point—most observers, like the editors of *The DePaulia*, still find student reaction to homosexuality to be negative. Again, it goes to show that administrative policies and outreach may not necessarily affect student beliefs and actions.

EDITORIAL: RELIGION VS. SEXUALITY AT DePAUL

Staff Editorial

THE DEPAULIA (Chicago, Ill.) 04/24/1998

It has come to our attention that some members of the DePaul community think that due to the Catholic nature of the university, issues concerning the gay community have no place on the front page of the DePaulia.

The picture that ran on last week's front page of the DePaulia, which showed two men kissing next to two women kissing, was intended to inform the community about Pride Week. We have received numerous complaints about this picture, most of which center around the fact that DePaul, because it is a Catholic institution, should not condone or publicize gay interaction.

People forget that one of the most important tenets of Christianity is "Love thy neighbor." People don't have to agree with gay lifestyles, but everyone deserves the same amount of respect regardless of their sexual orientation.

We find it odd that last year when a picture of two heterosexual people kissing ran in Fallout, the DePaulia's literary supplement, we received no complaints. This picture was much larger than the picture that ran on last week's front page. The fact that so many people have protested last week's picture tells us that homophobia is alive and well at DePaul, which means that organizations such as Pride DePaul are definitely still needed at this university.

The "Queer Kiss In" was meant to desensitize the community so that the sight of two gay people kissing would not generate the usual "Oh my God" response. However, the complaints that this picture has generated tell us that people's attitudes regarding gay rights haven't changed much since the 1950s. ∎

Drinking

You might be surprised that problems with alcohol occur almost as frequently on religious college campuses as they do at other universities. A 1998 poll of St. Bonaventure University students by *The Bona Venture* showed that 70 percent consumed alcohol with the intention of becoming intoxicated—that's 18 percent higher than the national average found by a Harvard University study. On the campuses of religious colleges nationwide, security forces deal with the same problems with alcohol-related incidents that they do on other college campuses. The problem seems to be universal, and it seems to be growing. *The Lariat* from Baylor University reports on the disturbing increase in alcohol violations on their campus.

ALCOHOL PROBLEMS ABOUND AT BAYLOR U.

By Brittney Partridge

THE LARIAT (Waco, Texas) 11/03/1998

Already this year, Baylor has experienced increased difficulties involving the consumption of alcohol by minors, and unfortunately, other universities are encountering these same problems.

According to Chief Jim Doak of the Baylor Department of Public Safety, their officers received a number of party calls this past weekend and issued five minor in possession charges in and around the campus area. As of Oct. 31, Baylor Police have issued 29 MIP's already this year, compared with 28 issued last school year.

"We've already gone past what we did all of last year, so you can only imagine what lies in store during the big months of the spring," Doak said. "It's not something that is unique to Baylor. It's definitely a common problem at all the other universities as well. We're just seeing an increase in student involvement and irresponsible drinking patterns."

Other universities are indeed experiencing problems with alcohol consumption among their students. According to the Phoenix House, a national non-profit substance abuse organization, America's 12,000,000 college students drink 430,000,000 gallons of alcohol each year.

Captain Nick Doran of the Southern Methodist University Department of Public Safety said SMU has experienced some increase in alcohol related problems this year. No specific statistics were available at this time.

"It is probably no different here than at most schools," Doran said. "We don't allow drinking on campus in public places, and a lot of our students are caught with booze and beer, and a lot of them with phony identification cards. We have a zero-tolerance policy for alcohol violations, and we are enforcing it as best we can this year."

Texas Christian University, on the other hand, has not seen an evident increase in alcohol consumption on their campus this year.

"We haven't had many problems with drinking on campus this year, and I haven't noted a real increase," Assistant Chief J. C. Williams of the TCU Police Department said. "The majority of the MIP's that have been issued are from the Fort Worth Police Department."

The TCU Alcohol and Drug Education Center reported that 45.9 percent of their students admitted to having five or more drinks in one sitting, which is called binge drinking, in the previous two weeks before the survey, given earlier this year.

Unfortunately, binge drinking has become the norm on many college campuses today, and experts estimate that thousands of students die from excessive drinking each year.

"There's not much you can do except deal with it head on," Doak said. "There's just no advantage to drinking underage."

Amanda Gunter, a Midland freshman, said she believes alcohol is definitely a problem at Baylor, but she has not encountered any problems with it herself.

"I have a problem with people who go out and drink just to get drunk," Gunter said. "In college, the majority of the people don't drink responsibly. I think that the consequences of drinking underage far outweigh the benefits."

Gunter said although Baylor has experienced an increase in drinking problems, she believes other campuses probably have much more severe alcohol problems. ■

Depending on the religious college you attend, you'll be faced with varying alcohol policies, varying ways of combating the problem of alcohol abuse, and varying methods of punishment for infractions. Some religious schools, like Brigham Young University, forbid the consumption of alcohol; at BYU, drinking is considered a breach of the honor code. As you've just read, Southern Methodist University doesn't allow drinking on campus in public places and professes "zero tolerance" regulations for rule-breakers. Other universities are taking a softer approach to dealing with student alcohol problems. At Marquette University, resident assistants use Alcohol 101, an interactive CD-ROM designed by the University of Illinois, to really bring home the consequences of alcohol abuse. And Boston College's novel approach, as *The Heights* reports, shows students just how wasteful alcohol can be.

SPILLING DRINKS FOR COMMUNITY SERVICE AT BOSTON COLLEGE

By Adam Smith

THE HEIGHTS (Chestnut Hill, Mass.) 02/18/1998

The stage is set for drama to build, as under-age students are caught with alcohol on the Boston College campus. It is reminiscent of a scene from the Untouchables, when the police would raid a warehouse owned by Al Capone for massive amounts of bootleg alcohol.

Although prohibition is over, police still confiscate large quantities of alcohol on a frequent basis. An immense closet in Rubenstein Hall houses a variety of seized beverages including kegs, a multitude of beer brands, filled coolers and numerous types of hard alcohol. Bottles half opened and new ones, with the price tag still on them, are kept here.

Despite common rumors that police throw parties with this alcohol, Police Chief Robert A. Morse states, "It is routine everywhere that alcohol is dumped." At BC this disposal is performed as part of community service done at the BC Police Department (BCPD), which also includes cleaning squad cars.

This day, as part of his 20 hours of community service, a student is dumping out the contraband alcohol. After being written up three times, twice for alcohol, he was assigned by Dean Michael D. Ryan to the Police Department to perform his services to the community. He had already been doing it for an hour, and so far the task had not bothered him. However, he complains that it is strenuous lugging the heavy thirty packs of beer from the confiscation closet to the small locker room.

Morse said the community service of disposing of the alcohol is done about once a month, depending on the season, and occurs most frequently during the football season in the fall. Morse made it clear his officers do not specifically go out searching for underage students with alcohol. He said, "Alcohol by its nature draws you to the problem."

He also reaffirms that, "Every school is struggling with this issue." He tries not to be overly aggressive with the student body.

With the banning of central sources on campus (e.g., kegs and party-balls), along with more on-scene disposal, less alcohol has come into the department for the most part. That does not mean, however, that the problem has subsided. Morse stated, "The whole effort is to teach responsibility," not to necessarily go out and punish students.

When the alcohol is disposed of, the police donate the money received from can deposits to organizations such as the BC Campus School. In this way, Morse stated, "The bad could benefit someone else." He added, "Even though the law says twenty-one, we realize students are going to drink." Many perceive drinking as a right of passage in college. If done responsibly, one may never get in trouble. Thus the police realize this and try to deal with the problem accordingly.

The BCPD confronts underage drinking situations internally. Protective custody is one way they do this, which, by utilizing the infirmary, keeps outside authorities out of the problem. Morse points out that any offense committed could eventually end up on a record to which future employers would have access.

He feels this is a problem that needs to be dealt with publicly. "We try to make the community aware of alcohol issues in the student handbook," he stated.

When asked what his largest confiscation ever was, he said it was at a football game when someone in a compact car had 32 cases of beer in a vehicle. Although the driver was of age, Morse cited laws limiting the amount of alcohol you can transport without a liquor license for the cause of appropriation.

By utilizing BC students through the community service program, the police department hopes to illustrate the alcohol dilemma on campus. As community service workers dump thousands of dollars essentially down the drain, the BCPD want students to see the waste produced by this act.

Morse remarked about one last aspect of this issue. "There is only one person benefiting out of this, and that's the liquor stores," he said. That is unequivocally true, and until one realizes the severity of the problem, it cannot be dealt with correctly. ∎

Activism is alive and well on the campuses of religious schools nationwide. Because of the emphasis on service at many of their schools, religious school students are actively involved with both local and international causes. As we saw in the section on volunteering earlier in this chapter, these students work not only with individuals but also with organizations both small and large to make the world a better place. In fact, Marquette University has made *Mother Jones* magazine's list of Top 10 Activist Schools two years in a row, a distinction few schools can claim.

MARQUETTE AMONG MOST ACTIVIST CAMPUSES
By Brian Salgado

THE MARQUETTE TRIBUNE (Milwaukee, Wis.) 09/09/1998

For the third time in five years, Marquette University is ranked on a list of America's top 10 activist schools. This year, Marquette is ranked ninth on the list.

Mother Jones, an investigative magazine based in San Francisco, compiled the annual list, which was published in its September/October issue. The magazine polled 21 organizations, including the Center for Campus Organizing and Habitat for Humanity International, to create the list. These organizations were asked which schools take action, and where the action has the greatest effect.

University of North Carolina, University of Wisconsin-Madison, who has made the list all five years, and Marquette are the only schools from this year's list to make a repeat appearance in the top 10.

"Service provides an opportunity to take what students learn in the classroom and apply it to life," said the Rev. Pat Dorsey, assistant director of University Ministry. "They can get in touch with their own needs and desires."

Among the activities that drew the most attention toward Marquette was Hunger Clean-Up, a campus-wide service project in which over 2,000 students, faculty and staff participated last April, raising approximately $16,000 for five social service agencies in the Milwaukee area.

Dorsey said he believes that, through service, students have an opportunity "to proclaim the hallmark of our identity as a Jesuit institution."

Richard Reynolds, reporter for Mother Jones and compiler of the top 10 activist list for the five years of its existence, was especially impressed with Marquette's reputation of staying with the community surrounding its campus.

"A couple of schools are involved in international issues," Reynolds said. "A lot of the action taken (by Marquette) is closer to home."

Junior Susan Reed, president of Students for Life, said she is proud her name has become one and the same with student activism. "I have always been interested in service," Reed said. "It has become a part of my identity."

Aside from participating in Hunger Cleanup, Reed also participates in MUCAP, the Marquette University Community Action Program. This program is volunteer-run and gives students the opportunity to volunteer their energy and time in the neighborhood and feel comfortable while living around Milwaukee.

Reed also said the service opportunities at Marquette help students who are scared by its surrounding neighborhood to "see those who are affected by social injustices."

Service opportunities such as these help to give a student a better understanding of urban issues, she said.

Reed worked with Dorsey to launch the International Marquette Action Program. IMAP is a weeks-long service project that takes place in Kingston, Jamaica.

There are five students and two professors from the School of Dentistry in Kingston helping develop a new dental plan for the community.

"Ample opportunities have turned into reality, both in the city, nation, and internationally," Dorsey said. ■

Supporting a good cause is one thing; protesting against administration policies is quite another, especially at a religious school. Protesting is probably the last thing you'd expect to find religious school students doing, especially those who attend schools with more conservative philosophies. But some religious school students aren't afraid of a little dissent. Students at BYU recently showed that they were willing to confront church policy for the sake of great works of art.

PROTEST PROVES BYU HAS MORE THAN ONE OPINION ABOUT ART

By Kelleigh Cole & Kristen Sonne

THE DAILY UNIVERSE (Provo, Utah) 10/31/1997

"Don't ban Rodin, don't ban Rodin," chanted a group of students Thursday morning.

More than 200 students rallied outside the Abraham Smoot Administration Building at 11 a.m. Thursday to express their views on the decision of the administration and the Museum of Art to remove four sculptures from BYU's display of "The Hands of Rodin, a tribute to B. Gerald Cantor."

Students gathered near the Brigham Young statue chanting and waving signs. Charles Sones, a junior from Mississippi majoring in secondary education, held a sign that read, "Let John Preach," in reference to a sculpture of John the Baptist that was pulled.

"I think the administration needs to know the views of the students, especially the arts and the humanities students. They want to see these sculptures," said Carrie Lewis, a junior humanities major from Afton,

Wyoming. "We see them in books, we see them on slides, and if they are here on our campus, we want to see them in real life because there's a big difference between a picture and seeing the real thing."

On the other hand, an art student and museum worker said she thinks the administration made the correct decision.

"For me, I think BYU made the right decision, although I'd really like to see the pieces in the museum," said Mandi Mauldlin, a senior majoring in art from Lancester, Calif. "I also understand the standpoint of the museum, because it is part of BYU, which is part of The Church they have to make decisions that reflect the standards of The Church, so I can understand it that way."

"We have multiple audiences that we have to pay attention to," said Academic Vice President Alan Wilkins. "I can understand how people would have differing opinions about what should or should not be in the art museum; that's part of what art is about. There are different opinions about any work of art and so the kinds of criteria have to do with balancing community values and judging what is appropriate for this entire community."

The appropriateness for the community is not definite because the community encompasses a university, public schools and residents.

Wilkins said one audience was the 60,000 school children who have visited the museum during the past 10 months. However, Rogan Ferguson, a junior majoring in art from Great Falls, Mont. said there is a way to accommodate children and other audiences.

"If it is not appropriate for children, we could put it into a room where at certain hours, that part of the exhibit would be open," Ferguson said. "That way it would be open for people who specifically want to view those pieces without having to fear that school children who might be on a field trip may see those pieces."

The administration removed "The Kiss" because administration felt that "nude males and females who are engaged in lovemaking represent a sacred and private kind of expression, that we do hallow in ways that I think the world at large doesn't see. I think it's a beautiful sculpture," Bartlett said.

"Saint John the Baptist Preaching," a nude depiction of the prophet was removed because of LDS Church principles.

"In our reverence for prophets, the fact that we have a living prophet, makes it difficult for us to depict prophets naked," Bartlett said.

"Monument to Balzac" was taken out of the museum as well. He said the sculpture in the traveling exhibit is not the same one that is usually thought of.

"It is a preliminary study that was done and the figure is nude and very muscular and strong," Bartlett said. "There is more than a subtle suggestion he is engaged in an act that we would not want to discuss or to present to our family."

The fourth sculpture, "The Prodigal Son," is a more monumental figure. It is of a figure clothed in robes "with the genital area that is unusually prominent," Bartlett said.

"In an environment of mutual respect and open dialogue, we welcome further comment from students and faculty on this issue. Letters received by *The Daily Universe*, the Museum of Art, and by e-mail will be read and considered by members of the administration," according to a campus memorandum distributed at the protest. ■

Student Services

As with other colleges and universities, religious schools for the most part provide excellent services for all types of students. Like any college, there are strengths and weaknesses, and different students with different needs will not always be happy with the services they find on campus. But overall, the services you will find on the campuses of religious schools will be outstanding.

Administrators at religious schools want you to leave campus with a great job in hand. To this end, fantastic career centers are a part of life on religious college campuses nationwide. At Texas Christian University's Career Services center, students are wisely encouraged to use multiple techniques to ensure a job that best matches their goals and talents.

NETWORKING, CAREER CENTER AND INTERNET ALL A PART OF SUCCESSFUL JOB SEARCHES AT TCU

By Jeri Petersen

DAILY SKIFF (Fort Worth, Texas) 02/02/1999

Job search sites on the Internet often lead students to believe they can point-and-click their way to the perfect job.

But Melissa White, assistant director of Career Services at Texas Christian University, said it's not quite that simple, even though these services can be an effective way to research the job market.

White said the Internet has become a popular way to look for a job, but that the most effective way is still networking.

"Only 15 percent of jobs offered anywhere are listed on the Web," she said. "Most people find jobs through someone they know. Networking will never change, but the way we go about it does. At Career Services, we do encourage students to use the Internet, but not as their only resource."

John Olsen, who received an MBA from the M.J. Neeley School of Business in 1997, said he posted his resume on the Internet, but ultimately got a job through a graduate school contact.

"I used the Internet service through the career center and got an on-campus interview, although it didn't result in a job offer," he said. "I also got calls from Blockbuster about the resume I posted myself, but we weren't a good match. The Web is a good starting place, though."

Julie Markus, a 1997 graduate, said she found her job through Career Services.

"I didn't use the Internet for my job search, but I use it now in my job as a recruiter."

Markus said her employer recruits heavily from the Web. The company advertises on reliable sites and uses resume matches to hire computer professionals, she said.

"Internet job searches can be extremely helpful if you know exactly what you want and where to look for it," she said.

Most sites offer free services for job-seekers, although some charge a fee for posting a resume.

"I always discourage use of any site that charges, especially when there are so many good free services out there," White said. "In the first place, the student doesn't know what he or she is paying for. In addition, there is no guarantee the student will get anything in return."

White said the career center's Internet job search offers some advantages over searches students do on their own. First, students don't pay anything for the service. Second, Career Services screens employers, so when students arrange an interview, they know the employer is legitimate.

Career Services offers many resources in addition to Internet job searches. Counselors teach students how to compose a resume, cultivate networking sources and interview successfully.

"I would like to see students come in here as soon as they get to TCU," White said. "We can actually help students figure out what they want to do by exploring career paths at the beginning of their college experience."

Haley Dugas, a marketing major who will graduate in May, said she did just that.

"I went in to the Career Center my sophomore year and filled out my resume," she said. "I have gotten calls for interviews all along, but I wasn't really interested then. Now that I'm about to graduate, I have some interviews scheduled through the center." ∎

Campus health services are met with varying degrees of student approval at religious schools—as at any other school. While there are instances of poor or limited services, most, like the aid given to pregnant students at Villanova, are admirable.

VILLANOVA U. ASSISTS PREGNANT STUDENTS

By Leah Urbaniak

THE VILLANOVAN (Villanova, Penn.) 04/15/1998

The University gives a tremendous amount of support to pregnant students.

The University does not only offer aid, which ranges from medical to emotional assistance. It also accommodates students in housing, day care and scheduling to ease the trauma of perhaps one the most devastating situations a college student can experience.

The Crisis Pregnancy Forum that took place on March 25 made it evident that although most students are unaware of the resources on campus, there is a wealth of people willing to help.

The presence of the panelists served as a reminder of the support that exists both on campus and in the surrounding community.

The process of how the Villanova community offers help during and after a pregnancy was traced from day one as a means of evaluating our resources.

When a student goes to the Health Center fearing she is pregnant, the first objective is to confirm it. The Health Center offers confidential pregnancy tests.

Acknowledging that many in college do not want to have a child, the next step is to guide the student to seek help in this time of crisis. The Counseling Center welcomes her and the father with emotional support.

One of the most comforting options offered by the Counseling Center is hosting a joint session during which the student can inform her parents of her pregnancy with a counselor present.

The goal is to ease the student's strain, since one of her biggest fears will be telling her parents she is pregnant.

Many times, Campus Ministry deals with students who are afraid to look for help because they do not want it put on their record.

In response, Campus Ministry locates outside help for the students and even goes so far as to accompany students on visits to the doctor.

The University is equally accommodating to the academic life of pregnant college women and students with children.

Residence Life recognizes that most pregnant college women are concerned with privacy and therefore will facilitate a move to a single room or work with local realtors to find housing.

Byrnes noted there are approximately a dozen local families who have offered their homes as a housing option for pregnant students.

Villanova also allows pregnant women to drop down to part-time status while continuing to live on campus.

Byrnes pointed out the registration process can often ease the burden of child care if classes can be scheduled around day care.

Although the University does not have its own day care facility, a quarter-mile away, Rosemont College has an on-site day care that can be used by Villanova.

Overall, the consensus among the panelists is that no one seeking help with a pregnancy on this campus will be turned away.

This greatly pleased Foster.

"[Villanova is] a good example of what a school should be like right off the bat," she said. ∎

Fun Stuff

Students at religious schools want you to know that they're a lot of fun too! Don't think that everyone's life at a religious school is completely consumed by theological studies and activities. That's far from the truth. There are just as many chances for you to let your hair down and have a good time at religious schools as there are at any other kind of school. Festivals, concerts, and naked soccer are just some of the activities enjoyed by religious schools students.

DePAUL FEST DRAWS RECORD ATTENDANCE

By Mark McCarrell

THE DEPAULIA (Chicago, Ill.) 05/22/1998

The 1998 Fest was "well worth the investment," and "one of the best turnouts we've ever had," said staff advisor Darryl Arrington of the DePaul Activities Board.

Friday, DAB helped DePaul students and friends celebrate the end of the academic year by sponsoring the Fest at Wish Field on West Belden Avenue.

In its second year at the multi-sports field, over 3,000 people attended.

The day started at 3 p.m. as the band Lower Still took the stage for the small audience that came early.

Later, as more people filtered onto the field, Reign Dog performed.

La Querida D'Coretz pumped the crowd that was anticipating the headlining act, hip-hop group De La Soul.

As bands played, attendees purchased food supplied by area businesses and participated in amusement activities provided by student organizations, including a velcro wall sponsored by the Residence Hall Council, a fast-pitch baseball booth sponsored by Phi Kappa Theta fraternity and body painting by Delta Zeta sorority.

DePaul radio station WRDP had a table at which they sold posters and gave away tapes and compact discs. Alpha

Brett Fagan/*The Bona Venture*

Psi Lambda, a co-ed fraternity, had a raffle for Cubs tickets.

Students had mostly positive reactions to the performers:

"I really liked Lower Still," said Kari Levy. "Reign Dog sounded good too."

"The first couple of bands I really didn't listen to, but De La Soul was pretty good," said Lawrence Chapa.

The beer garden was another part of this year's Fest activities.

According to Arrington, the beer garden was different from years past.

"It was located further away from the stage and became a minor focus."

In addition Arrington said there was a lower beer garden attendance because of the new campus alcohol policy requiring two forms of identification.

Some students felt beer wasn't essential for enjoying the Fest while others felt the beer garden was too small. "I felt all caged up," said John Nicholson.

Other students less concerned with the beer garden saw the Fest as symbolic for the community.

"I think its great how this event brings the university community together," said Levy. ■

MIGHTY MIGHTY BOSSTONES COMING TO ST. MICHAEL'S

By Alethea Renzi

THE DEFENDER (Colchester, Vt.) 02/26/1999

The Student Association has confirmed that The Mighty Mighty Bosstones will perform at St. Michael's Ross Sports Center March 13.

Led by frontman Dicky Barrett, the Bosstones have been a staple in the Boston music scene since 1985. They received national prominence with the number one single "Impression That I Get" from the album "Let's Face It" in 1997. The album had two other major hits the next year with "Royal Oil" and "The Rascal King."

As special events directors for the SA, senior Tom Michaels and sophomore Dan DiTullio are responsible for organizing campus concerts and P-Day.

Michaels says that booking the spring concert was especially tough this year, due to the fact that there were only four dates all semester that Ross was available.

"It was a matter of matching up the dates and prices for available bands," Michaels says.

Michaels said he and DiTullio got the idea to have the Bosstones after they held a discussion in The Defender Online chatroom last November. They put in a bid on Jan. 25 for the band, which was accepted Feb. 8

"Tom and Dan put an amazing amount of hours trying to get the best band possible to come to St. Mike's. It's going to be one of the best shows we've had in the past few years," Lael Croteau, secretary of programming says.

The band, aside from Barrett, includes Kevin Lenear and Tim Burton on saxophone, Joe Sirois on drums, Dennis Brockenborough on trombone, Nate Albert on guitar, Joe Gittleman on bass, and Ben Carr, the band's "Bosstone."

"I think it's cool that we're finally going to get a big band here. It's going to be a lot of fun," sophomore Julie McIntosh says.

"Frankly, I would be surprised to see them come. I've heard plenty of rumors of great, big-named bands that we have sought and they never showed," junior Sam Dixon says.

The Bosstones will provide its own opening act, which is currently unknown. ∎

NAKED SOCCER AT LUTHER COLLEGE NOT CONDONED BY ADMINISTRATION

By Seth Ansorge

CHIPS (Decoran, Iowa) 05/08/1998

With graduation only weeks away, President Baker and Ann Highum, vice president and dean of student affairs, have issued a statement about their plans to curtail the "tradition" of naked soccer. The statement concludes, "We will not condone nude soccer on the Luther campus."

During senior week last year, six students were fined for their participation in naked soccer, and one, Mircad Zahirovic ('99) was arrested. This year, the administration is hoping to stop the "tradition"before it starts.

"We don't want this to turn into a confrontation like last year. The transition to graduation ought to be a positive one." said Baker.

Not included in the statement are the consequences for students if they participate this year. Highum was unable to comment fully at the time of the interview, yet she did note that anyone participating in naked activities on campus will not be denied their diplomas, despite rumors to the contrary.

Security Services Supervisor Jim Ahles also declined comment on what actions will be taken against participants.

Last year, publicity of the event soared after the Cedar Rapids Gazette became aware of naked soccer through the police arrest record of Zahirovic, and printed a front-page story. The next day, the Associated Press picked up the story and the media blitz began.

According to Jerry Johnson, director of public information, approximately 1,200 newspapers, magazines, radio stations and television stations across the nation (including Rolling Stone) covered the event.

Steven Shank ('98), who was fined $90 for indecent exposure, remembers being "shocked" when he heard that his name had been on the radio in northwest Iowa two weeks after the event. News of naked soccer also went international, as Johnson received e-mails from Germany, Austria, France and Great Britain.

Johnson explained the media hype.

"Every year around spring time, editors from newspapers across the country look for a crazy, college prank story dealing with graduation. Last year was our turn. Naked soccer at Luther College is an editor's dream: there is a Christian institution, lots of naked people, and an arrest of one student. In the P.R. world, that's a home run," said Johnson.

Highum said she wishes Luther could have avoided all the publicity, but also knows such an event will naturally draw a lot of media attention. She expressed concern about the publicity, which she views as negative.

"I don't think [naked soccer] has a place at Luther," said Highum. "It is not consistent with the image I want for Luther, and I feel that many students agree with that."

Johnson, however, feels the publicity was not detrimental to Luther's image.

"The name 'Luther College' often conveys an image of a conservative, Christian, Midwestern school that might not be so attractive to prospective 18 year olds. The publicity we received helped dispel that image," said Johnson.

"Last year was not a P.R. nightmare or a crisis. Yes, it was a busy time, but a crisis means you incur damage. Damage for the Luther's institutional image was low. We got more national and international name recognition than at any other point in my 11 years here," said Johnson.

Students have responded in different ways to the administration's crack-down on naked soccer. Kirsten Setterlund ('98) offered another idea. "Why don't people start their own tradition?

"Except this time, don't tell everyone about it. This one has gotten out of hand." ∎

New York—*Continued*
Manhattan College
Mirrer Yeshiva
Niagara University
Practical Bible College
St. Bonaventure University
St. John Fisher College
St. John's University

North Carolina
Brevard College
Campbell University
Chowan College
Elon College
Gardner-Webb University
Lenoir-Rhyne College
Meredith College
Peace College
Pfeiffer University
Piedmont Baptist College
Queens College

North Dakota
Trinity Bible College
University of Mary

Ohio
Ashland University
Baldwin-Wallace College
Capital University
Cincinnati Bible College and Seminary
College of Mount St. Joseph
Franciscan University of Steubenville
John Carroll University
University of Dayton
The University of Findlay
Walsh University
Xavier University

Oklahoma
Mid-America Bible College
Oklahoma City University
Oral Roberts University
Southern Nazarene University
University of Tulsa

Oregon
Cascade College
Eugene Bible College
Linfield College
Multnomah Bible College and Biblical Seminary
Northwest Christian College
University of Portland

Pennsylvania
Baptist Bible College of Pennsylvania
Beaver College
Cabrini College
Chestnut Hill College
College Misericordia
Duquesne University
Eastern College
Gannon University
Gwynedd-Mercy College
Immaculata College
Lancaster Bible College
La Roche College
La Salle University
Marywood University
Philadelphia College of Bible
St. Charles Borromeo Seminary, Overbrook
Saint Francis College
Saint Joseph's University
University of Scranton
Valley Forge Christian College
Villanova University

Puerto Rico
Pontifical Catholic University of Puerto Rico
University of the Sacred Heart

Rhode Island
Salve Regina University

South Carolina
Charleston Southern University
Columbia International University
North Greenville College

South Dakota
Presentation College

Tennessee
Aquinas College
Belmont University
Christian Brothers University
Free Will Baptist Bible College
Johnson Bible College
Martin Methodist College
Trevecca Nazarene University
Tusculum College

Texas
Abilene Christian University
Amber University
Baylor University
The Criswell College

Dallas Baptist University
Dallas Christian College
David Lipscomb University
Hardin-Simmons University
Houston Baptist University
Our Lady of the Lake University of San Antonio
St. Edward's University
St. Mary's University of San Antonio
Southern Methodist University
Southwestern Assemblies of God University
Texas Christian University
Texas Wesleyan University
University of Mary Hardin-Baylor
University of St. Thomas
University of the Incarnate Word
Wayland Baptist University

Utah
Brigham Young University

Vermont
Saint Michael's College

Virginia
Averett College
Liberty University
Lynchburg College
Marymount University
Shenandoah University

Washington
Gonzaga University
Northwest College
Pacific Lutheran University
Saint Martin's College
Seattle Pacific University
Seattle University
Walla Walla College

West Virginia
Appalachian Bible College
Ohio Valley College
West Virginia Wesleyan College
Wheeling Jesuit University

Wisconsin
Cardinal Stritch University
Carthage College
Edgewood College
Maranatha Baptist Bible College
Marian College of Fond du Lac
Marquette University
Viterbo College

Two Year Schools

Arizona
Arizona Western College
Glendale Community College
Mesa County Community College
Pima Community College

California
City College of San Francisco
Fashion Institute of Design and
    Merchandising
Santa Monica College

Colorado
Bel-Rea Institute of Animal Technology
Colorado Community College and
    Occupational Education System
Colorado Mountain College

Connecticut
Briarwood College
International College of Hospitality
    Management
Mitchell College

Florida
Art Institute of Fort Lauderdale
Florida Community College
International Fine Arts College
Miami-Dade Community College

Georgia
Bauder College

Illinois
Cooking and Hospitality Institute of
    Chicago
Lincoln College
Lincoln College at Normal
MacCormac College
Morrison Institute of Technology
Northwestern Business College

Indiana
Holy Cross College
Indiana Business College

Kansas
Cowley County Community College
Independence Community College

Massachusetts
Dean College
Fisher College Boston
Franklin Institute of Boston

Massachusetts Communication College
Mount Ida College
Newbury College

Maryland
Baltimore International College

Minnesota
College of St. Catherine-Minneapolis

Missouri
Wayne County Community College

New Hampshire
Hesser College

IN THIS CHAPTER

Albuquerque Technical Vocational Institute
Borough of Manhattan Community College
City College of San Francisco
Cowley County Community College
Florida Community College
Glendale Community College
Independence Community College
Linn-Benton Community College
Mesa County Community College
San Jacinto College
Seattle Central Community College

McIntosh College
New Hampshire Technical Institute
White Pines College

New Jersey
Atlantic Cape Community College
Berkeley College
DeVry Institute
Middlesex County College

New Mexico
Albuquerque Technical Vocational Institute
New Mexico Military Institute

New York
American Academy of Dramatic Arts
Borough of Manhattan Community College
Finger Lakes Community College
Globe Institute of Technology

Maria College
Monroe College, Bronx
New York College for Wholistic Health
    Education & Research
Paul Smiths College of Arts and Sciences
Sage Junior College of Albany
State University of New York College of
    Agriculture and Technology at
    Morrisville
State University of New York College of
    Environmental Science and Forestry,
    Ranger School
State University of New York College of
    Technology at Canton
State University of New York College of
    Technology at Delhi

Oregon
Linn-Benton Community College

Pennsylvania
The Art Institute of Philadelphia
Bradley Academy for the Visual Arts
Central Pennsylvania Business School
Community College of Allegheny County
Harcum College
Manor Junior College
Pennsylvania College of Technology
Restaurant School
Valley Forge Military College
Allentown Business School

South Carolina
Spartanburg Methodist College

Texas
The Art Institute of Dallas
Art Institute of Houston
San Jacinto College

Vermont
Vermont Technical College

Washington
Centralia College
Green River Community College
Seattle Central Community College

West Virginia
Potomac State College of West Virginia
    University

Two Year Schools

Two-year schools are defined here as community colleges, junior colleges, and vocational-technical schools, which focus on either career preparation and certification or liberal arts and sciences education with an eye toward transferring to a four-year school. Students who complete the liberal arts and sciences program are awarded an associate's degree. Although some four-year schools do offer two-year associate's degrees, they are not included in this chapter; the schools here only focus on two-year programs.

Most, but not all, are public institutions that receive the majority of their funding from local, state, and federal sources. Most have "open door" enrollment, which means that you'll have to fulfill very few requirements for admission. Many give priority in admissions decisions to students from the communities they serve, but that doesn't mean that only the "locals" will go to two-year schools. In fact, you'll find a large population of international students at two-year institutions.

If you decide to attend a two-year school, expect flexible course scheduling. Two-year colleges are known for accommodating students with all kinds of outside commitments. You'll be able to take classes at all hours, including on the weekends. In fact, some two-year schools also have distance learning opportunities, where you can work toward a degree in your home via videotaped courses or courses on the Internet. Expect a diverse student body—you'll find married students, students with kids, older students, part-time students, and students of all races and religions. Expect the focus to be on you, your future, and your career. Since you'll only have two years to prepare for your degree or certification, you'll need to decide on a course of study fairly early on. Of course, this "what-are-you-going-to-do-next?" pressure will often get overwhelming. Luckily, you can rely on intense counseling to help you figure all of this out.

What makes a two-year school different from the rest? Their intense focus on preparing you with the job or study skills that you need to succeed in the future. Your success is very important to them. That's why classes are flexible and small. That's why career placement facilities are top-notch and placement rate data are a big deal. It's why two-year schools fight to get their credits accepted at four-year schools. If you attend a two-year school for career preparation or certification, you will leave with an identifiable skill set that you can take right to the workplace—and you may even graduate with a job in hand. If you complete a two-year program with a liberal arts and sciences focus, you'll leave not only with an associate's degree but also proven study skills that you can use in further education if and when you choose to pursue it.

Some of you may think that

attending a two-year school comes with a certain stigma. Let's talk about some of the myths surrounding two-year schools.

- A two-year college won't get me anywhere in life. If I want a good job making good money, I have to get a four-year degree.
- If I don't think college is right for me, going to a two-year school won't be any different than going to a four-year college.
- Because there aren't many extracurricular activities, I won't learn anything outside the classroom; my college experience will be limited to classwork.

First and foremost, if you go to a two-year college, you'll be trained for a great job upon graduating, especially if you enroll in career preparation coursework. Of the ten occupations with the *fastest* predicted employment growth from 1996-2006 (according to Bureau of Labor Statistics data), you can get training for seven at a two-year college: computer support and technicians, personal and home care aides, home health aides, medical assistants, desktop publishing specialists, physical and corrective therapy assistants and aides, and occupational therapy assistants and aides. The same is also true for six of the ten occupations with the *largest* predicted job growth from 1996–2006: registered nurses, truck drivers, home health aides, teacher aides, nursing aides, and receptionists.

Even if you think college life isn't for you, you still might want to check out the programs offered by two-year schools. Many find

two-year schools a great way to ease into the college experience. You can attend classes part time—in fact, over 64 percent of community college students are part-time students (defined as those who take fewer than 12 credit hours)—and work your way up from there. And, as we said before, they are really focused on you; two-year schools are known both for high-quality instruction by caring professors and for intensive counseling to help you choose a major and a career. If you think a four-year college might be in your future, two-year schools can help you get there—and get a bachelor's degree.

Finally, if getting involved in extracurricular activities or sports is important to you, you'll find ample opportunities to do so at a two-year school, (although if you want to go Greek you'll need to go somewhere else). Most important for your extracurricular life, however, will be the education you'll get from your exposure to students from all walks of life. Think of a two-year school as a microcosm of the world at large. If you look at it that way, you can only imagine what you'll be able to learn from the diversity of the students around you (and how much better is that than some chess club?)

Because two-year schools enroll students from all walks of life, it's hard to describe what a typical day might be like for you if you attend a community college or vocational-technical school. If you're a parent, you'll have to wake up extra early to make the kids breakfast and get to the on-campus day care on time. As you race to your first class, you see lots of students from your high school—and some of their parents, too, for that matter. If you're a

vo-tech student, maybe you're off to auto mechanics; a liberal arts student, English 101. After class, you drop by your adviser's office to see if you're on track for the credits needed to transfer to Big State U and then run to the career center to check if you've gotten any bites on the resume you put out on the Internet—gotta make sure you cover all those bases. You pick up the kids and make it home just in time for *Teletubbies* and dinner. Thankfully, mom's coming by tonight to watch them while you're back to campus for your advanced desktop publishing course. Afterward, you meet your friends downtown for coffee (how could you live without it?). Back to your apartment in time for a bedtime story for the kids, but it's not bedtime for you. You still have to hit the books for some reading for your weekend course, since you won't have time later this week—you're scheduled for the next three days at your part-time job at the bank. Whew!

As time goes by, you'll come to see yourself as a master juggler, and you might even come to enjoy the crazy pace (adrenaline can do some weird things, you know). You'll find the classes that best fit your schedule and, as you develop a personal relationship with faculty and counselors, you won't be intimidated by "the whole college thing." You'll seek out and join clubs to fill your spare time—yes, you'll figure out how to make some of that, too. You'll develop valuable skills that will make you an asset to any employer or four-year school. And before you know it, the two years will have flown by. Now why didn't you do that sooner? ∎

Academics

According to the American Association of Community Colleges, two-year schools are the first stop for about four in ten college-bound high school graduates. Currently, nearly 10 million students attend community colleges. With such a large number of students enrolling each year, it's clear that these schools have a lot to offer. What types of academic programs will you find?

Basically, two distinct types of programs are offered at two-year schools: liberal arts programs and vocational-technical programs. Community colleges award over 480,000 associate of arts degrees yearly, and while some students complete their education after receiving an associate's degree, many use two-year schools as stepping stones to a traditional four-year college education. "Exploring Transfer Program Encourages Students To Trade Up" reports on a program offered by the Borough of Manhattan Community College that encourages its students to enroll in coursework at Vassar, one of the nation's top colleges. Comprehensive liberal arts programs at two-year schools not only provide remediation in skills you may need to develop before enrolling in a four-year school, but also, in many cases, offer the exact same courses you can get at a four-year school. In fact, in a Florida law now requires both two- and four-year schools to have the same requirements for the same courses. Many states, including California, Florida, and Illinois, have very generous transfer policies between two-year schools and four-year state schools. Thomas Nelson Community College in Hampton, Virginia, for example, has agreements with several four-year colleges in that state to accept its credits. And while making the move from a two-year school to a four-year school may be intimidating to some, as described in "School transition can be collegiate challenge," the encouragement and support you'll find at two-year schools will keep you on track if that's the way you choose to go.

Attending a two-year school is also a great way to get professional training and certification in certain occupations. Each year, two-year schools award nearly 200,000 professional certificates. At vocational-technical schools, you can enroll in career preparation programs that you'll find only on the campuses of two-year schools—cosmetology, culinary arts, or auto mechanics, for example. "Independence CC cosmetology program in 20th year" describes one such career-preparation program that has withstood the test of time. Two-year schools with a career training focus also often look toward new curricula that will keep students on top of workplace needs, as reported by the *TVI Times* in "Albuquerque TVI to offer new trades programs in fall '99." Vocational and technical programs can also help those who are already employed beef up job-related skills. *The Guardsman* from the City College of San Francisco reports how that outstanding two-year school emphasizes workplace skills across its entire curriculum.

Students who attend two-year schools invariably point out that the professors who teach there are enthusiastic about their subjects and their students. In all likelihood, the professors at the two-year school you attend won't be involved in outside research; that means that first-year survey courses will be taught by professors (*not* by grad students) and that your teachers will have time outside of class to help you should you need it. In fact, many choose to teach at two-year schools because they consider teaching, not research, their first priority as educators. On top of that, two-year schools enjoy small class size—usually limited to around 30 students—so you'll enjoy the benefits of individualized instruction right from the start.

Interested? Then read on to find out more about the great academic programs offered at two-year schools nationwide.

Admissions

For the most part, admissions policies at two-year schools are not competitive. More often than not, spaces are filled by application on a first-come, first served basis. While some two-year schools require that applicants have a high school diploma or GED equivalent, others, like the City College of San Francisco, offer classes that will help you get your high school diploma before you move on to more advanced coursework. Oftentimes, international students will need to obtain certain scores on the Test of English as a Foreign Language, or TOEFL. Some schools, like Oregon's Linn-Benton Community College, reserve the right to give higher priority to residents of the district they serve. Others, like Independence Community College (ICC) in Kansas, require incoming freshmen to take placement tests in English, math, and reading to ensure proper class placement. ICC also allows you to apply military service toward course credit.

Many two-year schools, like Linn-Benton, have open enrollment for students who want to attend classes part-time without being formally admitted to the school. If students decide they like the coursework and want to go on to pursue a degree or certificate, then they must undergo the formal application process.

Admissions policies may vary based on the program you'll be pursuing within the school. At Florida Community College in Jacksonville, students who are interested in pursuing associate in sciences or arts degrees or technical certificates must submit ACT/SAT scores. At Linn-Benton Community College, programs in Engineering Systems Technology, Nursing, Wastewater Technology, and Dental Assisting have admissions standards that go beyond the school's usual "open door" policy. Mesa Community College recently changed its admissions policy for nursing majors. As you'll see, not all students are happy with their change from required GPA to first-come, first-served admissions practices.

NURSING MAJOR HOPEFULS NOT HAPPY WITH NEW ADMISSIONS POLICY

By Teri Dillion

MESA LEGEND (Mesa, Ariz.) 02/25/1999

As dusk fell over the Valley on Valentine's Day, many of MCC's pre-nursing majors were not looking forward to a nice, relaxing night with their loved ones. They were camping outside of the admissions office, waiting nervously until 8 a.m. Tuesday for the doors to open up and let them into the nursing program.

Students are now admitted into the program on a first-come first-served basis, rather than on academic performance, according to Jo Wilson, associate dean of Instruction. The first 50 in line would be accepted into the program if they had all their prerequisites in order. If they were not one of the first 50, they have to wait until next semester to try to be accepted.

Students used to have to maintain a 3.8 G.P.A. for admission to the program, but that requirement was dropped this semester.

"We've gone through hell . . . it comes down to this, when we got to stand in line and wait to get in . . . it's a direct slap to everyone involved," said the husband of pre-nursing major Lori Blezinski, who was waiting with her and their two young children.

Judy Weidholz, was the first applicant in line at 4:30 a.m. Sunday. "We have all worked hard for two, three, four years . . . we've spent this time fighting to get good grades, and then we finally get here and they're telling us it doesn't matter . . . it's who stands in line," Weidholz said.

Some of the concerns of those in line were for others who have worked hard but were not able to camp out. Weidholz used as an example a fellow pre-nursing major named Jeanette.

"Jeanette . . . who has finished everything, deserves to be in the program, (but) she has no family here, no one to take care of her kids," she said.

According to those waiting, the program has added new prerequisites and conditions of acceptance and keeps on changing. There are anywhere from 300 to 600 applicants for the 50 available positions.

"They're trying to say that they're making the standards higher by making us take all these other classes . . . but yet we have to sit out here like we're waiting for concert tickets," said Mary Utley, one of the first in line on Sunday.

Pre-nursing major Kristin Nevin found the new prerequisites hard to accept. "A lot of us had all our coursework done and we're just waiting to get in, and then they added 11 units, and new requirements," Nevin said. "They make changes . . . and there is no end to it."

After two semesters, students can become licensed practical nurses. In order to get an Associate degree in nursing, students must first be accepted into the program, and then take four more semesters of training.

According to Dean of Administrative Services Ron Etter, students have been receptive to the new system. "They're (the students) upset because the rules have changed . . . but they've been super," he said. ∎

Teaching & Research

While some who attend two-year colleges may question certain admission policies, especially when they change midstream in a student's academic career, no one will question the quality of instruction you'll receive at a two-year college. At these schools, faculty members are often expert instructors with real life experience in their fields; this is especially true when it comes to vocational and technical training programs. They are enthusiastic about helping you learn. If you are attending a two-year school in preparation for transferring to a four-year college or university, you can bet that your teachers will prepare you for further studies with top-notch liberal arts coursework. Although the majority of two-year college faculty members teach more courses per year than their four-year counterparts, most are not required by their schools to do outside research, so they have more time outside of class to meet with you. In fact, individualized attention is a hallmark of two-year schools.

Two-year college instructors are committed to you and your education. They are passionate about the subjects they teach and have that "extra something" that it takes to get their message across. As *The Cowley Press* notes, faculty members at their two-year college use a combination of humor, patience, knowledge, and desire to see students succeed for award-winning results. They are in touch with their fields and keep their talents honed through involvement in the community and the school; Glendale Community College's David Schmidt is a case in point. And the profile of Daniel Norton of Seattle Central shows just how dedicated these professors are to helping students think critically and get involved in pursuits beyond the classroom.

FANTASTIC FOUR EARN MASTER TEACHER AWARD AT COWLEY COUNTY CC

By Zabrina Wilson

THE COWLEY PRESS (Arkansas City, Kan.) 03/11/1999

Four Cowley instructors have been chosen to receive the Master Teacher Award. They are Pat Moreland, math instructor; Pam Smith, chemistry and physical science instructor; Dave Bostwick, humanities instructor; and Slade Griffiths, EMS and MICT instructor.

"The satisfaction I feel when students finally understand a concept is what I enjoy about teaching," says Moreland. She believes her strengths in the classroom are the knowledge of the subject and a strong desire to make each student successful. She teaches College Algebra, Intermediate Algebra,

Calculus, and Calculus for Business and Economics. This is Moreland's third year at Cowley College and her 25th year of teaching.

Smith says, "I really enjoying coming to class and seeing everyone smiling. I'm sure the students aren't as happy to see me as I am to see them, but I really like to get to know my students. The students are what makes the job fun." Smith teaches chemistry and physical science. She has been at Cowley College for three years. Before she came to Cowley she taught as a graduate assistant at Wichita State University for four years in the chemistry department.

Every semester Bostwick says he enjoys being around a variety of students and their viewpoints. Bostwick says, "I try to use humor in the classroom whenever possible. Sometimes this helps keep students interested, especially in required classes such as Composition I and Composition II. Also, I scan the newspaper for current events topics that may fit that week's lessons." This is Bostwick's third year teaching all the journalism courses as well as some composition courses at Cowley College.

Griffiths says he enjoys "seeing the light bulb coming on in the students' eyes. It is very fulfilling." Griffiths says his strengths in the classroom are his ability to relate to the students and his patience with them. He teaches paramedics programs. He has been at Cowley College for three years. The Master Teacher Award is an international award given only to community college instructors. The four master teachers will be traveling to Austin, Texas, in May to receive their awards. ■

GLENDALE CC MUSIC INSTRUCTOR DAVID SCHMIDT: PASSION AND ALL THAT JAZZ

By Jayne Nixon & Rachael Jacob

THE VOICE (Glendale, Ariz.) 02/18/1999

He is considered an expert jazz ensemble player and receives requests to perform several times per week. He is David Schmidt, music instructor at Glendale Community College.

This is Schmidt's ninth year teaching at GCC, and he has accomplished much. His latest achievement is the production of a CD of recordings by GCC Big Bands and the jazz combo. It will be released at a concert March 8, 7:30 p.m., at the Performing Arts Center.

"When students give back in accomplishments what I have given them, I feel the energy," Schmidt said of GCC jazz students, who have placed 2nd at the Fullerton Jazz Festival 3 years in a row.

As part of his involvement, Schmidt created the "combos," a group of jazz students who play on a less formal level than the Big Band groups. He has also improved and expanded the improvisation classes. After all this, he finds time to critique and recruit high school students—all important for a good program.

It is experiences like these that keep Schmidt dedicated to teaching.

Schmidt had the honor of playing the National Anthem at a Phoenix Suns vs. Utah Jazz game and can be seen Sunday nights at Beeloe's Underground, a nightclub in Tempe. While performing, Schmidt enjoys the spontaneity, improvisation, and creativity among each player and the audience.

"I'll never be happy with [my performance]," Schmidt said. "I haven't arrived where I want to be." Despite his personal criticisms he loves "to move [the audience] musically. It is interactive and fascinating to create a product that moves them intelligently."

Interestingly enough, Schmidt didn't begin playing the saxophone in the 4th grade because of the music alone.

"[I] picked it because that's what my sister's boyfriend played, and I thought he was cool," He said. After years of practice and hard work, he earned a music scholarship at Arizona State University and a Masters degree in saxophone. Currently, he is not only committed to his music and his students, but to his family and "being a dad."

Being passionate about life's work is such an achievement. Listen to David Schmidt's music and know the truth of this in his life. ■

Two-year colleges place great emphasis on hiring a diverse faculty to support their diverse students' needs. This entails looking for professors not only from many backgrounds but also those who are committed to the unique aspects of two-year college education. *The Guardsman* of the City College of San Francisco describes the techniques its administration uses in their exhaustive search for the absolute best faculty members.

CITY COLLEGE OF SAN FRANCISCO TO EXPAND FACULTY

By Pedro Tuyub

THE GUARDSMAN (San Francisco, Calif.) 03/22/1999

Chancellor Philip Day Jr. announced on January 26 that City College will hire approximately 85 new faculty members.

Some of the new hires will replace the 21 to 31 teachers who are retiring at the end of this term. The Partnership for Excellence Task Force, in a series of recommendations on the expenditure of $973,0000 in funds, proposed to the Academic Senate Executive Council the hiring of 26 new faculty in addition to filling the 31 retirement positions. These recommendations will not preclude any agreement already reached through negotiations between the American Federation of Teachers (AFT) and the District.

The faculty retirement was first announced by AFT president Sue Conrad at an Academic Senate Plenary Session meeting on January 19. According to president Conrad, there will be at least 26 new full-time positions for the 1999 Fall term, the largest increase since the implementation of AB 1725 (guidelines for hiring practices, especially for faculty) in 1991.

In the process of recruiting instructors and counselors, City College has participated in two Affirmative Action Job Fairs in Los Angeles and Oakland. Sponsored by the California Community Colleges and hosted by the Human Resources Department, these two events attracted 635 potential applicants. "We are recruiting teachers all over the country," said Human Resources acting director Gary Tom.

In its efforts to hire the best educators, City College has also participated in various conferences, such as the Mayor's Committee for Employment Disabilities, the Latina Leadership Network, San Francisco State University's Centennial Career Expo, Stanford University's Career Expo 1999, and UCLA Career Fair. "We want to aggressively recruit highly qualified applicants to apply, particularly people from diverse backgrounds," said Provost Frances Lee.

The City College employment qualifications require all applicants to meet both the state minimum qualification as well as the additional minimum qualifications of City College. Among these requirements, all applicants must hold a fully-satisfied LIFE California Community College Instructor Credential, a master's degree or equivalent, or a bachelor's degree or equivalent in some vocational areas.

The applicants must also demonstrate sensitivity to and understanding of the diverse academic, socioeconomic, cultural, sexual orientation, disability, and ethnic background of community college students. Furthermore, they must provide verifiable teaching experience, the ability to teach college classes, coordinate large courses, and familiarity with current educational technology.

In attempting to widen the search area for specialists, the departments have resorted to various publications such as *The Advocate, AsianWeek,* the *Chronicle of Higher Education, Hispanic Outlook in Higher Education, Black Careers Now,* the *San Francisco Examiner/Chronicle Sunday Edition,* and Web sites for *Diversity Link,* the *Modern Language Association,* and *Playbill.* "We ask all the departments to submit to us the names of publications and organizations related to the department to expand our contacts," said Tom. ∎

Community College Distance Learning Network

Some two-year schools offer interesting "distance learning" programs. The Community College Distance Learning Network (CCDLN), for example, is a consortium of eight regionally accredited two-year schools that offers courses, certificates, and degree programs through a variety of formats, including the Internet, mixed media, videocassette, print, and audiocassette (to find out more about CCDLN, access their Web site at http://ccdln.rio.maricopa.edu).

A problem facing many community college instructors, despite their demonstrated commitment to students and outstanding qualifications, is their part-time status. As this article from *The City Collegian* in Seattle points out, only 35 percent of community college teachers in Washington state are full-time employees of the schools at which they teach. This status can sometimes create tensions on campus.

WASHINGTON STATE PART-TIME TEACHERS MARCH FOR EQUAL PAY

By Joseph Drake

THE CITY COLLEGIAN (Seattle, Wash.) 12/03/1998

Today at Central a rally to protest low pay for part time teachers drew more than 100 people despite blustery winds and bone chilling cold.

After years of quiet acceptance of a two-tiered system of teacher pay, part-time college professors throughout the state are rallying, marching and demanding recognition. Faculty, students and other supporters used speeches, pickets signs, buttons and songs to drive home their message.

Plans presented at the rally included going to the state legislature and the Governor to demand more money, carrying the cause to the public, and, if necessary, refusing to sign a new contract as a prelude to an eventual teachers strike. A 10-foot-high petition being prepared for the Governor said, "Part-time teachers are the majority of faculty in the state and earn 40 percent of the pay their full time colleagues earn for the same wages."

After the 45-minute rally about 40 marchers paraded down Broadway to carry the message to the general public.

Central teacher Capri St. Ville called on teachers and other middle income workers to tear down the walls separating themselves into isolated interest groups.

Sandra Schrader, a former president of Central's teachers union, was introduced as a "an inspirational model for us all."

Schrader said, "This is my college and if I weren't here I should have my butt kicked." She added that she was "trying to get us poised for what we have to do next."

Schrader said that the union cause "gave me fire in my belly." She called for justice, equity and money for part time teachers.

Rosa Aguirre, an organizer from Jobs with Justice, spoke and compared the part-time teachers' struggle to the situation of part-time UPS workers that brought sympathy and support nationwide back to the union movement.

Verna Wilder of the King County Labor Council said, "We stand with you in solidarity" Wilder also said, "If you go on strike we will be out there to stand by your side."

T-shirt and button sales promoting the cause were brisk. Passing supporters signed post cards to the Governor calling him to act. About 50 placards from teachers not present indicated much wider support on the campus. A leaflet distributed by the union asked supporters to tell politicians that "you support 100 percent pro-rated pay for part-time instructors at our community and technical colleges."

"Part-time Equity Needs Attention," a song from the union sung to the tune of "Solidarity Forever," said, "Our Colleges are suffering—while legislators shirk."

Although they are only indirectly affected, about one third of the crowd, by a show of hands, indicated they were full-time teachers.

According to the union, there are nearly 10,500 community and technical college instructors state-wide, with only 3,500 holding full-time positions—a marked contrast to teacher employment in primary and secondary schools. That leaves about two-thirds of the teachers receiving 40 percent less of a pay scale than the remaining teachers.

Workers cleaning up leaves on Centrals' front lawn demonstrated solidarity with the teachers by turning off their blowers.

Ed Ciok, a negotiator for the teachers said, "I think we were successful." ■

Funding

Data from the American Association of Community Colleges shows that, of our nation's 1132 community colleges, the vast majority—995—are publicly funded. The majority of funding for community colleges, 70 percent, comes from local, state, and federal funds; 20 percent is from tuition; and 10 percent is from other sources. Because they are so reliant on government money, two-year colleges often find themselves wading through miles of red tape to get funding. Also, as recently noted by *The Chronicle of Higher Education*, two-year schools traditionally have not gotten as much money per student as four-year colleges have. When money is awarded, dividing it up becomes quite a process, as the students, administration, and faculty at the City College of San Francisco found out.

CITY COLLEGE OF SAN FRANCISCO GETS MULTIMILLION DOLLAR FUNDING

By Nino Padova

THE GUARDSMAN (San Francisco, Calif.) 11/16/1998

City College is set to receive $3.6 million in performance based funding as part of the California Community College system's Partnership for Excellence Program (PEP).

This program is an agreement between the state of California and the CCC system to increase the contribution of community colleges to the state's socioeconomic success.

An ad hoc task force formed by Chancellor Philip Day will formulate recommendations on how to allocate the $3.6 million for the 1998/99 fiscal year.

After funding enrollment growth and cost-of-living adjustments, the state has committed to an annual investment of $100 million to be distributed to districts over the next three years on a Full Time Equivalent Student basis.

Since PEP is considered performance based funding, the system has set forth a series of rigorous goals intended to measure student success on the community college level.

The goals, implemented by the state chancellor in concurrence with the California Post-secondary Education Commission, the Department of Finance and the Legislative Analyst, will be proposed to the board of governors in a Dec. 1, 1998 meeting.

One criticism of performance based funding is that the system "pays for grades" which could force institutions to lower standards and show greater up-front selectivity in hopes of meeting system goals.

The 24-person task force, consisting of administrators, faculty, classified staff and students, will assess the college's resources and recommend funding directions that will help achieve system performance outcomes.

The task force held its first of four scheduled meetings in the Rosenberg Library Oct. 29, where members were informed of the PEP allocation process before breaking down into smaller groups that concentrate in specific areas of program planning.

According to student economic chair and task force member, Kristen Bartok, "Students are present in all task force sub-groups to ensure that we play a major role in determining what is best for our success, not anyone else.

"We're looking at keeping the library open longer hours during the week and maybe on Sundays. We're also exploring ways for students to access reference materials from their home PCs."

Open forums have been conducted by task force members at both the John Adams and Phelan campuses in hopes of getting students suggestions for possible funding options.

One concern is the possibility of a spending package "top heavy" with personnel costs. "Those costs continue to go up even if this funding doesn't go up," said Chief Operating Officer Peter Goldstein.

Another concern the task force must take into consideration is the practicality of the performance goals.

In regards to transferring, Dean of Student Affairs Frank Chong said, "Simply because we're preparing students to transfer to four-year schools doesn't necessarily mean that they will."

"In fact, the number of community college students applying to UC has decreased over the last year," he added.

According to Chong, the four-week time frame in which the report must be submitted to the chancellor is, "intense, but the incentive is that the money is already there."

There is also mounting concern from the Chancellor's office that PEP, which ends in 2005, could switch from system based funding to district based funding as early as 2001.

On the uncertainty of PEP's future Chancellor Day said, "If there's $100 million out there, I'm willing to role the dice and play this game."

"I just don't know right now the way the rules are going to be played after this year, and I don't think anybody does," he added. ■

Academic Resources

While you won't find the same kinds of massive facilities at two-year schools that you will at most four-year colleges, the resources you'll find will be more than enough to meet your needs. Mesa College's MultiUse Labs provide access to state-of-the-art networking and a variety of software on multiple platforms at a variety of locations on its campus. Cowley County Community College's Renn Memorial Library houses tens of thousands of volumes and microform periodicals, provides Internet access, has automated its library collection, and provides access to academic databases. Oftentimes, because their libraries are smaller, two-year colleges have great interlibrary loan programs to ensure that you have access to all kinds of research materials. According to the American Association of Community Colleges, over 95 percent of community colleges are Internet connected. One such two-year college, the City College of San Francisco, is currently dealing with the joys and despairs of putting its students on the information superhighway.

INTERNET RESOURCES AT CITY COLLEGE OF SAN FRANCISCO

By Lara V. Desmond

THE GUARDSMAN (San Francisco, Calif.) 11/02/1998

With all the world spending more time online than worshipping their respective deities, it's only natural for City College to be providing free Internet access to students. What better research tool than the information superhighway? But with a sea of links to entertaining, ludicrous and tawdry curiosities, is this service more of a distraction than a learning tool? Or does it actually support educational focus?

Reference librarian Agnes Szombathy believes that the Internet's informative value definitely deems it worthy of being supplied by the school. "I think it is a wonderful thing. And I think it should be available to all students, all the time." She explained that no one ever questioned if the school needed this resource. "It was just a question of when."

For the Rosenberg Library, "when" was from the very beginning. Internet workstations have been available there since the doors opened in Dec. 1995. Since then the number of workstations have increased with demand. There are currently almost 100 stations open to students in the library labs alone, not to mention the rest of the various campus labs.

What issues are raised in maintaining high-technology learning facilities? One of the main concerns, according to Rita Jones, Dean of Library and Learning Resources, is network limitation. The system, originally designed to serve one hundred users at a time, is currently serving almost twice that. This slows the whole works up. Jones and others are in the process of negotiating a system upgrade.

Another issue is upholding academic integrity in the utilization of this powerful resource. Numerous sets of guidelines govern use of the computers and the internet. The Library/Learning Resources Responsible Use Policy for Internet Resources, for example, states, "Acceptable uses of the Internet are activities which support learning and teaching." It asserts the library's attitude of non-censorship and holds individuals responsible "for using these resources in an ethical and lawful manner." And it lists several specific prohibitions such as copyright infringement, commercial use, participation in chat rooms, game playing or online shopping.

The City College Computer Usage Policy states that violators of laws or regulations are subject to "the full range of disciplinary sanctions including the loss of computer privileges, dismissal from the college, and legal action." It's interesting that without even knowing that such policies exist, the majority of the student body apparently follows them precisely.

Jeremiah Danielson, a lab assistant and computer science major, has observed that students "come [to the lab] to get straight to work." If anything, he thinks the most common distraction to their studies is only as scandalous as Hotmail, a free e-mail service on the web.

As far as policies, Danielson agrees that they exist for good reason and need to be enforced. Recently, he had to tell someone to leave the lab and not return. The student in question ignored warnings that his knack for surfing World Wide Web porn was distracting and offending other lab patrons. Danielson says that instances like this are by far the minority.

How can students take advantage of this free and wonderful resource? It's simple. All they need to access the labs is a current student ID with the library barcode attached. The barcode is obtained at the library. The reference desk at the library keeps a handy list of all the computer labs' locations, hours and services available. There are always assistants on duty to answer questions, and printouts cost a minimal ten cents a page. Researching online is an amazing tool, but don't forget you can take library books home with you. ■

Academic Opportunities

As we mentioned earlier, the kinds of programs you'll find at two-year colleges can basically be divided into two different areas of focus: liberal arts programs that award you an associate's degree and can prepare you to transfer to a four-year college and vocational-technical programs that award either associate's degrees or professional certifications while providing career training for many types of professions.

Two-year college programs with a liberal arts focus offer great preparation for those who may want to continue their studies at a four-year college. The benefits of beginning college at a two-year school are many: Two-year schools often have lower student-teacher ratios, which means you'll have more opportunities for individualized instruction; two-year schools offer basic instruction in areas in which you may need to build strengths before moving on to a four-year college; and tuition at two-year schools is much lower, which means that you'll save lots of money along the way. Students who transfer from two-year to four-year colleges usually transfer to large state schools, which more readily accept transfer credits from community colleges. The *Mesa Legend* from Mesa Community College reports on the good and bad points about transferring from a two-year college to a four-year college.

SCHOOL TRANSITION CAN BE COLLEGIATE CHALLENGE

By Donna Taffe, Dylan Fields & Kim Larson

MESA LEGEND (Mesa, Ariz.) 02/25/1999

Some students who have transferred to Arizona State University from Mesa Community College feel they can compete academically with ASU students, but miss MCC's smaller classes. "It's so much easier to ask questions in a class of 40 than 240," said Elisha Griffin, an ASU communications major. "At MCC, the classes were so much smaller, but it was also too much an extension of high school."

According to MCC's Office of Research and Planning, 24 percent of ASU transfers came from MCC in the 1997–98 school year. The average G.P.A. for students from MCC was 2.82 and the average number of credits transferred was 27.2.

Over the last four to five years, statistics have shown that 90 percent of ASU students who transfer from MCC graduate. "Students often tell me they attend community college because classes are easier and less expensive," said Donna Landers, an academic adviser in the College of Liberal Arts and Science at ASU.

Landers estimates that about 40 percent of transfer students are able to graduate on time. However, Landers credits this success to many transfer students' decision to postpone choosing a major. ASU requires mandatory advising for anyone who transfers with less

than 12 hours which is designed to help students who are unsure about their majors.

Emily Penrod transferred from MCC last fall with more than 50 credits and was only able to enroll in nine hours of art courses that counted toward her major. Penrod said she is disappointed that her classes are taught by graduate assistants. "I think (graduate assistants) know their stuff, but their instructions are often vague," she said. "They aren't necessarily good teachers."

Business management major Mike Cocci found MCC to be a beneficial transition from high school to ASU. "I'm a little bit ahead of people that went straight (to ASU) because . . . they got hit with everything all at once . . . all while I stayed back awhile and eased into it."

Marketing major Darren Kooi thinks that the faculties on both campuses are great. "I don't feel any disadvantage to having started at MCC," he said. "I'm just better off financially than I would have been." However, not everyone starts at MCC and winds up at ASU. Sometimes it works the other way around.

"Well, I went to ASU first and then I was forced to go to MCC due to some . . . lower grades," said journalism major Chris Handel. "After going (to MCC) for a while, I think that ASU is a lot easier than it was the first time."

John Brown, a former MCC student and a business major, thinks he is equal with other students at ASU. "(MCC) was a little easier and less strict but pretty close to (ASU)," he said.

Jennie Moser, an accounting major, found trouble in having to adapt to two different environments. "People who came straight here had (their) freshman year to adjust . . . while I had to adjust (both) to my MCC freshman year and now to (ASU)," Moser said. "I think it would have made it easier to come straight here, but I couldn't afford it." ■

It's a mistake to think that studies at a two-year school won't be academically challenging. The Exploring Transfer program at the Borough of Manhattan Community College offers students a chance to enroll in intense studies at Vassar, one of the nation's most selective colleges. In fact, some students in this once-in-a-lifetime program have transferred to and received their bachelor's degrees from Vassar. And as those who have attended two-year colleges like Mesa Community College can tell you, the rewards for successfully beginning your studies at a two-year school can be many.

EXPLORING TRANSFER PROGRAM ENCOURAGES BOROUGH OF MANHATTAN CC STUDENTS TO TRADE UP

By Jacqueline Forde-Stewart

VOICE OF THE VOICELESS (New York, N.Y.) 02/11/1998

Summer 1998 will mark Borough of Manhattan Community College's tenth anniversary in a program that urges students to explore the possibility of leaving the school without graduating—The Exploring Transfer Program (ET).

Unfortunately successful transfer applicants are often erroneously considered part and parcel of the number of dropouts that plague the system. While dropout suggests the end of a student's academic career, leaving for these students represents a new beginning.

Unlike many transfer programs available to City College of New York students, ET by its association with Vassar College offers students insight to a world many of them were never or would never be privy to.

ET is hosted and funded by Vassar college, and BMCC is one of the seven community colleges invited annually to send students to what Jenny Sanchez (ET, 1993) described as "an academic boot camp."

Over the years 59 successful BMCC applicants earned praises from Vassar Officials. Professor Pat Hough a longstanding member of BMCC's selection committee stated that the overall feedback on students is positive. She was told that "BMCC students are comparable, but last summer in particular was above average."

Successful applicants have appropriately been representative of the diversity that is BMCC. In 1995 there was a blind student accompanied by a seeing-eye dog, and Ana Daniels, secretary for the Ethnic studies department, is a former ESL student who attended ET in 1990. Hough also remembered parents and full-time employees who gave up their regular schedules to participate in ET.

Hough added that while six to ten applicants are selected annually, the BMCC selection committee receives and submits an average of "20 completed, high-quality applications." Funding for the program, however, significantly limits the total number of students accepted.

The five-week program that usually runs from June to mid July requires students to take up residence in Poughkeepsie on Vassar's campus. Tuition, room, board, meals and books are paid for in full by the program. This relieves students of the day-to-day burdens that challenge most non-traditional students at community colleges.

Past candidates say this relief, however temporary, made it easier to submerge themselves in the weeks of intensive intellectual pursuits. Lutchmin Indarsingh, ET 1997, reports that her required reading was a total of 25 books. She added, "Students are also encouraged to do extensive independent research using Vassar's library and online resources."

Students take two of three interdisciplinary courses that focus primarily on reading, writing and analysis. The courses are team-taught by faculty members from Vassar and the participating Community Colleges.

Tricia Yi-Chin Lin, a member of the selection committee and an English professor, represented BMCC the summer of 1997. The primary role of the BMCC selection committee is to recruit students, assist in the application process and provide moral support. The final decision regarding acceptance into the program rests with the selection committee at Vassar. Other members of the BMCC selection committee are Beryl Duncan Wilson, Pat Hough, Maria De Vasconcelos, and Carl Johnson.

There is a great emphasis on academia, but from all accounts the program's primary goal is to encourage highly motivated community college students to reach for the unimaginable and explore the possibility of leaving—transferring to a higher caliber institution. Most students agree that this introduction to "the rigor of academic study at a highly selective four-year residential liberal arts college" made a significant impact on their lives.

Gregory Girard (ET, 1991) described it as "an opportunity to measure my ability to handle such intense work and thus I concluded that one has yet to know his potential unless he is put to the test."

Students concede that they learn more than the facts concealed in the 20 or more texts and handouts that constitute the required reading.

Over the years, however, not many BMCC students transferred to Vassar. In the spring of 1998, Heather Griffith Gonzales became the fourth BMCC student from the program accepted to continue her studies at Vassar. Gonzales attended ET 1997, and like most

non-traditional students found at BMCC had a hiatus between high school and college.

Simon Byron of ET 1991 and Diedra Anderson ET 1995 were the first two successful applicants. They have both already received their Bachelor's degree from Vassar.

Vianni Gonzalez, who transferred to Vassar in Fall 1997, is a true success story. Gonzalez took the initiative and applied both to the program and as a transfer student. He was accepted for both; therefore he bypassed the summer and started classes. Vianni and Heather are currently attending Vassar.

Professor Hough believes most students developed ties during the break between high school and college. This makes it difficult to entertain the possibility of spending two years at Vassar in Poughkeepsie, which is two hours by car from New York City.

Their reasons are many, continued Hough, including "family commitments, older students who did not want to share coed dorms or showers, and jobs."

Hough communicates regularly with the program coordinator at Vassar, Tom McGlinchy, in an attempt to keep abreast of opportunities for students as well as up-to-date on the happenings involving students. Hough said judging from the information supplied by McGlinchy and to the best of her knowing, "Students do not apply to Vassar after returning from the summer program."

While their critics continue to point accusatory fingers and selectively highlight figures of low graduation rate, BMCC continues to recruit students for ET. The selection committee remains committed to offering students this opportunity to expand their options.

Unlike the early days, Hough promises that prospective applicants can look forward to meeting past ET students eager to testify of their experiences and encourage others to embark on a journey that many agree changes the course of their lives. She believes that students will be more excited and inclined to try the program if they hear from actual participants as opposed to from second hand reports from professors. ■

At two-year schools, hands-on career preparation is offered in as many fields as you can imagine. Many career training programs try to create the atmosphere of the workplace you'll be entering. In some programs, such as the Independence Community College's cosmetology program, you practice the skills you're learning on people from the community (after many hours of training, of course); in turn, the community benefits from services you're providing, which are often free of charge or at a very low cost.

INDEPENDENCE CC COSMETOLOGY PROGRAM IN 20TH YEAR

By Jayme Lickteig

THE BUCCANEER (Independence, Kan.) 02/11/1999

The pleasant chatter of hairstylists and manicurists. The sweet smell of shampoo. The sour smell of perm solution. A gushing faucet. A roaring blowdryer. The fizzle of hairspray.

ICC cosmetology students learn their trade hands-on in an atmosphere identical to that of a fully furnished professional beauty salon.

The department, now located in the basement of the Independence Corporate Offices, offers classes and training in hair and nail technology and provides a work area for students to practice their skills on the public at low cost. The program covers the basics of hair, nails, facials and scalp treatment.

"We try to make it as much a salon atmosphere as possible, realizing that it is a school," says Cosmetology program instructor/director Mike Clark.

"We are open to the public from 9 a.m. to 3:30 p.m.; we take our very last haircut at 3:30, and schedule perms earlier."

ICC offers a 10-month certificate in cosmetology. The course covers 44 credit hours of cosmetology classes including Cosmetology I, II, III and IV, with an optional 10-hour Manicure/Onychology course. Approximate cost of the course is $1,850.

Students who receive a cosmetology degree must pass the State Cosmetology Examination to get a license. The exam takes two days and consists of one day of written theory and related work and one day of demonstration and oral examination.

Cosmetology students may continue general education classes to receive a two-year Associate of Applied Science degree.

"I encourage my students to continue to go to school and take courses that will help them succeed in their business," Mr. Clark says.

As part of their vocational training, students who have completed 320 hours of instruction may begin scheduling appointments with clients at the salon. This is endorsed by the school and mandated by the state.

"You have to like people, because this is a people business," says Mr. Clark.

Prior to working with clients, students practice a variety of hairstyles on mannequin heads. These plastic dummies have realistic faces and real hair to hold the chemical styling applied by stylists. The students sometimes sign a head they are particularly proud of with their name and date.

"When somebody starts here, we don't just 'throw them out on the floor,' so to speak, to start working on the public," says Mr. Clark. "They have to be in training at least two months before they begin working on the general public. Students continue to attend theory classes in hair and nail technology even after they begin taking appointments, adds Mr. Clark.

While students work on clients, they are continually supervised by Mr. Clark and Lila Goff, a cosmetology instructor for 10 years. Compliant with state requirements, all staff members are licensed and certified by the Kansas State Board of Cosmetology.

"Ideally, if they make mistakes we want them to make them at school so there's someone to help them," says Mr. Clark.

"Our students are really conscientious—they don't want to mess up; they want to do the absolute best job they can. Sometimes it takes a little longer than the professionals, because they are learning, but they don't want to mess up."

In its 19 years of operation, over 600 students have graduated the ICC cosmetology program. Many area stylists are former students of ICC, he says.

"I have had people who have gone to school here in order to put themselves through school. They have moved to Emporia, Manhattan, Lawrence and Pittsburg to continue their education; they practice cosmetology during afternoons and evenings and actually pay their way through school." ∎

Two-year schools are constantly redefining their curriculums to offer courses that students want and need to succeed. To do this, two-year college administrators have to be experts at keeping abreast of workplace trends and demands. New programs like those offered at Albuquerque Technical-Vocational Institute, described in these next two articles from the *TVI Times*, show that college's desire to accommodate students with a wide variety of interests and to provide new opportunities that will keep students on the cutting edge.

ALBUQUERQUE TVI TO OFFER NEW TRADES PROGRAMS IN FALL '99

By Donovan Kabalka

TVI TIMES (Albuquerque, N.M.) 03/23/1999

TVI's governing board has approved two new programs that will begin in the fall of '99. The first is an associate degree in cosmetology.

Based on data compiled from surveys done on the needs of community businesses, TVI has found "over 500 companies available to hire people with these credentials," said Joseph Rodman, Dean of Educational Services Student Learning. This program has been anticipated for quite some time

"Ron Apodaca, who does our recruitment tours, says that high school kids are always asking when we are going to start a cosmetology program," continued Rodman.

Students will be able to jump right into this program, but, "they will have to be ready for college-level A&S courses," Rodman said. The fees up and above TVI's tuition/registration fees will include a $300 kit exclusive to the cosmetology curriculum (essential tools used in this field). "This is a heck of an opportunity," said Rodman "because specialized schools in this trade can charge anywhere from $3,000–8,000."

The second program approved by the board is a one-term certificate in Manufactured Housing Set-up. This program comes in the midst of an extremely strong job market. "About 51 percent of new houses across New Mexico are manufactured homes," said Rodman.

The need for properly trained people in this job market is so strong that the New Mexico Manufactured Housing Association (NMMHA) has helped fund the program; they have also contributed in the development of the curriculum. According to Mr. Rodman, the biggest complaint from customers about their manufactured home is improper set-up. "We are very excited about this new program," said Rodman, "We hope the partnership [with NMMHA] will continue." The new programs will be offered every term, and will concentrate on evening and weekend offerings to benefit the working student. However, course times will also be offered for the traditional student.

One key element of both of these programs is that they offer a great opportunity for self-employment, which is a thinning aspect of business today, according to Rodman. With the influx and influence of big companies, most independently owned businesses are being shutout in many fields today. These new programs offer students the chance to be an independent entity in the business world. ∎

WEB BUSINESS PROGRAM ON THE WAY AT ALBUQUERQUE TVI

By Scott Quintanilla

TVI TIMES (Albuquerque, N.M.) 03/23/1999

The advent of the Internet has changed the way business is conducted. Or as expressed by Lois Carlson, Dean of the Business Occupations Department (BOD), business is changing by the second.

"Every 1.67 seconds there is a new user on the Internet, one potential new customer," said Carlson, when trying to convince TVI's Governing Board to consider Resolution 1999-7 at a meeting held March 9.

If resolution 1999-7 were put into effect, TVI could offer a new associate of applied science degree and certificate program in E-Commerce (in short, a way of conducting business over the Internet). The board voted in favor of the resolution.

"To be successful, you must let the business problem define your choices in technology," quoted Carlson from Internet Business. "The days of using the latest whiz-bang Net technology just for its bells and whistles are over. Now the Internet means business first, technology second. The rules and functions of business, including communications, marketing sales, customer support, and procurement—to name a few—all have to be addressed on the Web. And here's a warning: If you don't act now, you're toast."

The resolution contained a request for $43,587.50, which would cover a full-time E-Commerce faculty and includes 25 percent benefits. Carlson says in the past they have taken from the budget that exists for other programs.

"We can't do that anymore, we are stretched to the limit," explained Carlson. Even with a new skilled instructor, current faculty will be called upon to cross-teach courses. The BOD will help the E-Commerce faculty gain any needed skills through professional development. This could mean sending instructors to successful Internet businesses, such as Amazon.com and Broadcast.com, to obtain further Internet knowledge.

"They have the talent and understanding; they can teach this," said Carlson.

The E-Commerce program will offer 7 new courses, ranging from Web Accounting to Online Business Law. Carlson also pointed out that computer security is a big issue and that it will be emphasized in all proposed e-commerce courses.

Currently there are no E-Commerce degrees or certificates offered in New Mexico and to best of the department's knowledge, TVI is the first community college to look into these possibilities. In a survey of 450 Albuquerque businesses conducted by BOD, beginning salaries for graduates of the program would range from $16,000–$22,000 per year. Eighty-one percent of businesses that took part in the survey said they would hire E-Commerce graduates over applicants that received on-the-job-training.

Alan Greenfield, in charge of information systems at First State Bank, spoke in behalf of BOD stating that they are in need of people skilled in Internet business and are already in need of an intern.

"As long as you can guarantee you're moving forward from here, I am for you," stated Carmie L. Toulouse, Governing Board member in support for the new program. "I am excited and hope this is just the beginning." ∎

Two-year colleges also provide academic programs for those with degrees who want to advance in an existing career. These innovative programs build on the student's existing education to award another degree. Because of their ability to take into consideration the many requirements of working professionals with families, offerings like the Bachelor of Applied Science program described by *The Voice* from ASU West are immensely popular with working students.

ASU WEST HELPS PROFESSIONALS GET BACHELOR'S DEGREES

By Victor Allen

THE VOICE (Glendale, Ariz.) 02/18/1999

Individuals thinking about a job shift within a company they already work for may find themselves in need of a higher degree than the one they currently hold. Persons holding an Associate of Applied Science degree in fire science, law enforcement, paralegal or any specialized degree program can now earn a bachelors degree to satisfy educational needs to facilitate promotion.

Arizona State University West now has a program open to assist in getting that bachelor's degree and getting that job!

Taking an innovative approach to the demands of the ever changing job market, ASU West has developed a new Bachelor of Applied Science program tailor-made for students and their career goals. It is the first new degree to be approved by the Arizona Board of Regents since 1995.

This new degree program allows anyone with an AAS degree to obtain a BAS degree by accepting 60 credit hours from an AAS in a single block. This differs from previous BS programs that required a two-year course-by-course review. This is welcome news for those people who need a BS degree to change their career direction but don't have time to do a traditional BS program.

"The new degree program is focused on helping the student advance himself or herself within an existing job situation. For instance, a firefighter may want to advance to a public relations office, or a police officer may want to transfer into a job with the responsibilities of communicating and coordinating in the school districts," Dr. Elaine Maimon, Provost for ASU West said. "Courses are also conducted at a slightly faster pace than traditional courses taking into consideration the time constraints for the working student and recognition of an already developed educational capacity."

"Everyone is welcome to take advantage of the program. In fact, even though the program was just introduced in January, some students read about it in the Arizona Republic and quickly got on board," Dr. Maimon said.

"Our campus is state of the art and has full access for the handicapped. Ramps, Elevators, and push button doors went into the ground stage development of the campus.

"Child care is available for those who need it," Dr. Maimon said. "Our facilities specialize in the care of 3 and 4 year olds."

The program has a 60 semester-hour requirement for completion. The course outline is as follows: 21 semester hours in arts, computers, writing, ethics, and career development; 13 semester hours in lab science, history, global awareness and cultural diversity; 18-21 semester hours in classes with a thematic focus of the students choice based on goals and interests; electives; and 0–8 hours in classes to strengthen an area of specialization or explore new interests. ■

BEYOND THE Classroom

Quite frankly, if you attend a two-year school, chances are your life beyond the classroom won't be taking place on campus. The average two-year college student is 29 years old; most have families, jobs, and friends in other places. Two-year college students are just too busy living their lives to get involved in many extracurricular activities. Of course, that doesn't mean that great ways to get involved outside the classroom won't be available to you should you have the time and the interest. At Linn-Benton Community College in Oregon, you can become part of the Drama Club, Christians on Campus, or S.I.F.E. (Students in Free Enterprise), to name just a few. At Independence Community College in Kansas, you can join the Blue Note Band, play tunes on KGGF radio station, or be invited to become a member of the Beta Omega chapter of Phi Theta Kappa, the international academic honor society for two-year colleges. In fact, two-year colleges encourage all kinds of clubs and student-run organizations on their campuses. "San Francisco Community College's Inter-Club Council opens Its doors" describes how that school's administration works hard to support groups that contribute to the campus community. And the diverse groups described here, from those who keep the tradition of the "Anna Plays" alive at Independence to the guys who put the pedal to the metal at Linn-Benton, show that student organizations are alive and kicking at two-year schools. But don't worry: If you just can't find the time it takes to get involved in a club, you'll have plenty of chances to enjoy interesting lectures (a one-night-only commitment) like the one described in "PBS' 'Africans in America' highlighted at Seattle Central Community College symposium."

You won't find any articles about Greeks in this chapter. That's because, try as we could, we just couldn't locate any two-year colleges that house traditional fraternities and sororities. (If any of you are out there, please let us know!) Why could this be? Chances are, because students are only enrolled for two years at these schools and most kids at four-year schools don't join a fraternity of sorority until the end of their first year or beginning of their second year, it just doesn't work out timewise. Besides that, can you imagine a 29-year-old with two kids at home and a full-time job in business as a fraternity of sorority pledge? No, we didn't think so.

More encouraging, however, is the situation with sports at two-year schools. You'll find that two-year schools field teams in most of the "bigger" college sports—football, basketball, baseball, golf—and also offer clubs for other sports like soccer, archery, or tennis. As at any other college, a winning sports team brings a lot to the school: "Glendale CC's men's golf team takes tourney to win" tells the tale of that team's come-from-behind win, which generated enthusiasm campuswide. And the three stories from the City College of San Francisco *Guardsman* show how closely that school follows their football team. Tradition is also big in two-year-school sports; you'll read here about the loyalty that Florida Community College of Jacksonville's baseball coach—who's been with the team for 30 years—inspires around campus.

All in all, if you want to get involved at a two-year school, there'll be plenty of chances to do so—as a spectator, a fan, an athlete, an artist, a club president, and much more.

Student Groups

Students who attend two-year colleges live hectic lives. Oftentimes, they juggle full-time jobs with family responsibilities and schoolwork. Most times, they live off campus and commute to classes. This doesn't leave much time for extracurricular activities. But that doesn't mean that these opportunities aren't available. If you enroll at a two-year college and have the time to do so, you'll find many groups with which you can get involved. In fact, two-year colleges like the City College of San Francisco encourage the formation of campus groups, which can offer students a welcome diversion from their usual crazy pace.

GOVERNMENT

CITY COLLEGE OF SAN FRANCISCO INTER-CLUB COUNCIL OPENS ITS DOORS

By Mike Kushner

THE GUARDSMAN (San Francisco, Calif.) 11/02/1999

The City College Inter-Club Council (ICC) held its first open meeting Monday, January 25, in the upper level Student Union to officially accept applications from new and returning clubs for the Spring 1999 semester.

The Associated Student-sponsored ICC represents groups of students joined together by similar interests. Students volunteer their extracurricular time to join or form clubs, to socialize, plan activities on and off campus and hold special events for the student body. The clubs help students learn, share ideas, have fun and explore other cultures in an effort to build a community.

The ICC recruits members by word of mouth, publication of event schedules and mandatory open meetings, which are made accessible to the student body by posting schedules on designated bulletin boards throughout the campus. Some posting locations are by the cafeteria entrance, near the arts building and in the upper level Student Union. Another way to find out about club proceedings and events is to read the campus calendar section in the *Guardsman*. You can also go to the Student Union building, where most of the student government, council officers, and activities information is located.

In order to be officially recognized and receive funding, a club must submit a packet of forms and a checklist. The packet contains the petition for club recognition, budget forms, signature cards, advisor contracts, member lists, mission statements and club meeting schedules.

Each club must have at least 10 participating members, a faculty advisor who supports the group, a president and a treasurer. The club must then send a representative to an A.S. council meeting in order to be present and counted when the council opens its vote for official recognition. New club presidents, treasurers and advisors must attend special activity orientation workshops designed by Biehn. The workshops, held weekly, are to inform club officers of adopted policies and procedures and to inform them of their rights and responsibilities.

Each club makes its own charter, following ICC guidelines, copies of which are available through the student activities office. A representative is expected to attend the regular meetings of the ICC, which take place on Monday afternoons, 1-2 p.m., and include such items as agendas, campus news, job openings and student leadership courses.

In order to remain in good standing, each club must perform 20 service hours towards the good of the student body, and plan a campus-wide event open to all. Some benefits received by ICC officers and members are: e-mail and voicemail accounts, web pages on the college online information service and use of the electronic billboards for club announcements, as well as use of the P.A. system, the gas barbecue pit, the school van and available classrooms for meetings and events. A club may also petition for more money through a proposal, with the approval of ICC representatives.

A drive to recruit new members, create new clubs and encourage students to become more involved in student government and activities is now being undertaken by continuing ICC clubs and the Associated Student Council.

Hasani Gomez, ICC assistant, said, "A bigger and better club member recruitment day is now being planned for this semester by the ICC. We are going to concentrate our energies on pooling individual clubs and resources for a concerted effort at reaching the entire student body.

"The vision for the Spring Club Fair is the setting up of club information booths in Ram Plaza, so the council and member drive becomes more visible and accessible to all students. We are also going to have food, information and entertainment to publicize our activities." Gomez is also enthusiastic about the re-opening of the Martin Luther King center, located on the ground floor of the student union, which was closed in the fall due to vandalism. "This semester we are hiring an MLK monitor for security purposes to be available and accessible to answer questions relating to the ICC."

Last semester 60 clubs were organized with a variety of themes and purposes. They held student performances, lectures, field trips, dances, plays, films, social gatherings, intercollegiate conferences, raised money for scholarships, aided in the relief effort for Hurricane Mitch victims in South America, held food and clothing drives, fashion shows, food sales, ethnical and cultural focus seminars and invited guest speakers on a rainbow of important current topics to keep us informed of politics and communities outside our campus.

Highlights last semester included a blood donor drive, a women-of-color art show, Karaoke contests, a volleyball competition, an Indian pow-wow, an Asian-Pacific heritage week, Filipino pride events, viewing of the Leonid meteor shower, and speeches on civil rights by Muslim leaders.

This spring will see the Student Union Mural Project, which invites all students to participate in the planning and design of a new mural on the front facade of the Student Union building. The mural workshop will be directed by master muralist Susan Cervantes, founder and director of Precita Eyes Muralists, and will meet Fridays from 1 to 3 p.m. in the Student Union lounge.

Cresanti thinks participating in student activities is a must for all students. "Learning and becoming a part of student government and student leadership programs is essential for future success. We are a microcosm of the working world, so participating in student activities prepares you for getting along with different people, understanding the hierarchy of procedures and gets you ready to deal with the job market and related responsibilities."

Some returning clubs include the Latino Support Group, the Press Club, Bi-Gala, Women's Multicultural Group, La Raza, Muslim and Christian Associations, the Hong Kong Students Club, the African-American Achievers and the Polynesian Club, as well as clubs for Music, Drama, Comic Books, Martial Arts and many others. ■

The articles featured in this chapter point to the fact that student media is an important and vital force on the campuses of two-year colleges. Two-year colleges offer excellent opportunities for students interested in newswriting, sportswriting, cartooning, and all other branches of print and broadcast media to enhance their skills and keep the community around them informed. Students at two-year colleges can also compete for awards in these fields. Such competitions garner much-deserved recognition for both individuals and the school, a fact to which the students who contribute to *The Guardsman* in San Francisco can attest.

MEDIA

CITY COLLEGE OF SAN FRANCISCO GUARDSMAN HONORED AS ONE OF THE BEST

By Evan Ross

THE GUARDSMAN (San Francisco, Calif.) 11/02/1998

The City College Journalism Department, the Guardsman newspaper and the Guardsman Web site proved they are among the elite of community colleges by taking home 26 awards at the annual Journalism Association of Community Colleges (JACC) Northern California Conference Oct. 17 at San Jose State University.

A total of 277 students representing 27 colleges from Northern California came together for the day long conference and competition to compete, share ideas, participate in seminars and network with local professionals.

Articles, cartoons and layout work from the 1997-1998 school year sent in ahead of time were some of the categories judged for the mail-in division of the competition.

"Winning an award gives you an idea that you're headed in the right direction," said journalism student Michael Kushner, who won an honorable mention in the sports news writing mail-in competition.

Kushner added, "I knew nothing when I came here. The awards are a strong reflection on the school."

Juan Gonzales, Guardsman faculty adviser and Northern California JACC faculty president, attributes City College's success to the students and the stories.

"The number of awards we won speaks highly of our abilities," he said. "Our students pick up skills quickly and we have good variety and great stories. We have what it takes to win and we're committed to excellence."

Topping the list of awards for City College is the General Excellence award, regarded as one of the most prestigious honors the JACC bestows.

Some professionals on hand to lend their expertise were John Carne, a local attorney who spoke about journalists' rights, and Rich Rocamora, a Bay Area photo journalist who gave students tips on photojournalism techniques. The keynote speaker was William Woo, former editor of the St. Louis Post Dispatch, who gave a well-received talk on ethics.

The Northern California competition is a prelude to the state competition, which will be this April at Fresno State University, with 60 to 70 schools from California, Arizona and Nevada in attendance.

"The caliber is high at the state level," said Gonzales. "But our chances are good." ∎

At two-year colleges, there's no limit to the kinds of clubs you'll be able to join. Students with a song in their heart can raise their voices or play a tune through many fine musical groups. Glendale Community College's Chamber Singers are a great example of the kind of vibrant extracurricular life taking place at the campuses of two-year colleges.

MUSIC

A HARMONIOUS BLEND OF TALENT, DIVERSITY AT GLENDALE COMMUNITY COLLEGE

By Denise Williams

THE VOICE (Glendale, Ariz.) 02/18/1999

Try and find somebody who doesn't like music at Glendale Community College—it just can't be done.

Now find students who aren't content to just listen, but be actively involved by breathing life into musical compositions.

Some of these people are GCC's own Chamber Singers.

"The GCC Chamber Singers are an auditioned group of approximately 20 to 24 singers," says the Chamber Singers instructor Craig Peterson. "Some of the students are voice majors but many are not. They meet three times a week and perform mainly a cappella music from the renaissance through the 20th century as well as some vocal jazz music.

In the past, the Chamber Singers have gone on tour with the Concert Choir to such places as California, New Mexico and Colorado.

"I have found my time in Chamber Singers to be both enjoyable and challenging," says Chamber Singer A. L. Burrows. "Mr. Peterson's musical selections are great and have opened my senses to new styles of music. Chamber Singers is a great experience that I would recommend to everyone!"

The selections the Chamber Singers are working on now are the madrigals' "Matona mia cara" by Orlando Lassus and "Weep Oh Mine Eyes" by John Bennet. They are also rehearsing a French piece entitled "Belle et Ressemblante," which means beautiful and resembling; "Ballad of Green Bloom" by Benjamin Britten; and an a cappella jazz piece by Bobby Troup called "Their Hearts Were Full Of Spring."

The Chamber Singers' main concerts for the spring will be held on Thursday, March 11, and Thursday, May 6.

All performances are free and begin at 7:30 in the Performing Arts Center.

Students and community members looking to broaden their musical horizons, or maybe even those who just simply enjoy fine musicianship, need look no further than the GCC Chamber Singers. ■

Can't carry a tune but still want to be on center stage? Through opportunities to participate in theater at two-year colleges, you can showcase your talents without letting everyone know you're tone-deaf. At two-year colleges like Independence Community College, students can direct and star in theatrical productions that are steeped in over 40 years of tradition. As an added benefit, over the years ICC's Anna Plays have enhanced the bond between the school and the community by getting townspeople involved in the productions.

THEATER

40 YEARS OF INDEPENDENCE CC HISTORY EMBODIED IN 'ANNA PLAYS'

By Adam Viceroy

THE BUCCANEER (Independence, Kan.) 02/11/1999

Don't look now but the 40th annual 'Anna Plays' will soon be upon us. Each year students from the ICC Theatre Department direct and act in these plays.

But what exactly is the concept and history behind these plays?

To understand the history of these plays, you need to go all the way back to 1960, when theater instructor

Margaret Goheen started the Anna Plays. She started the plays and the award ceremony as a way to instill enthusiasm for the theater department while honoring Anna Ingleman, the very first theater and drama instructor at ICC.

Anna Ingleman taught at ICC for 21 years before she retired in 1946. Mrs. Ingleman was very instrumental in the development of two of ICC's most famous alumni.

One of them was William Inge, who went on to write many plays and has a festival named after him here at ICC.

The other student was actress Vivian Vance. Her name might not sound familiar, but the character she played on television might ring a bell—she played the nosy neighbor Ethel Mertz on "I Love Lucy."

The concept behind the Anna Plays is that students from the theater department must plan, cast and direct a play of their choice.

Each student is allowed to choose a play they might want to try, but the students are responsible for getting information on royalties and copyright laws. After they have picked a play, they then must start planning out how they are going to turn the words on the paper into a live-action play.

The student directors are also responsible for holding auditions to find people to play their characters. The student directors are allowed to choose almost anybody they want in their play—people from school or from the Independence area.

However, they must be able to work and get along with these people, so it's very vital for the directors to choose people who are responsible and won't bring down the quality of the play.

The plays are judged by people involved in the theater department, who determine who will win awards in the many available categories.

For some students, the awards may be the biggest driving factor to succeed; for others the simple thrill of accomplishment is enough.

But the awards are a tradition of the 'Anna Plays': they are the Oscars and Golden Globes of the ICC Theater Department.

Awards traditionally are given for: Best Play, Best Director, Best Actor or Actress. The People's Award, is

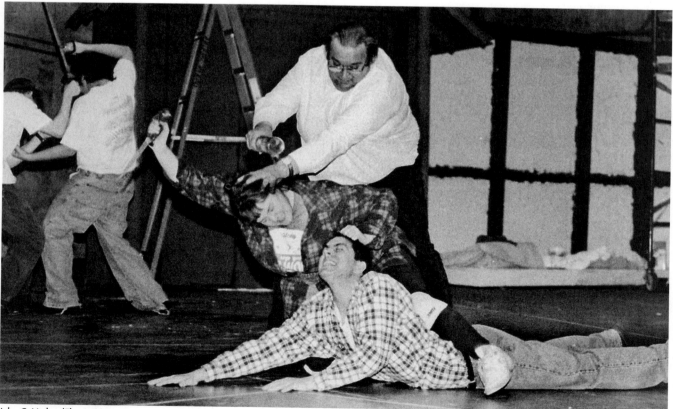

John C. Vrakas/The Argus

a new award that allows the audience to choose their favorite play.

Each year the competition gets stiffer, but win or lose, the thrill of being involved in an ICC tradition is gratifying enough.

So, the next time you hear somebody mention the Anna Plays or you watch the Anna Plays, remember that there is plenty of hard work and determination involved in this ICC tradition. ■

You might think that students who attend two-year colleges would be too busy to volunteer. In fact, quite the opposite is true at Cowley County Community College in Kansas. This two-year college requires its students to volunteer at one of ninety sites across the state. As the writer for *The Cowley Press* notes, even the busiest student has something to gain from volunteering.

VOLUNTEERING

VOLUNTEERS IMPROVE SURROUNDINGS AT COWLEY CCC

By Charlie Potter

THE COWLEY PRESS (Arkansas City, Kan.) 03/11/1999

When you're driving down the highway, what do you think about? Your daily plans? Your significant other? Do you ever stop to think about the upkeep of the road? Probably not. Without volunteers, our highways would be cluttered with empty McDonald's cups and beer cans.

Volunteers play an important part in the lives of everyone. From tutoring to candy striping to highway upkeep, those involved in service work for a goal and receive no monetary payment. Their compensation is of a much larger nature: pride and ownership in the community. The importance of the volunteer effort is greatly underestimated.

"Rock the Vote" campaigns urge voters to break the chain of apathy that plagues our nation. This virus has spread across the nation; few people are informed of the issues facing the country. Volunteers force us beyond this indifferent attitude. They serve and work to make a difference, not to earn wages. Volunteers saved taxpayers $201 billion dollars in 1995. Figures like these display improvement in the daily lives of all Americans. Most college students (being naturally skeptical) doubt the true impact of these numbers. The volunteer hours required for Freshman Orientation, Sociology and Psychology classes often change their minds.

Cowley has a placement office which offers students service selection from 90 sites in a five-county area. Students walk into the office with an apathetic attitude, ready to complete their penance. After their service, students usually return with a smile and renewed outlook on volunteerism.

Volunteerism is obviously good for the community; the volunteers, however, are the ones who truly gain from service. "We make a living by what we get, but we make a life by what we give," Winston Churchill once said.

Community service adds variety to life. Opportunities to serve can lead to careers and friendships. Volunteerism looks excellent on a resume. The difference they make, the smiles on the faces of children, the excitement of community members, and a job well done are the real rewards for volunteers.

Next time you're traveling down the road in your beat-up El Camino, give some thought to those who keep that highway attractive. They create convenience and allow you to take menial labor for granted. They receive no money; the enrichment of their own life and the lives of those around them is enough. Have you hugged a volunteer today? ■

Sports

Plain and simple, sports don't get the same emphasis at two-year colleges that they do at four-year colleges. This isn't to say that two-year college students don't play and enjoy sports or that loyalty to sports teams isn't in evidence at two-year schools. Because so many two-year college students have so many outside responsibilities, the fact is that they just don't have the time to participate in athletics or play the part of crazed fans at the same level that students at four-year colleges do.

That being said, sports teams and the athletes who compete do receive much-deserved recognition at two-year colleges. The crowds may not be as big, the dollars brought in by athletics may not be as plentiful, but the enthusiasm and respect for college athletes is still in evidence. In the final analysis, no matter what school you attend, certain truths will hold: When the team wins, like the Glendale Community College men's golf team, you're up; when they lose, like the Florida Community College women's basketball team, you're down. That's life, sports fans.

GLENDALE CC'S MEN'S GOLF TEAM TAKES TOURNEY WIN
By Matt Batman

THE VOICE (Glendale, Ariz.) 02/18/1999

For the first time since 1995, Glendale Community Colleges' men's golf team placed first in an Arizona Community College Conference tournament.

Not only did the Gauchos win, but they also defeated the number one team in the nation, Scottsdale Community College.

After what coach Don Ulm predicted would be a slow start at the first tournament in Tucson, the Gauchos golf team stunned everyone, including Ulm, and took first place out of 11 teams at the South Mountain Invitational at Cottonfields Golf Club.

Perfect conditions set up a better than normal start for the GCC team, and they placed second after the first round—six behind Pima and two in front of the team everyone loves to hate, Scottsdale!

Leading the way for Glendale was Basile Dalberto from France who was at even par, one off the pace.

At the end of the first day Ulm said, "Gauchos always bounce back!"

True to Ulm's word, bounce back they did!

Before beginning the second round Ulm told the boys that he expected Scottsdale to come back hard, and if put under pressure Pima might fold.

Ulm sent the team out to play with the message "hang tough" and more importantly "have some fun!"

Matt Batman, an Australian sophomore, came in early with a 66 that matched the low round of the tournament, setting the stage for a close finish.

The result could have gone either way, coming down to the last few putts.

Dalberto showed great concentration by holing a 4-foot par putt on the 18th green, for a two-stroke Gaucho victory.

"The boys deserved this today. They did the hard work and got the results," Ulm said. "The boys totally surprised me because I honestly thought we might take another week or two to get close to this level."

Ulm was perplexed by the team's unexpected results.

"I don't know what it is about the Gauchos team, but year in, year out they always seem to get off to a slow start and come home hard," Ulm said.

Taking individual honors for the Gauchos were the two international players, Batman and Dalberto, finishing tied for 2nd place.

Kevin Rail and Mike Plate narrowly missed finishing in the top six.

"We have a good mix of young men this year," said Ulm.

"A few sophomores to add maturity, and a few more freshman; that keeps everyone, including me, on their toes. This is the most comfortable I've ever felt with a group of players."

Ulm compares the current atmosphere of the team to the team of 1995 when the GCC team won twice.

"I think that it would be fair for me to say that this year's team has the potential to surpass past Gaucho performances, including the 1995 team," Ulm said. "I can say this without adding extra pressure to them (the team), because I think once they realize that they can mix it with the best, then only good things will come from it."

Ulm has raised the bar higher, but not without the players' affirmation.

Rail, the only returning player from last year's starting five, believes that Scottsdale may be somewhat of a threat.

"I think that we can beat Scottsdale again, but it's going to be a lot of hard work to take their number one ranking from them," Rail said.

Scottsdale won the first tournament at Randolph Golf Club by a massive 30 shots.

Comments from coaches and returning players were that this year's Scottsdale team was better than last year.

Scottsdale Community College seems to attract the best junior college players in the country.

The Scottsdale teams would have no trouble competing with the top division one teams in the country.

E.J. Harris/*The Commiter*

"This team has a real chance of doing something no other Gaucho team has done," Rail said. "Our goals still haven't changed much; we still want to place in the top five in the nation. But if we can compete with Scottsdale week in week out, then we might have to re-assess."

Two weeks before the boys got off to a bad start again, placing 5th after the first round at Randolph GC and 22 shots behind the leaders, Scottsdale.

Showing real Gaucho spirit, the team pulled back to finish third with a strong second day result, led by Plate who again narrowly missed a spot in the top six.

The team has to place in the top four of the conference in the end of year standings to get a berth at the nationals held in Alabama.

This year's Gauchos golf team seems well on track to accomplish their goal of reaching the national competition. ∎

FLORIDA CC AT JACKSONVILLE'S WOMEN'S BASKETBALL HITS SLUMP

By Justin Barney

CAMPUS VOICE (Jacksonville, Fla.) 03/09/1999

At the beginning of the season, the FCCJ women's basketball team set out to accomplish two things—win the Mid-Florida Conference and follow that with a state championship. "Our team goals were to win the conference and go on to state and win that," said Stars coach Debra Woods. "I felt like we had a good chance at winning the conference and at least, finish second." After an impressive start that saw FCCJ coast to a 20-3 record, the Stars crumbled, losing their final six games and finishing with a 20-9 mark.

"Everything was clicking in December," said Woods. "One loss to Central Florida and we started to slide. Our morale went down." The Stars 69-62 loss against CFCC on Jan. 27 ended a 13-game winning streak and sent FCCJ's season into a tailspin. Losses against Daytona Beach on Jan. 30 (70-52) and Santa Fe on Feb. 6 (49-48) put the Stars at a decided disadvantage in the race for the postseason, but they still had their chances.

After a trip to Sanford on Feb. 13 to face Seminole Community College, the Stars struggled. FCCJ failed to get into an offensive rhythm, and fell to the Raiders 69-53. Crystal Davis led the Stars with 16 points, followed by Melita Dennis with 12. "We had problems scoring," said Woods. "We had one, maybe two people looking to score. To win games, you have to have three people in double figures." Looking to salvage what was left of their season, FCCJ traveled to Ocala on Feb. 17 to face Central Florida, the team that abruptly ended their longest winning streak of the year.

Despite 24 points from Taylor, the Stars' fall from grace continued, as FCCJ was belted 92-76 by Central Florida. Their final game of the season came at home against Daytona Beach on Feb. 20, and what a game it was. The two teams battled back and forth, trading baskets almost at will. It took two overtimes, but DBCC finally prevailed with a 73-68 victory over the Stars. Daytona, the Mid-Florida Conference co-champions, held on despite 14 points and an impressive 24 rebounds from FCCJ's Mikel Taylor.

"When you're at the top, people want to attack you," said Woods. "People were hungry for us and we weren't prepared for that. It was the walking wounded as far as team spirit." Despite their late season swoon, the Stars still have reason to celebrate. After an impressive 20-win season, the freshman-laden team should return nearly every member next year, including Margie Mobley, who was the team's leading scorer before academic woes forced her to the sideline. All indications are that FCCJ should return stronger than ever.

"They'll be veterans and they'll be seasoned," said Woods. "They'll know more what's expected of them. This was a good learning experience." Coupled with a top-flight level of newcomers that is sure to feature some talented players, Woods says that next season's recruiting class, although possibly not from the area, should feature some playmakers.

E.J. Harris/*The Commiter*

"Were looking at some All-Americans and trying to sign a couple," said Woods. "If you look at all the teams in the state that are competitive, a lot of their players are not from in the city. We want to service the community, but then again you want to win." Individually, the Stars were led this season by a host of players, most notably Crystal Davis and Mikel Taylor.

Davis, a native of Augusta, Ga., led the team in scoring with 17 points per game and was named to three postseason teams, including the All-Conference, All-Freshman and All-State. "She has been a constant force for us all season," Woods said of Davis. Taylor, a 6' 2" rebounding machine from Palatka High School who averaged 7.7 rebounds per game, was also named to a pair of postseason teams—All-Freshman and All-Conference. "She has stepped up her game from the beginning of the season," Woods said, when asked about Taylor. ■

The article from Florida CC's *Campus Voice* raises an interesting point about athletes at two-year schools. What you may not realize is that some student-athletes start out at two-year colleges to hone and prove their skills in order to get noticed by and selected for big-name, four-year schools. Other student-athletes whose grades may not be up to par start out at two-year schools to train themselves academically before moving on to the role of scholar-athlete at a four-year school, which, as we've already seen, is a tough job to fill. Starting out as an athlete at a two-year school won't work to your detriment, as the last article proved; in some cases, talented athletes move on to Division I teams and eventually to the big leagues. *The Guardsman* writes about one such athlete at the City College of San Francisco.

CITY COLLEGE OF SAN FRANCISCO'S CURTIS HOLDEN LEADS BY EXAMPLE

By Nate Cohen

THE GUARDSMAN (San Francisco, Calif.) 11/16/1998

At 19, Curtis Holden has already set his eyes on the NFL, although he admits that it would be a long haul and a lot of hard work to get there.

A native of San Francisco, Holden was born in the Fillmore District until his family moved to Hunters Point near Candlestick Park. Living under the shadow of the park, where football legends earn their stripes, could have some degree of influence on Holden, the defensive standout of the City College Rams.

A sophomore majoring in computer programming, Holden intends to play football as hard as he can to attain greater heights and to finish a degree. "I'll play football to get an education," said Holden, who at his young age stands 6 feet 2 inches and weighs 245 pounds.

For Holden, finishing his degree is a priority. "I'll be the first in my family to go to a university," he said. Through hard work and perseverance, he may be able to land in the NFL after he gets his diploma.

As a young boy Curtis says his favorite players were Jerry Rice and Steve Young of the 49ers and Junior Seau of the San Diego Chargers, who he described as intense players. He admits these football luminaries greatly influenced him.

Holden started as a linebacker and a runningback at J. Eugene Mcateer High School where he graduated. As far as staying power in the game of football Holden says, "Speed is very important to move on to the next level. You can't be a big slow guy. Speed (as a linebacker) is more important than bulk or size." Holden pointed out, "There are some big guys who are quick."

To discipline himself in this sport, Holden resorts to weightlifting in addition to the rigorous training he receives from his coaches.

Holden has a feeling of esprit de corps among his teammates. He's very proud of the team and their long history of winning championships.

"We have a great team. We play together, we work hard, we're coached very well, and we play hard," he says, stressing, however, that, "I just think defense should be given more credit in what they do."

Holden holds a special compliment for George Rush, the Rams' head coach, for building the team into what it is now. And the feeling is mutual. Rush says of Holden, "He is a good man."

But alas, for fans of Holden, this young man in a hurry has two more months left at the College before he bids adieu to enroll at a yet-to-be-decided university.

As Holden leaves City College to tackle the challenges of university life, he has fond memories of the school that he says has prepared him a lot.

"It is one of the best in the nation. It has a great academic atmosphere. I think City College has adequately prepared me to go to a university," he said.

For all his academic preparations and rigid discipline on the playing field, there's no doubt that this young man could someday find himself into the apex of his chosen career, and, possibly, find himself hall of famer. Who knows? ∎

Interesting Speakers

Because of their close ties with the community, two-year schools often feature great lecture and symposia series that are open to local residents as well as students. Speakers at two-year colleges address issues affecting the community as a whole and the students who are a part of it. One area that gets a lot of attention is diversity. As two-year schools enroll the most diverse student populations of any type of educational institution in the nation, this is a topic that must be dealt with in meaningful ways. Seattle Central Community College recently tackled the subject of race and equality through its discussion of slavery in America.

PBS' "AFRICANS IN AMERICA" HIGHLIGHTED AT SEATTLE CENTRAL CC SYMPOSIUM

By Rita Heapes

THE CITY COLLEGIAN (Seattle, Wash.) 11/18/1998

On November 18th, Seattle Central Community College held a Symposium on the documentary series "Africans in America: America's Journey through Slavery," organized by humanities faculty J. T. Stewart and Carl Waluconis.

The master of ceremonies for the Symposium was Central student Deb Rodrigues. The Symposium featured speakers such as Tonya Jones from the local PBS station. Ms. Jones told the audience about a Web site credited to supplement the program. The Web site contains essays on the American journey through slavery plus a list of recommended movies, many of which can be rented from your local video store.

The symposium was a mine of information about African American affairs. The series took an historical view and asked questions such as: "How did Americans build a new nation based on the principles of liberty and equality while justifying the existence of slavery? Did American slavery and America's freedom have to exist side by side in our nation? How has this history shaped current views about race?"

"My hope is that 'Africans in America' offers an opportunity for open discussion of issues that Americans have not been comfortable talking about. If we recognize our shared history we're on the road to reconciling racial divisiveness," said the documentary's executive producer, Orlando Bagwell, in a statement.

The documentary is the tragic story of our nation's approval of slavery. Master and slave, enslaved and enslaver, we have all been changed and molded by this shared past. After watching the documentary one wonders who is an "American" and what is "American freedom." It is no wonder we find ourselves overwhelmed by a past we all shared yet felt and understood so differently.

History major and Central President Mr. Charles Mitchell spoke about the new information he had received from watching the series. Reminiscing about a recent family reunion at his ancestral home in Mississippi, Mitchell said, "The slave house and slave quarters are still standing and it was a very emotional experience for me."

We can all empathize with Mr. Mitchell as he thought about his grandparents and great-grandparents who had been enslaved there all those years ago.

The audience was held captive; many of them asked questions and some talked about having difficulty getting past their anger. Some visiting faculty members from Denver were present at the symposium. They came to Central to learn how to make their campus more diverse.

One Denver teacher commented "SCCC is a leader in college campus diversity and we are hoping to learn how to make our campus more like SCCC." ■

LIFE ON Campus

Many two-year students look at community colleges as a cost-effective way to get a college education. Overall, it's much less expensive per year or per credit to attend a two-year school than it is to attend a four-year school, whether it's a large state school, a liberal arts college, or a highly competitive university.

In fact, attending a two-year school for the first two years to save money and then transferring to a four-year college to complete coursework for a bachelor's degree is so common it has come to be known as the "two-plus-two" approach. In addition, over 30 percent of community college students receive some form of financial aid, so attending a two-year school is often a great way for those on a budget to receive valuable job training skills and certification or work toward a college degree.

The reason two-year schools can offer such great fees for the programs they provide is mostly because, like state schools, they're funded (for the most part) by taxpayers. But two-year schools also save a lot of money in other ways. Many don't have dormitories, so you don't have to pay room and board (the down side, of course, is that you might have to live with your folks for just a few more years). As we discussed in the last section, two-year schools don't fund student clubs and organizations to the same extent that four-year schools do. Because sports aren't as big of a deal at two-year schools, you won't see your money paying for new football uniforms every year or the construction of sports complexes that could house professional teams. All of this contributes to the cost savings you'll enjoy at a two-year school.

Don't think, however, that this means that two-year schools scrimp on their students. Not by a longshot. Of course you'll receive a fabulous education if you attend a community college or vocational-technical school, but you can also rest assured that the student services you'll find there will be top-notch. "City College of San Francisco's Chancellor listens in" reports that administrators at two-year schools are always ready to listen to your concerns. Two-year schools are also known for their intensive guidance counseling and career-placement facilities. At a two-year school, helping you achieve academic and career success is job number one; you can be sure you'll get all the attention you need to do so through services like those described in "Career Link provides free services to job seekers and employers" and "Independence CC's ACE is the place for study help, tutors and workshops." Moreover, the diverse student body they serve demands that two-year schools be especially tuned-in to the needs of all types of students; single parents are a case in point. But through programs like those outlined in "Scholarships, grants help Florida CC student parents pay for child care" and "Single mom balances schoolwork, daughter at Linn-Benton CC," two-year schools make sure that the unique needs of this population—or any other, for that matter—won't prohibit them from getting the education they desire.

You can see that diversity will be a big part of your life if you attend a two-year school. You already know that you'll be taking classes with full-time students and part-time students, students who are both young and old, single students and married students, students with kids and students without kids, students with jobs and students who are unemployed, students who want a traditional liberal arts education and students who want to be trained for a specific career, and students from all socioeconomic backgrounds. It should come as no surprise, then, to find out that the students at a two-year school will also represent many different parts of the globe. The number of international students at two-year colleges is quite high, and two-year colleges also enroll a large percentage of our country's racial and ethnic minorities. You could say that getting to know all of these students just might be the best part of your education.

Paying for College

Many students look at attending a two-year college as a great way to cut the cost of earning a degree without sacrificing high-quality education. The average tuition and fees at a two-year school, according to the American Association of Community Colleges, is $1,518 annually. Compare that to some of the schools we've quoted prices for already, and you can see what a difference taking this route might make to your budget. Price-conscious students who want to get a four-year degree but also save some money along the way often start out at a two-year college and then transfer to a four-year school to get their bachelor's degree. Sounds great, but it's not always that easy. Remember, not all four-year colleges have liberal transfer policies. Large state schools are the most liberal when it comes to accepting transfer credit from two-year schools; highly competitive schools are the least willing to accept two-year college credit. If you decide to take this route to save some money, you'll want to check out the credit and transferring policies of both the two-year and the four-year schools in which you're interested.

Regardless of the lower amounts involved, however, when the issue of raising tuition rears its ugly head, students are sure to take notice. No college student likes to have his or her tuition fees raised year after year, and two-year college students like those enrolled in the Maricopa Community College District are no exception. And if you're one of the tens of millions who will be repaying student loans each month after you graduate, maybe you should skip over "Students Weary to Repay Tuition Loans"—it'll just depress you.

HIGHER EDUCATION AT GREATER COSTS PER PROPOSED TUITION INCREASE

By Evan Marshall

THE VOICE (Glendale, Ariz.) 02/18/1999

The Maricopa Community College District (MCCD) Governing Board is being asked to study a proposal for a $2 per credit hour increase in tuition for the 1999–2000 school year.

This increase would raise the cost of tuition and fees from $38 to $40 per credit hour. Therefore, the increase for a full time student enrolled in 15 credit hours would be an additional $30 per semester.

The estimated impact of this increase is about $2.98 million in additional funds for the MCCD. The main reasons for this increase and additional information were presented on Feb. 23 during a public student forum in the GCC student lounge.

At this meeting, Debra Thompson, Director of Financial Planning and Budget for MCCD, talked about the proposed tuition increase and how this additional money would be spent.

"We try to adapt a budget that meets the demands of services," Thompson said.

According to Thompson, one of the main reasons that extra money is needed is to support the growing number of students. Enrollment at Maricopa Community Colleges is expected to grow 3 to 5 percent over the next year. A big part of these additional funds is planned to cover costs of hiring more faculty and allowing for new and additional courses to be offered.

"It's to allow us to serve people better," Thompson said. "These added dollars are also planned to help provide better student services and activities, including more money for scholarships.

"There was a particular emphasis on adding some scholarship money," Thompson said. She also stated the need "to add new activities and expand on what we have."

Other reasons given for the tuition increase were to cover inflationary costs, make all computer systems Y2K-compatible, and build a performing arts center at South Mountain Community College.

At the student forum, Thompson conveyed all of these advantages that would come with the extra money and explained how the District's main intention is to help the colleges grow and provide students with the best services possible. However, a number of students are still wondering whether or not this tuition increase is really necessary.

Some students expressed concern about possible continuing increases in tuition price that could eventually make college unaffordable to many people in the future, noting that just last year tuition was raised $1 per credit hour.

Thompson stated that there are no current plans for future increases because budget issues are decided on a year to year basis, but added that "pretty much every year tuition has gone up."

Even considering the proposed $2 increase, it would raise tuition and fees to a total of $1,200 a year for a full time student, still lower than the national average for public two-year institutions which is $1,381.

Although the increase has been proposed, it is not set in stone just yet. The proposal was submitted to the five-person elected governing board as an "information only" item on Feb. 23, and the board will be asked to vote on it March 23. If it is approved, it will then be forwarded to the Arizona Board of Directors for Community Colleges for a vote on April 16. If the measure is passed, the tuition increase will be effective July 1, 1999. ■

STUDENTS WEARY TO REPAY TUITION LOANS

By Donna Taffe

MESA LEGEND (Mesa, Ariz.) 02/25/1999

Mesa Community College (MCC) student loan default rate falls well within the national average, according to Joan Grover, director of Student Financial Services. Grover said that, student anxiety regarding loan default results from students failing to consider the issue of repayment prior to borrowing. Shannon Kissick, a full-time employee at America West Airlines, fears retribution each tax season since borrowing funds to pay tuition in 1993 for her first year at Phoenix Community College. Six months after receiving the loan, the $50 monthly payments began.

"Fifty bucks is a lot when you don't have it," said Kissick, who has struggled to pay her school loans as well as support herself since she turned 18. Despite consolidating her loans in an effort to get out of debt, Kissick is still having trouble making ends meet. Consequently, her debt has grown to $3,500. While continuing to work toward her degree, Kissick has been denied further financial aid. Although her wages have not been garnished, that threat is ever present in Kissick's mind. Kissick acknowledges that she did not consider how she would have to pay back when she borrowed more money than needed for tuition.

U.S.A. Funds, the nation's largest student loan guarantor, reported their lowest default rate in recent history for the 1998 fiscal year at 3.96 percent. However, in 1990, The U.S. Department of Education reported an all-time high default rate of 22.4 percent. As a result, in 1992 Congress enacted legislation in an effort to control the situation. Under the law, guarantors are now able to garnish wages and withhold tax refunds, as well as file adverse credit reports. Missy Mortenson, now an elementary teacher in Gilbert, found out the hard way that student loan payments can add up quicker than expected. "I thought loan payments would be about $50 a month, but by graduation, I had three separate loans totaling $564 a month," Mortenson said.

"When I decided to consolidate, I found that (one loan) would be wiped out because I was teaching. That was a nice surprise, but I never dreamed I would be this far in debt." While grace periods differ depending upon the loan agency, the usual grace period is about six months with the average payment ranging around $50. However, because loans are issued one year at a time, unless a student goes through consolidation, each loan could exceed $50 a month. ■

Diversity

A quick glimpse at the profile of those who attend two-year colleges shows that these students are quite a diverse lot. According to the American Association of Community Colleges 46 percent of all African-American students in higher education, 55 percent of all Hispanic students in higher education, 46 percent of all Asian/ Pacific Islander students in higher education, and 55 percent of all Native American students in higher education are enrolled at community colleges. Two-year colleges are also home to those of all faiths, ages, and abilities and from all socioeconomic backgrounds. A large number of international students enroll at two-year colleges to adjust to life in the U.S., improve their English in small classes, and learn the most advanced technical skills in the world. Many, but not all, use two-year colleges to ease into the academic environment of the states before moving on to a four-year college.

We saw in earlier chapters that the coming together of those from many ethnic and racial backgrounds has a significant effect on campus life at both large state schools and highly competitive schools. Because students at those schools take classes together and live together, both the good and the bad aspects of student body diversity become highlighted. Is the same true at two-year colleges, where all parts of students' lives aren't as intertwined? Since students don't spend all of their time together in the way that four-year college students do, is race a big issue at two-year colleges? Apparently so, and not just on campus, but in the community outside campus as well, as the *Mesa Legend* points out. While black students feel that race relations on the MCC campus are good, for the most part, many find the community around them not as tolerant.

RACE RELATIONS ISSUE FOR STUDENTS ON, OFF CAMPUS

By Dennis Welch & Dana Archibald

MESA LEGEND (Mesa, Ariz.) 02/25/1999

Black History Month is a time to celebrate the past, look toward the future and evaluate the present. In the eyes of some MCC students, race relations on campus have never been better. However, the reality off the protective atmosphere of campus is not viewed in the same manner. According to Nathaniel Williams, a 19-year-old African American sports medicine major, "everybody feels safe on campus."

"When you get across the street, everyone looks at you like you are the next thug," he said. While pointing out a scar he received from a stab wound, he remembered an all-too real incident.

According to Nathaniel, he and two of his friends were attacked by approximately 30 white men at the Brunswick bowling alley on Southern Avenue, about 50 yards away from the MCC campus. Oscar Tillman said Mesa residents should not feel as though their neigh-borhoods are any safer than anyone else's. "Race relations are a problem throughout the country, Mesa included."

Williams, however, does not believe the problem is in the city of Mesa alone. "This is a racist state," he said. "This is one of the most racist states I have ever been to." Williams, who moved to Mesa from Denver, feels that moving to Arizona was like stepping 25 years into the past. While most students feel that race relations on campus are not a major concern, Crystal Messer, an aerospace engineering major, holds an opposing view. "If you look into a classroom all the different races are sitting together." She added, "Everyone still hangs out in their own groups."

Messer believes that many issues regarding race have become more subtle, but the problems are still there. "People might not shout out racial slurs, but they are still telling racists jokes, and that contributes to ignorance," she said.

"The problems are still there." Williams agrees. "Everything is all good once you're at school, but even once you get in the parking lot, purses get held tighter and doors get locked when you walk by." Tillman believes that education is a key element in bringing about better relations between races.

While education is important, Williams believes that people need to take steps individually in order to make changes. In regard to college campuses, Tillman believes students have made great changes in thinking

in the past ten years by "breaking the status quo." Tillman attributes a lot of the change and advancement of civil rights and race relations to students. He hopes to see the role of the NAACP move into that of a mediator, rather than a confrontational agency in the next decade. "Some colleges are striving to make things better," Tillman said.

Williams feels that Black History Month is important but that focusing on the future is equally important. "You've got to learn your history, but you've got to pay attention to what's going on today," he said. ■

The *Mesa Legend* article raises an interesting question: If you attend a community college and the "community" it's located in is seen as racist (or sexist, or homophobic, or biased in any other way) by the student body, will that affect your opinion of the college itself? Or will you be able to separate the town from the school? How much a part of the community are community colleges? The answers may not be easy, but it's something to think about.

Most importantly, what we need to emphasize from the *Mesa Legend* article is that the majority of MCC students find race relations to be good on their campus. That's because two-year schools give students from all backgrounds the freedom to have a voice, point out areas of weakness, and work together to affect college life. BSU at Seattle Central Community College is one such group working toward unity.

SEATTLE CENTRAL CC BLACK STUDENT UNION STRIVING FOR CHANGE

By Terez Wea

THE CITY COLLEGIAN (Seattle, Wash.) Fall 1998

There are many clubs on campus; one is the Black Student Union (BSU). As described by president of the BSU Maliuka White, "the club is committed to improving success in the areas of academics, unity, and conditions in communities through student outreach. The club is also viewed as a meeting spot for African-American students to share ideas and create solutions to problems that may exist on or off campus".

To reach this goal, the club has set up numerous internal groups. These groups include study groups, recruiter services, the BSU connection, mis-education tutors, and a school board council. These programs are held weekly.

The study group meets Thursdays at 12:00 pm in

the Central library. Using this program, students can study with other students who may have the same class, or had the same class. "We do this to encourage group learning, because sometimes it works better for certain students," stated Maliuka. The program consists of tutors that work with local junior high school students. The meeting place for this particular program is the Central library, Tuesdays at 10:00 am.

The recruiter program consists of Central Students who go out and speak with potential students or current students and give them information concerning the BSU and their involvement with the school. The BSU connection is a link between the different BSU clubs at schools all over Washington. Recently the Central chapter of the BSU hooked up with the

University of Washington chapter. Through this connection, ideas for later programs and possible linkage between the two were discussed.

This quarter the BSU held a potluck dinner and is hoping to have more activities for students next quarter. "We need support, we do not have a vice president any longer and we want a stronger membership," Maliuka said. ■

If you're an international student planning to attend a two-year college, you'll find plenty of support there. International students are included in all areas of campus life at two-year schools. At Cowley College in Kansas, one international student found her niche in that school's outstanding music program.

MUSIC MAKES THE WORLD GO 'ROUND FOR INTERNATIONAL STUDENT YUMI OCHIAI

By Dena Cosby

THE COWLEY PRESS (Arkansas City, Kan.) 03/11/1999

Music wasn't on Yumi Ochiai's mind when she left Japan to attend Cowley College. Her goal was to obtain a hotel management degree, but being around Cowley's music department sparked her interest to become a musician. Ochiai, a 21-year-old international student, came straight to Cowley from Japan in the fall of 1997. She is a member of the jazz band and has been an asset to Gary Gackstatter, instrumental director, and Connie Wedel, vocal music director. Not only does she play an instrument for Gackstatter, she is also his work-study assistant.

"Work-study for Gary has its crazy moments," said Ochiai. "But I really, really like him." Ochiai has played piano for Wedel at several choir concerts and caroling activities. Wedel also asked her to play last semester during choir class.

"This was a wonderful experience for me and I thank Connie a lot for it," Ochiai said. Ochiai has been playing the piano since she was 6 years old. After her first three months, though, she took a break from the piano to find a different teacher.

"My teacher was very mean," Ochiai said. "She hit my hands when I messed up." Ochiai found a better instructor when she was in third grade and continued to take lessons for several years. Ochiai will be graduating from Cowley in the spring of 1999. Now, after surrounding herself with so much music and playing the piano for so long, she wants to return to Japan and pursue a musical occupation.

"Music makes me happy," she said. "It is everything for me." She is sad about leaving in May. She says she has met many great people and made a lot of friends. Her best friend, Josh Childers, a member of the jazz band, will be the person she will miss the most. "I have had many great times with him," she said. "Friendship is so important. Friends are so important in my life. This is what I've learned here at Cowley." ■

Drinking

You might bet that alcohol and drug abuse wouldn't affect the student population at two-year schools to the extent that it affects those at other schools. These students are usually older, don't live on campus, and have kids to take care of and jobs to go to; they're probably far to busy to party, right? Probably not. Alcohol and drug use and abuse are not limited to four-year schools. The problems wrought by controlled substances, especially illegal substances in the wrong hands, affect every sector of our society. It would be naive to think that these problems wouldn't have an impact on students at two-year colleges, too.

As you'll see from these articles from *The City Collegian* and *The Buccaneer*, the consequences of drug and alcohol abuse loom large in the minds of two-year college students across the nation. The problems pointed out here are twofold. They address the lack of clear rules that everyone stands behind and the lack of education about the problems that drugs and alcohol create. Surely that's something that everyone, college student or not, can relate to.

DRUG POLICY AT SEATTLE CENTRAL CC
By Lisa Sutter

THE CITY COLLEGIAN (Seattle, Wash.) Fall 1998

What is the drug policy at Central? According to the handbook, "It is the policy of the Seattle Community Colleges to prohibit the abuse of alcohol and the unlawful manufacture, distribution, possession, and use of illicit drugs. This policy applies to all employees and students of the Seattle Community Colleges while they are on district property, or while they are conducting college business, regardless of location."

OK. Fine. The security office, which holds the official rules and regulations, was far more cryptic. Basically, if you are on campus, regardless of who you are; student, personnel, or staff, you cannot have in your possession any of the following: marijuana, heroin, alcohol, methamphetamines, and any other opiates. You can not have anything with which you could inhale, inject or otherwise introduce into your bloodstream. The school has a strict no tolerance policy, and if you get caught with any of these items, you will be prosecuted to the fullest extent of the law.

VUSCA (Violation of Uniform Controlled Substance Act) is the law that explains which drugs are good (considered medicinal) and which drugs are bad (drugs with no therapeutic value). For example, heroin and morphine are very similar drugs. But heroin has no therapeutic use, versus morphine, which you could

carry on campus with a prescription and a doctor to back up your reason for having it.

Depending on what you are caught with and how much, you can get a gross misdemeanor (a pipe or any paraphernalia) or a Class A felony, intent to sell. Also included on the list of don'ts are prescription drugs that have been stolen from an individual or a pharmacy and resold on the street.

Surprisingly enough, many drug-related incidents at school do not involve students. Central campus is a big, warm, well-lit place, ideal when looking for a bathroom to use in. Overdoses are particularly problematic because of the severity of the situation. "You've got somebody who needs revival, medical attention on the bathroom floor. Sometimes they walk out," said Sgt. Sheldon, head of security.

She's been with the school seven years and has noticed an increase in heroin use. "Of course, it could be because we're better staffed now, we can be more proactive in patrolling. We used to have one person on in the day and one at night. You don't do a lot of patrolling by yourself. Who are you going to call for back up?"

When the security officers do detain someone, they try to control the scene, identify the person(s), let base know and call the Seattle Police Department. Often, they will wait for the police to arrive before they search the individual so they have more witnesses. Unfortunately, the Capitol Hill area is not as safe as it seems. There's so much drug abuse in the area that law enforcement officers can pick and choose whom they detain. The laws are there to protect the students and provide them with a safe environment to learn in. Says Sheldon, "We just want the students to be safe." ∎

COLUMN: DRINKING AGE LAWS ARE NOT WORKING HERE, BUT DRINKING EDUCATION DOES WORK

By Katia Ushakova

THE BUCCANEER (Independence, Kan.) 03/11/1999

Ways and styles of living and the rules and laws that guide us are very different from country to country.

I am an international student at ICC, so I have had a good opportunity to compare and see the differences, especially the differences between the United States and my country, Kazakhstan, a place of 17 million people bordering Russia and China.

Differences I want to talk about are those in the laws pertaining to drinking.

Before coming to the U.S. to study at ICC, I knew about the existence of the drinking-age law. It seemed absurd to me. But, then I didn't know what caused setting the legal drinking age up to 21 years.

In Kazakhstan, we don't have a law that prohibits drinking at a certain age. When I tell this to Americans, many say "Wow, you probably have 12-year-old alcoholics over there!" Surprisingly for them, we don't. Parents there teach their children how to drink reasonably at home. Having wine at the Graduation Day in high school is a tradition.

Here, in the USA, I found that the main reason for setting the drinking age at 21 years was the pressure from Mothers Against Drunk Driving (MADD). Prior to their activities, many states allowed drinking at 18. When the drinking age was raised to 21, there was a decrease in drinking and driving, according to research. Since 1982, annual alcohol-related traffic deaths have been reduced 36 percent.

The law is not solely responsible for the decrease. Education, drinking establishments, etc. influenced the improvement in the drunk driving problem.

Drinking, it seems to me, is a much bigger deal in the U.S. than it is in Kazakhstan.

I don't know why, but as soon as something becomes a law, there appears to be a great desire to break it.

I have spent seven months in the USA, and I know that almost everyone drinks before the age of 21. The drinking age law makes alcohol a "forbidden fruit" that everyone is tempted to taste. Drinking, to the young, is a symbol of a mature person, of an adult. Teenagers seem to need to prove to themselves and to others that they are adults. So there's a way to prove it—get drunk!

Before writing this article I did some research on the Internet because I needed some support for my ideas. First I got a bunch of Web sites, where some 16-year-olds wanted to set the drinking age back to 18. I found some sites published by exchange students that also compared drinking problems in America and in their countries. But all this information wasn't strong enough to make people think.

Finally, I found some articles based on research and statistics. They were published on the Net by Ruth C. Engs, Applied Health Sciences Professor, and Roderick Park, Chancellor of the University of Colorado. They both say "the minimum drinking age of 21 is not working."

Statistics show that today nearly 76 percent of the high school students in the U.S. drink alcohol. Nearly 30 percent of the high school seniors are heavy drinkers. This rate is a much higher percentage than among adults. After the legal drinking age became 21, the rate of cutting classes after drinking jumped from 9 percent to 12 percent, missing classes because of hangover—from 26 percent to 28 percent, getting low grades because of drinking—from 5 percent to 7 percent, and getting into fights after drinking—from 12 percent to 17 percent.

Park says we have to accept the reality that young people are going to drink, even if it's illegal. He says people don't "magically become wise or thoughtful at any arbitrary age." So instead of vetoing drinking before 21, it's better to teach young people how to drink reasonably and responsibly. ∎

Student Services

Two-year schools are renowned for providing services that are considerate of and responsive to their students' needs. Because there are so many different kinds of students for them to think about, two-year schools must go to great lengths to ensure that everyone's concerns are accommodated. This task can be quite daunting, but, given their "open door" policies, two-year school administrators find it to be integral to the success their institutions enjoy. Forums for students to voice larger concerns can be informal, like the City College of San Francisco's "listening sessions," or formal, like Independence Community College's Academic Center for Excellence. Both exhibit the kind of undivided attention you'll get at a two-year college. Whatever two-year school you attend, you'll be sure to find plenty of caring administrators like Gary Musgrave of Independence Community College, who sees your success as his number one priority.

CC OF SAN FRANCISCO'S CHANCELLOR LISTENS IN

By Amanda Wheeler

THE GUARDSMAN (San Francisco, Calif.) 11/02/1998

Chancellor Philip Day has initiated a series of listening sessions, which began in early December and will continue into the spring semester. These sessions are made up of faculty, alumni, students, and educators from other schools. The sessions give the chancellor the opportunity to identify areas where City College can improve.

The most recent session was held at the Phelan campus on Jan. 26 and included a broad range of speakers and panelists. Prior to each session, speakers who have been active at City College, or might be interested in the future of the college, are chosen. Each speaker is sent a packet about City College and is asked to prepare answers to five different questions about the campus.

The questions are: How can the college best prepare our students and help them acquire the skills and knowledge needed in the work force? What roles might the college take on to best serve the community? How can the college maintain the "open door" policy and expand access for those requiring our services? How can City College best address the need for innovative programs while maintaining traditional ones during a time of limited financial resources? What are the key issues the college should address in the future to best serve the community?

The speakers are organized into special focus panels according to his/her field of interest, and each is given 5 to 7 minutes to speak.

On Jan. 26, a panel of students, alumni and education specialists spoke before the chancellor and the board of trustees. The panel included Eddie Chin, Mary Hernandez and Jill Wynns, all from the Board of Education of the San Francisco Unified School District. Father John P. Schlegel, University of San Francisco President, spoke, as did Dr. Genaro Padilla, Vice Chancellor of the University of California at Berkeley.

Day feels the educators were an asset to the listening session. "Representatives from San Francisco State University, the University of California at Berkeley, the University of San Francisco and others gave us some very good ideas about our transfer program," he said.

Other speakers included alumni, student representatives, current Phelan campus students and panelist students from all the other City College campuses. Student suggestions included a campus-wide smoking ban. As alumnus John Caldera put it, "Why should everyone breathe second hand smoke and put up with the garbage generated by cigarettes?" Caldera would also like to see a low-cost health care plan available to all students.

Guardsman Calendar Editor Michael Kushner was chosen as a panelist due to his active involvement on the campus. While he also feels a smoking ban is a good idea, his speech focused on another issue. "It is my sincere belief that the Hebrew identity is either being ignored or forgotten on this so-called diverse and equal campus," he said. Kushner further feels that students should have input into any new faculty being hired. Kushner was responding to a statement by the chancellor in his opening speech that City College will have to hire over 50 new faculty members this term.

Student Representative Anthony Kenyon, of The Native American Study Organization, was also chosen as a panelist. Kenyon has been very involved in student government and an active member in the revamping of the financial aid process through "gripe fests," held last semester. Kenyon spoke on a broad range of topics, from financial aid and committee scheduling to electrical problems on campus and accessibility to locked areas.

Kenyon also spoke on instructional issues as well as leadership development. After speaking, Kenyon voiced a concern for the listening session process. "I hope the board utilizes the information. They asked us to present our grievances and suggestions from the point of need and experience as students. I've conveyed the message, important things to me and my club, and tried to relate concrete examples of problems which many students encounter during their stay here. I hope they really listen and do something this time. I hope it's not just lip service."

Members of the outside community were also asked to speak at the listening sessions. Don Price from the Sunny Side Coalition felt that City College needed to "promote better relations through community input, keep the community informed of changes to campus facilities, and revamp the lighting, walkways and landscaping on the Phelan campus near the tennis courts.

A speaker from the ICC, Jeff Trinidad, student and member of PEACE (Filipinos for Education, Art, Culture, and Empowerment), a club on campus, also expressed concern about the effect of the listening sessions. "So they finally agreed to listen, now will they do anything about our suggestions? Action taken by the board on behalf of the student speakers and their ideas must be forthcoming or this is a waste of time. I hope they move quickly and obviously when they institute the changes."

Day, who instituted the listening sessions here at City College, has had great success with a similar program in the Maryland Community College System.

After listening to over 50 speakers for the better part of the day, the chancellor was understandably tired. "It was great but exhausting. I'd give it an A+." The chancellor was also impressed with the feedback he received from all the different speakers. "We had an excellent cross section of students and alumni who shared their experiences and thoughts to help benefit the campus." The chancellor was also pleasantly surprised to receive positive feedback. "The alumni had really super positive things to say. Even though we have problems, they reflect back on [City College] as one of their educational highlights." ∎

INDEPENDENCE CC'S ACE IS THE PLACE FOR STUDY HELP, TUTORS AND WORKSHOPS
By Jayme Lickteig

THE BUCCANEER (Independence, Kan.) 09/17/1998

From tutors to workshops to financial aid assistance, the Academic Center for Excellence, or "ACE," is designed to help students succeed.

ACE is a student support program that offers a wide variety of services. The main purpose of this program is to provide student support services for a smooth transition into college life. It is federally funded, so there is no cost to students.

The ACE program provides all students with help in class work, test review and study skills. Staff advisers, staff tutors and peer tutors specialize in basic academic skills and in specific courses. Specialized instructors are available for language arts and math.

ACE instructors are usually available on a walk-in basis. Students seeking help with a large assignment, however, should schedule a meeting.

The center also offers workshops for development of academic skills, personal growth, career planning and continued study opportunities.

Assistance in acquiring financial aid is also available. Other responsibilities of the ACE include providing academic advising, career planning and personal development counseling and making sure that students with documented disabilities are given equal access to academic services.

Tutoring is available for all students, but other services are reserved for students who are first-generation college students or who have specific income levels or documented physical or academic disabilities.

Dr. Gary Musgrave, new dean of student services at ICC, encourages students to "take advantage of the program early." He recommends seeking help before minor questions become huge problems and students fall behind. ∎

A key concern facing students on any college campus is safety. Students want to know that the environment in which they'll be living and learning is crime-free. Because of the large number of students attending two-year schools in the U.S., safety is of the utmost importance, and administrators and security forces alike are always looking for new ways to make their campuses even safer. City College in San Francisco, home of all those famous hills, has just added a bicycle police unit to its security force—let's hope their legs are up to the challenge!

CITY COLLEGE OF SAN FRANCISCO'S BICYCLE PATROL IS UP AND ROLLING

By Louise Knapp Bowser

THE GUARDSMAN (San Francisco, Calif.) 11/16/1998

Campus police officer Mario Villalta's presence will be more visible and his patrols more flexible thanks to the donation of a new $650 Trek bicycle by the Associated Students in Aug. 1998.

Villalta's idea for bicycle patrols won immediate support from the campus police department when he presented it to them in June 1998. "There is a need for us to be able to patrol areas not accessible by car," he said.

According to Villalta, once the bicycle patrols are up and rolling, "I guarantee crime will go down." Villalta also believes the campus police will be more approachable to students when they are on bicycles rather than behind the wheel of a car.

In June 1998 when Villalta first approached the A.S. and San Francisco Community College District with his plan, then A.S. President Mario Magallon agreed to donate a bicycle right away. According to Villalta, it wasn't until the college district's budget was decided in July 1998 that there were sufficient funds for a second bicycle and that his plan was given the OK.

Before Villalta and three other chosen officers could begin their patrol, they had to take a one-day training course on how to maneuver bicycles slowly through crowds. The course, which was unavailable through mid-October and paid for by the district, included officers Ted Russo, Beatrice Ramirez and Julie Torres. A more intense three-day course will begin Nov. 18.

Villalta used his first day on patrol, Oct. 26, to inspect the pathways and areas on campus previously inaccessible by car. Villalta says he is looking forward to the district finally getting through all the red tape and producing the second bicycle.

"The ideal situation would be two officers patrolling the campus on bicycle and one in a car. This way we can cover the whole campus," he said.

The district will pay for all bicycle maintenance and uniforms consisting of shorts, shirt, jacket, shoes, helmet and gloves. Uniforms cost as much as the bicycle. Said Villalta, "It's worth it. You can't put a price on the safety of the students."

Student reaction has been positive so far. CIS major Glen Jameson, 32, said, "If it makes the police do their jobs better, cover more territory, then maybe it's a good thing." "However," Jameson added, "police should not be able to take the bikes home and use them recreationally." ∎

Preparing you for a career is an important focus at two-year schools. For this reason, before you enroll you'll need to look closely at the placement rate data of any two-year program with an emphasis is on career preparation. The placement rate—or the percentage of graduates who leave with job offers in hand or who get jobs very soon after finishing their education—will tell you just how effective the program is at finding employment for students.

From helping you prepare and send out your resume to providing you with access to job listings and working with you on interviewing skills, career service centers at two-year schools—like the high-tech Career Link center at City College of San Francisco—will find you a great job faster than you can say, "Which way to the bank?"

CAREER LINK PROVIDES FREE SERVICES TO JOB SEEKERS AND EMPLOYERS

By Margarita Chavez

THE GUARDSMAN (San Francisco, Calif.) 11/02/1999

City College is involved in a dynamic new community based partnership with San Francisco's One-Stop system that offers free assistance to both employers and job seekers.

Career Link is a large and complete career center, where all resources and services are free and available through self-service, groups or classes and individual services.

It offers career counseling and information on local employers and provides data on projections on wages and areas of job growth in the Bay Area.

Career Link is a partnership between the college, the Employment Development Department (EDD), National Council on Aging, Private Industry Council, Department of Human Services (DHS) and the Department of Rehabilitation.

In November 1997 the program evolved into a full-service center and moved from the Assessment Center at 33 Gough Street to its present location in the EDD building at 1320 Mission Street, near the corner of Cesar Chavez Street.

After moving to its present site Career Link added new services, upgraded its existing technology and hired additional staff to meet the increasing demand for more employment and training resources.

Career Link is still in its infancy. Its history dates back to 1992 when EDD, City College and DSS (now the Department of Human Services) began their partnership with the opening of the Assessment Center, which provided career and education counseling, testing and training referrals.

New federal legislation in the mid-1990s created grants and funds for communities to increase their career and employment resources. With more funds and more partners, Career Link evolved into a one-stop full service center.

Last year a second career center was opened at the Southeast campus in partnership with EDD, DHS and the Private Industry Council. Additional services are expected to be added in 1999.

Career Link offers the following self-service tools: career development software; CALjobs/Internet job searches; video library; bulletin boards for job listings; video viewing; fax /copy machines and phones to use for unemployment insurance claims.

You can also participate the following groups and classes: job clubs; resume workshops; interview workshops; PIC (Private Industry Council) orientation; "Intro to LMI" (Labor Market Information); Internet introduction classes; "Jump start your job search" classes; "Computer Basic" classes and "Using career information resources" classes.

Individuals can also participate in career counseling; Veteran's assistance; one-on-one job counseling; jobs for youth; CALWORKS employment specialists and a Deaf Counseling and Referral Agency.

Career Link has a child care center, staffed by a DHS employee experienced in caring for children and who is certified in First Aid and CPR. Children age 2 years and older can use the play area provided at the 3120 Mission Street site. ∎

Another great aspect of two-year schools is their emphasis on helping students with children. The average age of a community college student is 29, so many men and women who attend two-year schools are married or single with families, including small children, when they begin coursework. This could present a problem if two-year schools didn't provide quality care for their students' children.

Two-year schools acknowledge this dilemma and take decisive steps to ensure that their students with families have access to conveniently scheduled classes as well as day care facilities. Florida Community College in Jacksonville even awards scholarships and grants to help students defray the cost of child care facilities. As the young mom from Linn-Benton Community College poignantly tells us, being a single parent and trying to get an education isn't an easy road; two-year schools recognize this and work hard to give these aspiring individuals the much-needed help they deserve.

SCHOLARSHIPS, GRANTS HELP FLORIDA CC STUDENT PARENTS PAY FOR CHILD CARE

By Rabiah Ryan

CAMPUS VOICE (Jacksonville, Fla.) 03/09/1999

As the mom tried to juggle books and bags, her children ran across the parking lot at South Campus. She called out, pleading for them to be careful. Rearing children while attending classes can be a hair-raising experience, but one way to alleviate the stress is on-campus childcare.

"It's such a blessing that I can bring my kids here after work," said Florida County Community College of Jacksonville night student Stacy Petite. "It saves me so much time." Petite, 29, is a part-time night student and single mother of two who works full time and is

the sole custodian of her 6- and 7-year-old boys. She is one of a growing number of students taking advantage of scholarships and grants offered by the college to help eligible parents with the cost of childcare needs while they attend classes.

The FCCJ Child Development Center at South Campus is one of three school-wide on-campus facilities that offers day and evening child-care for a minimal fee. There is still plenty of space, although students get first priority, said Gwendolyn Thomas, the FCCJ scholarship coordinator. The other centers are at North and Downtown campuses. Kent Campus refers

Jeremy Parker/*The Commuter*

their students to St. Catherine's Episcopal Preschool, less than a five-minute drive from the campus.

Supplemental scholarships and grants are also available to currently enrolled students and may cover a large portion of all the costs and fees for an entire

semester, Thomas said. Though grants are based on need, the majority of the students who apply are approved, Thomas said. Students, she said, are encouraged to use the on-campus services, but they do not have to. ■

SINGLE MOM BALANCES SCHOOLWORK, DAUGHTER AT LINN-BENTON CC

By Lizanne Southgate

THE COMMUTER (Albany, Ore.) 02/17/1999

For Cherina McQueen, study time may not even begin until 10 p.m., when 14-month-old daughter Cyndia is finally asleep.

By then the trips back and forth to pick up and drop off Cyndia are over for the day, the food has been prepared and served, classes attended, the work study hours put in and the dishes done.

Now, it's time to get to work. McQueen is one of many single parents attending LBCC who face the daunting task of squeezing school work, employment and family life into a 24-hour day. The hardest part of being a single parent and student, says McQueen, is managing the time and stress demands of the dual roles.

The 26-year-old mom is attending LBCC to complete a one-year certificate program in juvenile corrections. After that she plans to enroll in a wildlife program offered at OSU.

Eventually she wants to use this unique mix of training to run a combination juvenile foster home and wildlife rehabilitation center where kids and animals can help each other. As she says, "Something has to touch them."

Before returning to school, McQueen spent nearly four years working in plastics manufacturing. She was making "a whopping $7 an hour" when she quit.

McQueen now receives financial aid, including work-study, that also helps her work toward her degree. While she confesses she is still just as poor as before, now at least she is working toward a goal rather than merely putting in hours at a dead-end job.

Juggling her dual roles as mom and student leaves little time for socializing. "My social life is a joke," she

said. "I have a roommate who goes out all the time and does these fun things and I get depressed. If I can take Cyndia with me, then I'll go out."

While McQueen is in class or at her work study position in the Financial Aid Office, Cyndia stays with her grandmother and great grandmother. For now, she is still too little to be in the Family Resource Center on campus.

Although she can't make use of the FRC, McQueen is grateful for other services that are available at LBCC. She makes frequent use of the Learning Resource Center, "especially the Writing Desk when I need to know how to write something in a certain style."

Asked what other services a college might offer to single parents, McQueen replied that a study center with childcare would be helpful. That would give her a chance to use the computers, do her research and maybe even find another student to work with.

McQueen is taking a parenting class at LBCC to help with "coping skills." While she is quick to admit that being a student and single parent is hard, she keeps her focus on the future.

"Anything challenging is a good thing. I'm really glad to be back in school even though right now, in a way, I'm in a ghetto. At least I'm working toward something. One day I'm going to be in a better financial situation and be able to do whatever I want. I want my daughter to have a better life." ■

We've seen in every other chapter in this book that college campuses have a way to go before they're considered completely accessible to those with physical challenges. And it looks as though two-year colleges are no different than the others. While the Americans with Disabilities Act dictated that certain adjustments be made to ensure accessibility, many claim that the Act does not touch on all aspects of a physically challenged person's life. This means that deficits remain to be addressed. Because two-year schools don't operate with the same huge endowments that many four-year colleges and universities do, and because they rely so heavily on local, state, and federal funds, money for handicapped accessibility may be slow to make its way to these campuses. What's important is that two-year schools like Mesa Community College recognize problems of accessibility and are working toward remedying them.

MESA CC STUDENTS STRUGGLE THROUGH CAMPUS

By Jeremy Williams

MESA LEGEND (Mesa, Ariz.) 02/25/1999

Opening a classroom door. Moving freely in and out of a campus restroom. Walking without difficulty along a school sidewalk.

For most Mesa Community College students, these things can be achieved without a second thought. But for members of school's population who use a wheelchair, these tasks have proved anything but easy. "Opening doors is a big factor," said MCC student Gene Heppard, who works in the Disability Resources office and relies on a wheelchair to get around. "The doors swing in and getting out of them is a problem. A lot of disabled students have limited use of their hands," Heppard said.

According to statistics provided by Disability Resources and Services, there were 744 disabled students on campus from the fall of 1997 to the spring of 1998. These disabilities ranged from blindness to multiple sclerosis. Over time, MCC's administration has made several adjustments to better serve its disabled students. "The major problems are the buildings (on campus), which are 30 to 35 years old and were never designed with handicap access in mind," said Ron Etter, dean of Student Services. "Accessibility was not a concern of the architecture of the time." In recent years, however, Etter has seen to it that the campus be made more accessible to those with disabilities. About three years ago, a push button door was installed at the library's entrance, as well as other locations on campus. While disabled students would like to see more automatic door openers, Etter explains that is just not feasible.

"Automatic door openers are expensive," Etter said. "(It costs) $1400 per door." Cutting curbs for easier wheelchair access, as well as resurfacing walkways to make them smoother, are just a few of the recent improvements that Heppard was glad to see. "The campus is very accessible," Heppard said. "It's flat with curb cuts. I have no complaints on that at all."

However, many agree that restroom access remains a problem. Ray Bonnett, president of Students with a Cause (SWAC), an on-campus organization consisting of disabled students, is also confined to a wheelchair.

"The top priority, in my opinion, are the restrooms," he said. "(People are) getting caught in doors and there's not enough room to turn around (in a wheelchair)." According to ASMCC President Tyrone Hanks, specific points of concern are the restrooms in the Kirk Center's game room, as well as the restrooms across from the advisement center.

Hanks, in conjunction with SWAC, has brought these locations to the attention of Etter with hopes that improvements can be made. "Tyrone has been very supportive of the whole thing," Bonnett said. "Dean Etter is working with us very diligently." Both Bonnett and Heppard agree that there is at least one convenient bathroom on campus. "The bathroom upstairs in the Kirk Center," Heppard said. "It's big and roomy." Bonnett agrees, but points out the drawback to this particular restroom. "There are restrooms upstairs, but when you're in a rush to get to class, they're not convenient," he said. Etter is seeking student feedback in the process to make the restrooms more accessible.

"What I've asked some of them to do is provide a list of which restrooms are problems," Etter said. "Students (need to) visit restrooms and let me know what changes they'd like to see; then we can make changes based on a priority system." Another problem is the way the Americans with Disabilities Act dictates adjustments. "The adjustments are formula driven,"

Etter said. "Some of the modifications made did not benefit students but they met the formula." Bonnett attributes a lack of funding for additional improvements to a lack of perspective. "I think it's just that they're not sitting in a wheelchair or they're not blind," Bonnett said. "How can they understand if we don't speak up?" ∎

You may not find as many planned occasions for celebration on the campuses of two-year schools as you will at traditional four-year colleges. Because most students live off campus, attend school part time, have jobs, and need to get the kids to bed by 9, there just isn't the need for them. But don't worry; festivals and other events—like Homecoming Week at ICC or Black History Month at FCCJ—may not be as many in number, but that just means you'll enjoy them all the more!

BIG EVENTS PLANNED FOR INDEPENDENCE CC'S HOMECOMING

By Charissa N. Struble

THE BUCCANEER (Independence, Kan.) 10/15/1998

Five big events will wrap up Independence Community College's annual Homecoming week, and students are encouraged to show their school spirit by attending and participating in the week's activities.

The Pirate football team plays Garden City at 7:30 p.m. Saturday in Independence, and many events have been planned around the game.

Pre-game activities include a bonfire at 7:00 tonight behind the practice field located southeast of ICC's dormitories, the ICC Homecoming 1998 Luncheon at noon Friday in the ICC Field House and a

Ted Schurter/*The Daily Egyptian*

tailgate party Saturday before the game at Riverside Stadium.

The crowning of ICC royalty will take place at halftime of the game. Students voted for their favorite candidates Tuesday and Wednesday and all king and queen candidates will be introduced at the noon luncheon Friday. Along with the candidates, ICC will introduce its coaches, football team, cheerleaders and Blue Note band. Guest speakers also will be present and there will be chances to win prizes throughout the luncheon.

Other events that have taken place this week

include: voter registration, a powder puff football game, a pep rally and a student skating party.

Students showed their spirit even more on Wednesday by wearing the school's colors: blue and gold.

The ICC Student Senate coordinated the activities. Student Senate member Jeromy Brooks thought that it was worth the effort. "Though it's difficult and time consuming to plan activities that will be considered fun, they bring the students together," Brooks said.

Student Senate president Troy Smith agreed.

"We put a lot of time and preparation into Homecoming as an organization and so it's been really worth it. We've seen a lot of student participation, especially with voter registration."

A reported 75 students registered to vote this year.

Smith also feels that Homecoming is a way to get the community involved with the school.

"ICC is excited about all the interest Homecoming generates, not only in the school but also in the community." ■

'TALL STORYTELLER' TELLS TALES TO FLORIDA CC STUDENTS
By Hannah Crawford

CAMPUS VOICE (Jacksonville, Fla.) 03/16/1999

A crowd of about 50 people congregated in the auditorium at Kent Campus on Feb. 9 to hear Kala JoJo, the "tall storyteller," as part of FCCJ's Black History Month program.

His performance began with him pounding out a rhythm on a portable drum. As he concluded the dramatic cadence, he stepped up to the microphone and greeted the audience, who responded with enthusiasm. He then proceeded to enliven the crowd with a call-and-response chant that quickly led to laughter and hand clapping.

Using a combination of African-American and West African Jali traditions, he speaks to people of all ages. His first story, accompanied by the gentle, rhythmic plucking of a small stringed instrument, related the tale of Truth and the purpose of storytelling. A story within a story.

It enthralled the audience, who remained silent throughout the narration. He next told the true story of three brothers who were slaves in America. It ended with a lesson about the importance of standing up for one's friends and beliefs.

Kala altered his pace for the next presentation, changing the solemn mood established by the previous story. Selecting volunteers to participate onstage, Kala encouraged the audience to sing and dance. After a hearty round of applause for the lively volunteers, Kala resumed his tales with the legend of the lion king. Known to Americans through the popular Disney cartoon, this true story of the life of an African boy enchanted the audience.

By combining a variety of tales and techniques, Kala was able to maintain the interest of his audience. His use of music enhanced the performance by giving the audience something to hold the attention of the listeners, as well as giving them with something to watch. ■

NOTES

NOTES

NOTES

NOTES

NOTES